D0294626

Celebrating Shakespeare

On the 400th anniversary of Shakespeare's death, this collection opens up the social practices of commemoration to new research and analysis. An international team of leading scholars explores a broad spectrum of celebrations, showing how key events – such as the Easter Rising in Ireland, the Second Vatican Council of 1964 and the Great Exhibition of 1851 – drew on Shakespeare to express political agendas. In the USA, commemoration in 1864 counted on him to symbolise unity transcending the Civil War, while the First World War pulled the 1916 anniversary celebration into the war effort, enlisting Shakespeare as patriotic poet. The essays also consider how the dream of Shakespeare as a rural poet took shape in gardens, how cartoons challenged the poet's élite status and how statues of him mutated into advertisements for gin and Disney cartoons. Richly varied illustrations supplement these case studies of the diverse, complex and contradictory aims of memorialising Shakespeare.

CLARA CALVO is Professor of English Studies at the University of Murcia. She is the author of *Power Relations and Fool-Master Discourse in Shakespeare* (1991) and co-authored *The Literature Workbook* (with Jean-Jacques Weber, 1998). She has edited, with Ton Hoenselaars, *European Shakespeares* (*The Shakespearean International Yearbook*, 8, 2008), a special issue of *Critical Survey* on *Shakespeare and the Cultures of Commemoration* (2010), and Thomas Kyd's *The Spanish Tragedy* for Arden Early Modern Drama (with Jesús Tronch, 2013). Her articles have appeared in *Shakespeare Survey*, *The Year's Work in English Studies*, and several other journals and collections of essays.

COPPÉLIA KAHN is Professor of English, *Emerita*, at Brown University. She has published widely on feminist theory, Shakespeare, Renaissance drama, and Shakespeare's place in American culture. She is the author of *Man's Estate: Masculine Identity in Shakespeare* (1981) and *Roman Shakespeare: Warriors, Wounds, and Women* (1997). She also co-edited *Making A Difference: Feminist Literary Criticism* (with Gayle Greene, 1985).

Celebrating Shakespeare

Commemoration and Cultural Memory

Edited by
CLARA CALVO AND COPPÉLIA KAHN

CAMBRIDGE
UNIVERSITY PRESS

CAMBRIDGE
UNIVERSITY PRESS

University Printing House, Cambridge CB2 8BS, United Kingdom

Cambridge University Press is part of the University of Cambridge.

It furthers the University's mission by disseminating knowledge in the pursuit of education, learning and research at the highest international levels of excellence.

www.cambridge.org
Information on this title: www.cambridge.org/9781107042773

© Cambridge University Press 2015

First published 2015

Printed in the United Kingdom by TJ International Ltd. Padstow Cornwall

A catalogue record for this publication is available from the British Library

Library of Congress Cataloguing in Publication data
Celebrating Shakespeare : commemoration and cultural memory / edited by Clara Calvo, Coppélia Kahn.
    pages cm
ISBN 978-1-107-04277-3 (Hardback)
1. Shakespeare, William, 1564–1616 – Appreciation.   2. Shakespeare, William, 1564–1616 – Influence.   3. Shakespeare, William, 1564–1616 – Anniversaries, etc.
I. Calvo, Clara, 1961-editor.   II. Kahn, Coppélia, editor.
PR2976.C337 2015
822.3′3–dc23   2015012534

ISBN 978-1-107-04277-3 Hardback

Contents

Illustrations

Notes on contributors

CLARA CALVO is Professor of English Studies at the University of Murcia. She has edited, with Ton Hoenselaars, *European Shakespeares* (*The Shakespearean International Yearbook*, 8, 2008) and a special issue of *Critical Survey* on *Shakespeare and the Cultures of Commemoration* (2010). With Jesús Tronch, she has edited *The Spanish Tragedy* for Arden Early Modern Drama (2013).

MARTA CEREZO is Lecturer in English at the Spanish Open University (UNED). Her areas of interest and publication are Shakespearean drama and contemporary English narrative in relation to literary gerontology. Her current research concerns the commemorative acts of Shakespeare's Quatercentenary and the presence of aging and stigma in contemporary English narrative.

SUPRIYA CHAUDHURI is Professor of English, *Emerita*, at Jadavpur University. She has published extensively on Shakespeare and Renaissance literature, as well as on cultural history, literary modernism, and narrative. Recent publications include *Petrarch: The Self and the World*, edited with Sukanta Chaudhuri (Calcutta: Jadavpur University Press, 2012).

AILSA GRANT FERGUSON is a Lecturer in Early Modern Literature at the University of Brighton, UK and an Academic Associate of the National Theatre, London. Her research focuses on early modern literature and culture and Shakespeare in performance, especially relating to counter culture, the First World War, and women's suffragism.

TON HOENSELAARS is Professor of Early Modern Literature and Culture at Utrecht University. He has written extensively on the reception history of Shakespeare worldwide. Books include *Images of Englishmen and Foreigners in the Drama of Shakespeare and his*

Contemporaries (1992), *Shakespeare's History Plays: Performance, Translation, and Adaptation in Britain and Abroad* (2004), and *The Cambridge Companion to Shakespeare and Contemporary Dramatists* (2012).

GRAHAM HOLDERNESS has published over forty books, mostly on Shakespeare, and many articles on criticism, theory, and theology. Recent publications include *Nine Lives of William Shakespeare* (2011), *Tales from Shakespeare: Creative Collisions* (2014), and *Re-writing Jesus: Christ in Twentieth-Century Fiction and Film* (2014). He is currently writing a historical fantasy novel on Shakespeare and the Gunpowder Plot.

PETER HOLLAND is McMeel Family Professor in Shakespeare Studies in the Department of Film, Television, and Theatre at the University of Notre Dame. He is editor of *Shakespeare Survey* and co-editor of the Oxford Shakespeare Topics and *Great Shakespeareans* series. His edition of *Coriolanus* for the Arden Shakespeare appeared in 2013.

COPPÉLIA KAHN, Professor of English, *Emerita*, at Brown University, is author of *Man's Estate: Masculine Identity in Shakespeare* (1981) and *Roman Shakespeare: Warriors, Wounds, and Women* (1987). She has written on Renaissance drama, feminist theory, and Shakespeare commemoration. She was president of the Shakespeare Association of America in 2009.

DOUGLAS M. LANIER is Professor of English at the University of New Hampshire. He specializes in early modern literature and Shakespeare's cultural afterlife. His book *Shakespeare and Modern Popular Culture* appeared in 2002. He is currently writing a book on *Othello* on film and a volume for the Arden Language and Writing series on *The Merchant of Venice*.

GORDON MCMULLAN is Professor of English and Director of the London Shakespeare Centre at King's College London, a general editor of Arden Early Modern Drama, and a general textual editor of the *Norton Shakespeare*, 3rd edition. His publications include *Shakespeare and the Idea of Late Writing* (2010) and the Arden edition of *Henry VIII*.

PHILIP MEAD, Winthrop Professor and inaugural Chair of Australian Literature at the University of Western Australia, is the author of *Networked Language: History and Culture in Australian Poetry* (2010) and studies of literary education in Australia, Shakespeare memorialisation, poetry and inauthenticity, contemporary Indigenous writing, and Australian literature in the world.

ANDREW MURPHY is Professor of English at the University of St Andrews. His authored books include *Shakespeare for the People: Working-class Readers, 1800–1900* (Cambridge University Press, 2008) and *Shakespeare in Print: A History and Chronology of Shakespeare Publishing* (Cambridge University Press, 2003).

ADRIAN POOLE is Professor of English at the University of Cambridge, and a Fellow of Trinity College, Cambridge. His monographs include *Shakespeare and the Victorians* (2004) and *Tragedy: A Very Short Introduction* (2005); he is a General Editor of *Great Shakespeareans*.

KATHERINE WEST SCHEIL is Professor of English at the University of Minnesota, Twin Cities. Her most recent book is *She Hath Been Reading: Women and Shakespeare Clubs in America* (2012), and she is completing a book on the afterlife of Anne Hathaway Shakespeare.

RICHARD SCHOCH is Professor of Drama at Queen's University Belfast. He is the author of *Shakespeare's Victorian Stage* (2006) and *Not Shakespeare* (2002), and the editor of *Great Shakespeareans: Macready, Booth, Terry, Irving* (2011). He is currently writing a book on British theatre historiography from the Restoration to modernism.

NICOLA J. WATSON is Professor of English at the Open University, having previously taught at Oxford, Harvard, and Northwestern Universities. Her publications include *England's Elizabeth* (with Michael Dobson, 2002), *The Literary Tourist* (2006), and *Literary Tourism and Nineteenth-Century Culture* (2009). Her new study, *The Author's Effects: A Poetics of Literary Object, Place, Pilgrimage*, explores afterlives through writer's house museums.

Acknowledgements

Clara Calvo wishes to thank the Folger Shakespeare Library for a Short Term Fellowship (2013) and for access to their collections, the Shakespeare Centre Library and Archives and the Shakespeare Birthplace Trust for accommodating research visits at short notice, the Fundación Séneca for funding Research Project 12014/PHCS/09, 'Great War Shakespeare II: Myths, Social Agents and Global Culture' and the Spanish Plan Nacional de I+D+i 2008–2011 (MICINN-MINECO) for funding Research Project FFI2011-24347 'Cultures of Commemoration II: Remembering Shakespeare'. Coppélia Kahn wishes to thank Brown University for generous funding. We both wish to thank the following institutions for venues at which the editors and authors of this book found a hearing: the Mahindra Humanities Center at Harvard University, the Société Française Shakespeare, sponsor of Shakespeare 450 (Paris, April 2014), the Shakespeare Association of America, the Deutsche Shakespeare-Gesellschaft, the European Shakespeare Research Association, the Shakespeare Institute at Stratford-Upon-Avon (University of Birmingham), the Humanities Institute at the University of South Florida and the Massachusetts Center for Interdisciplinary Renaissance Studies. Sections of Chapters 1 and 11 have previously appeared in *Shakespeare Jahrbuch* 151 (2015). We are grateful to Sabine Schülting for granting permission to include this material.

We are also very grateful to our editors at Cambridge University Press, Sarah Stanton and Rosemary Crawley, for their help, patience and understanding; to Helen Hargest and Melanie Leung for their expertise and help in locating illustrations; and to Peter Holland, for introducing us to each other.

Every effort has been made to secure the necessary permissions to reproduce copyright material in this work, though in some cases it has proved impossible to trace copyright holders. If any omissions are brought to our notice, we will be happy to include appropriate acknowledgements on reprinting in any subsequent edition.

Introduction: Shakespeare and commemoration

COPPÉLIA KAHN AND CLARA CALVO

This book participates in the worldwide commemoration of Shakespeare in 2016, the four hundredth anniversary of his death. Like the performances, exhibits, academic conferences, television shows, film festivals, t-shirts, tea towels and postage stamps likely to mark that special year, this volume can never fully succeed in the chimerical goal of making Shakespeare a monument, something permanent, the same throughout time, an 'ever-fixéd mark.'[1] Yet for centuries, commemoration of Shakespeare has persisted, and recently, with digital technology to beam it across the globe, increased.

Whatever Shakespeare has become in the four hundred years since he died, the diverse practices of commemoration have had a lot to do with it. No one could deny that Shakespeare deserves to be famous for his myriad achievements as a writer, but it must also be admitted that his fame has outstripped both the man and his writings. He is still, as he has been since the eighteenth century, an icon of Englishness wherever English is spoken, but he is now woven into the cultural fabric of many nations. His name is current almost anywhere in the world, and especially in the USA, Australia, New Zealand, India and Europe. Shakespeare has indeed become what Graham Holderness calls 'the Shakespeare myth': 'A powerful cultural institution, constructed around the figure of Shakespeare, that [can] be analysed to some degree separately from the person of the Elizabethan dramatist, and the texts of his works'.[2] This myth, refurbished as tastes, technology, interpretive fashions or political interests change, sustains the poet's cultural presence as a 'timeless' figure even as, through time, it changes.

Though this book was called into existence by the Quatercentenary, its fifteen essays, we believe, differ from other anniversary observances

---

[1] William Shakespeare, Sonnet 116, line 5, in *Shakespeare's Sonnets*, ed. Stephen Booth (New Haven: Yale University Press, 1980), 100.

[2] Graham Holderness, *Cultural Shakespeare: Essays in the Shakespeare Myth* (Hatfield, Herts: University of Hertfordshire Press, 2001), ix.

1

because they offer a critical perspective on the very activity in which they participate. They bring analytical scrutiny to the diverse forms commemoration takes, the political interests it has engaged, the philosophical questions inherent in it, the kinds of cultural work it does in the name of praising Shakespeare. Commemoration has a long history, beginning with the edition of Shakespeare's plays collected and published by John Heminge and Henry Condell in 1623. *Celebrating Shakespeare* isn't intended to be a comprehensive survey, however, though several essays deal with significant historical high points: the Garrick Jubilee of 1769 and the anniversary festivities of 1816, 1864, 1916 and 1964, for example. Rather, these essays present ways of understanding why and how Shakespeare has been celebrated at certain moments: not only according to the calendar of anniversaries, but in many other forms as well, and always in dense social contexts: war, international relations, tourism and commerce, modernism, imperialism, popular culture, social conflict. By not offering a survey of anniversaries, we aim to transcend the 'cult of the centenary' and explore forms of commemoration which are often excluded from official celebrations, such as gardens, cartoons, replicas or parodies. Through these case studies, we aim to understand how various modes of celebrating Shakespeare depend on certain tropes, but may also transform them; what discourses they appropriate, what debates they engage in, how they influence and perpetuate the poet's presence in the world.

Modes of celebration are diverse, to be sure, but we discern several problematics underlying that diversity: unresolvable contradictions and theoretical issues that run through these essays. The first is the dilemma of any memorial: in the face of inexorable change, how to represent a lost object of the past to an audience in the present. When Ovid, probably the poet who most inspired Shakespeare, came to the end of the *Metamorphoses*, he proclaimed that it would last as long as the Roman Empire lasted:

> And now my work is done: no wrath of Jove
> nor fire nor sword nor time, which would erode
> all things, has power to blot out this poem ...
> And everywhere that Roman power has sway,
> in all domains the Latins gain, my lines
> Will be on people's lips ...
> Ovid, *Metamorphoses*, XV[3]

---

[3] *The Metamorphoses of Ovid*, trans. Allen Mandelbaum (San Diego, New York, London: Harcourt, 1993), 549.

As it happens, his poem has outlasted that empire; in the original or in translation, we still speak his lines. However, as Supriya Chaudhuri says in this volume, 'Texts and their readers exist in time... the "afterlives" of texts and artefacts negotiate multiple temporalities.'[4] So do theatres, audiences, cities, schools, governments. Graham Holderness, in this volume, offers a helpful distinction between 'rehearsal' of Shakespeare as a figure 'alien, incongruous, from the distant past' (an image on a bank note, for example), and 'remembrance', which cultivates in the present an 'antiqued' poet (as in the annual Stratford-upon-Avon birthday celebrations).[5]

The Shakespeare we celebrate in 2016 is simply not the same author celebrated one or two hundred years, or even a decade, ago. Tradition would freeze the past for consumption today, but consumers eventually come to embrace, if not to crave, innovation. The performance tradition upheld by Betterton, for instance, which was believed to descend from the playwright himself, lasted two centuries until, as Richard Schoch explains, Henry Irving sensed that 'if the theatre were to survive it would not be through veneration of the past, but through overt renewal'.[6] As many essays in this book attest, memorialisation is nearly always belated: what is intended to be eternal eventually goes out of date. In 1926, when Henry Gullett's heirs managed to erect the statue of Shakespeare in Sydney that their forebear had envisioned before he died in 1914, Philip Mead notes, the statue and the urban niche created for it 'represented a backward-looking gesture of late-Victorian-Edwardian memorialisation'.[7] The statue or memorial, as in Ovid's lines, may survive fire, sword and time, may last in its physical form, but it will cease speaking to its viewers. It will no longer prompt them to remember Shakespeare, but rather will slip into a limbo of the outmoded, the done with and long gone – or, as Robert Musil declares, 'Everything permanent loses its ability to impress.'[8]

---

[4] Supriya Chaudhuri, 'Remembering Shakespeare in India: colonial and postcolonial memory', Chapter 5 in this volume.

[5] Graham Holderness, 'Remembrance of things past: Shakespeare 1851, 1951, 2012', Chapter 4 in this volume.

[6] Richard Schoch, 'Commemorating Shakespeare in performance: Betterton and Irving', Chapter 2 in this volume.

[7] Philip Mead, 'Lest we forget: Shakespeare tercentenary commemoration in Sydney and London, 1916', Chapter 11 in this volume.

[8] Robert Musil, 'Monuments', in *Selected Writings*, trans. and ed. Burton Pike (New York: Continuum, 1986), 320–2.

Yet, as Ton Hoenselaars points out, certain statues of the poet 'have become canonical worldwide', proliferating not only in squares and parks but also in everyday objects such as key chains and bookends.[9] Clara Calvo notes the visual hallmarks of the image of Shakespeare in tercentenary cartoons: doublet and hose, receding hairline, ample brow – visual tags still current in 2016.[10] It is easy to dismiss such images as mere clichés. Nonetheless, as Hoenselaars demonstrates, they possess 'sizeable cultural capital'. Furthermore, the histories of their creation, and in some cases eventual disappearance, reveal both passionate cultural investment in the poet and the vulnerability of such investment to the transience of tastes and to the violence of war: a statue of Shakespeare donated to the city of Paris in 1871 was melted down in 1941 for the war industry.[11] Similarly, topical, ephemeral cartoons, as Calvo shows, display a rich and healthy ambivalence toward the venerable poet, whose 'presence is memorialized and questioned simultaneously' in them.[12]

But what do we mean when we speak of remembering, or commemorating, 'Shakespeare'? In commemoration, the slippage between the man and his works in the familiar metonymy becomes problematic. We can no longer assume that the playwright who didn't even own his play scripts (they belonged to the Lord Chamberlain's or the King's Men) wrote them only to be performed, or showed no interest in publishing them.[13] Still, it fell to his colleagues Heminge and Condell, the otherwise undistinguished actors, 'to keepe the memory of so worthy a Friend, and Fellow, alive', by publishing the best copies of his plays they could find in a handsome Folio volume.[14] To them, he was both friend and colleague, but the mode of memorialisation they chose evokes Shakespeare not as friend but rather as author: they kept the man's memory alive by preserving his writings, so that his words might still be on our lips, centuries later. That is the form of commemoration in which Ovid trusted.

---

[9] Ton Hoenselaars, 'Sculpted Shakespeare', Chapter 13 in this volume.
[10] Clara Calvo, 'Brought up to date: Shakespeare in cartoons', Chapter 12, *passim*.
[11] Hoenselaars, Chapter 13.   [12] Calvo, Chapter 12.
[13] See Lukas Erne, *Shakespeare as Literary Dramatist*, 2nd edn (Cambridge University Press, 2013), *passim*. Erne argues that Shakespeare consciously aimed to have his plays published as well as performed.
[14] Quoted in David Scott Kastan, *Shakespeare and the Book* (Cambridge University Press, 2001), 55.

It was Ben Jonson who first articulated the problematic that sub-tends the metonymy of man for writings, in his poem, 'To the Memory of My Beloved, The Author William Shakespeare: And What He Hath Left Us', one of several prefatory poems included in the Folio edition of 1623. To memorialise Shakespeare, Jonson adopts a time-honoured trope of poetic fame used by Horace, Ovid and Shakespeare himself:

> Thou art a Moniment, without a tombe,
> And art alive still, while thy Booke doth live,
> And we have wits to read, and praise to give.[15]

Jonson creates a metonymy for Shakespeare as an author in his 'Booke'. Though the author is physically dead, metonymically he lives on in his book, because those living in the present moment read his work. Similarly, Ovid proclaims that his poem will survive the ravages of time because in posterity, readers will speak his lines. 'Thy Booke', the Folio, in attracting readers, is meant to displace and render super-fluous any ostentatious 'Moniment' gracing the tomb of a once-living human being. Because this metonymy has become a cliché, we no longer attend to the conditional phrase that limits it: Shakespeare is 'alive still' only '*while* ... we have wits to read' what's in his book. Like Ovid, Jonson wants the poet's lines, more than the poet as man, to be remembered. We *mis*read Jonson's metonymy when we con-found Shakespeare the man with his writing, as commemoration of Shakespeare over subsequent centuries has, with few exceptions, con-founded it. The cult of Shakespeare as man, rather than an appreci-ation of his works, has largely dominated commemoration.

It is possible that neither the man nor his works, extraordinary as they are, might have survived to be commemorated today. Samuel Schoenbaum notes, in his study of biographies of Shakespeare, that the poet 'did not in his day inspire the mysterious veneration that afterwards came to surround him. No playwright in that day did, and certainly no actor.'[16] Between the 1623 Folio and, say, Rowe's edition of 1709, any eminence won for the poet by the Folio might well have vanished. Between his death in 1616 and the Restoration in 1660,

---

[15] Ben Jonson, 'To the Memory of My Beloved, The Author William Shakespeare, and What He Hath Left Us', lines 22–4, in *The Complete Poetry of Ben Jonson*, ed. William B. Hunter, Jr (New York University Press, 1963), 372–4.

[16] Samuel Schoenbaum, *Shakespeare's Lives*, new edn (Oxford: Clarendon Press, 1991), 36.

the Folio was reprinted only once, in 1632, and though scores of his contemporaries' plays were published, only three of his were reprinted. Plays by his contemporaries were staged despite the law forbidding it, but only three scenes from his were performed by vagabond players. Though his works were 'occasionally ... plagiarized or echoed or quoted', or 'summarily judged in passing', no extended discussion of them in that forty-four year period exists.[17] He was rescued from a likely oblivion mainly by the enterprising theatrical manager William Davenant, his godson. When the theatres re-opened in 1660, Davenant begged a few old Shakespeare scripts considered less desirable than those of Beaumont and Fletcher, and his innovative productions of these plays drew crowds.[18] Till the end of the seventeenth century, however, 'most people who saw his plays performed could not have known that Shakespeare wrote the plays they were seeing', because those plays were adapted by contemporary playwrights to suit contemporary tastes. It wasn't his name, but rather, acclaimed actors and the social cachet of theatre going, that drew audiences.[19]

Without the pre-eminence of David Garrick as actor, theatrical manager and publicist, it is doubtful that we'd be celebrating the four hundreth anniversary of Shakespeare's death this year. True, the proliferation of eighteenth-century editions brought new attention to his 'Booke', and his plays were performed more and more, but it was Garrick who inaugurated the commemoration of the poet not, as Jonson stipulated, by reading that book, but rather by the social practice of festivities celebrating the man. Of course, Garrick had already won the adulation of theatre-goers by his stunning performances in Shakespearean roles, and that fame enabled him to engage the general public in his Jubilee, putting the poet on England's cultural calendar in a way that no other English author had so far enjoyed or ever would.

Garrick established rituals of bardolatry that endure to this day, notably in the annual Shakespeare's birthday celebration in Stratford-upon-Avon. First of all, in calling his celebration of Shakespeare a 'jubilee', Garrick linked it to the calendar, and paved the way for

---

[17] Gary Taylor, *Reinventing Shakespeare: A Cultural History from the Restoration to the Present* (Oxford University Press, 1989), 11–12.

[18] Taylor, *Reinventing Shakespeare*, 14, 23, 36.

[19] Don-John Dugas, *Marketing the Bard: Shakespeare in Performance and Print, 1660–1740* (Columbia, MO: University of Missouri Press, 2006), ix, 7–9.

such celebrations to be repeated periodically, for the word denotes a special anniversary – a twenty-fifth, fiftieth, sixtieth or seventy-fifth anniversary. Jubilees having long been appropriated by the Catholic Church to designate years of special plenary indulgence, however, in 1769 had become politically fraught. As Peter Holland explains in this volume, 'jubilee' struck a cultural nerve by associating the national poet with practices considered alien and papist.[20] We cannot document, even today, the exact date of the poet's birth, for the parish register records only his baptism.[21] Since that date was close to 23 April, the day celebrating St George, England's patron saint, when the poet's fame had been well established, 23 April became his birthday.[22] The date wasn't determined by fact but driven, rather, by the Shakespeare myth. Nonetheless, in pegging a lavish public celebration of Shakespeare to a regular calendrical interval, Garrick initiated a cultural habit that took firm hold. Arbitrary as birthdays are, they recur regularly; they are the subalterns of commemoration.

As is well known, Garrick's three-day extravaganza didn't include a single performance of Shakespeare's plays or even a recitation of his poems. What was performed over and over again in various modes was an *idea* of Shakespeare, or rather, of Garrick's partnership with the Bard, for Garrick had long linked his name to Shakespeare's.[23] The actor had reintroduced neglected plays, and built a temple to Shakespeare at his estate in Hampton; Gainsborough had painted him with one arm draped around a bust of the poet.[24] The acme of Garrick's several Jubilee expressions of adulation for the poet at the Jubilee was his 'Ode ... to Shakespeare', which he had written himself and which he declaimed to great effect, invoking Shakespeare in the memorable epithet, 'The god of our idolatry!'[25] Again, the emphasis falls on the man, not the works.

---

[20] Peter Holland, 'David Garrick: saints, temples and jubilees', Chapter 1 in this volume.

[21] Schoenbaum, *Shakespeare's Lives*, 7–8.

[22] Peter Holland, 'William Shakespeare', *Oxford Dictionary of National Biography Online* (Oxford University Press, 2004): www.oxforddnb.com. Accessed 15 October 2014.

[23] Christian Deelman, *The Great Shakespeare Jubilee* (New York: Viking Press, 1964), 74.

[24] Deelman, *Great Shakespeare Jubilee*, 71, 97–9.

[25] David Garrick, *Garrick's Ode*, rpt. in Martha Winburn England, *Garrick's Jubilee* (Ohio State University Press, 1964), Appendix B, 251–3, line 14.

By calling Shakespeare 'Sweet Swan of Avon', Garrick's ode cemented a certain representation of the poet that Jonson's poem had forecast.[26] Garrick situated the Jubilee not in London, where the poet lived most of his life and where he probably wrote most of his works, but in the country town by the Avon, in Garrick's words, 'Where Nature led him by the hand, / Instructed him in all she knew, / And gave him absolute command!'[27] As Nicola Watson shows in this volume, Garrick's identification of Shakespeare with 'Nature' was extended, through the custom of Shakespeare gardens, to the 'topobiographical' idea of 'an organic continuity between land and poet mediated by flora'.[28] Similarly, Katherine Scheil's essay documents the role of Anne Hathaway's cottage not only in securing the image of Shakespeare as a Warwickshire poet, but also as a rural lover wooing Anne among fields and flowers. During the Second World War, a photo of the cosy thatched house was captioned, 'There'll always be an England!', identifying it, and Shakespeare, with a nostalgic idea of a pastoral, pre-industrial nation.[29]

Stratford-upon-Avon, no longer pastoral, is now sustained by the tourist industry, yet no matter how global or multicultural, post colonial or post modern the presence of Shakespeare has become in film adaptations, avant-garde theatrical performances, and video games, the 'Shakespeare calendar' continues to mark anniversaries of the poet's birth and death. As we emerge from the 2014 celebrations and plunge into those of 2016, it seems a good idea to ask how they perpetuate Shakespeare, and what kind of Shakespeare they perpetuate.

As French sociologist Maurice Halbwachs suggested in *On Collective Memory*, published posthumously in 1950, 'collective memory' is to be distinguished from written history based on documents pertaining to the past and produced by trained scholars. It also differs from autobiographical memories of events personally experienced by individuals. In contrast, collective memory is created by and within a group, and group experience is essential to its creation. That experience, says Halbwachs, creates the framework or context that enables

---

[26] Jonson, 'To the Memory of My Beloved . . . ', line 71.
[27] *Garrick's Ode*, lines 10–12.
[28] Nicola J. Watson, 'Gardening with Shakespeare', Chapter 14 in this volume.
[29] Katherine West Scheil, 'Anne Hathaway's Cottage: myth, tourism, diplomacy', Chapter 15 in this volume.

memory of any kind. Each person's memory may be particular to her or him but, says Halbwachs, 'We can remember only on condition of retrieving the position of past events that interest us from the frameworks of collective memory ... landmarks that we always carry within ourselves.'[30]

Building on Halbwachs's idea of frameworks and contexts, the anthropologist Paul Connerton stresses performance and repetition as key factors in the creation of collective memory. By coming together to perform rituals that they repeat regularly, he argues, groups form collective habits and collective memories. Connerton identifies a 'rhetoric of reenactment' in which everyday life is 'envisaged as a structure of exemplary recurrences'. This rhetoric consists of 'calendrically observed repetition' – celebrating the same thing on the same day at regular intervals, through verbal and gestural repetition.[31] These kinds of repetition make up rituals, and the important thing about rituals is that people have to perform them. They have to say certain things, make certain motions, and repeat them from one year to the next. When they do, they create cultural memory.

Eric Hobsbawm, the influential British historian, connects the foregoing ideas of collective memory to a historical moment in which 'invented tradition' began to shape public symbolic discourse. His idea of tradition has strong affinities with Connerton's 'rhetoric of reenactment'. Defining tradition as 'a set of practices ... governed by rules of a ritual or symbolic nature, which seek to inculcate certain values and norms ... by repetition, which automatically implies continuity with the past', Hobsbawm argues that tradition is 'invented' most often when rapid social change 'weakens or destroys the social patterns for which "old" traditions had been designed'. 'Where the old traditions are alive', he writes, 'traditions need be neither revived nor invented.'[32] He identifies the period 1870–1914 as one in which numbers of 'new official public holidays, ceremonies, heroes or symbols' arose, spurred by the demise or decline of monarchies, revolutions that produced new nations, and the need to create 'an alternative "civic religion" for 'a

---

[30] Maurice Halbwachs, *On Collective Memory*, ed. and trans. Lewis A. Coser (University of Chicago Press, 1992), 172, 175.

[31] Paul Connerton, *How Societies Remember* (Cambridge University Press, 1989), 65.

[32] Eric Hobsbawm, 'Introduction', *The Invention of Tradition*, ed. Eric Hobsbawm and Terence Ranger (Cambridge University Press, 1996), 4, 5, 8.

relatively large, upper middle class élite'. In this era, for example, Bastille Day (made official only in 1880), the Internationale, the Olympic Games and anniversaries of the British royal family (notably, Queen Victoria's Golden Jubilee in 1887 and her Diamond Jubilee in 1897) became major public events, ritualised, participatory and spectacular.[33] These rituals convey and sustain an image of the past, though they are in fact recently invented. In like fashion, at Stratford-upon-Avon Shakespeare's birthday is celebrated annually in a ritual initiated in 1824. A procession led by the boys of King Edward VI Grammar School starts at the Great Garden of New Place and ends at Holy Trinity Church, where an actor impersonating Shakespeare hands a quill pen to the head boy of the school, who carries it inside the church to Shakespeare's grave, thus 'symbolizing', says the website, 'Shakespeare's journey from the cradle to the grave'.[34] Despite the symbolism of the quill pen, again, the emphasis falls not on the literary heritage that the poet bequeaths, but rather, on his basic humanity.

It may be revealing to compare these calendrical commemorations to one centring on place: Shakespeare's so-called 'Birthplace', the house on Henley Street in Stratford-upon-Avon. If the rituals through which we celebrate Shakespeare are in large measure invented, so is the mystique surrounding the birthplace, which literally re-placed the house first associated with the Shakespeare Myth, New Place, when the latter was demolished in 1759, and took on its rituals of literary tourism.[35] Even more than birthday and centennial celebrations, the Birthplace mystique depends, as Julia Thomas argues, 'on the idea of Shakespeare as a real man to whose life the building bore witness'. At the Birthplace, as it was recreated and presented during the Victorian era, that 'real man' was shown to have 'an affinity with common people'; he lived according to 'the values of a pre-industrial community', and was represented, says Thomas, in terms of nostalgic yearnings for an uncomplicated past.[36]

[33] Hobsbawm, 'Mass-producing Traditions', in *The Invention of Tradition*, 263, 269, 292.
[34] See www.shakespearesbirthday.org.uk.
[35] See Richard Schoch, 'The Birth of Shakespeare's Birthplace', *Theatre Survey* 53:2 (2012), 181–97.
[36] Julia Thomas, *Shakespeare's Shrine: The Bard's Birthplace and the Invention of Stratford-upon-Avon* (Philadelphia: University of Pennsylvania Press, 2012), 16, 5, 9.

The house on Henley Street is consonant with historian Pierre Nora's assertion:

There are *lieux de mémoire*, sites of memory, because there are no longer *milieux de mémoire*, real environments of memory ... If we were able to live within memory, we would not have needed to consecrate *lieux de mémoire* in its name.[37]

Nora's notion of the original, lived *milieux de mémoire* as 'primitive or archaic societies' in which even the most everyday gesture 'would be experienced as the ritual repetition of a timeless practice', however, is itself nostalgic.[38] Yet the distinction between the two terms rightly calls attention to the construction of authenticity involved in sites of memory.

Whatever cultural capital such places may create for the poet, they are, no matter how authentically 'restored', markers of death, discontinuity, loss. As Aleida Assmann says, 'Something is still present here, but what this demonstrates above all else is absence: the present relic denotes an irretrievable past.'[39] Literary shrines such as the Shakespeare Birthplace, quite apart from the commercialism that exploits them, inspire ambivalence: both the nostalgic wish to believe that the author was 'a real man', and an awareness that such relics are but simulations of his existence. Or, as Richard Schoch claims in his study of the Birthplace, the visitor aware that the experience offered by the site is not 'totally genuine' nevertheless accepts its tacit invitation 'to play the game of authenticity', entering into it as a performer.[40]

Many Shakespeare lovers, though, haven't sought the real man in either rituals or places of memory. Rather, they have brought Shakespeare into the real world through political action, finding in his works models of 'the political value of theatre and the theatricality of politics', as Andrew Murphy suggests in his chapter on the Easter Rising of 1916. James Connolly and Patrick Pearse, leaders of the rebellion, both 'heavily under the dramatic sway of Shakespeare', fashioned it as 'a

---

[37] Pierre Nora, 'Between Memory and History: *Les Lieux de Mémoire*', *Representations* 26 (Spring 1989), 7, 8.

[38] Nora, 'Between Memory and History', 8.

[39] Aleida Assmann, *Cultural Memory and Western Civilization: Functions, Media, Archives* (Cambridge University Press, 2013), 292.

[40] Schoch, 'The Birth of the Birthplace', 195, 197.

kind of theatrical event'.[41] On the other end of the political spectrum, in 1816, the anniversary of the poet's death was celebrated with a performance of *Coriolanus* starring the premier Shakespearean actor John Philip Kemble in the title role of 'the heroic individual defying the mob'. As Adrian Poole explains in his chapter, in the year after Waterloo when the French monarchy had been restored, this interpretation was congenial to those 'alarmed by the prospect of insurrection or even revolution at home'. Yet Shakespeare's plays don't easily submit to a single partisan interpretation. For Hazlitt, as Poole shows, the restoration of monarchy was a disaster, and Kemble's performance evoked the detestable 'superiority of the ruling class, endlessly reasserting itself'.[42] Both Kemble's performance and Hazlitt's interpretation of it were coloured and shaped by the volatile politics of the moment, interacting with Shakespeare's power to dramatise clashing ideologies. Or to transcend them: as Douglas Lanier demonstrates, when the United States celebrated the 1864 Tercentenary amidst a bitter civil war, Shakespeare poignantly became a figure for unification.[43] The globalisation of Shakespeare is likewise a political phenomenon, but as essays by Gordon McMullan and Philip Mead in this collection attest, that phenomenon began around the 1916 Tercentenary, far earlier than is commonly thought. Through his numerous actions as impresario of the Tercentenary, McMullan argues, Sir Israel Gollancz positioned Shakespeare 'at the pivot of the imperial and the postcolonial'. By re-locating commemoration from Stratford to London, and publishing *A Book of Homage to Shakespeare*, a collection of 166 tributes from all over the world, he re-cast the poet as an international rather than imperial writer. In his own contribution to that book, moreover, Gollancz marked 'his hybrid identity as a Jewish Briton of Polish extraction'.[44] In his interpretation of the tercentenaries celebrated in London and in Sydney, Philip Mead similarly finds commemoration marked by 'new antipodal, trans-Atlantic, and global changes' caused

---

[41] Andrew Murphy, 'Shakespeare's rising: Ireland and the 1916 Tercentenary', Chapter 8 in this volume.

[42] Adrian Poole, 'Relic, pageant, sunken wrack: remembering Shakespeare in 1816', Chapter 3 in this volume.

[43] Douglas Lanier, 'Commemorating Shakespeare in America, 1864', Chapter 7 in this volume.

[44] Gordon McMullan, 'Goblin's market: commemoration, anti-semitism and the invention of "global Shakespeare" in 1916', Chapter 9 in this volume.

by the First World War. The disastrous Gallipoli campaign in Turkey, carried out jointly by Australian and New Zealand forces in April 1915, turned Sydney's celebrations of Shakespeare into ambivalent rituals that invoked the poet both to mourn the faraway dead and to exalt the imperial cause.[45] In London, too, as Ailsa Grant Ferguson shows, the war transformed the very idea of celebrating Shakespeare: festivity now had to be 'frugal and patriotic, selective and pertinent'. As in the Tercentenary in Sydney, commemorating the poet reflected commemoration of war dead, 'in a *mise-en-abîme* of acts of remembrance', she comments. Yet wartime also fostered surprising modernist experiments. Performances of single scenes from Shakespeare interspersed with songs and speeches resembled music hall revues, blurring the boundary between élite and popular culture; actresses who were also pro-suffrage activists played men's roles and even directed performances; fragments of plays performed on the same programme implicitly referred to the wartime present, but in possibly clashing ways, or invited re-combination with each other, as in a modernist text.[46]

Thus acts of honouring and remembering a poet who had been dead for three hundred years became vehicles for the concerns of the moment, inverting any urge to recreate the poet's original moment, and inadvertently updating his works into what Supriya Chaudhuri calls, referring to Shakespeare in India after Independence, 'the time of a reformed present'.[47] In 1964, when Pope Paul VI sought to reform relations between his church and the Church of England, he turned to Shakespeare, and invited the Royal Shakespeare Company to perform at the Vatican. As Marta Cerezo argues here, the Pope wasn't only complimenting England on the four hundredth anniversary of its greatest writer: he was trying to use his praise of the poet's work as a kind of cultural bait to draw Anglicans closer to Rome.[48] Indeed, what is intended to remember the long gone poet often imagines him in new, futuristic guise, as Graham Holderness maintains in his study of the Great Exhibition of 1851, the Festival of Britain a hundred years later and the London Olympics in 2012. In each of these 'national

[45] Mead, Chapter 11.
[46] Ailsa Grant Ferguson, 'Performing commemoration in wartime: Shakespeare galas in London, 1916–19', Chapter 10 in this volume.
[47] Chaudhuri, Chapter 5.
[48] Marta Cerezo, 'Shakespeare at the Vatican, 1964', Chapter 6, *passim*.

celebrations of British culture', instead of being positioned within merry old England, Shakespeare is associated with the latest achievements of science and technology, and with a multicultural world beyond the boundaries of the British Isles – 'a kind of commemoration that remembers the future, as well as the past'.[49]

Commemoration, it seems, is a paradoxical operation that remembers Shakespeare best when it makes him new, like Sydney's Shakespeare Memorial 'clothed in bold and flamboyant dress' in order to 'wake up' the passers by who had ceased to notice it.[50] Or like the late nineteenth-century Indian playwrights who imitated not only Shakespeare's characters and plots but also his 'baroque extravagance' to create 'a new urban theatre of the masses'.[51] With original research in newly discovered archives, the essays gathered here unpack the hidden histories of such renewal, to explore the ironies of time and timing that sustain Shakespeare in cultural memory.

[49] Holderness, Chapter 4.   [50] Hoenselaars, Chapter 13.
[51] Chaudhuri, Chapter 5.

1 David Garrick: saints, temples and jubilees

PETER HOLLAND

I begin briefly with Shakespeare's birthdays, precisely and perversely because they will prove not to be relevant to what follows, neither the anniversary of the date of Shakespeare's birth nor the group of references to birthdays in Shakespeare. Of the latter there are four in all: Cassius' in *Julius Caesar* (5.1.71); Cleopatra's in *Antony and Cleopatra* (3.13.187); Thaisa's in *Pericles* (5.150–1); and Emilia's in *Two Noble Kinsmen* (2.5.36).[1] All four are in classical plays. No one in a play set in England or Britain is noted for having a birthday.

The tendency in early modern Europe was to celebrate not birthdays but name-days, the day of the saint with whom one shared a first name, something more pronounced in Catholic countries than in Protestant ones. I shall have more to explore on Shakespeare's link to saints' days later. Neither Garrick's Jubilee in 1769 nor the Shakespeare day that Goethe celebrated two years later with the speech for the Strasbourg commemoration had anything to do with Shakespeare's birthday. Whatever else may have been happening in the classical allusions that were part of celebrating and commemorating Shakespeare for Garrick and Goethe, no one seems to have connected the event either with Shakespeare's own birthday or his examples of birthdays. The link that is so natural to us – Shakespeare is to be celebrated on or about 23 April – does not figure at all. Celebrating Shakespeare was not for a day but for the whole year.

This tale of temples and monuments, idolatry and jubilation begins with a moment that I have usually considered simply as an act of cultural tourism, a sightseeing trip by three sisters visiting London

An earlier version of this chapter was given at the *Shakespeare 450* Conference in Paris in April 2014. My thanks to Dominique Goy-Blanquet for the invitation to lecture on Shakespeare's 'birthday'.

[1] All quotations from Shakespeare are from *The Complete Works*, ed. Stanley Wells, Gary Taylor et al. (Oxford: Clarendon Press, 1986). The passage from *The Two Noble Kinsmen* is from a scene usually attributed to Fletcher.

from Bristol, their home town, but which I want here to see in the complex context of the creation of the Shakespeare religion, something I will want to redefine as a moment as much of anxiety as of celebration as well as a moment of religious incoherence and imprecision.

When she was twenty-nine, Hannah More, the brilliant young playwright, spent the winter season of 1773–4 in London with her two sisters. Among the trips they made from the flat they rented near Covent Garden, one was along the Thames to Hampton to see the villa, set in six acres, that David Garrick had bought in 1754 and which, for more than twenty years, would be altered, extended and decorated on the advice of the innovative architect and designer Robert Adam, pretty much unknown when Garrick first hired him. Perhaps their connections made it possible to drop by as visitors but perhaps the house and grounds were already on the tourist trail.

When the sisters visited, the house was yet again undergoing building work, as it would need again after a serious fire in 2008, but Hannah was pleased 'infinitely' by Garrick's gardens and she visited Garrick's Shakespeare Temple, the 'grateful temple to Shakespeare' as Horace Walpole called it,[2] that in 1755 Garrick had had designed, possibly by Adam, about forty yards away from the house, on the river frontage. It is, as far as I know, the first temple dedicated to a writer; indeed, I am hard put to it to find another, since the so-called Dante Temple at the Villa Melzi on Lake Como acquires its name only because of the statue of Dante and Beatrice near it. Part of my concern in this article is precisely the sheer oddity of Garrick's project, magnified by the fact that no one seems to have found it odd.

The design of Garrick's temple, whoever the architect was, was clearly derived from the temple at nearby Chiswick House designed by William Kent, which was, in effect, a combination of a rotunda or cella, probably derived from the Pantheon in Rome, and a portico designed after the building often referred to then as the temple of Fortuna Virilis, now known as the temple of Portunus. As well as involving the young architect Robert Adam in the ongoing project of the villa, gardens and possibly the temple, Garrick also commissioned four paintings of the grounds from Johann Zoffany, then, like Adam, still in his twenties. The four showed the house and garden with Garrick reading; a garden view with two of his nieces playing; the

---

[2] Ian McIntyre, *Garrick* (London: Allen Lane/The Penguin Press, 1999), 233.

Figure 1.1 Johann Zoffany, *Mr and Mrs Garrick by the Shakespeare Temple at Hampton*, *c.*1762. Yale Center for British Art, Paul Mellon Collection.

Garricks taking tea in the garden with Colonel Boden, while Garrick's brother George fishes; and, the best known of the four, Mr and Mrs Garrick outside the Shakespeare Temple (Figure 1.1.). The last exists in two versions, one including their nephew playing in the portico and with a servant arrived from the house to serve tea, the other without these figures.[3] I emphasize the fact of this being a group of paintings because of the extent to which the villa was, for Garrick, the epitome of his status as a gentleman, complete with house, garden and garden folly.

The temple contained some of Garrick's greatest treasures. 'Here', wrote Hannah to a friend in Bristol, 'is the famous chair, curiously wrought out of a cherry tree' – she should have written 'a mulberry

---

[3] For the best study of these paintings and of Garrick's long and complex relationship with Zoffany, see Mary Webster, *Johann Zoffany 1733–1810* (New Haven: Yale University Press, 2011), esp. ch. 4, 'The Patronage of David Garrick', 75–91.

Figure 1.2 'Garrick's Shakspeare Chair', by William Hogarth (1697–1764). Private Collection/Photo © Liszt Collection/Bridgeman Images.

tree' – 'which really grew in the garden of Shakespeare at Stratford. I sat in it, but caught no ray of inspiration.'[4]

For Hannah, there was no epiphany from the chair (Figure 1.2), no transformational moment from this equivalent of the wood of the true cross (and, given the astonishing number of objects supposedly created from this one mulberry tree, it did have the prodigious powers of cloning itself that the true cross seems also to have had). Garrick seems to have had no doubt about the provenance of _his_ mulberry chair, even though in his play _The Jubilee_ he has two competing vendors arguing about whose goods are made from the real tree:

Don't buy of that fellow, your honor, he never had an inch of the Mulberry Tree in his life. His goods are made out of old chairs and

[4] George Winchester Stone, Jr, and George M. Kahrl, _David Garrick: A Critical Biography_ (Carbondale, IL: Southern Illinois University Press, 1979), 429.

stools and colored to cheat gentlefolks with. It was I, your honor, bought all the true Mulberry Tree.[5]

In the absence of such a sacred moment as Hannah More hoped to have from sitting in the chair, her experience returned to the human, indeed the emphatically somatic:

But what drew, and deserved, my attention was a most noble statue of this most original man, in an attitude strikingly pensive – his limbs strongly muscular, his countenance strongly expressive of some vast conception, and his whole form seeming the bigger from some immense idea [with] which you suppose his great imagination pregnant.[6]

The statue, which can be glimpsed through the door in Zoffany's painting, had been commissioned by Garrick in 1757 from the sculptor Louis François Roubiliac at a cost, Hannah More noted, of 'five hundred pounds' (other accounts suggested the price was only 300 guineas but that was still a huge sum). Garrick's fame was established on his special bond with Shakespeare and his plays but the statue was marked by a more particular identification than a quasi-religious adoration. The adoration was of course mixed with gratitude for Shakespeare's part in Garrick's successful career and the wealth it had brought him, the (good) fortune that had enabled him to buy the Hampton villa, build the temple and commission the statue. Nonetheless, the statue was seen and probably intended as more than that mix of awe and thanks: a widespread contemporary rumour suggested that the statue was not only *for* Garrick but also *of* him, that Garrick was the model as well as the patron, that Garrick was here performing or becoming Shakespeare, an assumption magnified for us by two strikingly similar paintings of Roubiliac working on the maquettes of two statues, one of Shakespeare (painted by Adrien Carpentiers) and one of Garrick (painted by Andrea Soldi). Roubiliac's pose is virtually identical in each, only the subject has changed – if it really has: in effect, Roubiliac sculpted Garrick twice.

I mentioned Walpole's description of the temple as a sign of Garrick's being 'grateful' to Shakespeare. Walpole, indeed, wrote for

[5] David Garrick, *Plays*, ed. Harry W. Pedicord and Frederick L. Bergmann, 7 vols. (Carbondale, IL: Southern Illinois University Press, 1980–2), II: 112.

[6] Stone and Kahrl, *David Garrick*, 429.

Garrick a motto to ornament the building: *Quod spiro et placeo, si placeo tuum est*. In a letter, Walpole offered a translation:

> That I spirit have, and nature,
> That sense breathes in every feature,
> That I please, if please I do,
> Shakespear, all I owe to you.

But, he wrote, 'his [Garrick's] modesty would not let me decorate it'.[7]

For Garrick, respect for Shakespeare was akin to – or perhaps identical with – an act of faith and this temple was not only jokingly the appropriate place in which to worship a divine being. As he wrote to a French friend, the translator and journalist Jean Suard, in 1765, 'I will not despair of seeing you in my temple of Shakespeare, confessing your infidelity, and bowing your head to the *god of my idolatry*, as he himself so well expresses it' and, anticipating a visit to Hampton by other French gentlemen, Garrick looked forward to a day 'when we shall throw all dramatic critics and critical refinements into the Thames, and sacrifice to Shakespeare'.[8] As Juliet encourages Romeo to swear 'by thy gracious self, / Which is the god of my idolatry' (*Romeo and Juliet*, 2.1.155–6), so Garrick's friend must bow to Shakespeare – and Garrick, like a high priest, was Shakespeare's earthly 'representative': in 1758, the *London Magazine* published some verse, supposedly 'dropt in Mr. Garrick's Temple of Shakespeare', in which Shakespeare's voice identifies Garrick anew:

> Unnotic'd long thy *Shakespear* lay,
> To dullness and to time a prey;
> But lo! I rise, I breathe, I live
> In you, my representative![9]

The appropriation of Juliet's line to Romeo to describe Garrick's reverence towards Shakespeare would reappear near the opening of Garrick's 'Ode' at the Stratford Jubilee. In response to the question

---

[7] Horace Walpole, *Private Correspondence*, 3 vols. (London: Henry Colbourn, 1837), I: 349.
[8] David Garrick, *The Letters of David Garrick*, ed. David M. Little and George M. Kahrl, 3 vols. (London: Oxford University Press, 1963), Letter 362, II: 463.
[9] Quoted by Michael Dobson, *The Making of the National Poet* (Oxford: Clarendon Press, 1992), 182. Little of this chapter would have been possible without Dobson's brilliant and pioneering work in this field.

> To what blest genius of the isle,
>> Shall Gratitude her tribute pay,
>> Decree the festive day,
> Erect the statue, and devote the pile?

comes the answer:

> 'Tis he! 'tis he! – that demi-god!
>> ... 'Tis he! 'tis he!
> 'The god of our idolatry!'[10]

And I find something troubling about Garrick's blandness – perhaps even blindness – to the oddity of this use. Shakespeare may be semi-divine but neither he nor Romeo is a god and what in Juliet seems to me to be a consciousness of the excess and of the sinful danger inherent in idolatry is turned in Garrick into unabashed glorying in this inappropriateness, in what the *Oxford English Dictionary* rather sternly defines as 'immoderate attachment to or veneration for any person or thing; admiration savouring of adoration' (*n.* 2). What kind of religion did Garrick want this new veneration of Shakespeare to be and how does it stand in relation to more conventional religion? I do not for a moment think he was particularly sure, least of all about its relationship to more conventional forms of Christianity. Garrick was, of course, a Protestant, descended from a Huguenot family, but his wife was a Catholic; when they married, on 22 June 1749, they had two ceremonies on the same day, the second a Catholic rite in the chapel of the Portuguese Embassy.[11] Certainly the confused and confusing nature of this new religion was an anxiety for some contemporaries. An attack on the Ode in a contemporary newspaper *The Public Ledger* comments first on Garrick's terming Shakespeare a 'demi-god': 'Had the Author been a little more conversant with the Pagan Mythology, he would have known that the title a Demi-God was never conferred but on Heroes. This is the first time it was ever applied to a Poet.'[12] But that shift from 'demi-god' to 'god' was even more troubling:

But, he [Garrick] seems to think, that even the rank of a Half-God was far too low for Shakespeare; and therefore, in a few lines after, he makes him a

---

[10] David Garrick, *The Poetical Works*, 2 vols. (London: George Kearsley, 1785), I: 57.
[11] Stone and Kahrl, *David Garrick*, 408.
[12] Reprinted in a defence of Garrick's *Ode*, *Anti-Midas* (1769), 23.

whole god ... Well said Christian! But it is no wonder he should endeavor to
make a God of Shakespear, since he has usurped the office of his High-priest;
and has already gained money enough by it, to make a golden calf, to be an
object of that idolatry which he recommends ... This extravagant expression, which is pardonable from the mouth of a young girl distracted with
love, and applied to her lover, he uses as his own serious sentiment, and
that of all the good People of this Realm, with regard to Shakespear.[13]

Eventually, inevitably, the transition from Shakespeare to Garrick
would occur: in his long poem *The Task* (published in 1785), William
Cowper found space to turn the god of our idolatry into Garrick, not
Shakespeare:

> ... Garrick's mem'ry next,
> When time hath somewhat mellow'd it, and made
> The idol of our worship while he liv'd
> The god of our idolatry once more,
> Shall have its altar; and the world shall go
> In pilgrimage to bow before his shrine.[14]

Roubiliac's statue was certainly not the first monument of and to
Shakespeare. The bust in Holy Trinity Church in Stratford-upon-Avon
was in place by 1623. The recognition of Shakespeare as a national
figure was signalled in 1735 by his being placed, along with Milton
and Pope, as one of the representative British poets among the sixteen
figures in the Temple of British Worthies created by William Kent for
Viscount Cobham in his gardens at Stowe and using some of the busts,
including Shakespeare, by John Michael Rysbrack that had earlier
stood in Gibbs's1728 Fane of Pastoral Poetry. Kent's temple is essentially not a space sacred to a divinity but to the memory of a hero or to
a heroic quality, here the modern worthies, positioned in the garden
to face the grander Temple of Ancient Virtue with its four statues,
exemplars of the arts of war, philosophy, poetry and law (Epaminondas,
Socrates, Homer and Lycurgus). So the British worthies included
poets and philosophers, monarchs and architects, eight for action
and eight for thought. Shakespeare's contribution to this is that, as the
tablet above the bust announces, he is the one 'Whose excellent Genius
open'd to him the whole Heart of Man, all the Mines of Fancy, all the

[13] *Ibid.*, 23–4.
[14] *The Task*, Bk 6, in William Cowper, *The Poetical Works*, ed. H. S. Milford, 4th
edn (London: Oxford University Press, 1934), 234.

Stores of Nature; and gave him Power, beyond all other Writers, to move, astonish, and delight Mankind'. Shakespeare may be excellent but he is not unique and, I would note, Hannah More was just as excited, before visiting Garrick's Shakespeare Temple, to see Alexander Pope's house and gardens, the 'haunts of the swan of Thames', for 'what an enthusiastic ardour I have ever had to see this almost sacred spot'.[15] Indeed, as Joseph Roach has intriguingly pointed out, Joseph Nickolls's painting of Pope's villa at Twickenham (*c*.1755) shows in the garden a temple and obelisk, neither of which was in fact ever in Pope's garden, as if either the Chiswick House temple (which has an obelisk in front of it) or Garrick's temple (which does not) had been transplanted there, so that, for Nickolls, the 'swan of Thames' is linked to the 'swan of Avon' via Garrick (as usual).[16]

If Stowe's temple is, in some senses, a sacred spot, it is an unusual one. Technically a roofless exedra, it is a temple without an interior, an open, public space, not one that defines its meaning by analogy to classical temples or churches. It is strikingly unlike any of the other temples at Stowe, for example, the Temple of Concord and Victory or the Gothic Temple. Its form desacralizes its meaning, turning its parade of worthies into something less than sacred, more heroic. One would not here expect to find that 'ray of inspiration', that semi-divine spark of genius that Hannah More hoped to find from the mulberry chair in Garrick's temple. The bust of Shakespeare at Stowe has no signs of the heroic body that she saw in the 'strongly muscular' limbs of Roubiliac's statue. As patriotic project, Stowe is not about the suprahuman nor about the bodily presence, that which lies below the head and shoulders of the bust, that which so overexcited Hannah More.

But the suprahuman, semi-divine Shakespeare has a long history, reaching its apogee long after Garrick's or Hannah More's conceptions of it in Sir Sidney Lee's proposal for a change in the nation's saint. In 1900, in a lecture on 'Shakespeare and True Patriotism', Lee began by comparing Shakespeare and St George as candidates for England's patron saint:

---

[15] William Roberts, *Memoirs of the Life and Correspondence of Mrs Hannah More*, 2 vols. (New York: Harper Brothers, 1834), I: 34.

[16] Joseph Roach, 'Shakespeare and Celebrity Culture', paper at the *Shakespeare and the Problem of Biography* conference, Folger Shakespeare Library, 4 April 2014.

If at the beginning of a new century a patron saint was chosen anew, and the choice lay between a mythical native of Cappadocia and Shakespeare, the native of Stratford-on-Avon, the straitest of cosmopolitan intellects among us could hardly defy the sentiment that gave the preference to the Englishman.[17]

The complete absence in Shakespeare's biography or afterlife of any of the prime requirements for sainthood, such as the performance of miracles through the saint's intercession, seems never to have crossed Lee's mind.

Shakespeare had already been defined as a saint long before. In 1660 John Phillips published his parodic almanac, *Montelion, 1660*. Parody almanacs became formulaic, based on the models of ones from the Interregnum, including, for instance, lists of the time since various events, some real, some not, some significant, others trivial, many jokey, often sexual or scatological. Each month listed its saints' days, as one would expect in any almanac, but with a radically unusual group of saints. January 1660 includes Ovid, Cicero and Petronius, and Chaucer, as well as Country Tom and Fair Rosamond. But 8 January is the day of '*Pericles* Prince of Tyre' and 5 January of 'Andronicus';[18] 2 May brings 'Jack Falstaff' and then, on 4 May, 'Shakespear' – the fact that the latter is not too far from Shakespeare's 'birth'- and death-day is, I am sure, no more than an accident.[19] *Montelion, 1660* is the only example I have yet come across in the parody almanacs that includes Shakespeare as a saint. But the *Montelion* for the following year, not by Phillips, has Falstaff again, now on 6 May.

In 1662 William Winstanley began his long series of 'Poor Robin' almanacs and Falstaff turned up frequently as one of the saints in the double calendar, one liturgical, one parodic, that Winstanley listed month by month. In *Poor Robin* for 1668, for instance, he is on

[17] Quoted by Peter Holland, 'Shakespeare and the *DNB*', in J. R. Mulryne and T. Kozuka (eds.), *Shakespeare, Marlowe, Jonson: New Directions in Biography* (Aldershot: Ashgate, 2006), 139–49, 140.
[18] George Thorn-Drury, *More Seventeenth Century Allusions to Shakespeare and his Works* (London: P. J. and A. E. Dobell, 1924), 4, listed the first but missed the second.
[19] Though the date looks like a Julian/Gregorian calendar discrepancy, England used the Julian calendar until 1752 and hence 4 May 1660 was the same as 4 May 1564. In addition, the baptismal register entry for Shakespeare had not yet been identified and therefore the extrapolation to the supposed birthday had not been made.

11 January, in 1675 on 31 January, in 1676 on 11 January and 1677 on 25 January. There is an exuberant energy in Winstanley's work; as Frank Palmeri comments,

Poor Robin's list draws its parodic saints from such widely disparate realms as picaresque and satiric literature, Greek history, English folklore, Italian literature, imperial Roman history, chivalric romance, criminal history, British political history, Shakespearean and other British drama, Elizabethan fiction, French fables, European mythology, the history of Catholicism and Anabaptism.[20]

Winstanley, who, not surprisingly, was running out of inspiration the longer the series continued, quoted the winter part of the final song in *Love's Labour's Lost* for a number of wintry months (for example, *Poor Robin* for 1670 and 1679) and peppered his pamphlets with Shakespeare quotations, allusions and references. The one for August 1677 mentions that 'we read in antient Chronicles of the *Merry Wives of Windsor*, and find the jolly *Dames of Wapping* celebrated by more modern Authors'.[21]

Winstanley would make his best-known contributions to the praise of Shakespeare first in one of the lives added to the second version of *England's Worthies* in 1684 (Shakespeare and Jonson as the examples of playwrights among the 72 worthies) and then expanded in his *Lives of the Most Famous English Poets* (1687), which covered 168 poets in all. Here Shakespeare is 'This eminent Poet, the Glory of the *English* Stage (and so much the more eminent, that he gained great applause and commendation when able Wits were his Contemporaries)'.[22] But the significance he accords Shakespeare can be seen in the frontispiece to the entire volume, which places a bust of Shakespeare between monuments to Chaucer and Cowley. Unnoticed until 2009,[23] this engraving by Van Hove clearly gives Shakespeare pride of place, even over Chaucer, whom Winstanley, quoting Peter Heylin, gives 'first place of our chiefest Poets', and Cowley, whom he calls 'the Glory of our Nation'.[24] The line from this bust to the one in Cobham's Temple of British Worthies is a

---

[20] Frank Palmeri, 'History, Nation, and the Satiric Almanac, 1660–1760', *Criticism* 40 (1998), 377–408, 384.

[21] Quoted in Thorn-Drury, *Seventeenth Century Allusions*, 15.

[22] William Winstanley, *Lives of the Most Famous English Poets* (1687), 130.

[23] Jackson C. Boswell, 'Yet Another "New" Shakespeare Image', *Shakespeare Quarterly* 60 (2009), 341–7.

[24] Winstanley, *Lives of the Most Famous English Poets*, 31, 182.

short one – and the connection of the name of Cobham's Temple with the title of Winstanley's *English Worthies* is, I suspect, no accident.

But, even as Cobham was having his temple built, there were signs of the campaign to have Shakespeare appropriately memorialized in marmoreal form in Westminster Abbey, a movement that gathered force once a bust of Milton had been placed there in 1737. The author of an early elegy on Shakespeare, William Basse, had argued that Shakespeare should be placed beside Chaucer, Spenser and Beaumont in the Abbey. It may be for Basse 'a sacred sepulchre' but we are a long way here from Shakespeare as saint, however ironically. Basse's proposal was, of course, one that Ben Jonson strongly resisted, proclaiming, in his elegy on Shakespeare printed in the First Folio, that Shakespeare did not need such a memorial:

> Thou art a Moniment, without a tombe,
> And art alive still while thy Booke doth live.

But others were not so sure and were determined that a monument in Westminster Abbey would be exactly what Shakespeare would have. Even if the body could not be moved from Stratford and buried in the Abbey, there was no reason why a memorial could not be in the capital's gathering of the great and the dead. The statue by Peter Scheemakers was unveiled in 1741. Often reproduced in prints and soon available as a small porcelain souvenir, it was a sign of Shakespeare's cultural value. It was a version of this statue, not the one in Garrick's temple, that would stand in the midst of the orchestra for the performance of Garrick's 'Ode' at the Jubilee (see Figure 1.3).[25]

The words in Shakespeare's voice about his being 'Unnotic'd long' hugely overstated the case for seeing the playwright as neglected before Garrick's arrival on London's theatrical and social scene.[26] But the myth continued, finding its place at the end of the century in an inscription on the plinth of another statue: a contemporary described the statue of Garrick put up in Westminster Abbey in 1797 as showing Garrick 'throwing aside a curtain, which discovers a medallion of the

---

[25] See also the print, e.g. at the National Portrait Gallery, NPG D7658, www.npg.org.uk/collections/search/portrait.php?search=ap&npgno=D7658, accessed 3 June 2014.

[26] See, among much other work, Don-John Dugas, *Marketing the Bard: Shakespeare in Performance and Print* (Columbia and London: University of Missouri Press, 2006).

Figure 1.3 'Mr. Garrick delivering his Ode at Drury Lane Theatre, on dedicating a building and erecting a statue to Shakespeare', 1769, engraving by John Lodge (fl.1782–d.1796). Private Collection/Bridgeman Images.

great Poet ... The curtain itself is designed to represent the Veil of Ignorance and barbarism, which darkened the drama of the immortal bard till the appearance of Garrick', while the inscription explains the meaning further:

> Tho' sunk in death the forms the Poet drew,
> The Actor's genius bade them breathe anew.
> Tho', like the Bard himself, in night they lay,
> Immortal Garrick call'd them back to day.[27]

Visit Garrick's Shakespeare Temple now and you will not find the Roubiliac statue, only a reproduction of it. In his will, as the symbolically placed second item, after the disposition of the Hampton estate, Garrick left the statue to the British Museum, where it stood in the King's Library until the opening of the new British Library, where it stands at the foot of the main staircase. Garrick plainly wished to have it seen as occupying a different kind of space from the temple: no longer part of religious fervour but instead as part of the national collection of the genius of the country that the new museum and its central feature, the library, were intended to symbolize. In many ways, Garrick's Shakespeare religion was always a matter of celebrating the genius of the nation. One might worship at the Shakespeare Temple or by reading in the British Museum or by going to the theatre or even by going on pilgrimage to the birthplace of the saint. That this was not exactly thought through is only appropriate: Garrick was an actor-manager, not a theologian, and his aim was always a Shakespeare cult, rather than a church. The transpositions of location for the act of faith is therefore characteristic and, for Garrick, probably desirable.

Even before the Shakespeare temple was built at Hampton, Garrick had redefined where the sacred space of Shakespeare should be, no longer in Westminster Abbey nor in Holy Trinity Church in Stratford-upon-Avon. In his prologue for the new season in 1750, Garrick defined the Shakespeare religion as belonging in the theatre itself:

> Sacred to Shakespeare was this spot design'd,
> To pierce the heart, and humanize the mind.

---

[27] Quoted by Vanessa Cunningham, *Shakespeare and Garrick* (Cambridge University Press, 2008), 8.

But, as Garrick well knew, especially given his responsibilities as manager, it all depends on the audience's taste – even a sacred spot can remain empty:

> But if an empty House, the Actor's curse,
> Shews us our Lears and Hamlets lose their force:
> Unwilling we must change the nobler scene,
> And in our turn present you Harlequin.[28]

And Harlequin, as Garrick would have remembered from one of his first appearances on the London stage, was perfectly capable of absorbing Shakespeare and even the celebration of Shakespeare as statue, playwright and divinity. Henry Giffard's *Harlequin Student* (1741), in which Garrick took the role of Harlequin when Richard Yates fell ill, ends with the arrival of Jupiter announcing that 'Immortal Shakespear's matchless Wit revives, / And now the Bard in speaking Marble lives', after which 'The Scene draws and discovers the monument of Shakespear, exactly represented, as lately erected in Westminster Abbey'.[29]

But, by 1769, Garrick had allowed the sacred spot to shift again, this time to Stratford-upon-Avon in the event that would be explicitly established as a religious one in its very title, the Jubilee. Garrick set out to privilege the birthplace over the rival attractions in Stratford:

The Gothic glories of the ancient Church, the modern elegance of the Civic Hall, cease to be regarded, when it is remembered that the humble shed, in which the immortal bard first drew that breath which gladdened all the isle, is still existing; and all who have a heart to feel, and a mind to admire the truth of nature and splendour of genius, will rush thither to behold it, as a pilgrim would to the shrine of some loved saint; will deem it holy ground.[30]

Not quite a manger but the next best thing, this shed was to be more even than the shrine of a saint. Think back to William Cowper (quoted above) on Garrick 'fram[ing] the rites'. James West noted on a letter from Garrick about the Jubilee on 19 May 1769, 'In Stratford, Garrick bows to Shakespeares Shrine.'[31] Long after the Jubilee, as Garrick

[28] Brian Vickers, *Shakespeare: The Critical Heritage* (London and Boston: Routledge & Kegan Paul), 6 vols., III: 365–6.
[29] Quoted in Dobson, *Making of the National Poet*, 163.
[30] Quoted in Jonathan Bate, *Shakespearean Constitutions: Politics, Theatre, Criticism, 1730–1830* (Oxford University Press, 1989), 31.
[31] Garrick *Letters*, Letter 538, II: 644.

wrote to Stratford's mayor to outline future annual events which 'should be on his *Birth*-day', he encouraged the mayor to ensure the cleanliness of the town to 'allure Every body to Visit yᵉ *holy Land*', as if Stratford and Bethlehem were indeed indistinguishable.[32] And the very notion of a jubilee, as Garrick hatched the plan with the burgesses of Stratford-upon-Avon, was designed to evoke pilgrimage and religion from its origins in Leviticus through Pope Boniface VIII's institution in 1300 of a period of remission from punishment for sin consequent on pilgrimage to Rome. Whatever else it was, the Stratford Jubilee was to be the creation of a national religious cult of Shakespeare worship.

I do not of course want or need to go over the events in Stratford, well described by Deelman and England,[33] beyond pointing out Garrick's commissioning Gainsborough to rework the portrait of Garrick with the bust of Shakespeare that had been exhibited in 1766, with Garrick in a cross-legged stance that deliberately echoes both the Westminster Abbey statue and the Roubiliac in Garrick's temple. The function of the event as ritual, its liturgical patterning, has been beautifully explored by Péter Dávidházi,[34] from the lunch for 700 people with its toasting Shakespeare in wine (shades of the Last Supper here) to Garrick's song in praise of the mulberry tree cup with its clear signs of Eucharistic adoration of this version of the Holy Grail:

> Behold this fair goblet, 'twas carv'd from the tree,
> Which, O my sweet Shakespeare, was planted by thee;
> As a relick I kiss it, and bow at the shrine,
> What comes from thy hand must be ever divine![35]

What most intrigues me is not the events in Stratford but the repossession of the event by the theatres in London and the pamphleteering and

---

[32] Garrick, *Letters*, Letter 625, II: 728, dated 8 March 1771.

[33] Christian Deelman, *The Great Shakespeare Jubilee* (London: Michael Joseph, 1964); Martha W. England, *Garrick's Jubilee* (Ohio State University Press, 1964).

[34] See Péter Dávidházi, *The Romantic Cult of Shakespeare* (Houndmills, Basingstoke: Macmillan, 1998), *passim*; and his '"He drew the Liturgy, and framed the rites": The Changing Role of Religious Disposition in Shakespeare's Reception', *Shakespeare Survey 54* (Cambridge University Press, 2001), 46–56. See also Kate Rumbold, 'Shakespeare and the Stratford Jubilee', in Fiona Ritchie and Peter Sabor (eds.), *Shakespeare in the Eighteenth Century* (Cambridge University Press, 2012), 254–76.

[35] Garrick, *Poetical Works*, II: 431.

other publications that also, at times, recreated the Jubilee as drama. And, within that process, there is a continual anxiety over the term 'Jubilee' itself, with its Catholic origins. Punningly, the Jubilee also linked to the controversy over the Jewish Naturalization Act of 1753, often referred to as the 'Jew-bill', an Act, promoted by the Whigs and fiercely opposed by the Tories, that, in gratitude for Jewish support during the Jacobite rising of 1745, allowed Jews to be naturalized as British citizens but which was inevitably attacked as an abandonment of the Christian basis of the country.[36] If Garrick's own version of the Shakespeare religion is something I have been defining as unconcernedly incoherent, the consequence of the remediation of its most public manifestation at the Jubilee was only a magnification of that incoherence and conflictedness, itself a source of cultural anxiety rather than reassurance, now by contemporary playwrights and critics, literati and literary hacks, playgoers and readers.

To document something of the scale of the response to the events in Stratford I need first to offer a short table of the Jubilee plays and prologues for London and a few of the associated pamphlets published in the capital:

1. Barely a week after the Jubilee had begun, on 13 September 1769, Samuel Foote added a speech for the Devil in his play *The Devil upon Two Sticks* that offered a definition of a Jubilee as 'a public invitation … to celebrate a great poet whose works have made him immortal by an ode without poetry, music without melody, dinners without victuals and lodgings without beds'.[37]
2. George Colman's prologue, 'Scrub's Trip to the Jubilee', was performed by Weston at Covent Garden on 19 September.
3. Francis Gentleman's play, *The Stratford Jubilee*, was intended for Samuel Foote's company at the Haymarket but was never performed. It was published, with Colman's prologue, on the same day.
4. *Garrick's Vagary*, an anonymous satire in dialogue-form, was advertised on 22 September.
5. Garrick performed the Ode on stage at the Theatre Royal, Drury Lane, on 30 September and repeated it on a few days thereafter (Figure 1.3).

---

[36] On this see James Shapiro, '"Shakespur and the Jewbill"', *Shakespeare Survey 48* (Cambridge University Press, 1996), 51–60.
[37] Deelman, *The Great Shakespeare Jubilee*, 272.

6. Foote announced that his theatre would perform a Burlesque Jubilee Ode with a parody of the Drury Lane procession of characters, dressed in rags, but was eventually dissuaded from doing so. *Drugger's Jubilee*, a reference to Garrick's role in Jonson's *The Alchemist*, was still being anticipated in May 1770.
7. George Colman's play *Man and Wife*, hastily rewritten to include satire on the Jubilee and including a pageant of Shakespeare's characters, was first performed at Covent Garden on 7 October 1769.
8. Garrick's *The Jubilee* followed at Drury Lane on 14 October.
9. *Anti-Midas*, a pamphlet defence of Garrick's Ode, was probably published in November.
10. Edward Thompson's poem, *Trinculo's Trip to the Jubilee*, also appeared in November.
11. Henry Woodward's pantomime, *Harlequin's Jubilee*, opened at Covent Garden in January 1770.
12. And Peter Barnes's play *Jubilee* was first performed by the Royal Shakespeare Company in the Swan Theatre, Stratford-upon-Avon in July 2001.

Put simply, I can think of no comparable case of such repeated remediation of an event into theatre, poem, pamphlet and parody. And in spite of the sustained mockery of the Ode, the rapacious inhabitants of Stratford, the weather and other such failures, there is really no mockery of the idea of celebrating Shakespeare in some such extravagant fashion. Only in the last two items on my list is there a thought of an alternative. Barnes's play envisages a very different celebration. As Hermione, the maidservant in Mrs Ross's brothel puts it,

why celebrate Shakespeare?... While you celebrate him, the real world is being forgotten for a verb or a noun ... What does Shakespeare know of the terror of my life...? Don't cry over his verse, cry over my life ... Celebrate me! Celebrate me![38]

Woodward's play was not published, but its songs were and Woodward's parody of Garrick's song 'The lad of all lads was a Warwickshire lad' as the competition between two pubs, both called The Magpie, that traded on the London Road, ends with a recognition of where power really lies:

---

[38] Peter Barnes, *Jubilee* (London: Methuen, 2001), 43.

Pro Publico bono will shew his best skill,
For the will of all wills is the Public's good will;
Public's good will!
Matchless still![39]

The farce ended with a hymn of praise to Lun: 'Songs grotesque, and jocund raise, / To LUN, who merited our praise!' As a reviewer described, the play closed 'with the descent of the statue of the late Mr Rich, under the name of Lun, which he always adopted when he performed the character of Harlequin', especially appropriate as, when Woodward played Harlequin, he used the name Lun, Jr.[40] The celebration of Lun's triumph is an ironic reversal of James Miller's *Harlequin-Horace* (1735), an attack on Rich exactly for his o'ertopping Shakespeare.[41]

Of course there is repetition among all these representations. Samuel Foote's mockery was taken over by many, most effectively by Garrick himself who turned it into a song: 'Odes, Sir, without poetry / Music without melody / Singing without harmony.'[42] The clash between London's fashionable elite, out for a good time, and provincial cunning, out for a profit, is an inevitable meme in most of these. But so is the repeated concern to define the Jubilee as nothing whatsoever to do with the decrees of the Pope and the remissions of sins sought by Roman Catholics. The word Garrick chose seems in this context to be recurrently troubling, even though there had been no shortage of uses earlier as part of national celebrations, such as the actor Richard Estcourt's ballad 'Britain's Jubilee' on Marlborough's victories over the French, published in 1708,[43] or Revd Joseph Acres' sermon preached on the accession of George I, *Great Britain's Jubilee or the Joyful Day* (1715). And Farquhar's play, *The Constant Couple*, subtitled *A Trip to the Jubilee*, a staple of the repertory throughout this period, made the actor Henry Norris famous as 'Jubilee Dicky' and mocked the foolish

---

[39] Henry Woodward, *Songs, Choruses, &c., As they are performed in the new Entertainment of Harlequin's Jubilee* (London, 1770), 7.
[40] Quoted in Dobson, *Making of the National Poet*, 216n.
[41] See Marcus Risdell, 'Picturing Rich', in Berta Joncus and Jeremy Barlow (eds.), *'The Stage's Glory': John Rich, 1692–1761* (Newark: University of Delaware Press, 2011), 266–72.
[42] Garrick, *Plays*, II: 107.
[43] In *Windsor Castle: A Poem* (London, 1708), 15–16.

character Clincher Senior for wanting to go to the Jubilee when all he can say about it is 'why the *Jubilee* is – faith I don't know what it is'.[44]

In 1769 the separation of the Stratford celebrations from the events in Rome, most recently in 1750, seemed crucial. Otherwise the country would have been left with the assumption that, as a character in Francis Gentleman's *The Stratford Jubilee* put it, 'the Jubilee ... is a rank piece of popery.'[45] Here, for instance, is a character in Colman's *Man and Wife*: 'If it is a Jubilee, it must be nonsensical. – I was at the Jubilee at Rome some years ago.'[46] Or, again, from the same play, 'you care no more for Shakespeare, than I for the Pope of Rome'.[47] (Colman, incidentally, offers what is my favourite label for Shakespeare: 'Shakespeare, Mr. Marcourt – Shakespeare is the Turtle of Literature. The lean of him may perhaps be worse than the lean of any other meat; – but there is a deal of green fat, which is the most delicious stuff in the world.'[48] The phrase is probably an echo of the fact that an enormous turtle, 327 lb in weight, had been served at one of the Jubilee banquets.[49])

Garrick's play has Nancy announce to Sukey, 'I swear I know no more about the Jubillo and Shakespur, as you call him, tha[n] I do about the Pope of Rome.' Sukey, who 'cried for a whole night together after hearing his Romy and July at Birmingham', tells Nancy off: 'Had you lived at Birmingham or Coventry, or any other polite cities, as I have done, you would have known better than to talk so of Shakespur and the Jewbill.'[50] Garrick was, indeed, concerned before the event at rumours of the locals' suspicions, writing to William Hunt, Stratford's Town Clerk, on 16 August 1769,

I heard Yesterday to my Surprize, that the Country People did not seem to relish our *Jubilee*, that they look'd upon it to be *popish* & that we sh^d raise ye Devil, & w^t not – I suppose this may be a joke, – but after all my trouble, pains labor & Expence for their Service & ye honor of ye County, I shall think it very hard, if I am not receiv'd kindly by them – how ever I shall not be the first Martyr for my Zeal.

---

[44] George Farquhar, *Works*, ed. Shirley Strum Kenny, 2 vols. (Oxford: Clarendon Press, 1988), I: 168.

[45] Francis Gentleman, *The Stratford Jubilee* (1769), 4.

[46] Colman, *Man and Wife*: or, the Shakespeare Jubilee (London: printed for T. Becket and Co. and R. Baldwin, Row, 1770), 17.

[47] *Ibid.*, 22.   [48] *Ibid.*, 19.

[49] Deelman, *The Great Shakespeare Jubilee*, 234.   [50] Garrick, *Plays*, II: 122.

In a postscript he asked Hunt to 'pray tell me Sincerely what the Common People think & Say'.[51] He turned the joke to his own use in his play but the anxiety here sounds real enough.

At its most extreme, the comparison between a celebration of the national poet and the threat of a foreign and subversive religion was carefully and anxiously pursued in the pamphlet-dialogue *Garrick's Vagary*. The author spends page after page charting the similarities between the events of the Stratford Jubilee and the precise rituals of the jubilee at Rome, so that, for instance, for the moment when the Pope takes up the cross and enters St Peter's, 'Here we are to substitute our *Roscius*, entering the Booth at *Stratford*, followed by all his theatrical Tribe, of various Denominations; *and then, taking up* not *the Cross*, but the *Ode*, he begins to read...'.[52] The sign of Christianity becomes the poem in praise of Shakespeare, creating a remarkable analogy. It is Garrick who pinpoints the convergence of papacy and the Jubilee in the transformation of the Shakespeare monument in Holy Trinity Church, when Ralph, a Stratford local, says, with provincial wisdom, 'I knew something was abrewing when they would not let his image alone in the church, but had the show people paint it in such fine colors to look like a Popish saint.'[53] Shakespeare painted is Shakespeare the Catholic saint. The writer who in national pride signifies the triumph of Protestantism is painted into the Catholic tradition.

Garrick's Vagary opens with an attack on everyone in London,

running out of Town, pell-mell, after a Brat of *Judaism*, a since foster-Child of *Popery*, now, forsooth, revived by an Actor, to the very imminent and most alarming Danger both of Church and State – As a good Englishman, and a true Protestant, I feel much Concern, am patriotically hurt ... at so papistical a Manœuvre ... I wonder how our Bishops can remain quiet on so critical an Innovation...[54]

The new Shakespeare religion, the cult of Shakespeare, is a threat to the coherence of the country's view of state and church and a sign of the invasive otherness of foreign religions such as Judaism and Roman Catholicism. The interweaving of patriotism and anti-popery would reach a new stage a few years later when the Papists Act of 1778 led to

---

[51] Garrick, *Letters*, Letter 553, II: 660. My thanks to Michael Dobson for drawing this letter to my attention.
[52] *Garrick's Vagary* (1769), 16, 19.   [53] Garrick, *Plays*, II: 105.
[54] *Garrick's Vagary*, 3–4.

the Gordon Riots in 1780. The rise of the Shakespeare religion comes to pinpoint cultural anxiety, social vulnerability and national insecurities in the very Englishness it was aimed to celebrate.

It is no surprise, then, that the Stratford Jubilee would lead to a proposal of yet another quasi-religious structure, another Shakespeare Temple, not this time in the gardens of an actor who wished to appear a gentleman but as a public structure to celebrate the glory of the nation. Paul Hiffernan was another playwright, poet, critic, hack, eking out a living in London. Helped by Garrick's drumming up subscriptions, Hiffernan published in 1770 his study of *Dramatic Genius*, the first book of which sets out his 'PLAN of a permanent TEMPLE, to be erected to the memory of SHAKESPEARE, in a Classical Taste; with INSCRIPTIONS and DECORATIONS, suitable to the Objects chosen'.[55] The inscriptions were to be in Latin and English, 'the one for the sake of learned Foreigners unacquainted with our Language, and by whom we are now visited in greater numbers than usual heretofore' (3–4), a sign of Shakespeare's potential interest for the developing tourist trade. Whatever the Jubilee might have done for Stratford and whatever Garrick may have done at his villa in Hampton, Hiffernan wanted to see extended to the proper kind of shrine to the poet and his actor, with scenes from tragedies and comedies. The exterior inscription, in Hiffernan's own awkward translation of his awkward Latin, was to read:

> Nor gay THALIA's comic *Fane* stands here,
> Nor solemn *Temple of the* TRAGIC MUSE;
> But SHAKESPEARE's Shrine, they emulous have raised! (23)

When entered into the Temple, the first object for the curious spectator's attention, is the great Poet; over whom is to be a sun, rising in all its glory, after having dissipated from our British Theatre, the long incumbent clouds of Gothic ignorance and barbarism, that are to be seen flying from the victorious lustre... (16)

But, if that suggests the sun behind Shakespeare, the inscription shows that Shakespeare himself is the source of the light and power: '*Darkness' dark shades fly* SHAKESPEARE's *solar Beams*' (16).

---

[55] Paul Hiffernan, *Dramatic Genius* (London: printed for the author, 1770), v. Subsequent page references are given in parentheses in the text.

Shakespeare is the blessed sun, an Apollonian transfiguration; the saint in whose honour the temple is created as a 'shrine', Hiffernan's word, has become fully divine, the energy for the world or more especially nation. Not a place for Shakespeare's relics like Garrick's collection in his temple, mulberry chair and all, but a place of pilgrimage to see the classical divine and the beatified Christian united against foreign darkness. No wonder Hiffernan wanted the foreign tourists to understand the message. No wonder this supremely hyperbolic architectural vision was never built. Shakespeare commemoration may often be grand or even grandiose but nothing out-tops Hiffernan's fantasy.

In *Desert Island Discs*, the world's longest-running radio programme, a celebrity 'castaway' is asked to choose, as well as eight records, a book other than the Bible and the works of Shakespeare, which somehow have reached the desert island already. In the same way, the progress from Basse's poem, through the parodic naming of Shakespeare as a saint, through the temples and statues, idolatry and popish celebrations that I have charted, ends in an equivalence: the works of Shakespeare and the Bible are really the same thing: both the Word of God. As the philosopher Lichtenberg noted in 1775, the audience at Hamlet's 'To be or not to be' 'not only knows it by heart as well as they do the Lord's Prayer, but listens to it, so to speak, as if it were a Lord's Prayer ... In this island Shakespeare is not only famous, but holy.'[56] Lichtenberg was no more likely than Garrick to unpack the complex and conflicting notions of faith and adoration sitting within that short word 'holy'. As usual, the imprecision is central to the possibility of turning fame into sainthood.

---

[56] Margaret L. Mare and W. H. Quarrell, *Lichtenberg's Visit to England* (Oxford: Clarendon Press, 1938), 16.

2 | *Commemorating Shakespeare in performance: Betterton and Irving*

RICHARD SCHOCH

A basic question in the historiography of Shakespeare in performance is the relationship between actors and their predecessors, both near and remote. At any given moment in theatre history, do actors adopt the gesture, expression, rhythm, and pose of past performers, or do they break with tradition and give new shape to the actor's art? To what extent has Shakespeare in performance been regarded as a living archive, an embodiment and preservation of past performances? To what extent has performance been regarded as the opposite: a source of novelty and innovation that spurns its own past? To invoke this volume's guiding theme, is acting Shakespeare a matter of commemoration or, contrastingly, dismissal?

There has never been a single answer to this question. Using the principal – and sharply different – case studies of the Restoration actor Thomas Betterton (*c.*1635–1710) and the great Victorian actor-manager Henry Irving (1838–1905), I will demonstrate that both the commemorative tradition and its opposite have dominated concepts of theatrical excellence at different moments. Having established that narrative, I will then consider why each tradition enjoyed a period of dominance and what that dominance tells us about the theatre's changing perspective on itself. In brief, I want to argue that the Restoration theatre's idea about itself privileged continuity and commemoration, whereas on the cusp of the twentieth century English theatre understood itself as forcing an estrangement from the past. The place where those contrasting ideas were articulated and embodied was in the actor's art.

The belief that performances of Shakespeare were commemorative began at the earliest possible moment when such commemoration was historically thinkable: the Restoration, when the performances of Thomas Betterton were, whether realistically or rhetorically, traced all the way back to Shakespeare's instructions to the actors who created the parts. The idea that Betterton was himself a living archive of theatre history was doubtless helped by the fact that he enjoyed an unusually long and successful career on the stage, making his debut at the Cockpit Theatre in 1660 and giving his last performance five decades later, when, aged seventy-five, he played the war-hero Melantius in *The Maid's Tragedy*.

Fortunately for posterity, one person who saw Betterton on the stage many times and at close range was the equally long-lived John Downes, prompter for the Duke's Company and later for the United Company. Downes's career, from 1661 to 1706, overlapped almost entirely with Betterton's. Downes is best remembered as the author of *Roscius Anglicanus*.[1] Published in 1708, a few years before its author's death, the work is the first example of English theatre history as calendar: a roughly sequential list of plays performed by each company, with some indication of casting. Downes considers, in turn, the King's Company (1661–82), the Duke's Company (1661–82), the United Company (1682–94), Betterton's breakaway company (1695–1704), and, finally, Vanbrugh's management of the reunited companies at the Haymarket in 1706. Occasionally he comments on various productions, noting their popularity or unpopularity, and sometimes includes an anecdote or observation about scenery and acting.

The work as a whole is a rather splendid mess, a happy jumble of theatrical data that is correct in many cases. As a commercial venture, it was not successful. There was no second edition; and Downes, in the few remaining years of his life, seems not to have written anything else. Still, it is the only history of the Restoration stage written by someone who witnessed it – and not just witnessed it, but was part of it. Despite being mostly an awkward roll call of performances, *Roscius Anglicanus* comes into its own in two passages about Betterton and the actors who preceded him. Instead of adding one more colourful item to his laundry list about a given theatrical season, Downes quickly drives the narrative about a Shakespearean play all the way back to the moment when the King's Men first produced it. In other words, the author stops describing one moment in time and starts to think across time.

---

[1] John Downes, *Roscius Anglicanus, Or An Historical Review of the Stage* ... (London: H. Playford, 1708).

No longer just a scribe, he now becomes something new, and new for his time: a theatre historian.[2]

From a distance of nearly half a century, the veteran prompter recalls not just the afternoon performances but the morning rehearsals for *Henry VIII*, staged by the Duke's Company at Lincoln's Inn Fields in 1663. Before Downes explains how Betterton, then at the beginning of his career, learned the title role, he first remarks upon the splendid new costumes and scenery for a play full of pageants and processions:

> King *Henry* the *8th*. This Play, by Order of Sir *William Davenant*, was all new Cloath'd in proper Habits: The King's was new, all the Lords, the Cardinals, the Bishops, the Doctors, Proctors, Lawyers, Tip-staves, new Scenes; The part of the King was so right and justly done by Mr. *Betterton*, he being Instructed in it by Sir *William*, who had it from Old Mr. *Lowen*, that had his Instructions from Mr. *Shakespear* himself, that I dare and will aver, none can, or will come near him in this Age, in the performance of that part … [I]t being all new Cloath'd and new Scenes; it continu'd Acting 15 Days together with general Applause.[3]

What stands out most vividly is the division between what was *new* in the performance and what was *old*. What was new were the defining characteristics of the Restoration stage: sumptuous costumes, extravagant painted scenery, and actresses, as recorded in the cast list that Downes also provides. What was old was the acting. Not that it was stale or hackneyed, but the opposite: that it somehow preserved, freshly, and not as a dead artefact, the essence of the role as Shakespeare communicated it to the actor who first played it. As Downes would have it, Betterton was taught by Sir William Davenant, who was taught by John Lowin, who was taught by the playwright himself.[4]

Two degrees of separation between Betterton and Shakespeare. We have no idea on what basis Downes believed this, other than hearsay

---

[2] An insightful commentary on the historiographical significance of *Roscius Anglicanus* can be found in Peter Holland's 'A History of Histories: From Flecknoe to Nicoll', in W. B. Worthen and Peter Holland (eds.), *Theorizing Practice: Redefining Theatre History* (Basingstoke: Palgrave Macmillan, 2003), 8–29. Jacky Bratton touches upon the disciplinary importance of *Roscius Anglicanus* but overstates the extent to which it was imitated. See her *New Readings in Theatre History* (Cambridge University Press, 2003), 17–18.

[3] Downes, *Roscius Anglicanus*, C4v.

[4] The descent through Davenant offers a theatrical parallel to the tradition first recorded by John Aubrey in the 1680s that Davenant was Shakespeare's illegitimate son.

and theatrical legend. But the story is not impossible: old Mr Lowin, who survived until 1653, was still with the King's Men in 1635, when he spoke the Prologue to Davenant's *Platonic Lovers* at the Blackfriars. Tradition alone claims that Lowin played the title role in *Henry VIII* when it was first performed at the Globe in 1612 or 1613, but for this period in theatrical history the absence of documentary proof is the norm. What documents do survive – such as the cast list for Jonson's *Catiline* (1611) – place the actor with the King's Men at that time.[5] Against that, we might ask, for example, whether Shakespeare was present for rehearsals if, as other traditions maintain, he had by that time retired to Stratford. And wouldn't it have been more likely that if an author instructed Lowin how to play the part, that author wouldn't have been Shakespeare, but Fletcher?[6]

When it comes to the validity of Downes's claim about *Henry VIII* we will never know whether 'all is true'. Or even whether part is true. But that may not be such a problem, because, historiographically, what really matters about this passage from *Roscius Anglicanus* is not the accuracy of its theatrical 'begats' but the reason why they were needed in the first place. In other words, what matters is the cultural work that this particular genealogical narrative accomplished.

What it accomplished, in 1708, was nothing other than the restoration of a normative theatrical past. It wasn't just that theatre was once again part of public life and leisure; it wasn't just the resumption of theatrical performance after an eighteen-year hiatus; but rather that theatre was being resumed in a particular way. In the very strut and fret of the Restoration actor, Downes wants to tell us, acting as Shakespeare knew it, as Shakespeare *created* it, could still be seen. Theatres had been closed for nearly two decades, but nothing had been lost.

Downes's belief that past performances live within performances of the present day becomes clearer if we look at how he structured his

---

[5] The cast list is printed in the 1616 Folio edition of Jonson's works.

[6] In his *Memoirs of the Principal Actors in the Plays of Shakespeare* (London: The Shakespeare Society, 1846) John Payne Collier includes a biographical sketch of John Lowin but discounts the acting genealogy proposed by John Downes – he relegates it to a footnote (174) – precisely because it could not be supported by documents. Collier was not interested in the cultural work accomplished by 'remote stage-tradition' (252) but only in whether those traditions could be empirically verified.

account of *Henry VIII*. He begins with the tailor-made costumes ('new Cloath'd in proper Habits'), then switches to the continuity of a pedigreed acting tradition ('Instructions from Mr. *Shakespear* himself') and then, finally, returns to new costumes and scenery ('it being all new Cloath'd and new Scenes'). New – old – new. In the very structure of his writing, Downes is giving us a template for reading Shakespeare in performance historically. In the sequence of words on the page, just as in the audience's reception of the performance, the production's visual components, Downes seems to be saying, bracket, encase, or surround actors who are themselves preserving 'original practices', so to speak. If the production had to be condensed into one image, it would be an old body dressed in new clothes. Or to reverse the biblical metaphor, old wine poured into new wineskins. As for the text, it doesn't fall out of the equation, but gets absorbed into the actor's work, here presented not as discretionary – the actor doesn't decide how to play the part – but as tightly regulated by norms, what Shakespeare taught.

At least for Downes, acting Shakespeare is always normative. It's not simply that an actor must act well, but that acting well means acting *justly*. In his account of *Hamlet*, the other play for which Downes constructs a family tree of actors, his language is even stronger: Davenant taught Betterton 'every Particle' of the role, and it was by the younger actor's 'exact Performance' of what he had learned that his reputation rose:

The Tragedy of *Hamlet*; *Hamlet* being Perform'd by *Mr. Betterton*, Sir *William* (having seen Mr. *Taylor* of the *Black-Fryars* Company Act it, who being Instructed by the Author Mr. *Shaksepeur*) taught Mr. *Betterton* in every Particle of it; which by his exact Performance of it, gain'd him Esteem and Reputation, Superlative to all other Plays[.][7]

Roscius Anglicanus insists repeatedly that there is something beyond and prior to the actor – not the text, but the acting of it, the embodiment of it – which derives from its first theatrical incarnation and demands, therefore, his loyal fiduciary care. It wasn't just that Betterton worked from an existing script but that he worked from a long-existing way of performing that script, handed down from actor to actor through the years, like a family heirloom.

[7] Downes, *Roscius Anglicanus*, C3r.

An esteemed performance, a performance like Betterton's, is one that recreates the *first* performance – exactly, justly and in every particle – and then transmits it – whole, intact and undiluted – both to the audience and to the next generation of actors. Nothing added, nothing subtracted. In the strictest sense, the actor does not bring any value of his own to the performance, but rather safeguards and sustains the value that preceded him, and that ought to survive him, holding it in stewardship for the time being and the time to come. That is what theatre history means to John Downes. The rhetorical construction of a commemorative acting tradition from Shakespeare to Betterton was deeply significant to the author of *Roscius Anglicanus*, a work whose very title configures the theatrical present, in the person of Betterton, as the living instance of a classical precedent.[8]

Why is it so important to Downes that the present looks like the past? Because he is trying to do something more than to compile a stage calendar. He is trying, from within that welter of data, to extract – to shape – a theatrical canon. And for a canon to possess integrity and authority over time it must amount to something more than a miscellany. In its own awkward way, *Roscius Anglicanus* is to the history of the theatre what Gerard Langbaine's *An Account of the English Dramatick Poets* (1691) is to the history of printed drama, in that both works aspired to consolidate a national canon: Langbaine's for drama, Downes's for acting. Just as Langbaine describes himself as a 'Champion in the Dead Poets' Cause', and so defends Shakespeare, Jonson, and Fletcher, we might call Downes a 'Champion in the Dead Actors' Cause', in that he presents the actors who first performed Shakespeare, Jonson, and Fletcher as having inaugurated an unbroken tradition.[9] We never get the details of what constituted that embodied tradition – we don't get a picture of it. Rather, we are assured only that the

---

[8] Nicholas Rowe similarly maintained that Betterton was 'so much a Master' of Shakespeare that 'whatever Part of his he performs, he does it as if it had been written on purpose for him, and that the Author had exactly conceiv'd it as he plays it'. Nicholas Rowe, 'Some Account of the Life of William Shakespear', in Rowe (ed.), *The Works of Mr. William Shakespear*, 9 vols. (London: Printed for Jacob Tonson, 1709), I: xxxiv. Rowe had enlisted Betterton's help in gathering information for his biography of Shakespeare and so was hardly impartial. But the point remains that Betterton is constructed as Shakespeare's immediate and perfect heir, with no corrupting passage of time intervening between them.

[9] Gerard Langbaine, *An Account of the English Dramatick Poets...* (Oxford: Printed by L. L. for George West and Henry Clements, 1691), I3r.

tradition, whatever its substance, continues to exist and is exemplified in the person of Thomas Betterton.[10]

Yet no sooner does Downes establish a normative genealogy of Shakespearean acting than he undermines it. Betterton's performance is lauded for preserving a tradition, but one whose *continued* preservation is cast into doubt because his performance could not be matched. As Downes asserts, 'None can, or will come near him in this Age.' Obviously this was meant as praise for Betterton (and more than a hint that popular comic actors like Colley Cibber – whom Downes had once hired for walk-on roles at Drury Lane – weren't up to scratch when it came to tragedy), but the result is a historiographical melt-down.[11] So well does Betterton uphold every particle of the acting tradition that he annihilates it. No one can follow him. Betterton has theatrical forefathers, but no children of his own. Paradoxically, then, *Roscius Anglicanus* presents Betterton's acting as both history come alive and the death of history.

This is less an empirical failure – Downes getting wrong the degree to which Restoration actors imitated their predecessors, something he could not know first hand – than a methodological impasse. Downes was one of the first people to think historically about the stage; not just cumulatively – one performance after another – but historically. What did it mean, what *does* it mean, to say that the stage has a *history*? It means that the stage has a past that is comprehensible; a past that can be preserved, and therefore known by those who did not live through it; and a past that is worth knowing. We see this entirely in Downes's genealogy of acting: theatre is understood as the continuity of an acting tradition; the theatrical past is preserved in the work of contemporary actors; and the past is worth knowing because it sprang from original authorities. In his own ham-fisted way, Downes, in 1708, was orienting

---

[10] The interesting divergence is that the pre-Civil War repertoire, as Langbaine concedes, must be adapted in order to survive in the playhouse; but for Downes, the manner in which those plays are acted must *not* be adapted. A contradiction emerges: the Restoration actor performs in a purely Shakespearean manner (whatever that means) plays that are not purely Shakespearean. The text is altered but the acting remains the same. And yet in both instances the result is the same – a canon is established.

[11] 'Mr. *Cyber*, A Gentleman of his time has Arriv'd to an exceeding Perfection, in hitting justly the Humour of a starcht Beau, or Fop... [he would be] not much Inferior in Tragedy, had Nature given him Lungs Strenuous to his finisht Judgment'. Downes, *Roscius Anglicanus*, E2r.

himself towards performance in a new way, a way that allowed the phenomenon of performance to be understood more deeply.

It was bound to be ham-fisted not just because Downes was a neophyte author but because he had no one to guide him. There was James Wright's *Historia Histrionica* (1699), which was mainly a response to Jeremy Collier's attack on the theatre; there was Richard Flecknoe's *Short Discourse of the English Stage* (1664) – just nine pages long – and there was, less directly, Langbaine's *English Dramatick Poets*. For someone who wanted to write theatre history in the first decade of the eighteenth century, there wasn't much to go by.

The vitality of *Roscius Anglicanus* resides not in its dull serial format but in the moments when the author liberates his genealogical imagination. It's important to remember that during the period in question, genealogical material of whatever type was not static. Rather, it circulated in the form of antiquarian or chorographic treatises that were passed from hand to hand, letters that contained extracts from historical documents, and in conversations in libraries, clubs, and coffeehouses. Such information circulated because it was socially useful. Pedigree wasn't a fact to be dutifully recorded and then forgotten precisely because it had been recorded. It was, rather, an awareness of social reality, a commodity of immediate relevance, and metaphorical equipment for living.[12]

The theatre was far from alone in falling victim to a pedigree craze in the seventeenth and early eighteenth centuries; it was, however, unusually susceptible to genealogical hierarchies by virtue of its embodied nature and its intrinsic obsession with searching for originals. If you wanted to give full vent to ancestor consciousness in the Restoration, the theatre was a good place to start. Indeed, the eighteen-year closure of the public theatres made that undertaking all the more urgent: the line had been severed, and now must be restored. Just as ancestral and family privileges were jealously guarded in everyday life, they were also jealously guarded in the theatre, with actors claiming the mantle of exalted predecessors, or having it bestowed upon them by chroniclers such as Downes.

---

[12] For an excellent discussion of the genealogical imagination in the seventeenth and early eighteenth centuries, see Daniel Woolf, *Social Circulation of the Past: English Historical Culture 1500–1730* (Oxford University Press, 2003).

Ancestry was a claim to family honour and prestige, and the longer the ancestry the greater the honour and the prestige. It wasn't the only such claim – the upright character and virtuous actions of individuals, even their personal wealth, still mattered – but it was an important one. Indeed, the theatre was a privileged space for such claims because it was where *pedigree* and *individuality* combined. An actor might be the living embodiment of his ancestors on the stage, but he had only himself through which to embody them. Thus, Downes defined an excellent actor as someone who, like Betterton, is simultaneously an artist in his own right *and* the steward of a proud tradition. By 1700, as Daniel Woolf explains, family genealogy was no longer a pious example of ancestor worship or a 'pseudo-biblical' series of 'begats'; it had, instead, become a 'bridge' between past and present.[13] Within decades of the Restoration, the respect due to ancestors was inseparable from the achievements of their latest descendants. Ancient lineage still mattered, and would continue to be esteemed, but only to the extent that its effects were felt in the achievements of people in the present day. Consciously or not, John Downes internalized this shift in broad historical thought, because his esteem for great actors in the past and his esteem for the greatest actor of the present are fundamentally indivisible. In a way that has not yet been appreciated, theatre history's early interest in pedigree – and the way the theatre itself expressed that interest – put it in the vanguard of English historical culture in the late seventeenth and early eighteenth centuries. All this makes *Roscius Anglicanus* a much more revelatory work than its critics and readers have long supposed.

A century-long obsession in editions of *Roscius Anglicanus* as to whether John Downes is right or wrong on this point or that has blinded us to his real and lasting achievement, which is less historical than historiographical.[14] The old prompter's achievement was not to answer the question of whether performance can be an archive of itself, not least because he appears to answer both 'yes' and 'no'. His achievement was to *ask* the question. He was the first to do it. In asking that question he accomplished something that we now all take for granted, but almost no one in 1708 did: he made theatre historically thinkable.

---

[13] Woolf, *Social Circulation of the Past*, 136–7.

[14] See, especially, John Downes, *Roscius Anglicanus, Or An Historical Review of the Stage*, ed. Judith Milhous and Robert D. Hume (London: The Society for Theatre Research, 1987).

Thinkable, but how? Not as drama, not as the struggles of rival and sometimes reunited companies, not as a business, not as a building, not as a vehicle for celebrity, but as *practice*. As something done and redone. As performance. And within the doing and redoing that constitutes performance's perpetual present lies its own history.

2

The forces that influenced how the English theatre reflected upon its own history had changed greatly by the late nineteenth century, when Henry Irving (1838–1905) ruled the English theatre. Beginning with his idiosyncratic performance of Hamlet in 1874, Irving's fame and reputation rested on his ability to be *unlike* the great actors of the past. Throughout his career Irving advertised himself not simply as the latest personification of an acting tradition – the heir to Richard Burbage and David Garrick – but as a complete artist of the stage, to be judged by his own standards and not by those of his theatrical forefathers. Irving's performances articulated a distinctively *modernist* approach to Shakespeare: that a production expressed the upheaval of tradition, not its untroubled continuity. This change was tied to the theatre's sense that a point of exhaustion had been reached with acting traditions, and that if the theatre were to survive it would not be through veneration of the past, but through overt renewal. On the threshold of the twentieth century, an anti-commemorative rhetoric was needed to give England's theatre its future.

Master of the Lyceum Theatre for three decades, the most famous Shakespearean of his day, and the first British actor to be knighted, Irving was deeply aware of theatrical tradition. With exceptions like Tennyson's *Becket*, the Lyceum's repertoire of Shakespeare and melodrama looked backward, and the roles that Irving acted would not have puzzled audiences from the 1850s. The night Irving first played Richard III he was presented with the sword that Edmund Kean had used when playing the role. It was a gift from the veteran actor William Henry Chippendale, who had shared the stage with the elder Kean. This was not Irving's first theatrical relic. Baroness Burdett-Coutts, his patron, had already given him a ring worn by Garrick.[15] Irving would not have prized these gifts if he did not see himself as connected to his illustrious

---

[15] Austin Brereton, *The Life of Henry Irving*, 2 vols. (London: Longmans, Green, and Co., 1908), II: 222.

forbears. Without question he understood himself to be the inheritor of
a tradition upheld by Garrick, John Philip Kemble, W. C. Macready and
Charles and Edmund Kean.

But he did not – and this is the crucial difference – regard himself as
bound by the tradition that formed him. His career stands as the first
expression in England of the modern artist's desire to control the full
process of artistic creation. Irving became known not as a typical actor-
manager but as a figure more strategic, more conceptual, and, hence,
more powerful. As Clement Scott put it, he was the 'master-mind and
guiding spirit' who 'suggest[ed] and organise[d] what was so splendidly
carried out'.[16] Scott was one of Irving's most enthusiastic supporters – but
that is all the more reason to observe that calling Irving a 'mastermind'
was praise, not censure. Attending rehearsals for their joint production of
Othello (1881), the American actor Edwin Booth witnessed that 'from
first to last [Irving] rules the stage with a will of iron . . . At the Lyceum one
sees the perfection of stage discipline.'[17] Decades after Irving's death,
Gordon Craig – the pioneering theatrical modernist who had been an
apprentice in Irving's company – famously pronounced him not just the
perfect actor but his ideal of the Über-marionette: the puppeteer who, by
pulling all the strings, controls everyone else's actions.[18]

It was Irving who guided the standard for theatrical greatness
away from genealogy and towards exceptionality. His exceptionality
was performed onstage and off. Irving's distinctive appearance and
manner – tall and spindly, the spidery walk, the bohemian long
hair, the bookish pince-nez, the broad hat and flowing frock coat –
turned him into a memorable figure. As Percy Fitzgerald remembered,
'there were only three or four men whom people would turn to
look after in the street – Mr. Gladstone, Cardinal Manning and
Irving'.[19] Undergraduates wore their hair in the same raffish style
and women congregated outside the stage door at the Lyceum. He
became a cult-like figure, with autograph-seekers and searchers after
relics: cigar butts, gloves, a lock of hair – all became collectibles.

---

[16] Clement Scott, *From 'The Bells' to 'King Arthur'* (London: John MacQueen, 1896), 233.

[17] *The Theatre*, October 1883.

[18] Edward Gordon Craig, *Henry Irving* (London: J. M. Dent & Sons, 1930), 32.

[19] Percy Fitzgerald, *Sir Henry Irving: A Biography* (London: T. Fisher Unwin, 1906), 291.

Comparisons with his friend Oscar Wilde – another *fin-de-siècle* original – are not far-fetched.

It would have been ego, but nothing more, were Irving's claim merely to have outshone Garrick, Kemble and the elder Kean. His claim, however, was more audacious yet. It was not Shakespeare the artist and Irving his interpreter but Irving the artist and Shakespeare his raw material. George Bernard Shaw's accusation that Irving 'never in his life conceived or interpreted the characters of any author except himself' is more than an indictment of vanity.[20] It captures the moment when adherence to theatrical precedent began not to matter. Chief herald of the new drama, Shaw despised all that he believed Irving represented: worn-out melodramas, indifference to good writing, and enslavement to opulence. Even so, Shaw understood that Irving raised himself above the level of mere showmanship: 'Irving's art was the whole of himself; and that was why he sacrificed himself – and everybody and everything else – to his art.'[21]

And so it can hardly surprise us that when Irving delivered a lecture on 'Four Great Actors' – Richard Burbage, Thomas Betterton, David Garrick, and Edmund Kean – at Oxford University in the summer of 1886, his goal was not to commemorate his predecessors but to construct a history of acting that anticipated – and refuted – the criticisms then levelled against him.[22] A deeply partisan observer of the past, Irving admitted no distinction between the history of the theatre and the history of himself. Thus, the 'censure' directed at Betterton for cluttering the stage with scenery led directly to the self-flattering admission that '[i]f it be a crime against good taste ... to heighten the effect of noble poetry by surrounding it with the most beautiful and appropriate accessories, I myself must plead guilty to that charge'. He dismissed attacks on Garrick for the strangeness of his pronunciation – attacks also made against Irving – as motivated by 'envy [of] the very universality of his success'.[23]

The motivating zeal that Irving manifested as both actor-manager and occasional chronicler of the stage brands him as an artist of the

---

[20] George Bernard Shaw, review of *Cymbeline, Saturday Review*, 2 January 1897.
[21] George Bernard Shaw, *Pen Portraits and Reviews* (London, 1932), 167.
[22] Irving's lecture was published as 'Four Great Actors', in *The Drama: Addresses by Henry Irving* (New York: Tait, Sons, & Co., 1896).
[23] Irving, 'Four Great Actors', reprinted in Jeffrey Richards (ed.), *Sir Henry Irving: Theatre, Culture and Society* (Keele University Press, 1994), 58, 60.

late nineteenth century, someone preoccupied with pursuing an ideal, no matter what the cost. This same zeal helps to explain why Irving took criticism seriously, perhaps too seriously, treating hostility to him as an assault upon the entire theatrical profession. It was as if even a single dissenting voice was somehow illegitimate, because it failed to appreciate that the artist's *intent* mattered more than the result. 'I plead for the actors', Irving declared in 1878 at a working men's institute in Birmingham. 'Their work is hard, intensely labourious – feverish and dangerously exciting. It is all this even when unsuccessful.'[24]

The intense prosecution of Irving's artistic ideal is usually analysed through the majestic synthesis of the kinetic, visual, and aural elements of the stage that marked his great Shakespearean revivals at the Lyceum.[25] But I suggest that the rupturing of theatrical tradition that Irving's ideal demanded can best be understood in terms of his individual acting style. His desire to extricate himself from the very performance genealogy in which he had been trained did not develop gradually. It was, in fact, manifested in his first Shakespearean effort in London, the 1874 *Hamlet*. Irving knew better than anyone else that he had no business performing that part. Although he had played the Dane on the occasional benefit night in Oxford and Manchester a decade earlier, that hardly prepared him for the role by which all great actors of the time were judged. But perhaps the audacity of the under-taking was what liberated him.

The story, which has long ago passed into theatrical legend, is that the opening night audience sat in confused silence until the 'nunnery' scene, when the newness of Irving's interpretation finally became apparent. Such was the arresting novelty of his performance – he neglected the acting 'points' hardened into tradition; he subscribed to William Hazlitt's theatrically risky proposition that Hamlet's ruling passion was not to act, but to think; he moved with 'short and frequently jerky' steps, so unlike Kemble or Booth – that it was hailed as the beginning of an era in Shakespearean production.[26] That was an overstatement: no one but Irving merited recognition and there was but scant *mise-en-scène*. Still, the performance must have felt shockingly

---

[24] 'The Stage', *The Theatre*, March 1878.

[25] See, for example, Alan Hughes, *Henry Irving, Shakespearean* (Cambridge University Press, 1981).

[26] *The Athenaeum*, 7 November 1874.

modern. Here was a Hamlet who made you stop and think, just as the character himself did.

Whether Irving showed himself a genius was a question quickly taken up in a war of pamphlets, with William Archer and Robert Lowe scornfully branding the Lyceum's leading man as the 'indiscriminately belauded . . . interpreter of Shakespeare to the multitude'.[27] But it was beyond dispute that this Hamlet was unusual. Gone was the blond wig of Charles Fechter's colloquial prince and gone was the plumed finery of Kemble's haughty aristocrat. Here, instead, was a mournfully contemplative young man dressed in black (save for a gold chain and dagger), the colour set off by his wintry pale complexion. Upon long, thin legs he slouched and lurched across the stage. The actor was mocked, but the edgy physicality conveyed Hamlet's anxieties: like the time, he was out of joint.

'We in the audience see the mind of Hamlet', reported Scott. 'We care little what he does, how he walks, when he draws his sword. We can almost realize the workings of his brain.'[28] Though flattering, the remark nonetheless captures an important truth: that the audience was led to admire less the emotional depth of any particular characterization and more the actor's intelligence in crafting that characterization. Irving's delivery in *Hamlet* was so peculiarly static that he seemed not to embody the character at all. Indeed his performance approached a conceptual reversal of theatrical norms: instead of the actor illuminating the character, the character illuminated the actor. It was not that Irving failed to perform Hamlet but that he used Hamlet to represent himself as an uncommonly intelligent tragedian, as evocatively captured in Onslow Ford's life-size marble sculpture from 1883 of Irving the actor blended with Hamlet the thinker. During the 1864 Shakespeare Tercentenary the aspiring actor had recreated in a *tableau vivant* Sir Thomas Lawrence's 1801 famous portrait of Kemble as an Elizabethan Hamlet. But that sort of ancestor worship no longer suited the new star. As soon as Irving seized his opportunity to play Hamlet, he took the performance of the role *out* of history – no more imitations of the great Kemble – and placed it in an isolated present.

---

[27] William Archer, Robert Lowe, and George Halkett, *The Fashionable Tragedian* (Edinburgh: Thomas Gray, 1877), 3.

[28] Scott, *'The Bells' to 'King Arthur'*, 62.

The following season, in 1875, Irving attempted a second idiosyncratic interpretation of a Shakespearean tragic hero, but to less encouraging effect. Critics quickly faulted his performance as Macbeth – only his second Shakespeare role in London – for failing to imitate the manner, pose and gesture of yesterday's tragedians. Consider, for example, this review from the *Illustrated Sporting and Dramatic News*, which presumed that unless traditional acting 'points' were observed, Shakespeare's characters could not be 'represented':

> That there is much to be admired in many of Mr. Irving's readings cannot be denied; but, on the other hand, so many obvious points rendered familiar to us by such actors as the Keans, Macready, Phelps, and others, and vouchsafed by many generations of dramatic critics, were missed, if not absolutely perverted, by Mr. Irving in his striving after originality, that the Thane of Cawdor in its entirety cannot be truly said to have been successfully represented on the present occasion.[29]

Undeterred by such criticism, Irving persisted with departures from tradition. It was risky to attempt Othello in 1876, just ten months after the Italian actor Tommaso Salvini had taken London by storm with his nearly bestial incarnation of the Moor. Audiences could not so quickly erase from their memory the exotic picture of Othello in turban and burnous or Salvini's raw passion when he struck Desdemona across the face with the back of his hand. Austin Brereton, one of Irving's hagiographic biographers, later described the Italian as 'the true Moor, the veritable Moor, the only Moor that ever was, could, or should be'.[30] The mocking hyperbole aimed to trivialize; but no doubt Irving sensed that his only option had been to act the part as differently as possible. The actor felt the depth of his failure but blamed the audience for its parochialism. 'They expect to see Othello as something entirely Eastern and mysterious', he complained to Walter Pollock; 'they don't at all understand finding him dressed like other characters in the play. I ought to have thought of that and given up the idea.'[31] Here, the actor and his audience are out of sync, the actor no longer interested in commemoration, and yet the audience still expecting that each new production of Shakespeare will look like the last one it saw.

---

[29] *Illustrated Sporting and Dramatic News*, 2 October 1875.
[30] Brereton, *Life of Henry Irving*, I: 199.
[31] Laurence Irving, *Henry Irving: The Actor and his World* (London: Faber and Faber, 1951), 272.

Three years later another celebrated role gave Irving a better opportunity to succeed by disavowing theatrical precedent. In *The Merchant of Venice* (1879), Irving's Shylock towered above the taunting Christians who surrounded him. Irving believed that the Christians were the play's true hypocrites because they preached mercy but never showed it.[32] 'I look on Shylock', he explained, 'as the type of a persecuted race; almost the only gentleman in the play, and most ill-used.'[33] That perspective came through in performance, leading the critic Dutton Cook to declare that he had 'never [seen] a Shylock that obtained more commiseration from the audience'.[34]

Revealingly, Irving's sympathetic portrayal of Shylock rested chiefly upon an unscripted silent moment – a moment that could not participate in a discourse of veneration because there was no precedent to revere. After Jessica's flight with Lorenzo the stage was overtaken by a whirl of revellers and masquers upon whose festivities the act curtain fell. As the applause died down, the curtain unexpectedly rose on the same moonlit piazza, only now the stage was empty. From the far side of the bridge appeared a dejected Shylock, leaning heavily upon his cane, heading slowly home. Expecting to find solace in his daughter's company, Shylock knocked twice at the unopened door of his house and then looked upward in confusion towards Jessica's room. The curtain dropped just as the lonely father was about to enter his house and discover what the audience already knew: his daughter had abandoned him.

This brief interpolation unleashed an extraordinary emotional charge. Steeped in the Victorian cult of domesticity, the Lyceum audience could not help but feel sympathy for a man who had been unjustly abused in public and then returned home only to endure the pain of being abandoned by a disrespectful daughter.[35] This moment of pure invention was crucial to Irving's sympathetic portrayal of Shylock, a portrayal that was itself inventive. Shaw pronounced Irving's Shylock as neither good nor bad but 'simply not Shylock at all'. Ignoring the

[32] 'An Actor', 'The Round Table. The Character of Shylock', *The Theatre* (December 1879), 255.

[33] Joseph Hatton, *Henry Irving's Impressions of America*, 2 vols. (Boston, 1884) 226–8.

[34] Dutton Cook, *Nights at the Play* (London: Chatto & Windus, 1883), 391–3.

[35] Jessica was 'an odious, immodest, dishonest creature' because she betrayed a parent. *The Spectator*, 8 November 1879.

text, the actor 'positively acted Shakespear off the stage'.[36] Remember-
ing the performance from a distance of thirty years, the playwright
Henry Arthur Jones likewise described it as 'ex-Shakespearean'.[37]
Irving's more humane Shylock proved immensely popular; but, for
the analytical purposes of this chapter, that is a secondary matter.
The greater concern is that his performance became incomparable.

That Irving's performance represented an extraction from history
which was seen simultaneously as the perfection of history can be
observed in the racial and religious politics that surrounded his interpretation of Shylock. Without question, national pride was aroused by
Irving's distinctive performance. The starting point for that response
was the recognition that a sympathetic portrayal of Shylock – a man
proud of his Jewish heritage and subjected to the vicious intolerance of
hypocritical Christians – was itself a proud sign of Anglo-American
moral supremacy. Only a civilization devoted to tolerance, only a
civilization in the ascendant, could produce and value such an enlight-
ened interpretation, or so the self-laudatory rhetoric would have it. *The
Merchant of Venice* 'could not be played in any century but the
nineteenth', affirmed the *Chicago Tribune* during one of Irving's eight
American tours; 'and it could not be played by any but an English-
speaking actor'.[38]

Here, then, is testament to a changing consciousness about performance and about what makes a performance excellent. The distinctive
characteristic of Irving's Shylock – so distinctive that only an Anglophone audience could appreciate it – was its 'modernity'. By 'modernity', the critic elaborated, 'one means the liberality of the conception'.[39]
Again, the performance speaks not to its stylistic antecedents – from
which it is distanced and detached anyway – but to changing motivations from outside the domain of performance. To praise a performance for existing only in the present – a present time, a present
geography, a present culture, a present religion – which in this self-
regarding instance was nineteenth-century, Anglophone, and Christian – is to claim that history no longer matters. History, in fact, is
what has been overcome. In this particular performance, history was
swallowed by the present in the figure of Henry Irving's sympathetic

---

[36] George Bernard Shaw, *Our Theatres in the Nineties*, 3 vols. (London:
Constable, 1932), II: 198.
[37] Henry Arthur Jones, *The Shadow of Henry Irving* (New York: William Morrow
& Co., 1931), 53.
[38] *Chicago Tribune*, 1 October 1893.   [39] *Chicago Tribune*, 1 October 1893.

Shylock. In 1741, Alexander Pope was supposed to have praised Charles Macklin's performance of the 'Jew that Shakespeare drew'.[40] That family resemblance was gone – long gone – and not worth remembering, let alone reviving.

As evidenced in these various examples from *Hamlet*, *Macbeth*, *Othello*, and *The Merchant of Venice*, it would be hard to overestimate how great a conceptual shift Irving demanded of his audience. Theatregoers had been accustomed for generations to interpret performances as a series of well-known acting 'points', with today's tragedians judged against those of distant yesterdays. Such points had long since petrified into tradition, and diehard theatregoers knew them by heart and expected to see them replicated in performance. Indeed, it was such replication that gave value to the performance, authority to the critics, and satisfaction to the spectator. But Irving offered an alternative. Whether you liked or loathed his acting was in some ways irrelevant. What mattered was that you recognized that it belonged to *him*. No one else could have created it. Such a reversal of theatrical norms was sometimes accepted by the audience; sometimes praised; but at other times feverishly denounced. In his three decades at the Lyceum, Henry Irving continuously and effectively challenged the presumption that Shakespeare in performance must recall a lauded theatrical past and that such recollection is itself the precondition for the intelligibility of contemporary performance. Irving opened the door to theatrical modernism so that artists like Gordon Craig could walk through it.

3

The historiographical moments instantiated in the careers and achievements of Thomas Betterton and Henry Irving could not have been more different. Betterton embodied the moment when the resumption of public theatregoing after an eighteen-year hiatus called for a valorization of deep continuity, even though much about theatrical practice was changing. The way forward was the way back. By contrast, nothing seemed to be changing about theatrical practice in the closing decades of the nineteenth century. Grand pictorial revivals of Shakespeare had been the norm since the era of W. C. Macready and Charles

---

[40] Quoted in John Gross, *Shylock: Four Hundred Years in the Life of a Legend* (New York: Touchstone, 1992), 122.

Kean. If anything had changed, it was that London theatres were even better equipped to create overwhelming stage spectacles through the latest technology. Irving's refusal to use electric lights at the Lyceum is symptomatic of his unwillingness to reinforce the dominant theatrical narrative of his day. Standing in the gap between those chronologically adjacent and yet conceptually distant territories named 'Victorian' and 'modern', Irving realized that the way forward was, in fact, the way forward.

And yet both ways went through Shakespeare. Both ways were bound up in discourses of commemoration that announced themselves in different manners because they were responding to different historical pressures. Betterton's situation, whether in reality or the rhetorical constructions of John Downes, was obviously commemorative in that it enshrined a normative genealogy of acting traditions that began with Shakespeare himself. Irving's situation was equally commemorative, but less obviously so. It wasn't that the Lyceum's actor-manager disavowed Shakespearean commemoration – nothing could be less true – but that he disavowed how other people went about it. Here, the recognition of Irving's incipient modernist aesthetic is crucial, for it reveals that the actor commemorated Shakespeare in a decidedly modernist manner: by rewriting him, whether in the interpolated silent scene from *The Merchant of Venice* or in a novel performance of Hamlet. For all the inevitable stylistic differences – the one traditional, the other iconoclastic – the ways in which Thomas Betterton and Henry Irving acted Shakespeare were both predicated upon the desire to commemorate Shakespeare. But to commemorate him in a way that made sense for each actor's theatre in each actor's time.

3 | Relic, pageant, sunken wrack: Shakespeare in 1816

ADRIAN POOLE

In April 1816 Britain had better things to celebrate than the bicentenary of Shakespeare's death. It was less than a year after Waterloo. Wordsworth had been busy writing the 'Thanksgiving Ode', in which he hailed Carnage as the daughter of Almighty God.[1] The poet's thoughts were not on Shakespeare but on the war-heroes who would join 'England's illustrious sons of long, long ages' and be remembered in turn by 'their sons' sons, and all posterity', on 'Commemoration holy that unites / The living generations with the dead'.[2] Yet the ghost of Shakespeare was not entirely absent from his mind. In another poem, similarly addressed to the aftermath of 'Battle's whirlwind', a Spirit appropriates Hamlet's words to the ghost of his father ('Rest, rest, perturbed spirit' (I.v.182)), singing instead: 'Rest, rest, perturbed Earth! / O rest, thou doleful Mother of Mankind!'[3]

In the late summer of 1815 Walter Scott, as he then was, had been amongst the vanguard of British tourists swarming to the battlefield, 'this celebrated scene of the greatest event of modern times'.[4] Long before Tennyson's 'Ode on the Death of the Duke of Wellington' in 1852, the greatest British hero of modern times inspired any number of

---

I gratefully acknowledge Kate Pfeffer's research assistance in the early stages of work on this essay. Research for this article has been financed by Research Project FFI2011-24347 'Cultures of Commemoration II: Remembering Shakespeare', funded by the Spanish Plan Nacional de I+D+i 2008–2011.

[1] Published in the volume titled *Thanksgiving Ode, January 18, 1816, with other short pieces chiefly referring to recent public events* (London: Longman, Hurst, Rees, Orme and Brown, 1816). The line about Carnage was controversial at the time, and disappeared from editions after 1832.

[2] *Thanksgiving Ode*, 15–16.

[3] References in the text are to *The Riverside Shakespeare*, 2nd edn, general ed. G. Blakemore Evans (Boston and New York: Houghton Mifflin, 1997); 'Elegiac Verses. February 1816', in *Thanksgiving Ode*, 50.

[4] *Paul's Letters to his Kinsfolk* (Edinburgh: Constable and Company, and London: Longman, Hurst, Rees, Orme, and Brown and John Murray, 1816), 194. Hereafter *PL* with page references in the text.

monuments, beginning with Richard Westmacott's huge 1822 statue of Achilles at the south-western end of London's Park Lane. In the year that Tennyson's elegy was written, an impressive bronze statue of Wellington on a rearing horse was unveiled in Edinburgh's Princes Street, a hundred yards or so to the east of Scott's marble effigy, from the hand of the same sculptor, Sir John Steell, at the base of the Scott Monument. Other less fortunate heroes were honoured in words and in stone, most notably Admiral Nelson and Sir John Moore, icons of sacrifice at Trafalgar (1805) and Corunna (1809). There are ancient traditions for commemorating great wars and warriors, in triumph and in mourning.

It is clear enough what service the heroes who risk their lives perform for their country, their nation, their state. But a poet? As he prepared to leave his native land in late April 1816, never to return, Britain's most celebrated living poet, George Gordon Lord Byron, remembered the boast made by Shakespeare's Coriolanus on his exile from Rome: 'There is a world elsewhere' (III.iii.135).[5]

The year following Waterloo was not all triumph. For one thing there was severe climate change. The massive eruption of Mount Tambora in Indonesia activated a global cooling that made 1816 known as 'the year without a summer', with predictable effects on food production. The threat of insurrection in Britain had been ever-present throughout the war years, with notable outbreaks in the naval mutinies of 1797, the Irish rebellion of 1798, the Despard conspiracy of 1802 and the Luddite activities of 1812.[6] So far from the forces of discontent being pacified by the ending of war, they were all the more ready to break out. In May 1816 for example, high unemployment and rising food costs sparked riots in the East Anglian town of Littleport, near Ely. They were quashed by local militia and some Royal Dragoons. Eighty-two persons were tried and twenty-four convicted, of whom nine were sentenced to transportation and five hanged. There is a plaque on the wall of St Mary's Church, Ely,

---

[5] Letter to S. Rogers, 8 February 1816; also letter to J. C. Hobhouse, the same day: 'There is a world beyond Rome'. *Byron's Letters and Journals*, ed. Leslie A. Marchand, vol. V, *1816–1817* (London: John Murray, 1976), 25, 24.

[6] J. E. Archer, *Social Unrest and Popular Protest in England 1780–1840* (Cambridge University Press, 2000); E. Royle, *Revolutionary Britannia? Reflections on the Threat of Revolution in Britain, 1789–1848* (Manchester University Press, 2000).

Figure 3.1 Memorial plaque, on the south wall of the tower of St Mary's Church, Ely, to the five executed Ely and Littleport rioters, 28 June 1816. Licensed under the Creative Commons licence. Photograph by John McCullough, 9 September 2010.

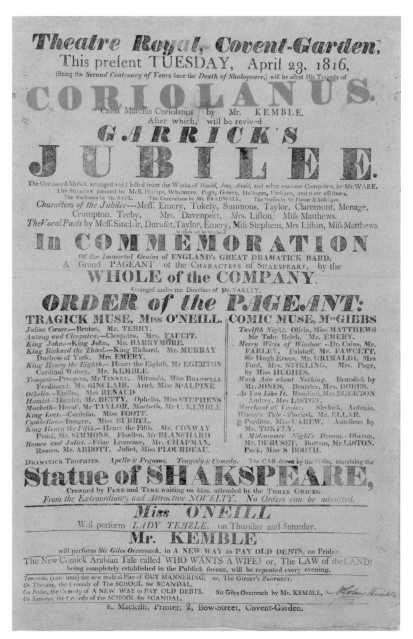

Figure 3.2 Poster for Theatre Royal Covent Garden, advertising a performance of *Coriolanus*, with John Philip Kemble in the title role, and a revival of Garrick's *Jubilee*, on 23 April 1816. ©The Trustees of the British Museum.

commemorating the execution on 28 June 1816 of William Beaviss, George Crow, John Dennis, Isaac Harley and Thomas South: 'May their awful Fate be a warning to others' (Figure 3.1). Later that year some 10,000 people attended a meeting in Spa Fields, north London, to protest against widespread food shortages and to demand parliamentary reform. Early in 1817 the Government passed a series of measures, suspending *habeas corpus* and criminalising such mass assemblies.

This is to sketch the context in which the choice of play to be performed at Covent Garden on the anniversary of Shakespeare's birth and the bicentenary of his death, 23 April 1816, takes on significance: *Coriolanus* (Figure 3.2). There is cause for reflection in the juxtaposition of these two memorial artefacts, the stone plaque and the flimsy playbill. The latter promises and preserves the memory of an evening entertainment at a Theatre Royal in London; the former records the capital punishment of five poor men on a modest church wall in East Anglia. Paper and stone, yet in their material form on the pages of this book these memorials are now equalised, levelled. To restore and disseminate these images is to raise the names they contain, however slightly, out of oblivion. The events they commemorate are very different, but they have in common that they mark the dramatic moment at which near-nobodies are lifted out of the crowd. The five men executed at Ely were singled out of the twenty-four convicted, who were themselves singled out of the eighty-two charged, who were in turn singled out of God knows how many more.

The story told by Shakespeare's *Coriolanus* has a painfully obvious relevance to the fate of the Littleport rioters, but the other attraction of the evening at Covent Garden provides a benign counterpart to the tragic events at Ely: that is, the revival of Garrick's Jubilee, culminating in 'A Grand PAGEANT of the CHARACTERS of SHAKSPEARE, by the WHOLE of the COMPANY', and the arrival, in a car drawn by the Muses, of the 'Statue of SHAKSPEARE, Crowned by FAME and TIME waiting on him, attended by the THREE GRACES'. Besides Shakespeare, David Garrick and John Philip Kemble, the bill sports the names of a large number of plays, players and the characters they represent, including Kemble's leading lady Miss [Eliza] O'Neill as the Tragick Muse (his sister Sarah Siddons had retired), Mrs [Maria] Gibbs as the Comic Muse, and a host of others well known enough to live in the memory (and the published memoirs) of those who saw them perform. The legendary clown Joseph (Joe) Grimaldi, for example,

appeared here as Sir Hugh Evans, and John Liston as Bottom, whose
other Shakespearean roles included Sir Andrew Aguecheek, Malvolio,
Pompey, Launce, Dromio, Polonius, Slender, and Cloten.[7]

Yet many of these names are obscure, in this respect more akin to
those of the five executed criminals than to Garrick's and Kemble's.
Some shrink into illegibility, especially in reproduction. We might
think of them as *near*-nobodies, for we can see that they do have
separate names, and so lives and deaths of their own, stories to be
told. In fact like Grimaldi and Liston, O'Neill and Gibbs, many of
them are indeed lodged in that great commemorative mansion, the
Oxford Dictionary of National Biography: 'Mr. Terry', for example,
representing Brutus, a close friend of Walter Scott's, responsible for
adapting his novels for the stage and providing him with antiquarian
bric-a-brac; 'Miss Foote', as Cordelia (and Virgilia in *Coriolanus*), led
a colourful and scandalous private life before marrying Charles Stanhope, fourth Earl of Harrington, in 1831; 'Mrs. Faucit', impersonating
Cleopatra (and Volumnia in *Coriolanus*), otherwise known as Harriet
Elizabeth Savill, née Diddear, mother of the leading Shakespearean
actress of the next generation, Helena Faucit.[8] It is harder to dig
out a story for 'Miss Plourdeau' (Juliet), 'Mrs. Dobbs' (Beatrice),
'Mr. Tinney' (Prospero) and 'Mr. Duruset' (Oberon): no room in the
ODNB for them. Nor for the five rioters executed at Ely. Yet these two
memorial artefacts remind us that for a moment or more each of these
individuals held everyone's attention, whether on the stage at Covent

[7] K. D. Reynolds, 'O'Neill, Elizabeth *married name* Elizabeth Wrixon-Becher,
Lady Wrixon-Becher (1791–1872)', *Oxford Dictionary of National Biography*
(Oxford University Press, 2004) [www.oxforddnb.com/view/article/1892];
Joseph Knight, 'Gibbs, Maria (1770–1850)', rev. J. Gilliland, *Oxford Dictionary
of National Biography* [www.oxforddnb.com/view/article/10602]; Jane Moody,
'Grimaldi, Joseph (1778–1837)', *Oxford Dictionary of National Biography*
online edn, January 2008 [www.oxforddnb.com/view/article/11630]; Jim Davis,
'Liston, John (*c.*1776–1846)', *Oxford Dictionary of National Biography*, online
edn, January 2008 [www.oxforddnb.com/view/article/16770]. All accessed
19 May 2014.

[8] J. Knight, 'Terry, Daniel (1789–1829)', rev. Klaus Stierstorfer, *Oxford
Dictionary of National Biography*, [www.oxforddnb.com/view/article/27147];
Joseph Knight, 'Foote, Maria [*married name* Maria Stanhope, countess of
Harrington] (1797–1867)', rev. K. D. Reynolds, *Oxford Dictionary of National
Biography*, online edn, May 2013 [www.oxforddnb.com/view/article/9807];
Carol J. Carlisle, 'Saville, John Faucit (1783?–1853)', *Oxford Dictionary of
National Biography*, online edn, January 2008 [www.oxforddnb.com/view/
article/49703]. All accessed 19 May 2014.

Garden or on the scaffold at Ely. A moment at which, for themselves and those watching, they were not blurred members of an anonymous mass, but singular, unique.

Certain of Shakespeare's plays – most notably the *Henry IV* plays and *Henry V*, *Macbeth*, and *Coriolanus* – provide salutary models of social order and disorder, of the disciplined army and the chaotic mob, which spoke urgently to the needs of a society in the immediate years after Waterloo, and through much of the subsequent century. If we look at how Shakespeare was being remembered in 1816, we can see him providing the means for staging and indeed performing some sharply contrasted motives. These include ways of remembering famous individuals and ways of remembering near-nobodies. The former isolate the exceptional figure of a Wellington or Napoleon, a Coriolanus or Henry V; the latter promote a more widely distributed interest in what Shakespeare's own plays call 'the commons', whether they are the riotous multitude of *Coriolanus*, or the band of brothers strenuously and temporarily concerted by Henry V.

Relic

How *was* Shakespeare commemorated in 1816? I shall focus on three activities: the first associated with the antiquarian John Britton and the 'Monumental Bust' in Holy Trinity Church, Stratford-upon-Avon; the second with the actor John Philip Kemble and the critic and essayist William Hazlitt; the third with the novelist Sir Walter Scott.

Though now largely forgotten, John Britton (1771–1857) educated himself out of obscurity to become a leading topographer and antiquarian of the age. Born just over a month before Scott, he shared some of the writer's passions and none of his genius. In partnership with Edward Wedlake Brayley he produced from 1801 onwards *The Beauties of England and Wales* in twenty-seven volumes; between 1807 and 1827 he completed the *Architectural Antiquities of Great Britain* in five volumes, and between 1814 and 1835 the *Cathedral Antiquities of England* in fourteen volumes.[9]

---

[9] J. Mordaunt Crook, 'Britton, John (1771–1857)', *Oxford Dictionary of National Biography*, online edn, Jan. 2008 [www.oxforddnb.com/view/article/3458]. Accessed 19 May 2014.

Britton was obsessed with the Monumental Bust in the Stratford church; it was, he insisted, the sole authentic image of the Bard. In 1814 he got George Bullock to make a cast of it. Shortly after, he attended a breakfast at which the result was scrutinised by Walter Scott, the artist Benjamin West and the phrenologist Dr Johann Spurzheim. Scott admired the forehead and lips but deplored the 'extraordinary' space between nose and upper lip. When it was pointed out that he had the same peculiarity, Scott refused to believe it. A pair of compasses was produced, and 'the modern Bard lost his wager by a quarter of an inch'.[10] So Scott was a quarter of an inch more extraordinary than Shakespeare? Size matters. This may have inspired Bullock to take the first cast of Scott's head; it was installed at Abbotsford, and the artist was employed to work on the library.

Meanwhile Britton laboured to propagate the image of Shakespeare's bust, and on 23 April 1816 he published an engraving with an essay contending that 'This invaluable "Effigy" is attested by tradition, consecrated by time, and preserved in the inviolability of its own simplicity and sacred station' (*Britton* 11). Britton waxed choleric at the scholar Edmond Malone for getting it painted white, and denounced all the pretenders, the fakes and the forgeries, past and future, urging that they 'be branded by the contempt and avowed indignation of every true Englishman, and lover of Shakspere' (*Britton* 14).

The engraving sparked much public debate. Wordsworth complained of the cheek and the jowl, that 'the former wants sentiment, and there is too much of the latter' (12 October 1816, *Britton* 15). But Nathan Drake rallied to support the idea of perfection embodied in the bust; he prefixed the engraving to the first of his two-volume *Shakspeare and his Times* (1817), describing it as 'this invaluable relic':

The impress of that mighty mind which ranged at will through all the realms of nature and fancy, and which, though incessantly employed in the personification of passion and of feeling, was ever great without effort, and at peace within itself, is visible in the exquisite harmony and symmetry of the whole head and countenance, which, not only in each separate feature, in the swell and expansion of the forehead, in the commanding sweep of the eyebrow, in

[10] J. Britton, 'Essays on the Merits and Characteristics of William Shakspere: also remarks on his birth and burial-place, his monument, portraits, and associations', in *Appendix to Britton's Auto-Biography*, Part III (London: printed for the subscribers to the Britton Testimonial, 1849), 1–44 (8). Hereafter *Britton* with page references in the text.

the undulating outline of the nose, and in the open sweetness of the lips, but in their combined and integral expression, breathe of him, of whom it may be said, in his own emphatic language, that

'We ne'er shall look upon his like again.' (quoted in *Britton* 15–16)

It is not only Shakespeare's forehead that swells and expands but Drake's own prose, for the capaciousness that Shakespeare embodies and inspires is crucial. No matter how wide ranging the mind, no matter how powerful the 'passion' and 'feeling', no matter how diverse the constituent items, this miraculous entity is 'at peace within itself'. Ghosts do not get more wholesome than this.

The engraving was more of a success than Britton's other efforts to celebrate the bicentenary with a national festival and the founding of an institute or club. He wrote to Scott, Byron, Southey, Moore, Bowles, Crabbe, Montgomery, Kemble, Wordsworth, Drake, Campbell, and others, to little avail (*Britton* 9). On 18 March 1816 Wordsworth replied politely commending his good intentions but declining to provide a poem. He was busy with other sons of memory and heirs of fame, the ones who had died fighting for their country. In Stratford itself there were some local celebrations on 23 April involving eating, drinking and fireworks. It rained, as usual. A new commemorative medal was struck, in imitation of Garrick's of 1769, inevitably declaring 'WE SHALL NOT LOOK UPON HIS LIKE AGAIN', in defiance of the number of 'likes' or 'likenesses' starting to stretch out to the crack of doom. *The Examiner* reported scornfully on 'the allurements of a public breakfast and a dinner – no small ones, perhaps, in a country, of which it is said that nothing can be done in it without a dinner'. No doubt this scorn would have been shared by the Littleport rioters. As an excuse for gluttony, it was 'a mere prostitution of his name to use it on such an occasion'.[11]

Britton was not a man to give up; he was full of what would become 'Victorian' virtues. On the fiftieth anniversary of Garrick's Jubilee, 6 September 1819, he delivered an address to an audience of three hundred at Stratford. The following year he started a project for 'the erection of a magnificent Edifice to the memory of Shakspere, in the nature of a Museum, Cenotaph, or Temple' (*Britton* 20). It ran into

---

[11] 'Another Shakspeare Jubilee', *The Examiner*, 21 April 1816, issue 434. *19th Century British Newspapers*, sourced from British Library: Gale Document Number: BB3200975193. Accessed 19 May 2014.

the kind of disagreement about its siting – Stratford or London? – that would become all too familiar. In 1835 he was involved in restoration of the chancel in the church at Stratford. Britton is a prime exponent of the kind of interest in commemorating Shakespeare that focuses on 'effigy' and 'edifice'. He borrows consciously and without embarrassment the traditional vocabulary of religious rites in speaking of relics, shrines and pilgrimage.[12] Words, whether Shakespeare's or anyone else's, are of secondary importance compared to sights and sites; they are mainly a means of getting things *done* and getting things *down* as matters of record, document, fact.

Pageant

It may seem strange to choose *Coriolanus* as the play most suitable for celebrating an anniversary at the end of a long war, in so far as it tells the story of a great warrior who defects to the enemy and leads an invasion intent on destroying his own country. But by the end of his career Coriolanus had become John Philip Kemble's signature role, and in any case, this was not the story told by his performance. It was the natural choice for the leading Shakespearean actor of his generation to enact on the bicentenary, as it would be for his farewell performance the following year. Yet Kemble's pre-eminence was no longer unchallenged. The mercurial Edmund Kean had burst on the scene in 1814, all energy, movement, surprise, and danger, as different as possible from the statuesque Kemble. But on 23 April 1816 Kean was out of town, getting into drunken brawls in Glasgow, so the Scottish papers reported.[13]

In another sense, as the Covent Garden playbill demonstrates, Kemble's Coriolanus was rivalled (or complemented or over-reached) by Garrick's Jubilee. Garrick's name is certainly more prominent. Kemble's *Coriolanus* may have been a Shakespearean play but it was not exactly Shakespeare's. As with most of the plays at this time it had been

---

[12] See P. Dávidházi, 'The Genesis of a Ritual: the Shakespeare Cult in English Romanticism', in *The Romantic Cult of Shakespeare: Literary Reception in Anthropological Perspective* (Basingstoke and London: Macmillan, 1998), 34–107.

[13] 'Students', *Caledonian Mercury*, 25 April 1816, citing the *Glasgow Chronicle*, issue 14728. *19th Century British Newspapers*, sourced through British Library: Gale Document Number: BB3205369910. Accessed 19 May 2014.

distinctly 'improved', a modified version of acting editions by Thomas Sheridan produced in 1755 and 1757. Kemble's *Coriolanus* followed Sheridan's, John Ripley explains, in depoliticising and aestheticising Shakespeare's text. As for the citizens of Rome, this version reduced them to 'little more than theatrical furniture – mindless, capricious lumps on whom Martius might vent his spleen and an apolitical mass ripe for exploitation by self-interested demagogues'.[14] But to exaggerate the nobility of Caius Martius and the degradation of the Roman populace is to make the play's politics speak differently rather than to eliminate them. The protagonist becomes the model of the heroic individual defying the mob, a view of the play congenial to audiences and readers alarmed by the prospect of insurrection or even revolution at home, this side of the Channel. Kemble had played the title role frequently from 1789 to 1797, and again from 1806, with annual revivals from 1814 until his retirement three years later. But it is significant that for the nine years between 1797 and 1806 he did *not* put it on, years in which the threat of invasion and the effect of bad harvests made the play too sensitive for performance.[15]

So we can readily imagine the actors compelled by this version of Shakespeare to impersonate 'mindless, capricious lumps' enjoying their more dignified roles in the grand pageant concluding Garrick's Jubilee, an orderly parade of more than forty characters from twenty plays, each catching the limelight for one loveable moment. Old favourites in more than one sense, not just Hamlet but 'Mr Betty', a decade older than when he had been the child prodigy 'Master Betty', 'the infant Roscius'; not just Fluellen but Willy Blanchard, later remembered as 'a mannerist, always walking the stage with his right arm bent, as if he held it in a sling'.[16] And although Drury Lane did not try to compete with Kemble's *Coriolanus* on 23 April, they did stage a similar pageant with key scenes from sixteen plays in pantomime. Reporting the shows at both Theatres Royal, the *Morning Post* noted that at Drury Lane the pageant had saved the evening. 'The Ode to Shakespeare' as originally

---

[14] J. Ripley, 'From Sheridan to Kemble: The Making of a Production Tradition (1752–1817)', in *Coriolanus on Stage in England and America 1609–1994* (London: Associated University Press, 1998), 94–142 (123).

[15] See Ripley, *Coriolanus on Stage*, 114.

[16] Dr [J.] Doran, *Their Majesties' Servants, or, Annals of the English stage: from Thomas Betterton to Edmund Kean*, 2nd edn, revised, corrected and enlarged (London: W. H. Allen, 1865), 407.

spoken and sung in 1769 was greeted with a storm of hisses. This mutiny was quelled by a view of the birthplace and a sing-song round the mulberry tree, but it was the pageant that 'turned neutrality into approbation'; by the time the statue of the Bard rose in a magnificent temple, 'complete reconciliation' had been achieved.[17] We can readily imagine the nostalgia on which the pageant drew for the now legendary pre-war era of Garrick. But the enthusiasm with which this revival was greeted suggests a deeper basis in gratified dream. Here were Shakespeare's characters triumphantly released from plot, from passion and pain, embodying a vision of history transcended.

To understand Hazlitt's extraordinary essay on *Coriolanus* it is vital to realise the sort of performance on which he was drawing, and the socio-political context in which he was doing so.[18] The restoration of the monarchy in France and the triumph of traditional forms of sovereignty across Europe seemed to those with liberal let alone radical convictions, such as Hazlitt, catastrophically complete. Caius Martius Coriolanus could seem to represent the 'sovereignty of nature' attributed to him by Shakespeare's Aufidius (IV.vii.35) – that is, the 'natural' superiority of the ruling class, endlessly reasserting itself. 'The language of poetry naturally falls in with the language of power', concludes Hazlitt. Borrowing from the description of Martius by his enraptured mother (II.i.158–9), he declares of poetry that 'before it "it carries noise, and behind it leaves tears"'. And borrowing the most shocking line from Wordsworth's recent 'Thanksgiving Ode', Hazlitt pronounces that 'Carnage is its daughter'. Poetry, he decides, is indeed 'right-royal' (IV, 214).

More authentically 'right-royal' than Coriolanus, King Henry V is the Shakespearean warrior more regularly summoned to rally the British (or English) in time of war. It had been a good role for a youthful Kemble in the earliest years of the French Revolution from

---

[17] 'The Theatres', *Morning Post*, 24 April 1816, issue 14122. *19th Century British Newspapers*, sourced from the British Library: Gale Document Number: R3209513850. Accessed 19 May 2014.

[18] See U. Natarajan, 'William Hazlitt', in Adrian Poole (ed.), *Great Shakespeareans: Lamb, Hazlitt, Keats* (London and New York: Continuum, 2010), vol. IV, 64–108 (86–9). First published in *The Examiner*, 15 December 1816, Hazlitt's essay was reprinted in *Characters of Shakespear's Plays* (1817): *Complete Works of William Hazlitt*, ed. P. P. Howe (London and Toronto: J. M. Dent and Sons, 1930), vol. IV, 214–21. All references to Hazlitt are to this edition, with volume and page references in the text.

1789 to 1792.[19] During the invasion scare of 1803, a broadside entitled 'Shakespeare's Ghost' recycled some of Henry V's most stirring speeches, along with some rousingly patriotic lines from *King John*. Now *this* was what our National poet was for: 'SHAKESPEARE often delights us on the Stage in the Hour of Amusement – let him now in the HOUR OF PERIL inspire us with that PATRIOTISM and COURAGE which animated our Forefathers to those DEEDS OF GLORY which he describes.'[20] Yet Kemble stopped playing the hero of Agincourt after 1811, and in the years around Waterloo *Henry V* held nothing like the aura with which he continued to endow *Coriolanus*. It was Roman stoicism that the ageing Kemble could do best, and what his audiences seemed to need.

Hazlitt saw in the two plays a crucial link between theatricality, sovereignty and political power. Of Henry V he concedes: 'We like him in the play. There he is a very amiable monster, a very splendid pageant' (IV, 286). 'Pageant' is a word to which Hazlitt often has recourse in thinking about royalty, spectacle, and credulity. Reflecting 'On the Spirit of Monarchy' (1823), he writes: 'Man is a poetical animal, and delights in fiction … We see the symbols of Majesty, we enjoy the pomp, we crouch before the power, we walk in the procession, and make part of the pageant' (XI, 256). It is instructive to see the word spreading its wings in the course of the nineteenth century. The first example cited by the *Oxford English Dictionary* for the following definition (3.b.) is from 1805 (Southey's *Madoc*): 'A brilliant or stately spectacle arranged for effect; *esp.* a procession or parade with elaborate spectacular display; a showy parade'. And yet when Hazlitt oddly describes Henry V, the king himself, as 'a pageant', he is harking back to a much older sense (4), dating back at least to Shakespeare's own time, and in the *OED*'s examples continuing up until at least 1990: '*fig.* Something empty or insubstantial; a delusion; a specious display or tribute'. The *OED*'s example nearest in time to Hazlitt is from James Mill's *History of British India* (1817): 'The sovereign, divested of all but the name of king, sinks into an empty pageant.' In this sense we

---

[19] E. Smith's Introduction to her edition of *King Henry V*, Shakespeare in Production (Cambridge University Press, 2002), 18–20.

[20] Printed in the *Gentleman's Magazine* LXXIII (July 1803), Part II, 664; reprinted in F. J. Klingberg and S. B. Hustvedt (eds.), *The Warning Drum: The British Home Front Faces Napoleon: Broadsides of 1803* (Berkeley and Los Angeles: University of California Press, 1944), 123–5 (125).

find the words 'empty' and 'insubstantial' and 'mere' commonly used to qualify 'pageant'.

Sunken wrack

Hazlitt was drawn to the 'insubstantial pageant' of Prospero's speech: 'the great globe itself, / Yea, all which it inherit, shall dissolve, / And like this insubstantial pageant faded / Leave not a rack behind' (*The Tempest*, IV.i.153–6). It was precisely for their rejection of pomp and pageantry that in 1825 he could still admire the young Wordsworth's *Lyrical Ballads*: '"the cloud-capt towers, the solemn temples, the gorgeous palaces," are swept to the ground, and "like the baseless fabric of a vision, leave not a wreck behind"' (XI, 87). What is it that is (or is not) left behind – a 'rack', 'wrack', or 'wreck'? High above it might refer to a wisp of cloud, but if we look beneath us, on the ground, under the earth, beneath the sea, it could be more substantial, and precious.

Here we alight on the third of the metaphors around which the memory of Shakespeare was being organised in the early years of the nineteenth century: buried treasure or 'sunken wrack'. The phrase comes from a speech by the Archbishop of Canterbury in *Henry V*. He is recalling the feats of the king's great-grandfather, Edward III, that made England's chronicle 'as rich with praise / As is the ooze and bottom of the sea / With sunken wrack and sumless treasuries' (I.ii.163–5). Hazlitt seizes on the lines as a means of epitomising Shakespeare's poetry. *Henry V* is a second-rate play after all, he says, but it is full of such riches as *this* (IV, 289). Again in 'Thoughts on Taste' (1818), he dismisses Voltaire's scornful concession that in Shakespeare's works there are 'a few pearls on his enormous dunghill'. Let us call them rather 'Rich as the bottom of the oozy sea, / With sunken wrack and sumless treasuries' (XVII, 57), replies Hazlitt. But of course the wrack and ruin have to be salvaged and treasured, if they are ever to be 'summed'.

Sir Walter Scott would not have agreed with Hazlitt about pageantry. If the magnificence of King George IV's coronation in July 1821 sharpened Hazlitt's acerbity, it whetted Scott's appetite for more. Just over a year later he stage-managed the monarch's triumphant visit to Edinburgh, the first by a reigning monarch since 1650. There was no lack of pageantry.

As for Kemble and *Coriolanus*, Scott was a friend and a fervent admirer, though not an uncritical one. He could see the inflexibility that put some Shakespearean roles beyond the actor: Macbeth, Lear, even Hamlet, where 'many delicate and sudden turns of passion slip through his fingers'. Kemble was best suited to 'characters in which there is a predominating tinge of some overmastering passion, or acquired habit of acting and speaking, colouring the whole man', such as Caius Martius and the Brutus of *Julius Caesar*.[21] And yet given the liabilities entailed by characters to whose stories violence, betrayal and treason were integral, there was a third, even more influential role: Joseph Addison's Cato. The later part of Kemble's career was devoted to impersonation of 'the Roman character', his biographer declared. James Boaden was not alone in concluding that in his performance of 'these illustrious stoics', Kemble's Cato was 'the superior effort', embodying 'a venerable unity of principle and purpose'.[22]

Scott limped through life with a club foot caused by childhood polio. This limited his participation in live combat and increased his eagerness to imagine it. When it came to immediate social unrest, and the threat of something worse, he did not hesitate to identify with a Kemble-style Coriolanus. When challenged by the Czar of Russia to name the action in which he had been wounded – this was Paris in 1815 after Waterloo, and Scott was sporting the uniform of the Edinburgh Light Horse – the writer was driven to recalling 'the affair of Moredun Mill'. The Czar must have been puzzled. 'Moredun Mill was where he had helped to put down starving and unarmed Scottish rioters', explains one of Scott's biographers.[23] In Scott's fiction, however, the representation of collective violence is a more complex matter, and the exploration of its causes and consequences a major aspect of his claims to greatness. As for the role played by Shakespeare in Scott's thinking about war, injury and memory, it is worth following him to Waterloo in the late summer of 1815, an experience he turned into *Paul's Letters to his Kinsfolk*.

It was almost disappointing to find the signs of carnage already gone, or going. 'These transitory memorials were in a rapid course

[21] J. G. Lockhart, *Memoirs of the Life of Sir Walter Scott, Bart.*, 2nd edn, 10 vols. (Edinburgh: R. Cadell; London: J. Murray and Whittaker & Co., 1839), vol. V, 208.

[22] J. Boaden, *Memoirs of the Life of John Philip Kemble, Esq., including a History of the Stage from the time of Garrick to the present period*, 2 vols. (London: Longman, Hurst, Rees, Orme, Brown, and Green, 1825), vol. II, ch. 8, 526–7.

[23] J. Sutherland, *The Life of Walter Scott: A Critical Biography* (Oxford: Blackwell, 1995), 187.

of disappearing, for the plough was already at work in several parts of the field' (*PL* 201). There was still a stench in the air. But there was also plenty of 'wrack' or 'wreck' scattered around and not yet sunken, like the all too hastily buried corpses. These relics of the carnage were being rapidly pocketed by the souvenir-hunters, of whom Scott was shamelessly one. He was particularly intrigued by the manuscript of some chivalric songs of love and war that he picked up, 'reliques' of French minstrelsy that got their interest from where they were found:

the gallantry and levity of the poetry compels us to contrast its destined purpose, to cheer hours of mirth or of leisure, with the place in which the manuscript was found, trampled down in the blood of the writer, and flung away by the hands of the spoilers, who had stripped him on the field of battle. (*PL* 214–15)

The bits and pieces were being eagerly marketed by the locals. Scott even instructed one of them on how to get more for his money. He wondered what would become of a door removed from a mansion. It would surely be cut up into trinkets like Shakespeare's famous mulberry tree in Stratford (*PL* 209): invaluable relics.

We can see an analogy between the material fragments scattered across the battlefield and the Shakespearean words scattered across the body of Scott's writings. He ransacks Shakespeare more freely than any writer of the age except – possibly – Hazlitt. Shakespeare is by no means the only provider. Of the thirty or so quotations from English authors in *Paul's Letters* (there is a handful from Latin, Greek, Scripture, German and French), the majority are from Shakespeare (eight), while the remainder are furnished by Spenser, Fletcher, Cowley, Dryden, Congreve, Prior and Swift (in fact Henry Brooke), and by more recent or contemporary poets including Home, Cowper, Chatterton, Sheridan, Campbell, Baillie and Byron (from his 'Ode to Napoleon Bonaparte').

There are occasions on which Scott's invocation of Shakespeare is pointed and purposive. As, for example, when he characterises the desperate loyalty of Napoleon's imperial guards, their determination 'to make good the boast, which had called France to rely "upon their stars, their fortune, and their strength"' (*PL* 78). Readers need to know their *King John* well to pick up the allusion to a speech by Constance denouncing Austria's failure to support her (III.i.126). And similarly their *Henry VIII* to recognise Wolsey's riposte to Surrey's accusation of treason (III.ii.252–4), with which Scott rebukes Ney's criticism of

Napoleon's conduct of the battle (*PL* 134). Scott dwells longer on the terrifying threat made by Henry V at the siege of Harfleur (III.iii.1–43); again this serves the purposes of rebuke, this time to those bloodthirsty compatriots who call for Paris to be razed to the ground. He invites them – as Henry invites the citizens of Harfleur – to imagine the havoc that would be unleashed (*PL* 354–5). In the central chapter that re-imagines the crucial day of battle itself, there are only two literary references: one is to Shakespeare, the other is to Homer. This is a special occasion, requiring supreme literary authority. It is the moment when the two heroic figures of Wellington and Napoleon should come face to face in mortal combat. All the signs and sounds lead everyone to expect that Buonaparte will lead the climactic charge. He fails the literary test.

None listened to the shout with more eager hope than our own great General, who probably thought, like the Avenger in Shakespeare [Macduff],

> ———— There thou shouldst be:
> By this great clatter one of greatest note
> Seems bruited. ————
> [*Macbeth* V.vii.20–2]

All indeed expected an attack headed by Buonaparte in person; and in failing upon this instant and final crisis to take the command of his Guards, whom he destined to try the last cast of his fortune, he disappointed both his friends and enemies. (*PL* 180)

Given the frequency with which the Scottish play is invoked by English writers from the 1790s onwards to figure the murderous chaos unleashed by regicide, the revenge is sweet indeed that can portray Napoleon here as a failed Macbeth.

But these are exceptions. Throughout most of the text, Shakespearean allusions slip in and out in much the same way as those to other literary friends and acquaintances. In this respect *Paul's Letters* epitomise the work done by allusions to Shakespeare throughout Scott's fiction, where they generally lighten and facilitate, as they might in casual conversation between friends. We could even say that they *casualise* what might begin to sound too solemn. This is very different from the ways in which a later novelist such as George Eliot remembers Shakespeare, to pointedly enforcing effects. For example in *The Antiquary* (1816) there is a dramatic scene in which four leading characters

are hauled up to safety from the face of a sea-cliff (chapter 8). In his
excitement the antiquary of the novel's title, Jonathan Oldbuck, makes
reference to Shakespeare four times in quick succession, to *Hamlet*, *King
Lear*, *The Comedy of Errors*, and *The Merry Wives of Windsor*. They
are a form of distraction. None of these references serves to intensify the
drama, any more than the lines about Dover Cliff from *King Lear* that
form the chapter's epigraph, or the narrator's reference to the 'beetling
precipice' in *Hamlet* (I.iv.71); rather, they serve to disperse it.[24]

Paul's Letters to his Kinsfolk is rarely now remembered by comparison with the novels which everyone has somehow *heard* of, including
Waverley at the very least, if only because the afterlives of Scott and his
characters have been so diffuse, and the relics of their existence so
substantial – the name of a railway station, a football club, towns and
streets all over the Anglophone world.[25] You cannot walk down Edinburgh's Princes Street without noticing the Scott Monument, the huge
Gothic pile designed by George Meikle Kemp, begun in 1840 and
inaugurated in 1846. This is how Shakespeare *might* have been commemorated, if the likes of John Britton had had their way. The brass
plaque buried beneath the Monument does indeed claim Scott and his
creations as the nearest thing to Shakespeare.[26] In the 1840s this would

---

[24] Oldbuck's allusions all occur on p. 64 of David Hewitt's edition of *The
Antiquary* (Edinburgh University Press, 1995); their Shakespearean sources,
along with the chapter motto from *King Lear* (61), and the narrator's references
to *Hamlet* and *King John* (62 and 66), are identified in his Explanatory Notes,
472–3.

[25] A. Rigney, *The Afterlives of Walter Scott: Memory on the Move* (Oxford
University Press, 2012); Nicola J. Watson, 'Sir Walter Scott', in Poole (ed.),
Great Shakespeareans, Vol. V, 10–52; and 'Afterlives', in F. Robertson (ed.),
The Edinburgh Companion to Sir Walter Scott (Edinburgh University Press,
2012), 143–55.

[26] The brass plaque carries this remarkable inscription by Francis Lord Jeffrey:
'THIS GRAVEN PLATE / Deposited in the Base of a Votive Building / on the
fifteenth day of August, in the Year of Christ 1840, / And never likely to see the
light again, / Till all the surrounding structures are crumbled to dust / By the
decay of time, or by human or elemental violence, / May then testify to a distant
posterity that / His Countrymen began on that day / To raise an Effigy and
Architectural Monument / TO THE MEMORY OF SIR WALTER SCOTT,
BART., / Whose admirable writings were then allowed / To have given more
delight and suggested better feeling / To a larger class of readers, in every rank of
society, / Than those of any other Author, / With the exception of Shakespeare
alone; / And which were therefore thought likely to be remembered / Long after
this act of Gratitude / On part of this first generation of his Admirers / Should be
forgotten.' See N. M. McQ. Holmes and L. M. Stubbs, *The Scott Monument:*

undoubtedly have seemed true, though Dickens would soon rival and in due course overreach his predecessor. Steell's statue of Scott is easily visible at near-ground level, but all the figures who fill the niches soaring above him are now (without help) illegible. This is how Shakespeare has been imagined in the visual arts, and in live performance, and Dickens too, surrounded by the multitude of their fictional creations, a grand pageant, a whole company. But not in stone, not on this scale. As for the Monument, it is tempting to recall Scott's own reflection on the ironic reversals of history. On entering Paris shortly after Waterloo, he contemplated all the memorials to Napoleon's now meaningless victories: 'No building among the splendid monuments of Paris, but is marked with the name, or device, or insignia of an emperor, whose power seemed as deeply founded as it was widely extended' (*PL* 292).

The Antiquary helps to return us to the world of John Britton, for Scott shared his title-character's passion for 'antiquities'. For all their manifest differences of political conviction and loyalty, Scott and Hazlitt both recognise the difficulty in valuing or 'summing' the wrack of the past. Hazlitt deplored the pageantry into the service of which Shakespeare could be pressed as vigorously as Scott enthused about it. But both understood the power of spectacle and performance, the strength of the will to believe in embodied memories, and the way in which 'the spirit of the age' was discovering the uses to which relics, souvenirs, memorials and monuments could be put: a whole new industry. Hazlitt knew he was not immune to such an allure, and Scott was ready to confess that some of the machinery was rubbish.

Or 'trumpery', the factitious inverse of Hazlitt's (and Shakespeare's) 'sumless treasuries'. One of the soldiers Scott met at Waterloo was scandalised by the interest he took in stuff that seemed to the combatant 'scattered as mere trumpery upon a field of victory' (*PL* 158). In the novel Scott wrote immediately after *Paul's Letters*, the antiquary's study is crammed with a 'wreck of ancient books and utensils'; every surface overflows with 'miscellaneous trumpery'.[27] Shakespeare could readily be turned into just such trumpery. In the modern world, it

A History and Architectural Guide (A City of Edinburgh Museums and Art
   Galleries Publication, 1979), 11.
[27] *The Antiquary*, ed. Hewitt (1995), 22. Y. S. Lee explores the connections
   between the novel and *Paul's Letters* in 'Sir Walter Scott on the Field of
   Waterloo', *Nationalism and Irony: Burke, Scott, Carlyle* (Oxford University
   Press, 2004), published online (Oxford University Press, 2007).

would become increasingly strenuous to raise the sunken wrack and shine a light on the ruins, and then to discriminate between trumpery and treasury.

The very ease with which Scott and Hazlitt and their Victorian successors appeal to Shakespeare suggests something essential about the means of remembering his works to best effect, both personally and collectively. Namely, that it requires active collaboration on the part of the reader, viewer or spectator, whether in the solitude of the study or the company of others. Otherwise it will all remain 'a pageant', as Hazlitt puts it, or mere 'trumpery'.

Warrior and artist

To return once more to Waterloo. At the time of writing tour operators are taking bookings for expensive trips to the battlefield and its environs on the bicentenary in June 2015. There is a whole industry at work transporting people to the battle sites of the First World War, and all over the world to sites of mass carnage. Waterloo enthusiasts have expressed disappointment at the failure of British politicians to support their bicentenary. They should hardly be surprised. The conduct of 'international relations' involves as much delicacy as brutality, the hostilities of yesterday turning remorselessly into the alliances of today, and vice versa. Artists normally play a pacific and indeed politic role in the opportunity they afford for soldering such alliances, in so far as their work can cross boundaries between nations and languages, drawing readers and audiences together from all round the globe. This is why in 2012 we had the World Shakespeare Festival to coincide with the Olympic games. Warriors like Wellington (and Napoleon) whose fame depends on great military victories (and defeats) can never hope to achieve such 'universal' appeal. The blood spilt at Waterloo after all was real, no more of a pageant than the battle of Agincourt (or 'Azincourt', as the natives insist on calling it).

Yet it would be wrong to make too sharp a distinction between the forms in which we remember the Warrior and the Artist, the Victor of Waterloo and the Bard of Avon. The material forms in which this memory is invested – the relics, the busts and the monuments – make powerful claims on the world around them. They take up more or less valuable space. So too do the forms of collective memory that require performance and active engagement, moving through time: pageants in the service of celebration, mourning, nostalgia, defiance and self-assertion.

These are two of the main ways in which I have tried to indicate that Shakespeare and his works were commemorated as early as 1816, adumbrating so many later developments. It is only when we reach the third form in which collective memory is invested that a distinction emerges between the warrior and the artist. The 'sunken wrack' of words presents possibilities for revival and renewal by others that deeds alone can never provide. In honouring the past, commemoration always looks to the future, but it is in this third and last form that it does so most actively, sociably, creatively. As Shakespeare in 1816 was beginning to bear witness.

4 | Remembrance of things past: Shakespeare 1851, 1951, 2012

GRAHAM HOLDERNESS

Rehearsal and remembrance

Ton Hoenselaars and Clara Calvo have defined the relationship between Shakespeare and the 'cultures of commemoration' as 'a series of more or less conscious or active attempts to rehearse Shakespeare in the present, as well as efforts to guarantee the remembrance of Shakespearean things past and present in the future'.[1] There are different ways of doing this. To 'rehearse' Shakespeare in the present might involve the 'quotation' of Shakespeare, by for instance inserting the Shakespearean image, or Shakespearean language, into contemporary popular culture: putting Shakespeare's image on a banknote, or a credit card; playing with Shakespearean tag-lines in stand-up or situation comedy. The focus of attention is on the present, and Shakespeare is appropriated as something alien and incongruous from the distant past. The other method is to commemorate by invoking an unbroken continuity of Shakespearean 'remembrance'. Hoenselaars and Calvo are more interested in such formal 'rituals of commemoration', which have punctuated popular interest in Shakespeare since David Garrick's 1769 Jubilee, are exemplified annually on 23 April by the 'Birthday Celebrations' in Stratford-upon-Avon, and concentrate intensively on Shakespeare centenaries and anniversaries of birth or death: 1896, 1914, 1916, 2014, 2016.[2] These public rituals, according to Hoenselaars and Calvo, 'promote a particular kind of social memory in relation to Shakespeare, as together, they paved the way for a combination of tourism and theater on which the Stratford industry still relies today'.[3] Though apparently grounded in tradition, such rituals in practice produce what Eric Hobsbawm

---

[1] Ton Hoenselaars and Clara Calvo, 'Introduction: Shakespeare and the Cultures of Commemoration', *Critical Survey* 22 (2010), 1.
[2] Hoenselaars and Calvo, 'Introduction', 3.
[3] Hoenselaars and Calvo, 'Introduction', 3.

called 'invented traditions', which claim to be both old and authentic, but are actually neither.[4]

Thus while one kind of commemoration makes Shakespeare anachronistically modern and local (the logo for the 450th anniversary celebration of Shakespeare's birth, 'Shakespeare 450', held in Paris in 2014, for instance, displayed a Shakespeare wearing sunglasses and an Eiffel Tower ear-ring); the other cultivates in the present a carefully 'antiqued' Shakespeare, inauthentically rooted in invented tradition (in the annual Stratford Birthday Celebrations, Shakespeare's funeral bust is provided with a new quill pen, a prop the original memorial did not, apparently, contain).[5] The deliberate anachronisms of a Shakespeare 'rehearsed' in the present highlight the innovation and inventiveness of the exercise, and acknowledge the constructed nature of the contemporary collision. By contrast, the repeated commemoration of a bygone Shakespeare occludes the anachronism, and projects contemporaneity into the past. The one calls attention to the vanishing of the subject and the need to reimagine him, like toasting an absent friend; the other pretends that the long-dead friend is still alive, and dwelling amongst us.

The distinction between these two different kinds of commemoration, which one might name (using Hoenselaars and Calvo's terms) 'rehearsal', and 'remembrance', raises some profound questions of intellectual ownership and authority. 'Rehearsal', with its semantic associations of repetition, duplication and theatricality, is much more amenable to academic analysis, since to produce it requires a sense of history, an awareness of difference, and an iconoclastic intelligence. These are qualities shared with the most inventive adaptations of Shakespeare in print, on stage, on screen, some of which have become modern classics in their own right, and receive their own share of critical attention. Public and popular 'remembrance', on the other

---

[4] Eric Hobsbawm, 'Introduction', in Eric Hobsbawm and Terence Ranger (eds.), *The Invention of Tradition* (Cambridge University Press, 1983), 1. For Garrick's Jubilee see Graham Holderness, 'Bardolatry: or the Cultural-Materialist Guide to Stratford-upon-Avon', in Graham Holderness (ed.), *The Shakespeare Myth* (Manchester University Press, 1988), 1–15; Michael Dobson, *The Making of the National Poet: Shakespeare, Adaptation and Authorship, 1660–1769* (Oxford: Clarendon Press, 1992); Robert Sawyer, 'From Jubilee to Gala: Remembrance and Ritual Commemoration', *Critical Survey* 22 (2010), 25–38.

[5] See Graham Holderness, *Nine Lives of William Shakespeare* (London: Bloomsbury, 2011), 27.

hand, takes place largely outside the academy, is conducted by amateur rather than professional agencies, and ignores or defies the normal rules and conventions of academic inquiry and interpretation.[6]

Before the 1980s, attention to these social and cultural contexts formed no part of Shakespeare study, criticism and teaching. There was an impassable gulf between the Shakespeare of the academy, and the Shakespeare of popular culture. Even the liaison between professional literary criticism and the theatre was a difficult, and at times conflicted, relationship. It was only when, under the influence of Marxist and post-structuralist theory (Althusser, Barthes, Foucault), criticism began to interpret Shakespeare in terms of 'social institution' and 'ideological apparatus', that the territories of public commemoration became even visible, let alone inhabitable, fields of intellectual inquiry.

Current work on commemoration is still strongly influenced by the methodologies and perspectives developed during the 1980s, and under the tutelage of those theoretical mentors. One particularly strong influence shaping the analysis of cultural practice in such fields was that of the Frankfurt School. It was *The Dialectic of Enlightenment* by Theodor Adorno and Max Horkheimer that introduced the now-familiar term 'culture industry'.[7] Within this conceptual framework, public and popular Shakespeare became both visible and discussable in ways that had never happened before. But the opportunity to broaden the scope of cultural inquiry also introduced new and enduring paradigms.

Hoenselaars and Calvo refer, in the 'Introduction' to their collection of essays on Shakespeare, to the 'Stratford industry' as a primary site of commemoration. Other contributors to the same collection deploy similar language. Robert Sawyer argues that Garrick's Jubilee, and the Royal Gala of 1830, 'represent the twin pillars of the Shakespeare industry today'.[8] Anita Hagerman proposes a link between 'Shakespeare's iconic status' and 'the cultural capital of commemoration'.[9]

---

[6] This distinction is by no means absolute, since academics both engage in their own forms of public commemoration (such as the centenary conferences of 2014), and participate in popular public events that may bear little relation to the priorities of Shakespeare criticism and theory.

[7] Max Horkheimer and Theodor W. Adorno, *The Dialectic of Enlightenment* (reprinted London: Verso, 1997).

[8] Sawyer, 'From Jubilee to Gala', 35.

[9] Anita Hagerman, 'Monumental Play: Commemoration, Post-War Britain and History Cycles', *Critical Survey* 22:2 (2010), 105–18, 107.

But there are inherent problems with this language, and with this tradition. The Adorno–Horkheimer argument was framed by a set of reactionary propositions shared with influential figures in literary criticism such as F. R Leavis and T. S. Eliot. They believed that the decline of traditional social institutions such as the family had produced an ideological crisis; that culture had lost all authenticity, and become reified into a manipulative industry; that the autonomous individual was in the process of destruction; and that only high culture preserved any critical value, while the mass media were irredeemably degenerate.

Some of the seminal influencers in the emerging field of cultural sociology based their thinking in the Frankfurt School. In the late 1980s, in a book entitled, after Adorno and Horkheimer, *The Culture Industry*, Robert Hewison coined the phrase 'heritage industry' to describe what he considered to be a sanitisation and commercialisation of the past when reproduced as 'heritage'.[10] Heritage was not a recuperation of the past, but an invention designed to capture a nostalgia for the past, as a lost 'golden age', in a context of economic and political decline. Hewison argued that the rise of heritage as a form of popular entertainment distracted from the development of a 'critical culture' which 'engages in a dialogue between past and present'.[11] Heritage presents culture as finished, complete and firmly in the past. He pointed to the widespread perception of cultural and economic decline that became a feature of Britain's perception of itself as a nation in the decades following the Second World War:

> In the face of apparent decline and disintegration, it is not surprising that the past seems a better place. Yet it is irrecoverable, for we are condemned to live perpetually in the present. What matters is not the past, but our relationship with it.[12]

Around the same time Patrick Wright published the influential book *On Living in an Old Country*.[13] Wright was also concerned with what he called the increasing 'museumification' of the United Kingdom, and

---

[10] Robert Hewison, *The Culture Industry: Britain in a Climate of Decline* (London: Methuen, 1987).
[11] Hewison, *The Culture Industry*, 144.
[12] Hewison, *The Culture Industry*, 43–5.
[13] Patrick Wright, *On Living in an Old Country: The National Past in Contemporary Britain* (London: Verso, 1985).

the ways in which heritage might act as a distraction from engaging with the issues of the present. Wright argued that various pieces of heritage legislation put forward by the Thatcher government could be read as a revival of the patriotism of the Second World War, and connected this Conservative patriotism to the events of the Falklands conflict (1982). Like Hewison, he was also critical of the 'timelessness' conferred on the past when presented as a 'heritage site'.

National heritage involves the extraction of history – of the idea of historical significance and potential – from a denigrated everyday life and its restaging or display in certain sanctioned sites, events, images and conceptions. In this process history is redefined as 'the historical', and it becomes the object of a similarly transformed and generalised public attention. Abstracted and redeployed, history seems to be purged of political tension; it becomes a unifying spectacle, the settling of all disputes. Like the guided tour as it proceeds from site to sanctioned site, the national past occurs in a dimension of its own – a dimension in which we appear to remember only in order to forget.[14]

Contemporary work on Shakespeare commemoration continues to be based in these Frankfurt School paradigms, which hold that public and popular commemorations are products of a 'Shakespeare' or 'Stratford' 'industry';[15] trade in 'nostalgia'; and above all represent concerted attempts to shape a sense of 'English' national identity by reference back to a sanitised and de-historicised past.[16] Under the twin pressures of commercial imperative and ideological interpellation, the industry continues to generate, through its commemoration rituals, a nationalist, patriotic, nostalgic, heritage Shakespeare. Meanwhile we, as academics (and therefore not part of any 'industry', and disinterestedly oblivious to commercial considerations!) strive to produce a 'critical culture', by insisting that Shakespeare is international, global and historic. Rituals of commemoration endeavour to transmit ideologies such as nationalism unimpeded to the participant. We work to disrupt that transmission, to cure the public of their ideological illusions and to replace values such as British patriotism, English nationalism and heritage nostalgia with internationalism, multiculturalism and an unillusioned grasp of history.

[14] Wright, *On Living in an Old Country*, 69.
[15] See Hoenselaars and Calvo (eds.), *Critical Survey* 22, 4, 35, 107.
[16] See Hoenselaars and Calvo (eds.), *Critical Survey* 22, 4, 28, 107–8.

Critical work on Shakespeare commemoration has tended to focus on a 'great tradition' of Shakespeare festivals held on centenary anniversaries, especially 1916. I will concentrate instead on the past as celebrated in key events of the kind that Hoenselaars and Calvo call 'official commemoration', 'gatherings that really concern the nation', and in which Shakespeare might be expected to play a minor role.[17] In this chapter I propose to exert some pressure on the Frankfurt School paradigm, by focusing on the re-contextualisation of Shakespeare in three major national celebrations of British culture: the Great Exhibition of 1851, the Festival of Britain 1951 and the London Olympics of 2012. All three festivals would be expected to produce, in their representations of the past, a classically patriotic, nationalist, nostalgic 'heritage' commemoration. Yet in all three we can find examples of 'rehearsal' as well as 'remembrance', in the form of a Shakespeare repositioned in relation to the modern disciplines of engineering, design and technology; to the place of British culture within a global and multi-cultural world; and to public and popular investment in rituals of commemoration.

1851: the Great Exhibition

On 12 July 1851, an art critic for *The Spectator* recalled his visit to the Great Exhibition:

Walking eastward along the nave, and disregarding those works of which we have made mention already, we are first struck by the admirable spirit and energy of Baron Afarochetti's colossal head of a horse. Lough's 'Mourners', and a statue of Shakspere from the Stratford bust, by Bell – a weak affair – come soon after.[18]

The statue of Shakespeare was listed in the catalogue as 'unfinished statue of Shakespeare, from the Stratford bust',[19] though in fact John Bell's white plaster effigy draws on both the Stratford bust and the Scheemakers statue in Westminster Abbey. It was not the first thing

---

[17] Hoenselaars and Calvo (eds.), *Critical Survey* 22, 3.

[18] *The Spectator*, 'Visits to the Great Exhibition' (12 July 1851), 14.

[19] Claire Pettitt, 'Shakespeare at the Great Exhibition of 1851', in Gail Marshall and Adrian Poole (eds.), *Victorian Shakespeare, Volume 2: Literature and Culture* (London: Palgrave, 2003), 61–83, 61.

the *Spectator* critic noticed, nor did it strike him as distinguished for its artistry. Another contemporary documentation of the same object, however, tells a very different story. The title page of the exhibition's souvenir folio, *Recollections of the Great Exhibition, 1851* displays a striking image of the Bell statue sheltering beneath a beautiful wrought-iron canopy (Figure 4.1).[20] In this form the statue stood at the entrance to the British nave in the Crystal Palace.[21]

The statue of Shakespeare may have been 'weak' and unremarkable, as the *Spectator* critic put it, but the dome containing it represented the cutting edge of modern technology and design. The structure was a cupola, fashioned from traceries of wrought iron, curved into an inverted flower-like shape, with slim iron columns supporting the dome, each one surmounted by a perching eagle. At the apex a cylindrical chimney tapered into a kind of spire, topped by a weathervane, and a figure of Eros.

The 'Coalbrookdale dome' came from the factory of Abraham Darby, who at the very beginning of the Industrial Revolution made significant advances in the smelting of iron, using coke as fuel. It was Darby's company that built the first iron bridge. The Coalbrookdale ironwork took pride of place in the Exhibition, as an example of the most advanced modern design technology. Housing the statue of Shakespeare, it provides a perfect synthesis of art and industry, of metallurgy and imagination.

In the illustration the Shakespeare exhibit is the centre of an active attention of spectatorship from a diverse, cosmopolitan, international and multi-cultural crowd, drawn from both within and outside the British Empire. A gentleman in top hat, mutton-chop whiskers, frock coat and white trousers, the very image of Victorian respectability, explains its form to two men from Persia, dressed in brilliant red, blue and yellow costumes, with baggy trousers and white turbans. A man in blue naval officer's uniform with gold-braided cocked hat stands by, his bonneted wife on his arm. Two little girls in frocks sit casually at the monument's base, poring over a printed catalogue. The elaborate flowered costumes and coolie hats of imperial China complement the flowing robes and turbans of India. A stout Englishman in brown broadcloth and gaiters stares at the monument with the ingrained truculence of a farmer.

---

[20] *Recollections of the Great Exhibition, 1851* (London: Lloyd Bros. & Comp., Sept 1st 1851). Lithograph by Jonathan Absolon.

[21] Pettitt, 'Shakespeare and the Great Exhibition', 61.

Figure 4.1 Shakespeare Statue by John Bell, Great Exhibition 1851. *Recollections of the Great Exhibition*, 1851. © The British Library Board, X.953.

Another contemporary depiction of the Shakespeare statue tells yet a different story. John Leech's picture of the Bell statue (without the Coalbrookdale dome) was published in *Punch* (Figure 4.2).[22] The

---

[22] *Punch*, 5 July 1851, 21:16. No. XX in the *Punch* series, 'Memorials of the Great Exhibition, 1851'.

Figure 4.2 'Dinner-time at the Crystal Palace', *Punch* 21 (1851), 16.

image shows a large group of common people standing and sitting around the monument, paying little attention to the statue, but completely at their leisure beneath the Bard's avuncular gaze. A red-faced woman, basket at her feet, holds out a glass to be filled with wine by an equally rubicund man. Two soldiers in military caps flirt loudly with a couple of pretty country girls. Children are everywhere: a small boy with his father's hand-me-down hat slipping over his ears; a little girl holding wool for her busily knitting mother; and at the centre of the pedestal, a nursing mother suckling her baby at her breast, her own mother looking indulgently on. The title of the published sketch was 'Dinner-time at the Crystal Palace'. An abandoned, inverted umbrella suggests both a relaxed carelessness and a social topsy-turveydom.

As Alan R. Young comments, Leech's satirical portrayal of a working class sufficiently at home in the Great Exhibition, and at the base of Shakespeare's statue, to enjoy their picnic, was underpinned by an awareness of the controversial location of the Exhibition in Hyde Park, near fashionable Belgravia and Rotten Row.[23] In practice, working-class visitors were not only welcomed but encouraged (the Commissioners reduced the entry price from 2s/6d to 1s on weekdays) to attend, and proved no threat to social order. The nursing mother may also be more than a touch of Hogarthian parody: Gideon Mantell recorded in his diary that in the British nave he observed 'many dirty women with their infants, giving suck on the seats with their breasts uncovered'.[24]

Leech added to the plinth of the statue an inscription from *Troilus and Cressida*, 'One touch of nature makes the whole world kin'.[25] The ultimate effect of the cartoon, despite its satirical inflection, is to suggest that there need be no separation here between Shakespeare and the common people. Putting the two illustrations together, since these observations derived from events that occupied exactly the same time and space, we find the common people enfolded within a cosmopolitan gathering of all nations, the focal point of which is the image of Shakespeare. Nothing could better exemplify the aspiration Prince Albert defined as the ultimate purpose of the Great Exhibition: to bring closer 'that great end, to which all history points – the realization of the unity of mankind'.[26]

---

[23] Alan R. Young, *'Punch' and Shakespeare in the Victorian Era* (Berlin: Peter Lang, 2007), 113.

[24] E. Cecil Curwen (ed.), *The Journal of Gideon Mantell* (London: Oxford University Press, 1940), 273. See also Jeffrey A. Auerbach, *The Great Exhibition: A Nation on Display* (New Haven: Yale University Press, 1999), 155.

[25] *Troilus and Cressida*, 3.3.169. Quotations from Shakespeare come from *The Complete Works*, ed. Stanley Wells and Gary Taylor (Oxford University Press, 1986).

[26] Inaugural Address of the Great Exhibition of the Works of Industry of All Nations, London 1851. Quoted in Michael Sorkin, *Variations on a Theme Park:*

The synthesis of art and industry visible in the Shakespeare exhibit replicated the aesthetic and technological achievement of the Crystal Palace itself. Its designer, Joseph Paxton, was a landscaper, and Head Gardener to the Duke of Devonshire at Chatsworth. The design he submitted to the selection committee, which included the great engineer Isambard Kingdom Brunel, showed extraordinary technical imagination. The model was based on a conservatory Paxton had built at Chatsworth, using new techniques in construction, combining wood, plate glass and cast iron. The Chatsworth Lily House was built to house the giant Amazonian waterlily, *Victoria amazonica*. Paxton used cast plate glass with a curtain wall system, so vertical bays of glass could be hung from cantilevered beams, producing a building with roof and walls of light. The model was the basis for the construction of the Crystal Palace. Paxton said that the ribbed floating leaves of the massive lily were his inspiration for this design: a perfect marriage of art and nature; of science and imagination; of architecture and engineering. Brunel was clearly impressed by the design, since he not only supported it in the committee but imitated the method, when he redesigned Paddington Station, and used the same construction company (Fox and Henderson).

The Great Exhibition was not simply a national celebration of British achievements in technology and the arts but an international gathering, a kind of industrial Olympics dedicated to a peaceful international competition of rival skills. It was 'an Exhibition of the Industry of all the civilized Nations of this World', as the illustrated catalogue put it, aimed at 'benefiting the great family of mankind', an aspiration naturally expressed in the language of Shakespeare:[27]

Other nations have devised means for the display and encouragement of their own arts and manufactures; but it has been reserved for England to provide an arena for the industrial triumphs of the whole world. She has offered an hospitable invitation to surrounding nations to bring the choicest products of their industry to her capital, and there to enter into an amicable competition with each other and with herself ... Whatever be the extent of the benefit which this great demonstration may confer upon the Industrial Arts of the world, it cannot fail to soften, if not to eradicate altogether, the prejudices

The New American City and the End of Public Space (New York: Hill and Wang, 1992), 209.

[27] *The Great Exhibition of 1851*, facsimile of *The Art Journal Illustrated Catalogue* (London: The Observer, 1970), xi.

and animosities which have so long retarded the happiness of nations; and to promote those feelings of 'peace and goodwill' which are among the surest antecedents of their prosperity; a peace, which Shakspere has told us –

> '... is of the nature of a conquest;
> For then, both parties nobly are subdued
> And neither party loses'.[28]

And so in that miraculous glass palace, modelled on the leaves of a lily; constructed by means of the most advanced engineering technology; at the heart of a Great Exhibition that gave equal emphasis to art and industry, stood the figure of Shakespeare, re-made in the image of the Industrial Revolution, assimilated to the new priorities of modern industrial Britain. Despite the conventionality of the statue itself, its incorporation within the Coalbrookdale dome made the monument an example of rehearsal rather than remembrance; a kind of commemoration that remembers the future, as well as the past.

1951: the Festival of Britain

In 1951 the post-war Labour government of Britain fostered a 'Festival of Britain', intended as a celebration and promotion of British culture, and coinciding with the centenary of the Great Exhibition of 1851. The purpose underlying the Festival was that of demonstrating the success of the nation's post-war recovery and reconstruction under a Labour administration: to display, in the words of a Board of Trade committee, Britain's 'moral, cultural, spiritual and material' recovery from the destruction and demoralisation of war. Robert Hewison commented:

The main thrust of the Festival was towards advertising British achievements in science, technology and design ... but the Festival was a significant cultural phenomenon, both in its conception and its reception. It is interesting to see how literary its treatment was, for the theme, in the words of the official guide, was 'The Autobiography of a Nation'. Those responsible for arranging the various sections of the shows were officially known as script writers, with the exhibition on the South Bank (the centre-piece, but by no means the only piece) divided into chapters of the 'island story'. The literary approach was essentially didactic and propagandist. This was to be 'a challenge to the sloughs of the present and a shaft of confidence cast forth

[28] *Henry IV, Part Two*, 4.1.315–17.

against the future', said the official guide, falling back on the language of the King James Bible.[29]

The Festival has been described as, to an extent, a continuity from the machinery of war-time propaganda: 'Both in its approach and its selection of personnel, the Festival of Britain betrayed its origins in the efforts and experience of the Ministry of Information and CEMA in wartime, when the idea of theme exhibitions with a confident message was first put into practice.'[30] CEMA, the Council for the Encouragement of Music and the Arts, had been established in 1940 and became the Arts Council in 1946; as an instrument of state patronage its importance had been growing, and it was allocated an extra £400,000 to spend on the Festival itself. But despite the centralised planning, the project was able to build on a very broad basis of national support created by the socialising influences of the war. A broad and active popular participation, familiar enough in traditional rituals such as coronations, jubilees, royal weddings and funerals, testified encouragingly to a degree of progress in the direction of a new democratic culture.

The main foci on Shakespeare in the 1951 Festival lay in Stratford and Birmingham, where the Shakespeare Memorial Theatre and the Birmingham Repertory Theatre staged ambitious cycles of the history plays.[31] But Shakespeare was placed also at the heart of the 'Autobiography of a Nation' on the South Bank. Among the permanent and temporary buildings and constructions – the still-existing Royal Festival Hall; the 'Skylon', a futuristic metal sculpture, suspended in the air with no visible means of support; an enormous dome resembling an alien spacecraft – stood a tall vertical barn-like building, with a timber trussed roof of oak that swept and curved upwards at the sides, and a façade of glass, named 'The Lion and the Unicorn'. Inside was an exhibition space telling the story of the British people. A large mural depicted scenes from British history, and the exhibition itself documented the history of British institutions, parliament, law and church.

---

[29] Robert Hewison, *In Anger: Culture and the Cold War, 1945–60* (London: Weidenfeld and Nicolson, 1981), 48–9.

[30] Hewison, *In Anger*, 49.

[31] See Graham Holderness, *Shakespeare's History* (Dublin: Macmillan, 1985), revised in *Cultural Shakespeare* (Hatfield: University of Hertfordshire Press, 2001), 37–55; and Hagerman, 'Monumental Play'.

In pride of place was displayed a copy of the First Folio of Shakespeare's works, alongside a King James Bible.

The Lion and the Unicorn of the building's title were intended to represent twin facets of the 'British character': 'on the one hand, realism and strength; on the other, fantasy, independence and imagination'. The exhibition's gallery was devoted to a celebration of the English language, 'with principal sections on the translations of the Bible into English, the works of Shakespeare and idiomatic uses of the present day'. The Bible was 'the great beacon of the language', while Shakespeare 'enshrined his mother-tongue in monumental plays'.[32]

Despite the imperial language deployed in the Lion and the Unicorn's guide-catalogue – 'Through the English language, once upon a time, a huddle of British islanders founded a mother-tongue. Through it, today, two-hundred and fifty million people can converse together' – the 1951 Festival appears strikingly insular, compared to the internationalism of the Great Exhibition. The organisers were still speaking the language of Empire, though celebrating a Britain emerging from a world war, victorious by virtue of a largely transatlantic and colonial alliance. International cultural influences were visible everywhere, especially the Scandinavian style of some of the South Bank buildings. The 'Skylon' presented a striking image of futuristic imagination.

Yet the Festival mood was inward-looking, almost parochial, seeking for the roots of British nationality in the distant past, and in close physical association with the land. Jed Esty claims that at the time Britain took an 'anthropological turn' in response to the shrinking of English influence.[33] Accustomed to global dominance, Britain was beginning to see itself as one culture among many, a crisis of national identity that produced 'the rise of an Anglo-centric cultural paradigm'.[34] At the time the global map was being redrawn, the Empire was in the process of dissolution, and an insular nationalism was no longer viable. As a public mood this insularity was hardly surprising. Only a decade previously, Britain had stood alone to confront Nazi Germany, surrounded by a Europe defeated, occupied, collaborating or fascist-led, and a United States reluctant to engage directly in

[32] Exhibition catalogue, quoted in Becky E. Conekin, *The Autobiography of a Nation: The 1951 Festival of Britain* (Manchester University Press, 2003), 95.

[33] Jed Esty, *A Shrinking Island: Modernism and National Culture* (Princeton University Press, 2003).

[34] Esty, *A Shrinking Island*, 1.

the anti-Nazi conflict. But for a post-war Labour government this adherence to the Dunkirk spirit represented a dangerous concession to a more reactionary form of nationalism. By the end of the year, war-time leader Winston Churchill had been returned to power in a Conservative election victory.

To subsequent critical commentators, the Festival of Britain appeared in retrospect to be less a 'shaft of confidence cast forth against the future', and more like the termination of post-war potentialities for progressive change. Michael Frayn argued that the Festival testified to the hegemony of a radical middle class, which favoured Labour's programme for achieving social justice, provided it was not permitted to change the fundamental basis of British society:

> With the exception of Herbert Morrison, who was responsible to the Cabinet for the Festival and who had very little to do with the actual form it took, there was almost no one of working-class background concerned in planning the Festival, and nothing about the results to suggest that the working classes were anything more than the loveable human but essentially inert objects of benevolent administration. In fact Festival Britain was the Britain of the radical middle classes – the do-gooders; the readers of the *New Statesman*, the *Guardian*, and the *Observer*; the signers of petitions; the backbone of the BBC.[35]

It is not surprising, then, that this particular 'Autobiography of a Nation' involved, at least in cultural terms, an attempt to establish links with the remote past, rather than a progressive vision of future change. The paradox is visible in the Jacobean language used by the official guide to express future aspiration, where the Festival seemed to embody reactionary hopes for re-establishing of past glories, rather than the socialist version of historical progress that might have been expected from a Labour government with strong popular mandate. The return to power of Churchill, Shakespearean orator and leader of the 'band of brothers' which saved Britain in her hour of peril, was a fulfilment of those reactionary dreams, visible here in tense contradiction with the progressive hopes of the Labour government's last cultural intervention.

There was, however, another, very different, manifestation of Shakespeare on display on the South Bank. Between 1951 and 1954,

---

[35] Michael Frayn, 'Festival', in Michael Sissons and Philip French (eds.), *The Age of Austerity* (London: Hodder and Stoughton, 1963), 319.

British railways introduced the 'Britannia' class of steam locomotives designed in Derby by R. A. Riddles, and built in Crewe. The new trains were applauded as examples of progressive technology and design, further evidence that Britain was recovering from the dark, drab days of war, and post-war austerity. Each locomotive was given a name, either from the pantheon of British military and political heroes or from the ranks of British writers. The fifth production, no. 70004, was called 'William Shakespeare'. Given a special finish, it was displayed in a static exhibition on the South Bank for the Festival of Britain.

Locomotive 70004 'William Shakespeare' was in many ways little different from existing rolling stock, but was much more beautifully designed, with clean lines and a stylish finish. The wheels were more discreet, half-concealed inside the bodywork, while the chimney stack had been flattened to give the locomotive a smooth, aerodynamic look. It was painted a bright green, with a bright red bumper. The machine was a beautiful piece of design engineering, sleek and classic in its lines, bright and modern in its decoration, exuding a quiet and confident

Figure 4.3 11 October 1951: the *William Shakespeare* locomotive, which powers the *Golden Arrow* train. Photo by Topical Press Agency/Getty Images.

sense of power. It was basically the same steam locomotive invented by Stephenson over a century before, yet in terms of craftsmanship, design quality and engineering precision it struck observers as excitingly modern. I have seen a photograph, now unfortunately inaccessible, of a crowd of ordinary people standing on a platform at Victoria Station inspecting the 'William Shakespeare' train: they laugh, point up at the red name plate riveted to the side of the locomotive, and converse with pleasure amongst themselves. Here Shakespeare was recontextualised, at the cutting-edge of modern design and technology, and firmly at the centre of public attention. Later in the same year the 70004 was assigned to the Golden Arrow route to Dover, helping to link London to the European mainland (Figure 4.3). Here we see the name of Shakespeare participating in a crucial element of post-war reconstruction.[36] As in the Coalbrookdale dome, Shakespeare remained not only central to British culture but intimately bound up with the principal social and economic drivers of the day, industry, engineering and design.

2012: London Olympics

This association of Shakespeare with industry became a key emphasis in the opening ceremony of the London Olympics in 2012, held at Stratford in East London. Here the ceremony's director, Danny Boyle, presented another 'Autobiography of a Nation', one strikingly different from that of 1951, and much more akin to the Great Exhibition of 1851.

Within the huge 100,000 seat arena was enacted an extraordinary history of Britain, achieved by a combination of stunning technical wizardry and mass performance. Initially the spectators were presented with medieval England, a pre-industrial landscape of fields and villages, meadows and woods, at its centre a mound, perhaps representing Glastonbury Tor. Smoke rose from the chimney of a thatched cottage. Actors playing the roles of rural labourers tilled the fields or played games, kicking a ball or dancing round a maypole. Victorian cricketers played their game on the village green. Meanwhile, a child's

---

[36] See Ton Hoenselaars and Clara Calvo, 'Shakespeare Eurostar: Calais, the Continent and the Operatic Fortunes of Ambroise Thomas', in W. Maley and M. Tudeau-Clayton (eds.), *This England, That Shakespeare: New Angles on Englishness and the Bard* (Farnham: Ashgate, 2010).

voice sang William Blake's poem 'And did those feet' from *Jerusalem*, a nostalgic celebration of England's 'green and pleasant land'.

A significant historical change was foreshadowed, when an old omnibus drawn by two shire horses entered the arena and deposited a group of men wearing the top hats and frock coats of Victorian capitalists. One of them, who seemed to be *primus inter pares*, strode ahead of the group, carrying a book. This was Isambard Kingdom Brunel himself. But he was played by actor Kenneth Branagh, famous for his Shakespearean roles and productions. Brunel stood on the mound, and in a declamatory voice spoke Caliban's lines from *The Tempest*.

> Be not afeard, the isle is full of noises,
> Sounds and sweet airs that give delight and hurt not.
> Sometimes a thousand twangling instruments
> Will hum about mine ears, and sometimes voices
> That, if I then had waked after long sleep,
> Will make me sleep again, and then, in dreaming
> The clouds methought would open, and show riches
> Ready to drop on me, that when I waked,
> I cried to dream again.[37]

The musical accompaniment, 'Nimrod' from Edward Elgar's *Enigma Variations*, evoked both the Victorian era and British nationalist sentiment.

Brunel's Shakespearean speech was a preface to a performed history of the Industrial Revolution. The rural populace began to drift away, while by some invisible technology the great tree on the summit of the mound rose into the air, revealing beneath its roots a pit emitting smoke and light. From this breach in the rural landscape there began to stream myriads of industrial workers, ragged with poverty and dirty with toil. Under the beneficent gaze of Brunel and his band of entrepreneurs, the working masses occupied the arena, beginning to roll up the green carpet of grass, and remove it to disclose hard surfaces of metal or glass. Fences were planted to represent land enclosure. Women and men were seen hauling laboriously at machines that triggered from the ground tall factory chimneys, six in number, that rose into the air and belched forth the smoke and steam of industrial production. Brunel strode cheerfully through the midst of this immense social upheaval, surveying the apparently infinite capability of human labour.

[37] *The Tempest*, 3.2.138–46.

The green grass of rural England disappeared, replaced by a brownfield industrial site full of machinery: a water wheel, beam engines, looms. At the centre of the display was a large circular trough, linked by a long channel to a crucible such as those used in steel production. A technical simulation of steel-smelting then began, using light effects and fireworks. A sparking river of molten steel appeared to pour into the channel and slowly make its way towards the central trough. Steelworkers busily hammered and sieved the glowing ore. Running around the trough, the molten steel appeared to form a perfect ring. Above the heads of the audience, four identical rings of light were hovering suspended in the air, slowly converging towards one another. The ring that had shaped itself in the centre also rose and moved towards the others. In a dazzling technological *coup d'oeil*, these five rings, which seemed to have the mass and density of metal, yet hovered ethereally in the air, effortlessly combined together to form an image, which then seemed to burst into flame and cascade showers of brilliant sparks down into the space of the auditorium. The symbol of the Olympics: all the nations of the world, linked together in peaceful competition.

The use of Caliban's lines puzzled Shakespeareans. James Shapiro commented:

Why you would choose Caliban's lines as a kind of anthem for the Olympics, I'm not sure. If you gave those lines some thought, especially in the light of the British Empire, it's an odd choice. The lines are quite beautiful, and I guess they wanted to rip them out of context and talk about how magical a place the British Isles are. Why give him the lines Shakespeare wrote for a half-man, half-beast about to try to kill off an imperial innovator who took away his island? I don't know. You would probably have to ask the people who designed the opening Games ceremony what their thinking was.[38]

Shapiro's bafflement was widely shared. Observers found the cultural conjunction effected by the juxtaposition inappropriate in two ways. Firstly, what does Shakespeare have to do with Brunel? The great engineer Isambard Kingdom Brunel, whose designs and inventions revolutionised both the machinery and the systems of transport, has

---

[38] Quoted in Michael Florek, 'Shakespeare Passage Features in Opening Ceremony', *USA Today* (27 July 2012). Available at http://usatoday30.usatoday.com/sports/olympics/london/story/2012–07–27/shakespeare-tempest-london-olympics-opening-ceremony/56548372/1

proved central to this study, his legacy being abundantly visible in the three national festivals discussed. But what has he to do with Shakespeare? This was the question in many minds, when frock-coated and top-hatted Kenneth Branagh voiced Caliban's lines from the summit of the Olympic mound.

In fact, Brunel was an art connoisseur and a Shakespeare enthusiast. In the late 1840s, he commissioned a set of paintings of Shakespearean subjects from some of the most distinguished English artists of his day, including Charles West Cope, Augustus Leopold Egg, Edwin Landseer, Frederick Richard Lee, Charles Robert Leslie and Clarkson Stanfield. The paintings were intended for display in the dining room of his house in Duke Street, St James's, which would appear to have become known, by the time of his death, if not earlier, as the 'Shakespeare Room'.[39]

On 27 December 1847, Brunel wrote to Landseer of his plans and their rationale. He had two objectives: to illustrate passages of Shakespeare – 'the choice of subjects I leave to the artist limiting only to selections from the *Acted* and *popular* plays of the *Author*' – and to promote contemporary British art, by making:

the rendering . . . of one of our most National of English Poets of *past times* the occasion or means of obtaining a collection of the best examples of the first English Artists of the *present* time and I should wish to make the more apparent object – the illustrations of the Poet – subservient in each case to the second object.[40]

Brunel thus had a very clear conception of how the past should be commemorated in the present, as 'rehearsal' rather than 'remembrance'. The homage to Shakespeare was to be subservient to the freedom of the contemporary artist to interpret the plays in whatever way he chose. The Shakespeare Room was to house a modern Shakespeare, appropriated to assist in the advancement of contemporary art and design, and to stage a 'dialogue between past and present'.[41]

The second impropriety was the juxtaposition of Caliban's lines with a figure of Victorian authority and power. Why was a Victorian captain of industry speaking lines from an oppressed colonial subject?

---

[39] 'Mr. Brunel's Collection of Works of Art', *The Times*, 23 April 1860, 7.
[40] Quoted in H. Faberman and P. McEvansoneya, 'Isambard Kingdom Brunel's Shakespeare Room', *Burlington Magazine*, 137, no. 1103 (1995), 108–18.
[41] Hewison, *Culture Industry*, 144.

As Erin Sullivan puts it, 'Why use a speech from Caliban – one of the most disenfranchised and politically dispossessed characters in all of Shakespeare's plays – to represent the dreams, ambitions and history of Great Britain, Empire and all?'[42] The speech was universally described as 'out of context'. But the 'context' it was felt to be 'out of' was not that of *The Tempest*, which from its inception has been subjected to wide diversities of interpretation and adaptation, from Dryden and D'Avenant's *The Enchanted Island* (1670) to the film *Forbidden Planet* (1956), but of a particular critical orthodoxy that identifies Caliban as the oppressed colonial subject and Prospero as the imperial oppressor. Brunel stands for nation, empire, colonial domination; Caliban for the subjects of imperial aggression, the wretched of the earth. One gets the impression that in general Shakespeareans would have preferred the lines to have been spoken by one of the colliers or steelworkers impersonated in the show, while Brunel soundly whipped him.

Caliban has another line in the play that seems to have been overlooked in these responses: 'This island's mine.' Who speaks for Britain? For Danny Boyle it was Brunel, and Shakespeare, and in the closing ceremony Winston Churchill, who emerged from a model of Big Ben to reprise Caliban's lines. The appearance of Churchill in a sense took up the narrative where the Festival of Britain left off. But the 'Autobiography' of the island nation these figures collectively represented was in fact an extremely left-wing and democrat version of history, which emphasised the struggle for political rights (the Suffragettes), immigration and the social integration of ethnic minorities (the arrival of the *Windrush*), and the establishing of the post-war Welfare State (the National Health Service). Equal emphasis was given to creative works of fantasy and imagination: J. M. Barrie, Tolkien, J. K. Rowling. In his introductory note to the programme, Danny Boyle deployed the language of utopian socialism:

But we hope, too, that through all the noise and excitement you'll glimpse a single golden thread of purpose – the idea of Jerusalem – of the better world, the world of real freedom and real equality, a world that can be built through the prosperity of industry, through the caring nation that built the welfare state, through the joyous energy of popular culture, through the dream of

---

[42] Erin Sullivan, 'Olympic Performance in the Year of Shakespeare', in Paul Prescott, Paul Edmondson and Erin Sullivan (eds.), *A Year of Shakespeare: Re-living the World Shakespeare Festival* (London: Bloomsbury, 2013), 3.

universal communication. A belief that we can build Jerusalem. And that it will be for everyone.[43]

Churchill, Brunel and Shakespeare were all speaking on behalf of an extremely diversified, multi-ethnic and multi-cultural British people. The representative claim is a wholly substantial one: in the league table of 'Great Britons', based on a poll conducted in 2002 by the BBC, Churchill and Brunel came first and second respectively, while Shakespeare was fifth.

In Danny Boyle's vision of Britain, Caliban is in fact the human and social cornerstone of the population. A man who lived in a wondrous isle, surrounded by the shapes of his imagination. An instinctive artist, a poet and a dreamer. He heard random noise as exquisite music, and saw the clouds open onto infinite possibility. Brunel too, in Boyle's fantasy, lived in an isle of wonders, and heard the same music. He listened to the random babbling of nature, and interpreted it into a common language. He dreamed the same dreams: dreams of space and time. And what he dreamed, he invented: his mind and hand went together. His imagination reached out across distance, abbreviated time and annihilated space, crossed rivers and linked towns, burrowed deep into the earth, and rode the pitching waves of the high seas. And from those visions, he conjured machines that made dreams into reality: bridges, ships, railways.

The ceremony chronicled and celebrated two British achievements, the Industrial and the Digital Revolutions. Thus the aesthetic technology of the 2012 opening ceremony, which depended in large part on the latter, took Brunel's machinery and rendered it back into dream again. This was a technology capable not only of construction but of creation. Engineering had entered the realm of poetry. Art and science had become one, as they were in the Renaissance. Shakespeare and Brunel no longer stood opposed, as the dreamer and the artisan, or the poet and the engineer. They had become one voice, one hand, one mind. And by the combination of their powers of vision and practice, the Olympic Opening Ceremony suggests, they had brought greatness back to Britain.

---

[43] Danny Boyle, *London 2012 Olympic Games, Opening Ceremony* (n.p.: Haymarket Consulting Media, 2012), 1.

From sceptred isle to isles of wonder

If we seek for the presence of Shakespeare not only in the 'great tradition' of centenary celebrations but in this alternative tradition of national festivals, we can find a Shakespeare 'rehearsed' rather than merely commemorated; a Shakespeare simultaneously celebrated as a cornerstone of British culture, and brought into intimate relation with the scientific, technological, international and popular priorities of the national festivals. In each case, what initially appears to be an incongruous juxtaposition becomes a surprisingly homogenous and harmonious reconciliation of Shakespeare with industry, science and technology, with global culture and with popular participation. These Shakespearean quotations also testify to a British culture capable of confidently staging a productive dialogue between the present and the past; patriotic but not xenophobic; nationalistic but also democratic; effortlessly combining high and popular cultures. From Shakespeare's 'sceptred isle' and his Caliban's island 'full of noises', through Churchill's 'island race' to Danny Boyle's 'isles of wonder', we can rediscover 'imagined communities' of a nation worthy of respect, admiration and love.

5 | Remembering Shakespeare in India: colonial and postcolonial memory

SUPRIYA CHAUDHURI

Texts and their readers exist in time, and as Shakespeare grows further and further away from us, 450 years after his birth, we may need to ask what the act of 'remembering' involves. It is obviously true that the operation of cultural memory works to destabilize our awareness of historical time, and the 'afterlives' of texts and artefacts negotiate multiple temporalities – as does the text or artefact itself in the instant of its making. For colonial readers, encountering Shakespeare both as literary master-text and as theatrical property, the experience was one that interrupted any prior sense of literary tradition and required an engagement with new forms of historicity. On the one hand Shakespeare was assured of a kind of perpetual life outside time and history, while on the other he was obviously the composite product of a historical process that left deposits of all kinds, some visible, some invisible, on the objects that passed through it. What resulted was an inevitable distortion, even a foreshortening, of the temporal perspective on a writer treated both as classic and as contemporary.

Walter Benjamin, commenting on the life of the artwork, placed it in the context of survival, through translation and adaptation, into later times. Adapting Aby Warburg's term, *Nachleben*, or afterlife, he said that:

The concept of life is given its due only if everything that has a history of its own, and is not merely the setting for history, is credited with life ... The philosopher's task consists in comprehending all of natural life through the more encompassing life of history. And, indeed, is not the continued life of works of art far easier to recognize than the continual life of animal species? The history of the great works of art tells us about their antecedents, their realization in the age of the artists, their potentially eternal afterlife in succeeding generations. Where this last manifests itself, it is called fame.[1]

---

[1] 'The Task of the Translator', in Walter Benjamin, *Illuminations*, ed. Hannah Arendt, trans. Harry Zohn (London: Fontana, 1977), 69–82, 71.

Shakespeare's extraordinary fame as a dramatist in colonial India was achieved primarily in two contexts: as part of a new educational curriculum designed for the training of the native bourgeoisie, and as an inventor of plots and characters that could be freely adapted and re-purposed for the use of the stage. Much has been written on both these aspects of influence and adaptation, from Shakespeare as a kind of 'mask of conquest' in the colonial curriculum (citing the title of Gauri Viswanathan's well-known book),[2] to re-appropriations of the plays in the popular theatre. The purpose of this paper is not to review these two traditions, but to reflect on memorial practice, particularly the *time* that Shakespeare inhabits in different forms of cultural appropriation. Three different kinds of time – the 'universal' time of the classic, the sedimented time of history, and the time of a reformed present – coincide in the perception of Shakespeare in India. I will suggest that this understanding of time has implications for the way in which the project of modernity itself is conceived, as for the fabrication of history. Looking at the cultures of memory that attach themselves to Shakespeare in the subcontinent over a period extending from the inception of colonial rule till after the demise of empire, and including two key dates, the Shakespeare Tercentenary of 1864 and the Quatercentenary of 1964, I will attempt to examine the nature of Shakespearean afterlives in relation to the 'time of the text'.

Shakespeare in the classroom

The first recorded performances of Shakespeare in India date from the late eighteenth century, and a translation of *The Tempest* into Bengali was produced by one Claude Monckton as early as 1809 at the Fort William College in Calcutta, established for the training of British colonial officers.[3] Shakespeare was prescribed for study as part of the literary curriculum of the Hindu College in Calcutta, in 1817 the first

---

[2] Gauri Viswanathan, *Masks of Conquest: Literary Studies and British Rule in India* (Delhi: Oxford University Press, 1998).
[3] See Sushil Kumar Mukherjee, *The Story of the Calcutta Theatres, 1753–1980* (Calcutta: KP Bagchi, 1982), 1–30; Amal Mitra, *Kolkatay Bideshi Rangalay* (Calcutta: Prakash Bhavan, 1967), *passim*; and Thomas Roebuck, *The Annals of the College of Fort William* (Calcutta: Hindustanee Press, 1819), 187.

secular institution of higher learning on the European model to be set up by the native gentry.[4] Students of the Hindu College acted scenes from the plays, following a practice already initiated by English-language schools such as Drummond's Dhurrumtollah Academy, where in 1822 the brilliant young Henry Louis Vivian Derozio achieved notice for his performance as Shylock, at the age of thirteen. Two years later Derozio wrote a prologue for a school play which declared:

> No mighty KEMBLE here stalks o'er the stage
> No SIDDONS all your feelings to engage
> But a small band of young aspirant boys
> In faintest miniature the hour employs.[5]

But as an iconoclastic leader of the Young Bengal group at the Hindu College, where he taught between 1828 and 1831, Derozio seems to have favoured Romantic poetry, and an early biographer comments that if he had 'devoted himself with as much ardour to the study of Shakespeare, Milton, and the old Dramatists, he would have had a deeper insight into human feelings'.[6] It was left to Derozio's successor, David Lester Richardson, to make Shakespeare central to literary studies in colonial India, to such an extent that no less a person than Thomas Babington Macaulay wrote to him, 'I may forget everything about India, but your reading of Shakespeare, *never*.'[7] This memory, which for Macaulay was capable of supplanting 'everything about India', is analogous in some ways to the 'shelf of a good European

---

[4] See 'A Sketch of the Origin, Rise, and Progress of the Hindoo College', reprinted from *The Calcutta Christian Observer* (Calcutta: Baptist Mission Press, June–December 1832), in Sakti Sadhan Mukhopadhyay (ed.), *Derozio Remembered: Birth Bicentenary Celebration Commemoration Volume* (Calcutta: Derozio Commemoration Committee and School of Cultural Texts and Records, Jadavpur University, 2008), vol. I: 44.

[5] *Song of the Stormy Petrel: Complete Works of Henry Louis Vivian Derozio*, ed. Abirlal Mukhopadhyay, Amar Dutta, Adhir Kumar, and Sakti Sadhan Mukhopadhyay (Calcutta: Progressive Publishers, 2001), 269. See also Ananda Lal and Sukanta Chaudhuri (eds.), *Shakespeare on the Calcutta Stage: A Checklist* (Calcutta: Papyrus, 2001), 23–4.

[6] 'Henry Louis Vivian Derozio', in Thomas Philip Manuel, *Poetry of our Indian Poets* (Calcutta: D'Rozario & Co., 1861), reprinted in Mukhopadhyay (ed.), *Derozio Remembered*, 136.

[7] Quoted in Taraknath Sen (ed.), *Shakespeare Commemoration Volume* (Calcutta: Presidency College, 1966), vii.

library' which, in his notorious Minute on Indian Education of 1835, he preferred to 'the whole native literature of India and Arabia'.[8]

Macaulay's Minute has been much discussed, but I would like to note here his signal employment of what we might call a trope of erasure, replacing the unwanted other with the cultural master-property of empire. To remember Shakespeare in colonial India was, as Macaulay's letter to Richardson suggests, founded upon a radical *forgetting*. Richardson's own teaching was famously linked to an impassioned reading of the plays, a declamatory practice for which we have further memorial testimony, and which became part of the pedagogic style of the college. In his classic work of social history, *Ramtanu Lahiri o tatkalin bangasamaj* (*Ramtanu Lahiri and the Bengali social world of his time*, 1904), the Brahmo scholar Sivanath Sastri wrote:

> No one had been known to read Shakespeare like him. As he read, he became almost intoxicated with passion, and he inflamed his students as well. Having heard Shakespeare read by him, his students were convinced that there was no poet to compare with Shakespeare, no literature to touch the English. They refused to look at anything native after that. Hatred of their own race became deeply entrenched in many of these youths. Liquor flowed freely among those who held such views.[9]

Swapan Chakravorty comments drily on this early link between Shakespeare and drunkenness, a conjunction that, through the century, binds the iconoclasm of Derozio's heirs, the Young Bengal group, as much to forms of wilful forgetting as to creative renewal.[10] It is worth remembering this link, since memory and forgetting are closely interdependent in colonial culture, and knowledge, as Sir Thomas Browne said, is made by oblivion.[11] The project of modernity, articulated with such power by the Young Bengal group, involved an effacement or obliteration of the past at the same time as its members sought to

---

[8] Thomas Babington Macaulay, *Speeches: with his Minute on Indian Education*, ed. G. M. Young (Oxford University Press, 1935), 349.

[9] Sivanath Shastri, *Ramtanu Lahiri o tatkalin bangasamaj* [Ramtanu Lahiri and the Bengali Social World of his Time, 1904], ed. Baridbaran Ghosh (Calcutta: New Age Publishers, 2007), 113. My translation.

[10] Swapan Chakravorty, *Bangalir Ingreji Sahityacharcha* [The Study of English Literature in Bengal] (Calcutta: Anustup, 2006), 13–14.

[11] 'Knowledge is made by oblivion, and to purchase a clear and warrantable body of Truth, we must forget and part with much we know.' Sir Thomas Browne, *Pseudodoxia Epidemica*, 3rd edn (London: R. W. for Nath. Ekins, 1658), 'To the Reader', A2r.

seize the future. In the event, however, Shakespeare came to belong neither wholly to the future nor decisively to the past.

Energetically promoting Shakespeare to the title of greatest of all poets, Richardson increased the number of Shakespearean texts in the literature curriculum, wrote essays on Shakespeare that illustrated his practice of close and sympathetic reading (including one on 'Shylock' and another on 'Othello and Iago'), and produced the first English literature textbook in the world.[12] In the Preface to his *Selections from the British Poets*, Richardson reflected on the capacity of great poetry to inhabit the soul, never relaxing its hold upon the memory, and becoming, in his phrase, 'a portion of our minds'. He comments, 'Since the time of Shakespeare two centuries and a half, loaded heavily with literary productions, have passed away, and yet Lear and Hamlet and Macbeth and Othello are as fresh as ever!'[13] Shakespeare's capacity to transcend time allows his writings to serve as a source of present, that is, *modern* literary illumination. Richardson's anthology offers explicit recompense to the youth of Bengal for their 'loss of riches', the material impoverishment of colonial servitude:

Let Milton and Shakespeare instruct the young natives of India how to appreciate the beauty which God has lavished upon the creation. He who is so taught has within his reach those sources of pure and serene delight that are wholly inexhaustible.[14]

By the middle of the nineteenth century, a literature syllabus similar to the one Richardson had devised was being taught at the four government colleges that had been established in Bengal, and, in 1858, the official incorporation of the University of Calcutta standardized the pattern of examination for a rapidly growing network of institutions of Western education.[15]

---

[12] For the Shakespeare essays, see David Lester Richardson, *Literary Leaves, or, Prose and Verse chiefly written in India*, vol. II (London: W. H. Allen & Co, 1840). See also his *Selections from the British Poets from the time of Chaucer to the Present Day*, with biographical and critical notes by David Lester Richardson (Calcutta: Baptist Mission Press, 1840). On Richardson's *Selections*, see Michael Hancher, 'College English in India: The First Textbook', in *Victorian Literature and Culture* (Cambridge University Press online journal, available on CJO2014. doi:10.1017/S106015031400014X).

[13] Richardson, *Selections*, 6.   [14] Richardson, *Selections*, 16.

[15] For an account of the establishment of the English literature curriculum, see Rangana Banerji, *The Origins of English Studies in Bengal* (Calcutta: Pages & Chapters, 2012), 59–125.

Shakespeare's Tercentenary

The success of Richardson's literature course, with its institutionaliza-
tion of Shakespeare worship, contributed to those imbalances of the
colonial education system that have been widely noted (usually by
way of a critique of Macaulay's Minute): not just the neglect of
Sanskrit or Persian poetry and philosophy, but also the emphasis upon
a humanities curriculum, to the exclusion of pure and applied sciences.
Nevertheless, Richardson's pupils, among them the poet Michael Madhusudan Dutt and essayist Rajnarain Bose, recalled their master and
his favourite poet with gratitude, and by the second half of the century
there is a kind of literary memorialization of Shakespeare that leaves its
cultural traces on a history of affect. In his autobiography, Rajnarain
Bose remembered Richardson's style of teaching Shakespeare, his close
and impassioned reading of the plays, and his links to contemporary
theatre, where his advice on Shakespeare performance was sought by
actors.[16] Unsurprisingly, Michael Madhusudan Dutt's five-act play
Sharmistha (1859, translated into English as *Sermista*) was influenced
by Shakespeare's *As You Like It* and written in blank verse. The
play was staged in 1873 with women performers in lead roles, to
general disapproval. Dutt's early poetry and drama show strong
Shakespearean influence, and he was himself mercilessly lampooned
by Dinabandhu Mitra in his popular Bengali farce *Sadhabar Ekadashi*
[*The Married Woman's Widow-Rites*, 1866] as an educated drunkard
(what else?) declaiming snatches of Milton and Shakespeare.[17]

Sadhabar Ekadashi was acted in 1866, two years after the Shakespeare Tercentenary, and it is at this point that we might pause to ask a
question about colonial time. We have no evidence for any celebration
of the Shakespeare Tercentenary in India, despite the fact that after
Garrick's belated and rained-out Jubilee in 1769, the 1864 celebrations
in Stratford were elaborate and substantial. The Archbishop of Dublin,
Richard Chenevix Trench, delivering the sermon in Holy Trinity
church, had asked his congregation to 'imagine this England of ours
without her Shakespeare ... the foremost poet whom the world has

---

[16] Rajnarain Bose, *Atmacharit* [My Life], in Naresh Jana (ed.), *Atmakatha*
[Autobiographies] (Calcutta: Ananya Prakashan, 1981), vol. I, 12.
[17] Dinabandhu Mitra, 'Sadhabar Ekadashi' ['The Married Woman's Widow-
Rites'] in *Dinabandhu Rachana-sangraha* [Collected Works] (Calcutta:
Saksharata Prakashan, 1973), 177–181.

seen, we are almost bold to prophesy, it will ever see'.[18] As Richard
Foulkes suggests, Trench was in effect responding to Carlyle's question
in 'The Hero as Poet', delivered as a lecture on 12 May 1840:

> Consider now if they asked us, Will you give-up your Indian Empire or your
> Shakespeare, you English: never have had any Indian Empire, or never have
> had any Shakespeare? ... should not we be forced to answer, Indian Empire
> or no Indian Empire, we cannot do without Shakespeare! Indian Empire will
> go, at any rate, some day; but this Shakespeare does not go, he lasts forever
> with us.[19]

'Lasting forever' invokes Shakespeare's own conceit of immortality, as
contrasted to time-bound colonial possessions, doomed to their ends in
history. But in 1864 both Shakespeare and Indian Empire seemed
secure enough, India having been officially transferred to the Crown
in 1858, after the turmoil of the 1857 Revolt. Yet there are no records
of special performances, lectures or commemorative events in Britain's
principal colony. It may be, of course, that the records have not
survived, though there is evidence of stage and other activity both
before and after. But the enthusiasm generated around the Tercentenary in Britain and France, even in Germany despite the wars of unification, does not appear to have affected India. Was Shakespeare's age
irrelevant, since he was so resolutely presented as being 'for all time'?
The colonial project was itself an interruption of, perhaps an assault
upon, notions of time and history. On the one hand it attempted new
feats of historiography, while on the other it required the supersession
of earlier kinds of temporal knowledge for what Christopher Prendergast, following Arjun Appadurai, calls Eurochronology.[20] Colonial
India was subjected to a kind of 'invention of history', its natives
derided for their persistent confusion of myths with truth, and requiring the intervention of British historical method as exemplified in John
Clark Marshman's *History of India* (1867).

[18] Cited in Richard Foulkes, *Performing Shakespeare in the Age of Empire*
(Cambridge University Press, 2006), 75.
[19] Thomas Carlyle, *Heroes and Hero-Worship* (London: Oxford University Press,
1963), 148.
[20] See Christopher Prendergast, 'The World Republic of Letters', in Christopher
Prendergast and Benedict Anderson (ed.), *Debating World Literature* (London:
Verso, 2004), 6. The term is used by Arjun Appadurai in *Modernity at Large:
Cultural Dimensions of Globalization* (Minneapolis: University of Minnesota
Press, 1996), 30.

The time of the classic

In his brilliant indictment of 'allochronic' discourse, Johannes Fabian speaks of the 'denial of coevalness' produced by Western anthropology, so that the time of the other is specifically not the time of the self.[21] While his critique is restricted to anthropological practice, it is worth noting how the terms 'medieval' and 'modern' came to be used in British Indian historiography, so that the pre-colonial inevitably presented itself as medieval. Shakespeare could not be placed within that undifferentiated space of pre-modernity. Yet Shakespeare's time – contemporary with the reign of the Mughal emperor Akbar – was in some respects both too near and too far. What strikes us most in accounts of early Shakespeare pedagogy in India is the emphasis upon the immediacy and accessibility of the Shakespearean text, an accessibility that was assured by liberal education on the Western model. 'Every home has its Shakespeare; everyone can open and read the original work,' wrote Bankimchandra Chattopadhyay, greatest of nineteenth century Bengali novelists and first graduate of the newly founded University of Calcutta, in an essay on 'Shakuntala, Miranda and Desdemona' first published in 1875.[22] Not only does this astonishing assertion convert the few beneficiaries of colonial higher education to an undifferentiated 'everyone', the essay also projects a time independent of history, the time of the classic, to which each educated person has equal access. This time is significantly different from the time of modernity, or modernization, to which Shakespeare also belongs – or belonged, when he was first made part of the colonial curriculum.

It was Sir William Jones who first instituted the comparison that Bankimchandra develops in this essay, recklessly inverting history to describe Kalidasa, a Sanskrit court poet of the fourth century CE, as 'the Shakespeare of India' in the Preface to his translation of *Sacontala, or the Fatal Ring* (1789).[23] The parallel is difficult to sustain, since Kalidasa wrote very few plays and is known principally for his long

---

[21] Johannes Fabian, *Time and the Other: How Anthropology Makes its Object* (Columbia University Press, 2002), 32.

[22] In Bankimchandra Chattopadhyay, *Bankim Rachanavali* [Complete Works], vol. II, ed. J. C. Bagal (Calcutta: Sahitya Samsad, 2004), 181. My translation.

[23] Kalidasa, *The Sacontala: or, the Fatal Ring*, trans. Sir William Jones, republished Jogendra Nath Ghose (Calcutta: Trübner & Co, 1875), iii.

narrative poems belonging to the golden age of Sanskrit poetry at the fabled court of Vikramaditya (usually identified with Chandragupta II, *c.*376–415 CE). Moreover, his plays bear the mark of a studied idealization of character on the lines recommended by that great manual of early Sanskrit theatre and the arts of performance, Bharata's *Natyashastra* (*c.* first century BCE). Nevertheless, the epithet 'Shakespeare of India' was repeated by the Sanskrit lexicographer Sir Monier Monier-Williams, and comparisons between Shakespeare and Kalidasa are standard to this day (attempted even by the well-known postcolonial theorist Harish Trivedi).[24] Parallels across periods and cultures – classic speaking to classic over the gulf of time – were not uncommon in late eighteenth century Europe, when Goethe greeted *Shakuntala* as the pinnacle of earthly and poetic perfection, but the anachronism of Jones's comparison appears studied and deliberate.[25] Kalidasa resembles Shakespeare, not the other way around. Not only is Shakespeare, as 'timeless' classic, the measure for all poets, he is co-opted into the Orientalist discovery of classical Sanskrit literature in late eighteenth-century Europe (later to be termed the Oriental Renaissance). The classic status of Kalidasa is deliberately affirmed in such a way as to resist and pre-empt Macaulay's own co-opting of 'Orientalist' knowledge when he dismissed all such comparisons in the following words: 'I certainly never met with any orientalist who ventured to maintain that the Arabic and Sanscrit poetry could be compared to that of the great European nations.'[26] Jones and Monier-Williams were maintaining exactly what Macaulay held in such abhorrence, yet the parallel that Macaulay was to draw between Europe's rediscovery of the Greek and Latin classics, and India's discovery of English, is implicitly sustained. 'What the Greek and Latin were to the contemporaries of More and Ascham, our tongue is to the people of India. The literature of England is now more valuable than that of classical antiquity,' wrote Macaulay.[27] Paradoxically,

[24] See Harish Trivedi, 'Colonizing Love: *Romeo and Juliet* in Modern Indian Disseminations' and R. A. Malagi 'Toward a Terrestrial Divine Comedy: A Study of *The Winter's Tale* and *Shakuntalam*', in Poonam Trivedi and Dennis Bartholomeusz (eds.), *India's Shakespeare: Translation, Interpretation and Performance* (Newark: University of Delaware Press, 2005), 74–91 and 123–40.

[25] See Dorothy Matilda Figueira, *Translating the Orient: The Reception of Sakuntala in Nineteenth-Century Europe* (Albany: State University of New York Press, 1991), on the European 'discovery' of Kalidasa.

[26] Macaulay, 'Minute', 349.   [27] Macaulay, 'Minute', 351.

therefore, the 'classical' perfection of Sanskrit must be claimed not by
comparison to another classical language, but by invoking the 'classic'
status of Shakespeare. Indeed, Richardson too asserted that

> The Indian students read our English poets, as English collegians read the
> poets of Greece or Rome, not only to familiarize their minds with beautiful
> images and pure and noble thoughts, but to acquire a thorough knowledge
> of the language in which the poetry is embodied.[28]

As in all accounts of the classic as opposed to the classical, what is at
stake here is not antiquity but value, not time but money. At a time
when courses on English literature are being initiated simultaneously in
India and England, Shakespeare serves as an imperishable token of
value in both, but for India, he also serves to *validate* what we might
call a literary ideal.

Shakespeare and modernity

It is worth reflecting, then, on the forms of *folding*, or folded time that
a renaissance – whether in Europe in the fifteenth century or in colonial
India in the nineteenth – involves. The idea of a Bengal Renaissance
was important to early and mid-nineteenth century writers and social
reform movements, distant though it may have been from Macaulay's
characteristically dismissive observations. Still, even for Macaulay
(and William Bentinck, co-signatory to his 'Minute') any revival of
arts and letters in India, on the model of that in fifteenth century
Europe, could only be accomplished by borrowing, from not only
a foreign but a modern literature. As a project of modernization
this might seem more logical than looking back to classical antiquity,
the method chosen by the Renaissance in Europe, a period also called
Early Modern. What complicates the process is the *desire for the
classic* (or perhaps, since desire is impossible to legislate, the tangled
yearning for the classical as classic), exemplified in Bankimchandra's
comparison of Shakuntala with Shakespeare's heroines Miranda and
Desdemona (later taken forward by his friend Shrishchandra Majumdar in an essay called 'Miranda and Kapalakundala', 1880, and by

---

[28] Richardson, Preface, *Selections*, 16.

Rabindranath Tagore in his essay 'Shakuntala', 1902).[29] During the crucial years around 1864, Bankimchandra, whose sense of history was acute and unerring, had Shakespeare very much on his mind. His novel *Kapalakundala* (published 1866), set around the turn of the sixteenth century, when Portuguese ships carried on a flourishing trade in slaves from Bengal, drew the first part of its plot from *The Tempest*. In his own words: 'While writing *Kapalakundala* the author I most read was Shakespeare.'[30]

Bankimchandra was under no misconception regarding Shakespeare's time or his own: for him Bengal's 'Renaissance', which he placed in fifteenth-century Nabadvip, was already long past. He knew himself to inhabit the 'time-lagged' moment of colonial modernity, and like several contemporaries including Michael Madhusudan Dutt, he was untiring in his efforts to create a modern Bengali literature by subjecting indigenous materials to the impact of new genres and the thought-systems of the European enlightenment. But of all the authors who formed part of the colonial curriculum, it was Shakespeare who haunted Bankimchandra's imagination and became an unstated presence in his novels. In his late novella *Rajani* (1877), a young man called Amarnath leafs through a picture-book containing portraits of Shakespearean characters, and comments that painting cannot capture the nuances conveyed by speech or action. Perhaps recalling Lessing, whom he may have read, Bankimchandra suggests that visual representation is relatively static and incomplete compared with the complexity of Shakespearean characterization.[31] In many ways,

[29] Shrishchandra Majumdar, 'Miranda o Kapalakundala', *Bangadarsan*, Shravan 1287/ July–August 1880; see also Kshirodbihari Chattopadhyay, 'Kapalakundala o Miranda', *Bharatvarsha*, Agrahayan 1325/ November–December 1918; and Rabindranath Tagore, '*Shakuntala*', in *Rabindra Rachanavali* [Complete Works] (Calcutta: Vishvabharati, 1942), vol. 5, 521–37, and trans. Sukanta Chaudhuri, in Rabindranath Tagore, *Selected Writings on Literature and Language*, ed. Sukanta Chaudhuri, Oxford Tagore Translations (New Delhi: Oxford University Press, 2001), 237–51.

[30] As cited in J. K. Chakravarti (ed.), *Kapalakundala* (Calcutta: Shridhar Prakashani, 1967), 7. On Bankimchandra's debts to Shakespeare, see Supriya Chaudhuri, 'The Absence of Caliban: Shakespeare and Colonial Modernity', in R. S. White, Christa Jansohn and Richard Fotheringham (eds.), *Shakespeare's World/ World Shakespeares* (University of Delaware Press, 2008), 223–36.

[31] In Bankimchandra Chattopadhyay, *Bankim Rachanavali* [Complete Works], vol. I, ed. J. C. Bagal (Calcutta: Sahitya Samsad, 2003), 457. It is not impossible that Bankimchandra knew Lessing's *Laocoön: or the Limits of Painting and Poetry* (1766): for an English translation, see Gotthold Ephraim Lessing,

Bankimchandra's 'memory' of Shakespeare (providing, among much else, chapter epigraphs for his novels) functions as a site from which he draws material for a major social and historical project, the renewal of Bengali literature and the rewriting of national history. That task was completed by his younger contemporary Rabindranath Tagore, who stands in a more critical relation to Shakespeare, though as a boy of thirteen he was asked by his tutor to render *Macbeth* into Bengali verse. In his *Reminiscences*, published in 1912, Tagore speaks of the tremendous impact produced on the relatively narrow and staid social world of his youth by the passion and colour of Shakespearean drama, which he viewed not so much as classic or romantic, but as a form of modern baroque, marked by the 'working out of extravagantly vehement feelings to an inevitable conflagration'.[32]

Shakespeare and nineteenth-century theatre

It was this baroque extravagance that Shakespeare brought to the 'rebirth' of Indian theatre in the nineteenth century, offering new possibilities for the representation of emotion and event. On stage, Shakespeare has a formative role in three early traditions: performance in English on colonial stages, especially in Bombay and Calcutta during the late eighteenth and early nineteenth centuries, modern vernacular theatre, drawing on new dramatic writing as well as on Shakespeare in translation, and Parsi theatre, the first professional popular theatre in India. A yawning gulf separates all of these from the classical Sanskrit drama, and nineteenth-century theatre is largely a new creation, however much it might have been influenced by Bharata's *Natyashastra* and by popular performance styles. As Aniket Jaaware and Urmila Bhirdikar show in their discussion of Shakespeare in Maharashtra, Shakespeare formed the basis for a theorization of tragedy, unknown to classical Sanskrit dramatists, and even where the nine *rasas* were invoked, a complex understanding of the 'pleasure' of tragedy, the structure of plots, and the nature of evil (or the role of the villain)

Laocoön, Nathan the Wise, Minna von Barnhelm, ed. W. A. Steel (London: Dent, 1930), 1–110.

[32] Rabindranath Tagore, *Jivansmriti* [My Reminiscences], in *Rabindra Rachanavali* [Complete Works] (Calcutta: Vishvabharati, 1954), vol. XVII, 374–5.

emerges both from Marathi theatre in the later nineteenth century and from contemporary scholarship.[33] In fact, the tragedies had a durable popularity on stage; the first Shakespeare play to be translated into Marathi was *Othello*, by Mahadevshastri Kolhatkar in 1867.

In Bengal, Shakespeare, described by Tagore as 'represent[ing] for us the ideal of drama',[34] served as the agent of theatrical modernity for the colonial bourgeoisie. He cast a long shadow on the new Bengali theatre (initiated in 1872 with the founding of the National Theatre, after an abortive beginning in 1795 through a short-lived venture by the Russian impresario Herasim Lebedeff). Its middle-class audience, able to draw upon its own memories of the Shakespearean text from classroom or study, was frequently critical of the quality of adaptation. In 1854, the editor of the *Hindu Patriot* comments: 'Nothing will give us greater pleasure than to behold Shakespeare springing into new life under the histrionic talent of our educated countrymen, but we cannot calmly look on while the old gentleman is being murdered or mangled.'[35] Yet close adherence to the original (as in Girish Chandra Ghosh's staging of his translation of *Macbeth* in 1893 at the Minerva Theatre, in 'authentic' Scottish costume and using English stage conventions) was not necessarily well received, and more thoroughgoing adaptation of names, places and costumes usually fared better. Early Shakespeare translation was compelled to negotiate, implicitly if not explicitly, with both genre and substance – moral, philosophical and dramaturgic – of the Shakespearean text. One recourse was 'to recast the dramatic form into narrative and to assign it to a new and pseudo-Sanskritic subgenre' (as in Ishvar Chandra Vidyasagar's choice of the term *vilasa* to categorize his narrative rendering of *The Comedy of Errors, Bhranti-vilasa*).[36] Even where

---

[33] See Aniket Jaaware and Urmila Bhirdikar, 'Shakespeare in Maharashtra, 1892–1927: A Note on a Trend in Marathi Theatre and Theatre Criticism', in Tom Bishop, Alexander Huang, Graham Bradshaw, and Sukanta Chaudhuri (eds.), *The Shakespearian International Yearbook*, 12 (Farnham: Ashgate, 2012), 43–52.

[34] Rabindranath Tagore, Introduction to *Malini*, in *Rabindra Rachanavali* [Complete Works] (Calcutta: Vishvabharati, 1940), vol. IV, 136.

[35] Quoted by Sarottama Majumdar, 'That Sublime 'Old Gentleman': Shakespeare's Plays in Calcutta, 1775–1930', in Trivedi and Bartholomeusz (eds.), *India's Shakespeare*, 266–7.

[36] See Sisir Kumar Das, 'Shakespeare in Indian Languages', in Trivedi and Bartholomeusz (eds.), *India's Shakespeare*, 54.

the Sanskrit term for formal drama, *nataka*, is used, the problem of genre remains, especially since tragedy was not recognized by classical Sanskrit dramatists. On stage, there was little evidence of interest in the specifically historical and philosophical dimensions of Shakespearean drama: indeed the history plays were the least translated, only *Henry V* and *Richard II* being translated into Hindi and none into Bengali before 1962.

Most successful, of course, was the use of Shakespearean plots and characters by the Parsi theatre (performing in Gujarati, Urdu and Hindustani/Hindi), many of whose principals were well acquainted with Western stage techniques, using them to create a flamboyant stage spectacle, with dazzling props and costumes complemented by extravagant acting styles, music and dance. It was this Parsi theatre, flourishing in the second half of the nineteenth century right up to the first quarter of the twentieth, and extending its reach from India's western coast to Mandalay, Bangkok, Java and even southern Africa, which 'translated' the passion and violence of Shakespearean drama to create a new urban theatre of the masses. That this commercial theatre gave birth, at a certain remove, both to the Marathi *sangeet-natak* (a form of opera) and to the Bombay film is now recognized, though its texts, critically disdained in their time and not always written down, have largely not survived. If the Parsi theatre made Shakespeare popular (its greatest figure Agha Hashr Kashmiri (1879–1935) was awarded the title 'Indian Shakespeare' at a reception in Delhi) it did so by a policy of thoroughgoing adaptation, frequently converting his tragedies into comedies and adding sensational and extravagant action and music.[37]

The ghost of Shakespeare is everywhere in the theatre of the nineteenth century. At least six hundred translations of the plays were produced in different Indian languages, the greatest number in Bengali, followed by Marathi, Tamil and Hindi. Many more were adapted in prose versions, some based on Lamb's *Tales*, and aesthetic and metrical experimentation drew upon Shakespearean genres. But whether

---

[37] See Javed Malick, 'Appropriating Shakespeare Freely: Parsi Theater's First Urdu Play *Khurshid*' and Rajiva Verma, 'Shakespeare in Hindi Cinema', in Trivedi and Bartholomeusz (eds.), *India's Shakespeare*, 92–105 and 269–90; and Rajiva Verma, 'Shakespeare in Indian Cinema: Appropriation, Assimilation, and Engagement, in *The Shakespearian International Yearbook*, XII: 83–96.

or not his texts are directly translated or adapted, it is his dramatic 'example' that operates behind the new vernacular drama, and even behind some forms of fiction. Moreover, Shakespeare remained central to the university literature curriculum up to Independence and thereafter, though there was little or no academic recognition of the process of 'Indianization' by which he had been publicly assimilated. Indeed, pedagogy might appear to overcompensate for creative licence by excessive attention to the niceties of Shakespearean text, as exemplified in the meticulously annotated editions of Shakespeare produced by H. M. Percival, Professor of English at the Presidency College in Calcutta from 1880. Exceptional, as always, was Rabindranath Tagore's brief but pointed critique of *The Tempest* as a play of power in his essay on Kalidasa's *Shakuntala* (1902).

The Shakespeare Quatercentenary

Let us move forward to 1964, the Shakespeare Quatercentenary, an event celebrated in India by way of both academic tribute and stage festivity, in marked contrast to the 'silence' of 1864. It might seem, indeed, that the time was now ripe for the emergence of a political, re-historicized Shakespeare in the era of decolonization, after fifty years or so of relative neglect of his plays during a period of intense nationalist agitation in the first half of the twentieth century. In many respects 1964, marked by the death of Prime Minister Jawaharlal Nehru on 28 May, increased tension on India's borders with China and Pakistan, economic recession, and a split in the Communist Party of India, was a critical year for the Indian state. In this climate of gloom and apprehension, the Shakespeare Quatercentenary turned out to be an intensely *memorial* event. It drew, among much else, a special number on Shakespeare in Indian languages brought out by the Sahitya Akademi journal *Indian Literature*, as well as a catalogue of translations (with 670 listed items) published by the National Library of India. Other kinds of tribute were also forthcoming. A commercial company, Indian Oxygen Limited, brought out a special number of *Oxygen News*, while a scholarly *Shakespeare Commemoration Volume* was edited by Taraknath Sen and published in 1966 from Presidency College, Calcutta, formerly the Hindu College where Derozio and Richardson had taught. There were numerous collections of critical essays, including

Shakespeare: A Book of Homage from Jadavpur University and the suggestively titled *Shakespeare Came to India*, edited by C. D. Narasimhaiah. Each of these publications sought to review a long history of transactions with Shakespeare on the Indian subcontinent, in effect laying claim to a Shakespearean inheritance. The tone was generally respectful, and the difficulty of negotiating a colonial legacy was eased by a strong claim for Shakespeare's universality. 'For the England of trade, commerce, imperialism and the penal code has not endured but the imperishable Empire of Shakespeare will always be with us', Narasimhaiah wrote approvingly.[38]

Of these books, the least memorial in content was actually the explicitly titled *Shakespeare Commemoration Volume*, mainly a collection of scholarly essays on Shakespeare without any specific Indian focus, but prefaced by an introduction that asserted a century and a half's tradition of Shakespeare pedagogy at the Presidency (earlier Hindu) College. In that introduction, Taraknath Sen, himself a justly celebrated scholar and teacher of Shakespeare, asserted a pedagogic tradition beginning with Richardson in the nineteenth century and extending through C. H. Tawney, H. M. Percival, and Manmohan Ghosh to the 'greatness and power' of Praphullachandra Ghosh in the early twentieth century.[39] Collectively, the histories of translation, adaptation and pedagogy made a strong case for the cultural embedding of Shakespeare in vernacular literary and dramatic practice, characteristically expressed as a proprietary claim, whether of Shakespeare to India or of India to Shakespeare. There is certainly some editorial unease about Shakespeare as colonial legacy, most commonly resolved by the counter-assertion of an imperishable literary empire of which India continues to be part. Fashioned as part of the celebratory *politesse* of official quatercentenary literature, these assertions seem today to be painfully uncritical and unreflecting. But what was achieved as part of this claim, an actual inventory of Shakespearean translation, adaptation and (to a lesser extent) commentary, that is an *archive*, was more important. In effect, this archive gave textual substance to cultural memory, unquestionably demonstrating more than a century's work with Shakespeare in the languages of the

---

[38] C. D. Narasimhaiah (ed.), *Shakespeare Came to India* (Bombay: Popular Prakashan, 1964), 5.
[39] Sen (ed.), *Shakespeare Commemoration Volume*, vii–xii.

sub-continent, work that, in its many angles of deployment, its gaps and silences, its transformations and distortions, could serve as a memory-site for the future. For the colonial intelligentsia, and even for the middle bourgeoisie, Shakespeare is indeed a memory-site in Pierre Nora's sense, a repository of the specific histories and engagements that had worked to produce the complex substance of 'colonial modernity'.

Yet it is arguable that the Quatercentenary in fact stood more or less at the culmination of a process of *liberation* from Shakespeare, rather than, as Rosa García-Periago has argued, his rebirth and 'Indianization' on the postcolonial stage.[40] Though 1964 was an intensely memorial year, Shakespeare's affable familiar ghost was, in the long run, in the process of being relegated to the status of an occasional visitant, rather than revived as genius of the stage, which he was for the theatre of the nineteenth century. The quatercentenary year itself, 1964, produced some respectful enactments, such as Ebrahim Alkazi's *Raja Lear* in Urdu for the National School of Drama, played in Western costume. In Bengal, the Marxist Utpal Dutt, who had begun his career playing Shakespeare in English with Geoffrey Kendall's Shakespeareana company in 1947, was by the 1950s taking Bengali Shakespeares from metropolitan locations to small towns and villages, using the open, *jatra* setting to emphasize the popular and social elements of the plays. Records for the Quatercentenary show a large number of adaptations for vernacular stages, in addition to performances in English by local groups and touring companies. Dutt's Little Theatre Group, linked to the Marxist Indian People's Theatre Association (IPTA) called on 17 April for a mass meeting to celebrate Shakespeare's fourth centenary at the foot of the Ochterlony Monument in Calcutta, where scenes from *Othello* were enacted.[41] This commenced one of several Shakespeare festivals during that year, with further full performances of *Othello*, *Julius Caesar* and *Romeo and Juliet*, all translated by Dutt, at the Minerva Theatre. A review of

---

[40] See Rosa García-Periago, 'The Re-birth of Shakespeare in India: Celebrating and Indianizing the Bard in 1964', *SEDERI* 22 (2012), 51–68.

[41] For an account, see Lal and Chaudhuri (eds.), *Shakespeare on the Calcutta Stage*, 78. For Dutt's theatre ideology, see Utpal Dutt, *Towards a Revolutionary Theatre* (Calcutta: Seagull Books, 2009).

Julius Caesar commended the performers' success in giving a 'modern shape to the ideological struggle' by locating the play in a fascist country.[42] The IPTA also independently staged *Julius Caesar* in a more humble proletarian location on the outskirts of the city on 23 April, announcing a month-long Shakespeare festival of its own. Dutt's Shakespeare, despite its agitprop roots and its political commitment to what its maker called 'Third Theatre', took no great liberties with the text or settings, though Dutt, like the IPTA, was influential in creating a politically engaged theatre of the people for the twentieth century. Unsurprisingly, it was from Bertolt Brecht that he borrowed the term (though not the form) 'epic theatre'.

Postcolonial Shakespeares

Yet paradoxically, to remember Shakespeare in 1964 was also to create the conditions for forgetting him. Certainly post-Independence urban theatre, receptive on the one hand to contemporary influences from Europe and attempting, on the other, to 'rediscover' indigenous performative traditions, such as *jatra*, *yakshagana*, *kathakali*, *nautanki* and much else, never re-established Shakespeare as cultural master-text in the way that colonial theatre inevitably had. Rather, experimentation with Shakespeare in some of these styles, such as B. V. Karanth's production of *Macbeth* (*Barnam Vana*) in *yakshagana* style at the National School of Drama in 1979, or Habib Tanvir's adaptation of *A Midsummer Night's Dream* as *Kamdev ka Apna, Basant Ritu ka Sapna* (1993, revived 1995 and many times thereafter) using an eclectic mix of folk theatre traditions and with tribal actors, or Sadanand Balakrishnan's Kathakali *Othello* (1996), and Lokendra Arambam's Manipuri *Macbeth, Stage of Blood* (1997), produced distinctive and extremely memorable Shakespeares that have been exhaustively written about in the context of postcolonial re-appropriation. For Shakespeare was not, of course, actually forgotten: he remained a significant cultural property, open to new kinds of indigenization and 're-purposing' in radically altered political and social contexts. But Shakespeare was not in any sense 'reborn' in 1964, nor did the Quatercentenary actually *commence* the process of indigenization and decolonization. Rather, he had been indigenized from the start, but decolonization

[42] Cited in Lal and Chaudhuri (eds.), *Shakespeare on the Calcutta Stage*, 109.

reduced his cultural importance and ubiquity, making him part of a dramatic repertoire that could be fitted to new contexts, genres, and performative styles.

I would like to suggest that time – postcolonial time, with its inescapable emphasis upon historicity, belatedness, and rupture, constitutes the necessary context for understanding post-Independence Shakespeares. Histories of Shakespeare adaptation, which naturally focus on striking individual productions, often do not convey sufficiently the *relative* place of Shakespeare with respect to adaptations from many other languages, and the nature of experimentation and originality in vernacular theatre in the phase of decolonization. While attention has been drawn to outstanding individual adaptations of Shakespeare, it should be noted that Brecht, Pirandello, Lorca, and to some extent Greek tragedy share space on the modernist stage with remarkable revivals of folk, traditional and even classical styles and materials. Between 1947 and 1980 there is a marked decline in translation activity, fewer actual performances, and, above all, less dependence on Shakespeare as a formative element in theatre culture.

It was not until the 1990s that India was caught up in another kind of engagement, this time with what might be called global Shakespeare, a distinctive and much-analysed phenomenon which leaves its mark as much upon the cinema as the theatre. We may think particularly of Vishal Bhardwaj's *Maqbool* (*Macbeth*), *Omkara* (*Othello*), and now his Kashmiri *Haider* (*Hamlet*).[43] These films suggest that Shakespeare is not forgotten, yet we should note that postcolonial remembrance is always a form of betrayal. Instead of the layered, or sedimented memory of the archive, so painstakingly built up through the nineteenth century, we have the instantaneous presence we are more accustomed to associate with the internet, or with its digital toy, the hyperlink. Global Shakespeare inhabits its own time, which is the time of the eternally contemporary, the time of the remake or remix. This is not Benjamin's *jetzeit*, a past charged with the time of now. It might seem that Shakespeare's continued presence takes its toll from the cultures of memory, but this is not quite so in practice. Rather, the Shakespeare of the contemporary Bombay film deliberately

---

[43] See Supriya Chaudhuri, 'What Bloody Man is That? *Macbeth*, *Maqbool*, and Shakespeare in India', in *The Shakespearian International Yearbook*, XII: 97–113.

erodes nostalgia, obliterating any awareness of the text's existence in historical, sedimented time. In such transactions, Shakespeare is no longer a classic in the old sense, that of the culture of veneration: rather, he is part of that constantly circulating capital that no one precisely owns, but on whom literary, theatrical or cinematic fortune may depend.

6 | *Shakespeare at the Vatican, 1964*

MARTA CEREZO

On 12 November 1964, during the third phase of the Second Vatican Council, a commemorative performance in celebration of the 400th anniversary of Shakespeare's birth was attended by many of the 2,000 Council Fathers residing in Rome at the time. Following the example of other states around the world, the Pope observed Shakespeare's Quatercentenary; celebrations at the Vatican included performances by a handful of Italian actors and some members of the Royal Shakespeare Company (RSC) invited by the English College in Rome.[1] The programme of events, arranged by the Pontifical Central Committee for Sacred Art in Italy and the Catholic Theatre Centre, included excerpts from the *Sonnets* (23, 65, 29), *The Passionate Pilgrim* (XII, XIII) and several plays.[2] The scenes, selected by Tony Church, were from *Richard II* (3.2), *Twelfth Night* (2.2; 2.4), *As You Like It* (2.7), *Henry VI III* (3.2), *Romeo and Juliet* (4.3), *The Merchant of Venice* (4.1), *Cymbeline* (4.2) and *The Tempest* (4.1). For the second half of the programme, Italian actors gave readings in Italian of *Hamlet* (3.3, 3.4), *Measure for Measure* (3.2) and *Henry VIII* (3.2).[3]

Research carried out for this article has been financed by Research Project FFI2011-24347 'Cultures of Commemoration II: Remembering Shakespeare', funded by the Spanish Plan Nacional de I+D+i 2008–2011.

[1] In October 1964 Tony Church received a call from David Brierley, General Manager of the RSC, asking him to organise the English part of the performance. Excerpts were given by Tony Church accompanied by Stratford company members Dorothy Tutin and Derek Godfrey, who were the only three RSC leading actors available at the time. Tony Church, *A Stage for a Kingdom* (London: Oneiro Press, 2013), 141.

[2] Special thanks to Helen Hargest, Archives and Imaging Co-ordinator at the Collections Department of the Shakespeare Birthplace Trust at The Shakespeare Centre, for kindly providing me with the programme of the performance.

[3] The Italian actors who took part in the performance were Sergio Tófano, Massimo Foschi, Giovanna Galletti, Sandro Ninchi, Michele Kalamera, Carlo D'Angelo, Nicoletta Languasco, Armando Spadaro and Ronaldo Lupi. Orazio Costa was in charge of the Italian adaptation and Giovanni Zammerine played the organ.

The event acquired a clear international resonance. Throughout the performance the Pope sat on a gold and scarlet raised platform set in the centre of the main aisle of the Auditorium in Palazzo Pio amid many of the Vatican ecumenical Council Fathers from all continents, the College of Cardinals and other dignitaries attending the Council, and most probably among them, the Anglican observers. Members of the diplomatic corps, the cultural world and journalists from the international press had also been invited to witness the ecumenical process. The performance was sponsored by the British religious communities of Rome and it was broadcast live by Programma Nazionale (today RAI 1).[4] The event was therefore embedded within a local, but also global, international religious, diplomatic and cultural setting where Shakespeare's texts came to life in a commemorative performance geared, at first glance, to celebrate the author's birth.[5] As this chapter will argue, the Pope conceived this Shakespearean performance as a commemorative act that celebrated Shakespeare's work but also, and mainly, as an occasion to diplomatically reinforce the bonds between European states and churches to further the Second Vatican Council's ecumenical policy.

The RSC visit to the Vatican has been discussed in relation to the company's attempt to have its *First Folio* blessed by the Pope and the misunderstanding that ensued when the Pope believed the volume was being offered as a present for the Vatican library.[6] This essay goes

[4] 'British Actors Stage Recital for Pope Paul', *The Hartford Courant* (1923–1984), *ProQuest Historical Newspapers Hartford Courant* (1764–1986), 13 November 1964, 14; 'Celebrazione di Shakespeare alla presenza del Pontefice', *La Stampa* 13 November 1964, 3, www.archiviolastampa.it (accessed 2 June 2014); Alan McElwain, 'Rome Letter', *Catholic Herald*, 20 November 1964, 2, http://archive.catholicherald.co.uk (accessed 2 June 2014); 'Shakespeare Folio Accepted in Error', *The Blade* 13 November 1964, front page, https://news.google.com/newspapers?nid=8_tS2Vw13FcC&dat=19641113&printsec=frontpage&hl=es (accessed 2 June 2014). Special thanks to Matteo Chiocchi, from the Customer Service RAI TECHE, for kindly providing me with the recording of the event broadcast by Programma Nazionale on 12 November 1964.

[5] In their announcements, Italian newspapers *La Stampa* and *Stampa Sera* (12 November 1964) described the act as the 'Celebrazione del IV centenario della nascita di Shakespeare' (See 'Oggi alla TV', 4; 'Oggi sul video', 1).

[6] For accounts of the incident see Paul Edmondson and Stanley Wells, 'The Limitations of the First Folio', in Christa Jansohn, Lena Cowen Orlin and Stanley Wells (eds.), *Shakespeare Without Boundaries: Essays in Honor of Dieter Mehl* (Plymouth: University of Delaware Press and The Rowman and Littlefeld Publishing Group, 2011), 23–34, 23; Eric Rasmussen, *The Shakespeare Thefts: In Search of the First Folios* (New York: Palgrave Macmillan, 2011), 59–63;

beyond the anecdote and shows how the 1964 RSC performance in Rome can be analysed from three different angles that have ecumenism and diplomacy at their centre. The first two revolve around Paul VI's closing address to the actors and the promoters of the commemorative performance. A close analysis of this speech shows, first, that the performance must be envisioned as a site of memory in which the inner mechanisms of what Melanie Hall and Erick Goldstein (2010) call the 'diplomatization of culture' are at work, as the Pope invited the RSC actors so as to foster institutional relations between England and Rome, and also between the Anglican and Roman Catholic churches. Second, as this chapter will also argue, Paul VI's speech on Shakespeare acquires further significance if read in the light of the doctrine advanced in the *Lumen Gentium*, the *Dogmatic Constitution on the Church*, which was promulgated precisely on 21 November, during the closing session of the third phase of the Council and just a few days after the RSC performance at the Vatican. Finally, the third part of this chapter analyses the RSC trip to the Vatican, taking into consideration two interconnected events at the time in which diplomatic relations played a central role: the drafting process of the Council statement on the relation between Catholics and Jews – in preparation since 1961 and finally approved on 20 November 1964 – and the controversy that arose in September 1963 as a result of the RSC production of German playwright Rolf Hochhuth's *The Representative* (*Der Stellvertreter*). The play denounced Pope Pius XII for not having publicly condemned Hitler's extermination of millions of Jews during the Second World War. Both events are crucial to our understanding of the implications of the performance of *The Merchant of Venice* 4.1 at the Vatican.

Stanley Wells, *Shakespeare: For All Time* (London: Macmillan, 2002), 371; Anthony James West, *The Shakespeare First Folio: The History of the Book, Volume II: A New Worldwide Census of First Folios* (Oxford University Press, 2003), 126. See also McElwain, 'Rome Letter', 2; 'Pope Gets a First Folio of Bard Through Error', *New York Times*, 12 November 1964, n.pag, www.nytimes.com/1964/11/13/pope-gets-a-first-folio-of-bard-through-error.html?_r=0 (accessed 2 June 2014); 'Shakespeare Folio Accepted in Error', *The Blade*, 13 November 1964, front page, http://news.google.com/newspapers?nid=1350&dat=19641113&id=MdpOAAAAIBAJ&sjid=TgEEAAAAIBAJ&pg=1723,628 6224 (accessed 2 June 2014).

The Pope's address

In March 1966, the Archbishop of Canterbury, Michael Ramsey, paid a visit to Pope Paul VI in Rome to set up an Anglican–Roman Catholic Joint Preparatory Commission. To strengthen diplomatic relations was an important item in the agenda of this preparatory encounter between Paul VI and Ramsey. The three meetings of the Commission at Gazzada, Huntercombe, and Malta were characterised by a willingness on both sides to achieve 'further reconciliation between Anglicans and Roman Catholics as also to promote a wider unity of all Christians'.[7] Ramsey's visit implied 'a new stage in relations between both Churches'.[8]

The socio-political and ideological forces at work at the Vatican during those years can be accounted for by Melanie Hall and Erik Goldstein's notion of the 'diplomatization of culture', i.e. the development of a diplomatic sub-structure on which the American and British governments 'could ultimately build a close, official, diplomatic bond' during the nineteenth century.[9] This sub-structure 'had marked a gradual transition from one of hostility, to mutual wariness, to growing amity, to seeking to mark common values, heritage and history, to finally one of diplomatic and military alliance' during the First World War.[10] Such a diplomatic concord resulted from 'the work of unofficial diplomats who built the groundwork for mutual understanding, [and] wove the personal networks that would facilitate cooperation'.[11] Hall and Goldstein locate these unofficial diplomats in areas such as 'the language and related literary cultures; areas touching upon religion; monument-making and growing interest in preserving evidence of (variously) a common past, heroes of the race, and literary homes and haunts'.[12] It is my contention that this notion of 'the diplomatization of culture' can be transferred from the political to

---

[7] 'The Malta Report: Report of the Anglican–Roman Catholic Joint Preparatory Commission', 2 January 1968, www.vatican.va (accessed 2 June 2014).

[8] 'The Malta Report'.

[9] Melanie Hall and Erik Goldstein, 'Writers, the Clergy, and the "Diplomatization" of Culture: Sub-Structures of Anglo-American Diplomacy, 1820–1914', in John Fisher and Antony Best (eds.), *On the Fringes of Diplomacy: Influences on British Foreign Policy 1800–1945* (Surrey and Burlington: Ashgate, 2010), 127–54, 128.

[10] Hall and Goldstein, 'Writers', 127.   [11] Hall and Goldstein, 'Writers', 127–8.

[12] Hall and Goldstein, 'Writers', 128.

the religious arena, to account for the importance of the RSC visit to the Vatican in 1964. On 24 March 1966, Paul VI and Ramsey signed a Common Declaration, which affirmed their intention to 'inaugurate between the Roman Catholic Church and the Anglican Communion a serious dialogue which, founded on the gospels and on the ancient common traditions, may lead to that unity in truth, for which Christ prayed'.[13] Over a year earlier, on 12 November 1964, the unity of both Churches was also promoted by the work of RSC actors performing at the Vatican as unofficial literary diplomats.

On 13 November 1964, one of *La Stampa*'s headlines read: 'Celebrazione di Shakespeare alla presenza del Pontefice'. The newspaper turned its attention from the commemorative nature of the event to what *La Stampa*'s correspondent at the Vatican considered had been its predominant feature: the Pope's dominant presence through his concluding speech, which showed that the RSC performance at the Vatican was seen as an important cultural precedent to the 'serious dialogue' between the Roman Catholic Church and the Anglican Communion that Paul VI and the Archbishop of Canterbury would be launching in March 1966. He presented Shakespeare's works as part of a common universal cultural background and as belonging to the 'ancient common tradition' that their joint declaration would highlight less than two years later.

In his speech to the actors and the promoters of the performance, the Pope recalled his visit, thirty years earlier, 'as an enquiring and hasty tourist, to the city and the home of Shakespeare in Stratford-on-Avon', and alluded to his first encounters with Shakespeare at school and in his private readings, through which he experienced 'fantastic riches and psychological truth'.[14] The Pope's account of his visit to Stratford-on-Avon emphasised his enjoyment of the work of the British author and his early contact with English culture; through his private remembrance of Shakespeare's life and work, the Pope showed he had positive memories of England, the birthplace of Anglicanism.

The day after the performance, the Italian and international press highlighted the Pope's celebration 'in this supreme writer [of] the

---

[13] Paul VI and Michael Ramsey, 'Common Declaration of His Holiness Paul VI and His Grace Michael Ramsey, Archbishop of Canterbury', 24 March 1996, www.vatican.va (accessed 2 June 2014).

[14] Paul VI, 'Address of Paul VI for the Fourth Centenary of the Birth of William Shakespeare', 12 November 1964, www.vatican.va (accessed 2 June 2014).

magnificent cultural tradition and artistic genius of the English people'.[15] Thus, it was not just Shakespeare who was celebrated on this occasion but also his country. To the Pope, as he would tell Jean Guitton years later, writers such as Shakespeare, Dante, Goethe, Cervantes or Pascal were representatives of 'the mind of a whole people'.[16] Through the glorification of Shakespeare, the Pope's welcoming of the English 'artistic genius' entailed an exaltation of English cultural and national identity, clearly meant to promote a rapprochement with Britain and the Church of England, an attitude which fits in with the ecumenical spirit of the Council and its aim of achieving a broad religious communion.

Previously, on 2 November 1963, *The Tablet* had published a note entitled 'Pope Paul's Affection for England'. It revealed details of a letter from the Pope to Archbishop Heenan of Westminster, in which he celebrated the reciprocal esteem in which the Holy See and the English people held each other by recalling 'many marks of regard and courtesy' such as the Queen's visit to Pope John and those of 'Christian leaders not in communion with this Holy See' who 'were warmly welcomed by him'.[17] The Pope expressed to Heenan his hope that 'the cordial relations already existing between us and the British people may continue, and that with God's help they may grow still more during our pontificate'.[18] The RSC commemorative performance was clearly presented by the Pope as one of those marks of regard, courtesy and diplomatic contact between Rome and England, and Shakespeare, as Alan McElwain stated after attending the event, was described as 'the most British of all international institutions'.[19]

Lumen Gentium

On 21 November 1964, nine days after the RSC performance, the *Dogmatic Constitution on the Church*, known as *Lumen Gentium*, was promulgated by the Council. This proclamation constituted, as

---

[15] Paul VI, 'Address'.
[16] Jean Guitton, *The Pope Speaks. Dialogues of Paul VI with Jean Guitton* (London: Weidenfield and Nicolson, 1968), 124.
[17] 'Pope Paul's Affection for England', *The Tablet*, 2 November 1963, 22, http://archive.thetablet.co.uk/page/2nd-november-1963/22 (accessed 2 June 2014).
[18] *The Tablet*, 22.   [19] McElwain, 'Rome Letter', 2.

Hubert Jedin notes, 'the climax and center of the conciliar decrees', since 'it ended the Church's quest for its self-understanding which had begun at the end of the thirteenth century' and 'for almost all other decrees of the council must be interpreted in its light'.[20] Paul VI's closing address makes more sense if read in the light of the doctrine and the language of the *Dogmatic Constitution*, whose Chapter 2 declares that the Church

fosters and takes to itself, insofar as they are good, the ability, riches and customs in which the genius of each people expresses itself. Taking them to itself it purifies, strengthens, elevates and ennobles them. The Church in this is mindful that she must bring together the nations for that king to whom they were given as an inheritance, and to whose city they bring gifts and offerings.

This characteristic of universality which adorns the people of God is a gift from the Lord Himself. By reason of it, the Catholic Church strives constantly and with due effect to bring all humanity and all its possessions back to its source in Christ, with Him as its head and united in His Spirit.[21]

A close reading of these two paragraphs helps to contextualise the meaning of the Pope's references to Rome in his final address as 'always avid and prompt as she is to honour the high achievements of the human spirit, and happy as she is today to celebrate, in this supreme writer, the magnificent cultural tradition and artistic genius of the English people'.[22] Though the Pope's words elevate the English nation and promote the affiliation between both nations and churches, it is actually Rome, as the symbolic city of God, ruled by the Pope, her king, which is being privileged over England in these words, since it 'fosters and takes to itself' the 'riches' of the English 'genius' and cultural tradition that she 'purifies, strengthens, elevates and ennobles' by hosting an act in remembrance of England's 'supreme writer'. The Pope's words show how, by welcoming the literary event and hosting the ecumenical Council, Rome 'brings together the nations' and receives from them offerings that reflect 'the high achievements of the human spirit'. The descriptions of Rome in the Constitution and the

[20] Hubert Jedin (ed.), *History of the Church, Volume X: The Church in the Modern Age* (Burns & Oates: London, 1981), 133.
[21] *Dogmatic Constitution on the Church Lumen Gentium*, Chapter 2, 21 November 1964, www.vatican.va (accessed 2 June 2014).
[22] Paul VI, 'Address'.

Pope's closing address are strikingly similar, as he includes the English nation in the womb of nurturing Catholic Rome portrayed in the Constitution; it is Rome that receives all humanity for its purification, and places 'all its possessions back to its source in Christ'. Therefore, the depiction of the city of Rome as the epicentre of the Christian world explains the Pope's assertive statement regarding the authority of the Catholic faith and of the Pontiff as 'the Vicar of Christ and pastor of the whole Church' who, in virtue of his office, has 'full, supreme and universal power over the Church' and 'is always free to exercise this power'.[23]

Accordingly, Paul VI's appearance at the performance, on a raised platform amidst all the Council Fathers, and the rhetoric used in his concluding address were part of his own performance aimed at consolidating the Roman Church and the Pope's primacy in a controversial section of the *Lumen Gentium*. A clear disagreement on Chapter 3 of the Constitution, dealing with the College of Bishops, took place around the time of the RSC's Vatican visit. Paul VI solved this problem by his intercession in the matter through the elaboration of a *nota explicatia praevia* that was submitted to the Theological Commission and later handed to the Council Fathers on 14 November, two days after the Shakespearean performance. As Jedin remarks, the note 'was supposed to exclude every encroachment on the doctrine of primacy by the doctrine of the College of Bishops developed in Chapter 3' and achieved its aim as the Chapter was finally approved with the votes of the defenders of collegiality on 18 November.[24] A day later, a new controversy arose over the vote to be taken on the *Declaration on Religious Freedom*, which the Pope, against the opinion of influential Council Fathers, decided would be reviewed in the next period of the Council. What Jedin calls 'the stormy general congregation of 19 November', produced yet another conflict in relation to the text of the *Decree of Ecumenism*, which was modified by the Pope after it had already been approved by the Council Fathers, though not yet promulgated.[25]

An appreciation of the tensions and dissensions within the Council that the Pope had to face and solve during those days is essential to an understanding of his closing address in Palazzo Pio. Though first oriented to establish links between religious beliefs and peoples, it

---

[23] *Dogmatic Constitution*, Chapter 3.   [24] Jedin, *History of the Church*, 131.
[25] Jedin, *History of the Church*, 132.

was also intended to assert his Papal authority among all nations in order to reinforce an essential teaching from the First Vatican Council 'about the sacred primacy of the Roman Pontiff and of his infallible magisterium'.[26]

Though, as already mentioned, the Pope's address opened with personal and intimate reflections on the personal resonance the performance had for him, it gradually gained a deeper religious significance. Paul VI appropriated Shakespeare's works by presenting them as a reflection of the 'religious understanding of the world' that was being written into the pages of the *Lumen Gentium* during those same days.[27] The choice of terms made by the Pope in his speech was not random but rather was intended to suggest a connection between his vision of Shakespeare's works and the contents of the *Dogmatic Constitution*, which was formulated in a metaphorical language, endowing the religious discourse with literary overtones as one of its introductory paragraphs confirms: 'In the Old Testament the revelation of the Kingdom is often conveyed by means of metaphors. In the same way the inner nature of the Church is now made known to us in different images'.[28]

To Paul VI, Shakespeare's works are pervaded by 'high moral lessons and admonitions', which are metaphorically portrayed as a 'valuable fruit',[29] a metaphor for the word of God that offers salvation, in Chapter 1 of the *Dogmatic Constitution*. At the closing of the Council, on 8 December 1965, the 'fruit' image reappears in the Pope's 'Address to the Artists' who, in his view, constitute the seed of beauty, which makes divine truth visible. The Pope suggests that artistic creation is essential to human salvation, and envisions it as an element of universal religious reunification. The Pope addresses artists as 'friends' of the Church, since they had 'aided her in translating her divine message in the language of forms and figures, making the invisible world palpable'.[30] He asks them not to 'refuse to put [their] talents at the service of divine truth',[31] which had become the epicentre of the Council:

This world in which we live needs beauty in order not to sink into despair. It is beauty, like truth, which brings joy to the heart of man and is that precious

---

[26] *Dogmatic Constitution*, Chapter 3.   [27] Paul VI, 'Address'.
[28] *Dogmatic Constitution*, Chapter 1.   [29] Paul VI, 'Address'.
[30] Paul VI, 'Address of Paul VI to Artists', 8 December 1965, www.vatican.va (accessed 2 June 2014).
[31] Paul VI, 'Address ... to Artists'.

fruit which resists the wear and tear of time, which unites generations and makes them share things in admiration.[32]

The papal conception of the artists sheds light on his concluding speech in 1964, in which he highlights how the beauty of Shakespeare's texts 'leads to the discovery of the moral laws, which make life great and sacred, and lead us back to a religious understanding of the world'.[33] Shakespeare's powerful language, says the Pope, 'induce[s] men to listen with reverence to the great verities he expounds, of death and judgment, of hell and heaven'.[34] The reiteration of the verb 'lead' in combination with the terms 'induce' and 'verities' is crucial to the interpretation of his speech. The Pontiff's words endow the work of Shakespeare with a sacred nature, portraying it as a book of faith designed to 'communicate the fruit of salvation to men'.[35] The religious force of Shakespeare's texts is compared to that in the Gospels; they must be read, listened to or followed with veneration, as they lead humanity to redemption. Again, these words become more pointed when read in the light of the opening lines of the *Dogmatic Constitution*:

Christ is the Light of nations. Because this is so, this Sacred Synod gathered together in the Holy Spirit eagerly desires, by proclaiming the Gospel to every creature, to bring the light of Christ to all men, a light brightly visible on the countenance of the Church.[36]

In this evangelical context, the Council Fathers attending the performance could easily have interpreted the Pope's final address as a clear reference to the *Lumen Gentium*, that is, the light of the people. The Pope presented the plots of Shakespeare's plays as a 'salutary reminder to modern man that God exists, that there is a life after this life, that evildoing is punished and good rewarded'.[37] Thus, the Bard's texts were being read as a universal artistic light whose beauty opens the way through spiritual darkness and unveils the divine truth imprinted in the different chapters of the *Dogmatic Constitution*. In his closing speech the Pope shared with the Christian world his perception of the commemorative performance, not just as an act of celebration of Shakespeare's art, or as a tribute to his nation's cultural pride, but as a re-enactment of the Word of God prior to salvation.

[32] Paul VI, 'Address … to Artists'.   [33] Paul VI, 'Address'.
[34] Paul VI, 'Address'.   [35] Paul VI, 'Address'.
[36] *Dogmatic Constitution*, Chapter 1.   [37] Paul VI, 'Address'.

The Merchant of Venice 4.1: the Vatican and the Jewish question

In his account of his experience in Palazzo Pio in 1964, Tony Church significantly foregrounds the performance of *The Merchant of Venice* 4.1: 'The programme lasted just three quarters of an hour and included, perhaps dangerously, an extract of the trial scene, with Dorothy repeating her performance as Portia which she'd done so brilliantly at Stratford, Derek playing Antonio and myself as Shylock.'[38] Church then remembers how, during the dinner with all the British bishops that followed the event, Archbishop Heenan, who had delivered the opening address of the commemorative performance, said to him 'how appropriate the Shylock scene had been and described how, with some difficulty, he had persuaded the conference to amend that ancient edict which had condemned all Jews perpetually for the crucifixion of Christ'.[39] Church's unease about the representation of the trial scene and Heenan's comment to the actor are crucial for grasping the significance of the RSC commemorative performance at the Vatican. Both are best understood in the light of two controversial and interconnected events: the preparation from 1961 to 1964 of the Council document on the relation between Catholics and Jews, and the controversial RSC production of Rolf Hochhuth's *The Representative* on 25 September 1963. Thanks to efficient diplomatic actions undertaken by the company, that production did not disrupt relations between Rome and England, as revealed by the Pope's letter to Heenan, showing his affection for England just a few weeks later.

Ever since Pope John XXIII's announcement of the celebration of an Ecumenical Council on 25 January 1959, the Catholic Church had been seen as nurturing tolerance and respect for non-Catholic Christians and also for other faiths, including the Jews. In 1961, coinciding with the preparatory phases of the Council, the trial of Adolf Eichmann in Jerusalem forcefully brought back painful memories of the Nazi genocide against the Jews. As Judith Hershcopf states, the trial reactivated moral questions that were self-critically formulated by religious spokesmen.[40] On 20 April 1961, for example, the *Catholic Sentinel* acknowledged how anti-semitism 'was not confined to Nazi

---

[38] Church, *A Stage*, 141.   [39] Church, *A Stage*, 143.
[40] Judith Hershcopf, 'The Church and the Jews: The Struggle at Vatican Council II', *American Jewish Year Book* 66 (1965), 99–134.

Germany, or limited to the time that Adolf Hitler ruled the Third Reich. Persecution of the Jews is a black mark on the history of Christendom.'[41]

The Council's ecumenical spirit of reform and renewal of its Church urgently called for the vanishing of such a 'black mark'. A *Secretariat for the Promotion of Christian Unity* was established and the Pope appointed Agustin Cardinal Bea as president, commanding him to prepare a conciliatory declaration on Catholic–Jewish relations. The draft statement was complete by May 1962 and was to be discussed in the conferences of the Central Commission in June; however, fierce opposition from the most conservative sectors of the Curia and from the Arab nations impeded its publication during the first session of the Council (11 October–8 December 1962).[42]

During the period between sessions the relation between Catholics and Jews was strongly evident in Cardinal Bea's agenda and the issue was gradually attracting attention worldwide.[43] In the midst of this religious controversy, on 20 February 1963, German playwright Rolf Hochhuth's *Der Stellvertreter*, directed by Erwin Piscator, was performed in West Berlin's Freie Volksbühne. Hochhuth's criticism of Pope Pius XII's refusal to publicly denounce Hitler's persecution of the Jews during the Second World War turned the issue into a full-scale global controversy.[44] The German première was followed by seventy-three productions in twenty-seven countries.[45]

---

[41] Quoted in Hershcopf, 'The Church and the Jews', 108.

[42] Cardinal Bea, 'Text of Cardinal Bea on Draft of Catholic Attitude Toward Jews', 19 November 1963 *Catholic News Service. Vatican II: 50 Years Ago Today*. http://vaticaniiat50.wordpress.com (accessed 2 June 2014); Hershcopf, 'The Church and the Jews', 109–12.

[43] Hershcopf, 'The Church and the Jews', 113–14.

[44] For detailed analyses of the relationship between Pius XII and the Holocaust see Pierre S. J. Blet, *Pius XII and the Second World War* (New Jersey: Paulist Press, 1997); John Cornwell, *Hitler's Pope: The Secret History of Pius XII* (London: Penguin Books, 1999); Michael Phayer, *The Catholic Church and the Holocaust, 1930–1965* (Bloomington: Indiana University Press, 2000); David I. Kertzer, *The Popes Against the Jews* (New York: Vintage, 2001); Robert G. Weisbord and Wallace P. Sillanpoa, *The Chief Rabbi, the Pope and the Holocaust: An Era in Vatican Jewish Relations* (New Brunswick, NJ: Transactions Publishers, 2008). For comprehensive studies on Hochhuth's play and its international impact see Eric Bentley, *The Storm Over The Deputy* (New York: Grove Press, Inc. 1964) and Dolores Barracano Schmidt and Earl Robert Schmidt, *The Deputy Reader: Studies in Moral Responsibility* (Illinois: Scott, Foresman and Company, 1965).

[45] Sarah Stanton and Martin Banham, *Cambridge Paperback Guide to Theatre* (Cambridge University Press, 1996), 169.

In Rome the play was banned and the answer from the Vatican to the original German version of the play was firm and implacable.[46] Gravely offended by Hochhuth's harsh condemnation of Pius XII, Giovanni Battista Cardinal Montini – Archbishop of Milan and recently elected to the Papacy on 21 June – sent a letter entitled 'Pius XII and the Jews' to the international Catholic newspaper *The Tablet* on 29 June 1963.[47] In it, he protested that Hochhuth's play was a mere manipulation of facts and entirely misrepresented the character of Pius XII. Cardinal Montini's letter to *The Tablet* did not explicitly mention the RSC's intention to produce the play in London in the autumn. However, it praised an article published by *The Tablet* on 11 May 1963, also entitled 'Pius XII and the Jews', which objected to the RSC's decision to stage the play.

In order not to present the British production as a head-on attack on the Pope or the Catholics, and most probably in an attempt to avoid diplomatic tensions between England and Rome, the company's steps before the première seem to me to have been carefully taken. A meeting attended by two members of the Council of Christians and Jews – Sister Louis Gabriel of the Sisters of Sion and Michael Wallach, Registrar of the Jews' College – as well as Clifford Williams, producer of *The Representative*, and John Roberts, general manager of the Aldwych Theatre, stands out as an example of the RSC's attempt to reconcile positions. Sister Louis Gabriel highlighted the helpful and understanding attitude of Williams and Roberts, who assured her and Michael Wallach that offensive references to Pius XII had been omitted, as they had no intention to libel the Pontiff. After being invited 'to see one of the rehearsals in time to discuss with them any relevant objections before the actual performance', both members of the Council finally showed their admiration for a staging they found 'splendid'.[48] To Sister Louis Gabriel, Hochhuth's play presented 'a gross caricature of the character of Pope Pius', which damaged the moral message of the play, that is, to 'challenge the whole of Christendom for its failure to

---

[46] 'Polemiche in Inghilterra per un dramma su Pio XII', *La Stampa* 22 September 1963, 5, www.archiviolastampa.it (accessed 2 June 2014).

[47] Cardinal Montini, 'Pius XII and the Jews', *The Tablet*, 29 June 1963, 18, http://archive.thetablet.co.uk/article/29th-june-1963/18/pius-xii-and-the-jews (accessed 2 June 2014).

[48] 'Play Report is Denied', *Catholic Herald*, 30 August 1963, 1, http://archive.catholicherald.co.uk (accessed 2 June 2014).

oppose the Jewish persecution'.[49] This self-critical interpretation was clearly in tune with the position of the progressive sectors of the Curia that demanded a clear statement from the Council acknowledging the responsibility of the Catholic Church in the Jewish persecutions throughout history.

The play was finally premièred in London on 25 September 1963. Four days later Paul VI would deliver the opening address for the second session of the Council. Despite ongoing opposition, Cardinal Bea's draft document was prepared for distribution among the Council Fathers on 8 November.[50] Conscious of the fact that the performance of *The Representative* at the Aldwych dealt with extremely current religious and political affairs, the RSC took care to present the play as a neutral ground in which both the Catholic and Hochhuth's viewpoints would be acknowledged. Before licensing the play, Lord Cobbold, the Lord Chamberlain, required the company to include a refutation from 'an authoritative Roman Catholic' in the theatre programme.[51] As a clearly conciliatory diplomatic strategy, the RSC chose Cardinal Montini's letter to *The Tablet*. In an article significantly called 'Interference', the *Baptist Times* described this act of censorship as 'an extraordinary, sinister and impertinent interference on his part [the Lord Chamberlain's]'.[52] The article continued by strongly denouncing the Roman Catholic pressure exerted on the British Foreign policy in educational and artistic matters and by demanding the withdrawal of the letter from the programme. But the letter was never withdrawn and, most importantly, Michael Kostow, the company's director of publications, announced the RSC's redoubled effort to give voice to the Catholic protests by releasing a special programme supplement which also contained the Pope's letter; an article by Desmond Fisher, editor of the *Catholic Herald*; a statement by the executive of the Council of Christians and Jews; short comments by the author, translator and designer of the play; and other articles on the controversy.[53]

---

[49] 'Play Report is Denied', 1.   [50] Hershcopf, 'The Church and the Jews', 116.

[51] Quoted in Dawn B. Sova, *Banned Plays: Censorship Histories of 125 Stage Dramas* (New York: Facts on File Inc., 2004), 77.

[52] 'Interference', *Baptist Times*, October 1963: n.pag.

[53] 'Theatre Gives Catholic View. Anti-Pope Play Controversy', *Catholic Herald*, 20 September 1963, 1, http://archive.catholicherald.co.uk (accessed 2 June 2014).

The British production of *The Representative* was amply covered by the press and TV in Britain, bringing about a reassessment of the Vatican participation in the Nazi exterminations and, despite the RSC's efforts to ease tensions, caused violent disturbances.[54] However, as we can infer from Tony Church's comment, the company did its best to avoid confrontations and to find common ground between themselves – as a company performing what was being considered an anti-Catholic play – and the Catholic community in England: 'At the end of each performance, there was a discussion with the audience conducted by a Roman Catholic priest, a remarkable man, who was a friend of the cast. The whole cast stayed. It was a sobering experience.'[55] At a time when 'Council Fathers of the English-speaking world presented a solid front in favor of the schema on ecumenism',[56] the presence of a Roman Catholic priest in the RSC's discussions after every performance of *The Representative* shows that the spirit of dialogue promoted by the English sector of the Council was, at the same moment, present at the Aldwych.

Cardinal Bea's declaration on the Catholic attitude towards the Jews was distributed to the Council Fathers as Chapter 4 of the *Schema on Ecumenism* on 8 November 1963. On 19 November 1963 Bea explained its content, which highlighted the strong bonds between the Catholic Church and the Jews and represented a clear sign of the Catholic Church's repudiation of anti-semitism – especially of the Nazi extermination of the Jews. He refuted the charge of deicide against the Jews, and asked Catholics to follow Christ and the Apostles' example of 'ardent charity', mercy, truth and patience towards the Jews.[57] Despite voices of dissent, Archbishop Heenan, acting as speaker of the English Council Fathers, was loudly applauded for announcing his 'welcome of the present schema with joy'.[58]

---

[54] 'Pope Play Posters are Defaced', *Daily Telegraph*, 2 October 1963, n.pag; 'Un interprete de "Il vicario" chiede protezione alla polizia', *Stampa Sera*, 2 October 1963, 8, www.archiviolastampa.it (accessed 2 June 2014); 'Threats to a Theatre "Eichmann"', *Daily Mirror*, 30 October 1964, n.pag.

[55] Church, *A Stage*, 125.

[56] Msgr. James I. Tucek, 'Discussions on Ecumenism Continue; Liturgy Votes Also Take Place', 20 November 1963 *Catholic News Service. Vatican II: 50 Years Ago Today*, http://vaticaniiat50.wordpress.com (accessed 2 June 2014).

[57] Cardinal Bea, 'Text of Cardinal Bea' 1963.

[58] Tucek, 'Discussions on Ecumenism'.

However, despite Heenan's and many other Council Fathers' support of Bea's declaration, a small but powerful minority among the bishops prevented it from being voted on before the end of the second session of the Council on 4 December 1963. Surprisingly, in the period between sessions it was secretly modified. The new document had deleted the rejection of the deicide charge against all Jews and seemed to reiterate the call for the conversion of the Jews.[59] On 14 September 1964 the third session of the Council opened and most Council Fathers urgently called for a return to Bea's draft of 8 November 1963. In October 1963, Heenan had declared that ecumenism was a synonym for 'dialogue' and 'reunion in charity' and 'must not be understood as an effort to convert those of other faiths to one's own convictions'.[60] Now, he openly expressed his opposition to the new document and declared: 'I humbly plead that this Declaration of ours shall openly proclaim that the Jewish people as such is not guilty of the death of our Lord.'[61]

As a response to the modification of Bea's draft, the Christian press accused Christians of using Jews to ignore their shared guilt in Christ's death and asked Christian repentance for the crimes committed against them. Even Council Fathers such as French Bishop Leon Elchinger considered that the Council should ask forgiveness in the name of all Christians.[62] On 20 November 1964, a final document, 'The Relationship of the Church to non-Christian Religions', was adopted by the Council Fathers with the Pope's support, and an overwhelming vote in its favour of 1770 to 185. It maintained the spirit of Cardinal Bea's first draft, as it highlighted 'the spiritual patrimony common to all Christians and Jews', 'condemn[ed] hatred and persecution of Jews', rejected the charge of deicide against all Jews, explained Christ's passion and death as a result of 'the sins of all men' and suppressed the call to conversion.[63]

Just eight days before this vote, on 12 November 1964, the trial scene of the *Merchant of Venice* was performed by the RSC before Paul VI and the Council Fathers. In the programme, the play is described as 'the drama of the victory of mercy over pitiless justice. The speech of Portia

---

[59] Hershcopf, 'The Church and the Jews', 121.
[60] 'Essential to Ecumenism is Dialogue, Not Conversion', *Catholic News Service. Vatican II: 50 Years Ago Today*, http://vaticaniiat50.wordpress.com (accessed 2 June 2014).
[61] Quoted in Hershcopf, 'The Church and the Jews', 124.
[62] Hershcopf, 'The Church and the Jews', 124.
[63] Quoted in Hershcopf, 'The Church and the Jews', 99.

(who appears in the robes of a judge) on mercy, contains scriptural and Christian references, as the greater part of Shakespearean allusions to this virtue'.[64] The scene deconstructs the conception of Christian mercy and compassion that the Duke, Portia and Antonio had previously presented as opposed to Shylock's unyielding and unmerciful stance, rejecting the money offered to him to save Antonio's life.[65] The strength of this scene, when contextualised within Bea's drafting process and within the Vatican–Hochhuth controversy, lies in its presentation of a Jew condemned for lack of mercy – for his refusal to save the life of a Christian – that dismantles what the Duke in *The Merchant of Venice* (4.1) calls the 'difference of spirit' between Jews and Christians. By comparing Christian ownership and treatment of slaves to his claim to Antonio's pound of flesh, Shylock is clearly questioning Christian mercy, while at the same time exposing Christian hypocrisy and unkindness by reminding them of their cruelty towards other human beings. By staging this scene for the Council Fathers who were to vote in favour of the document 'The Relationship of the Church to non-Christian Religions' just eight days later, the RSC actors Tony Church, Derek Godfrey and Dorothy Tutin were participating in the ongoing polemical Council debate on Christian responsibility for the historical persecution of Jews. Indirectly, they were pointing to Bea's insistence on Christian mercy as the only way to restore the relations between Catholicism and Judaism. Shakespeare's art was once again working as an 'unofficial emissary' which was, in this case, reinforcing Heenan's ecumenical spirit and strengthening the position of the most progressive sector of the Curia.

Despite the uncomfortable implications of this scene, Tony Church's initial concern about its inadequacy as a commemorative act in Rome proved to be unnecessary. The RSC spirit of dialogue, religious tolerance and respect shown during the weeks before and after the premiere of *The Representative* avoided any diplomatic tension between England and Rome to the point that it was Paul VI who invited them to participate in the event. Many members of the audience, and surely the Pope, associated Tony Church's performance of Shylock with his acclaimed performance as the Financial Advisor to the Pope in the

---

[64] 'IV Centenario della Nascita di William Shakespeare'. Auditorium Palazzo Pio, Roma 12 Novembre 1964. Programme of the Commemorative Performance.

[65] The interpretation of this scene is still much debated.

English version of the German play. It is also probable that the most informed members of the audience made a further link between *The Merchant of Venice* and *Der Stellvertreter*, as both plays had been produced a year before by Erwin Piscator at the Freie Volksbühne in West Berlin and dealt with issues of Christian guilt and responsibility for the Jews' extermination. Therefore, as we can infer from the vote of 20 November in favour of Bea's document, most Council Fathers must have regarded the performance of this scene from *The Merchant of Venice* as a timely and 'appropriate' – borrowing Heenan's term – rendering of issues, such as the conversion of the Jews and Christian mercy, which were, as we have seen, the cause of substantial disagreement within the Council. The performance of the trial scene from *The Merchant of Venice* also constituted a disturbing remembrance of the Holocaust, the inadequate Christian reaction to the Nazi crimes and Pius XII's role during the Second World War, at a moment when this historical controversy had also gained force world-wide thanks to Hochhuth's play.

Commemoration and ecumenism

Going beyond what Tony Church describes 'as an episode of unscheduled but sublime farce'[66] (when the Pope assumed that the actors offering the *First Folio* to him for his blessing meant it as a gift), it is true that the public presentation of the volume to the Pope at the closure of the celebration culminated a commemorative performance that achieved a diplomatic and religious significance. As this chapter has shown, the performance of Shakespearean scenes by British and Italian actors at the Vatican in 1964 served several purposes. First, the closing address of the Pope thanking the promoters and the performers turned the RSC actors and the work of Shakespeare into 'unofficial emissaries or diplomats', whose presence brought to the fore a common cultural background shared by British Anglicanism and Roman Catholicism. This common cultural background was crucial for the strengthening of international relations at a time when Paul VI was keen to promote the unity of all Christian churches. During the Second Vatican Council, this was certainly an item in the agenda that

---

[66] Church, *A Stage*, 142.

corroborated the Council's ecumenical spirit and its desire to achieve a far-reaching religious rapprochement.

Second, the RSC performance acquires further religious resonances if analysed in the light of both the Pope's closing address and the *Dogmatic Constitution on the Church* or *Lumen Gentium*. Taking advantage of the occasion, Paul VI used his commemorative speech on Shakespeare to assert his Papal authority and reinforce the power of his word among the Council Fathers with a view to putting an end to controversies and disagreements. The Pope's closing address at the quatercentenary celebrations also portrayed Shakespeare's works as sacred texts that could enlighten humanity and lead them to salvation by conveying the message of universal Christian faith that would be announced to the world just nine days later with the promulgation of the *Lumen Gentium*.

Finally, the representation of the trial scene of *The Merchant of Venice* had an obvious ideological dimension. Once it is contextualised within the all-embracing nature of the Council and within the Catholic Church's determination to renew and reform itself by acknowledging its share of responsibility for the historical persecution of the Jews, it is easy to imagine that the trial scene must have had a deep resonance. If nothing else, it actively inserted the performance within the religious and political debates that surrounded Cardinal Bea's drafting of the document on the relationship between Jews and Christians. The RSC's successful management of the diplomatic tensions brought about a year earlier by their London production of Hochhuth's *The Representative* was crucial for the Council's acceptance of the performance of a scene in which Christian mercy was put into question by a Jew. Therefore, commemoration was turned into a forceful ideological act that conveniently suited the agenda of a Vatican Council willing to engage in further ecumenical dialogue with other faiths and in particular with the Anglican Church.

7 | *Commemorating Shakespeare in America, 1864*

DOUGLAS M. LANIER

On 20 February 1864, William Winter, the eminent American drama critic of his day, writing under his accustomed pseudonym 'Mercutio', devoted his column 'Drama' in *Albion* to the prospects for a suitable commemoration of the Shakespeare Tercentenary later that year. Those prospects, he lamented, were 'not hopeful' even in Shakespeare's own England, and in America they were even less certain. Acknowledging that the nation was 'convulsed with civil strife', Winter implored his countrymen nevertheless to embrace reverence for Shakespeare as a principle over which they might unite, asking first 'actors, and men of letters, and artists, of all descriptions' to gather in honour of 'the most wonderful Genius ever sent down from heaven', and then to extend that spirit of unity outwards to America's relationship to the world, 'hold[ing] out hands of sympathy with all the world, in reverence for the illustrious memory of the world's poet'.[1] A number of journalists of the day shared Winter's fear that Shakespeare's birth risked going unrecognized in America. An editorial in the *Cleveland Morning Leader* on 20 April 1864 lamented the fact that though the Tercentenary was the first opportunity for 'the whole world' rather than just England to offer 'the incense of their grateful praise' to Shakespeare, Americans – and especially Clevelanders – were exhibiting 'a general inactivity and want of zeal' towards commemoration of the event.[2] These kinds of journalistic squibs might be seen as starting places for the notion that the 1864 Shakespeare Tercentenary went largely unobserved in America. This lack of commemoration would seem surprising given the critical consensus that Shakespeare was ubiquitous in mid-nineteenth-century American culture, a mainstay in

This article is part of Research Project FFI2011-24347 'Cultures of Commemoration II: Remembering Shakespeare' (Spanish Plan Nacional de I+D+i 2008–2011).
[1] In a scrapbook of William Winter's writings, Folger Shakespeare Library.
[2] 'The Birthday of Shakspeare', *Cleveland Morning Leader*, 20 April 1864, 3.

the theatre and in schools, a much-invoked touchstone in public discourse, a figure whose popularity crossed social classes.[3] In this chapter, I want to suggest that American commemoration of the 1864 Tercentenary was more robust than has been generally acknowledged. There are records of tercentenary celebrations in New York City, Rochester (New York), Boston, Lowell (Massachusetts), Utica (New York), Cleveland, St Louis, Philadelphia, Washington DC, Baltimore (Maryland), Detroit, Chicago, Cincinnati and no doubt others which have left no documentary record.[4] These celebrations – and the anxiety that America might not mark the Tercentenary and thereby expose the nation's cultural inferiority to the world – illustrate the complex relationship between Shakespeare and American culture in the middle of the century.

The most salient reason that Shakespeare's birth risked going unrecognized in America in 1864 is the most obvious: the nation was otherwise occupied with civil war, an enterprise which sapped civic resources and darkened the mood for celebration, especially in the bloody year leading up to the Tercentenary. Chastizing public leaders for their lack of interest in tercentenary celebrations, an editorial in the *Cleveland Morning Leader* adds that 'this may readily be excused by the plea that the distractions and discords of war ring louder in our ears than the melodious strains of any singer'.[5] The effect of the war was so acute in the South that in February 1864 the Confederate legislature contemplated suppressing theatrical performances altogether in an effort to conserve resources and honour memories of the dead. Though the legislation was never passed and stage performances continued in diminished form in Southern cities in the later years of the war, there are almost no records of substantial commemorations of the Shakespeare Tercentenary in Confederate states other than newspaper notices of the occasion on the appropriate day, and periodic, somewhat bemused press reports of the vexed state

---

[3] Lawrence Levine, 'William Shakespeare in America', in *Highbrow/Lowbrow: The Emergence of Cultural Hierarchy in America* (Cambridge: Harvard University Press), 11–82.

[4] There are also records of commemorations in Toronto, Halifax (Nova Scotia) and Nassau in the Bahamas.

[5] 'Birthday of Shakspeare', 3.

of tercentenary preparations in England.[6] Even though myriad anecdotes testify to the popularity of Shakespeare with Confederate readers and theatre-goers, evidence suggests that Shakespeare commemoration, in 1864 at least, was principally a Northern metropolitan phenomenon.[7] In addition to revealing just how resource-strapped and dispirited the South was in 1864, this may indicate the extent to which the intelligentsia of Northern cultural centres like New York, Boston and Philadelphia – clerics, newspapermen, scholars – were widely regarded as national arbiters of cultural taste and interpretation, and so the appropriate authorities for conducting tercentenary celebrations.

There is one important exception: the commemoration held in Norfolk, Virginia, exhaustively chronicled in an article in *The New Regime* on 24 April 1864. However, this exception tends to prove the rule. Norfolk had been under Union occupation for almost two years before the Tercentenary, and the detailed account of the Norfolk celebrations appeared in a Union-run newspaper. The lavish evening celebration, probably organized by Union forces for themselves, included a dinner, display of a Shakespeare edition (open to the banquet scene in *Macbeth*), English and American coats of arms, Shakespeare-themed engravings, extended toasts and speeches, an original poem, musical selections and singing.[8] The *New Regime* article opines that the Tercentenary provided an answer to those in the

---

[6] The Southern press did discuss the consequence of not marking the tercentenary. In the *Charleston Daily Courier*, 8 April 1864, 1, the editor argues that Shakespeare's birthday should be marked, for despite the seeming impropriety of doing so during war, 'no friends of the Confederacy abroad will be discouraged, or will abate their hopes and opinions concerning us because, notwithstanding the troublous times, we show some recognition of our rightful claim to our portion of birthright in SHAKESPEARE'. The wording suggests how Shakespeare was regarded in the South as a cultural property not fully its own.

[7] E. Merton Coulter notes that William H. Crisp, a prominent Southern actor, was called upon to help with a Confederate commemoration of the tercentenary, but nothing came of the effort. See *The Confederate States of America 1861–1865* (Baton Rouge: Louisiana State University Press, 1950), 507.

[8] The detailed press account does not identify who organized the evening commemoration, which was addressed to the professional elite of the city, though one account suggests it was the work of Union soldiers; the theatrical portion is credited to S. W. Glenn, local impresario and manager of the Norfolk Opera House. Troy Valos of the Norfolk Public Library notes that names of local families do not appear in the press account (private correspondence, 21 November 2014).

foreign press who charged 'us' with a 'barbaric element' in conduct of the war, for the commemoration offered 'our more intelligent citizens ... those intellectual pleasures of peace which the name of Shakespeare recalls to all'.[9] The notion that commemorating Shakespeare might answer the charge of Northern barbarity only underlines the extent to which Shakespeare was routinely associated with the North's cultural achievements, even though before the war Southern cities had a thriving tradition of Shakespeare performance.[10]

This is not to claim that Shakespeare's appropriation during the American Civil War had an exclusively Unionist cast. A joke using *Richard III* as its reference point, reprinted in many papers in 1864, lampooned Lincoln's love for the Bard and his delay in negotiating with commanders in the Confederate capital:

The President has declared his liking for Shakespeare. Now we can well imagine a position in which the words of *Richard* to *Stanley* in his mouth would be exceedingly appropriate – that is, with a very slight change to suit a circumstance. Thus:

Scene–White House. Time–Midnight.

Mr. Lincoln to Mrs. Lincoln: Look to your *sister*; if she convey letters to Richmond, you shall answer it.[11]

---

[9] 'Local Histories: Shakspeare in Norfolk', *The New Regime*, 24 April 1864, 2. I thank Troy Valos for this and other references to the Norfolk festivities. Of special note is J. S. Mulligan's response to a toast for 'the colored race of the age of Shakspeare'. At some length and with considerable scholarly citation Mulligan argues that Othello was a Moor and not a Negro or 'Ethiopian', for it is 'not so probable' that 'the negro race could have furnished to Venice the valiant captain he has portrayed' ('Local Histories', 2); his riposte drew loud applause. This episode suggests that, despite the festive atmosphere, there was evidently tension between those concerned to lend Shakespearean imprimatur to the dignity of black folk, and those eager to use Shakespeare to deny it. Later, M. Sullivan of the Custom House argued that Shakespeare was in fact an Irishman, though it is not clear whether his case was in earnest or in jest.

[10] The theatrical portion of the commemoration, at the Norfolk Opera House, involved a performance of the fourth act of *The Merchant of Venice*, with Shylock played by John E. McDonough, an actor based in Philadelphia who happened to be in Norfolk with his touring production of a burlesque *The Seven Sisters of Satan*; *Seven Sisters* appears on the tercentenary playbill as the main attraction. The performance culminated with a tableau of Shakespeare himself (played by the opera house's manager, S. W. Glenn) in his study, presumably surrounded by representations of his characters. See 'The Shaksperian Festival' and 'Amusements', *The New Regime*, 23 April 1864, 2 and 3 respectively.

[11] 'All Sorts of Shorts', *Daily Ohio Statesman* 31, 19 April 1864, 4.

In *Punch*, a British journal openly sympathetic to the Confederate cause, Lincoln, dressed as the murderous tyrant Richard III, appears at the tail end of the comic processional published in its tercentenary issue (see Figure 7.1).[12]

Most famously, John Wilkes Booth, the assassin of Lincoln, embraced *Julius Caesar*'s Brutus as an important precedent justifying his actions, his cry of '*sic semper tyrannis*' designed to recall the murder of Caesar in the service of republicanism.[13] (With his two brothers, Edwin and Junius, Booth had performed in a gala production of the play only months before on 25 November 1864 in New York City, a performance to benefit tercentenary efforts to erect a Shakespeare statue in Central Park.) Nonetheless, there was some reticence in explicitly enlisting Shakespeare to the Confederate cause. In his dedicatory ode for the opening of the New Theater in Richmond, Virginia, in 1863, Henry Timrod, perhaps the Confederacy's most accomplished poet, alludes at length to Shakespearean characters – Miranda, Juliet, Lear, Othello, Hamlet – as he portrays the stage as a 'fairy ring / Drawn in the crimson of the battle plain', a visionary, ameliatory space from which 'every loathsome thing / And sight and sound of pain / Are banished'. Yet when at the poem's end Timrod searches for a political model, a 'hero who can teach a hero's part / In this distracted time',[14] he chooses not from the obvious Shakespearean candidates but singles out William Tell, champion of the Swiss cause of liberty.[15] Shakespeare's status as

---

[12] *Punch's Tercentenary Number*, 23 April 1864, 4–5. In the preceding year *Punch* featured a cartoon in which a freed slave in the guise of Caliban, after being handed emancipation by Lincoln, offers to beat a Confederate general, a comic allusion to the enlistment of black regiments in the Union cause (*Punch* 45, 24 January 1863, n.p.). The caption, 'you beat him 'nough, Massa! Berry little time, I'll beat him too', alludes to Caliban's altercation with Trinculo in *The Tempest* ('Beat him enough; after a little time / I'll beat him too', 3.2.80–1).

[13] This connection is even more explicit in Booth's letter to the *National Intelligencer* (written 14 April 1865 and reconstructed afterwards) justifying the assassination. There he ends his diatribe against Lincoln and Northern tyranny with lines from *Julius Caesar*: 'O, that we then could come by Caesar's spirit, / And not dismember Caesar! But, alas, / Caesar must bleed for it' (2.1.169–71). For an extended discussion of this connection, see Albert Furtwangler, *Assassin on Stage: Brutus, Hamlet, and the Death of Lincoln* (Urbana, IL: University of Illinois Press, 1991).

[14] Henry Timrod, 'Address Delivered at the Opening of the New Theatre at Richmond', in James Shapiro (ed.), *Shakespeare in America* (New York: Library of America, 2014), 177.

[15] While on the run after Lincoln's assassination, and saddened by his national vilification, John Wilkes Booth pairs Brutus and Tell as champions of liberty in a diary entry of 21 April 1865: 'with every mans hand against me, I am here in

Figure 7.1 'Lincoln as Richard III', in *Punch* Tercentenary Number, 23 April 1864.

transcendent, vatic, even quasi-divine, and the association with his literary authority (as opposed to theatrical popularity) with Northern centres of cultural power seemed to militate against Confederate writers appropriating Shakespeare to legitimize the Southern cause.

American commemorations of Shakespeare's birth in 1864 took one of two forms: private, small-scale celebrations by fraternal societies or clubs, or larger public celebrations organized by committees or civic authorities. Of the two, small-scale commemorations were far more common, and the fact that they often left no physical memento and garnered little press coverage has contributed to the impression that Shakespeare's birth Tercentenary passed without notice in North America. One group especially active in organizing these small celebrations were St George's Societies, chapters of which were located in many metropolitan areas in America and Canada. The Society of St George was first founded in New York City by expatriate British citizens amidst the Revolutionary War to offer assistance to fellow countrymen; similar societies were formed throughout the nineteenth century in several American and Canadian cities. These societies soon evolved into organizations of expatriate Englishmen and those Americans with British lineages who were for various reasons motivated to celebrate English heritage. With membership restricted to men only until late in the twentieth century, these were male counterparts to women's literary societies of the nineteenth and early twentieth centuries, providing not only charitable work but also fraternal camaraderie with a distinctly Anglophilic flavour.[16] For obvious reasons, these societies held an annual banquet on 23 April, the feast day of St George, the patron saint of England, so it was convenient to append recognition of Shakespeare's achievements to the festivities. In most cases, tercentenary celebrations of this sort consisted of a toast to Shakespeare and a 'response' in the form of a eulogy, poem or lecture on the Bard added to the established roster of toasts, songs and cheers that followed dinner. There was, in other words, no separate commemoration of Shakespeare on the tercentenary date at these gatherings; instead, recognition of Shakespeare's birth was folded into more general celebrations of Englishness.

despair. And why: For doing what Brutus was honored for, what made Tell a Hero. And yet I for striking down a greater tyrant than they ever knew am looked upon as a common cutthroat.' William Hanchett, 'The Diary of John Wilkes Booth, April 1865', *Journal of the Illinois State Historical Society* 72.1 (1979), 41.

[16] See Katherine West Scheil, *She Hath Been Reading: Women and Shakespeare Clubs in America* (Ithaca: Cornell University Press, 2012).

From an American perspective, the Anglophilic quality of these St George's Society commemorations posed potential problems for the tercentenary celebration. Given the origins of the American nation in its break from Britain, the very notion of an American organization celebrating British heritage was controversial, and perhaps more so because the nation, in the midst of a civil war, was facing a challenge to its identity. The controversy was addressed directly by the president of the Cleveland St George's Society, Mr Outhwaite, in his annual address to his membership in 1864 (only moments before Shakespeare was toasted). Outhwaite publicly worried that Americans might be reluctant to join the St George's Society for fear that doing so would call their patriotic loyalty into question.[17] Implicitly, then, toasting Shakespeare in such a gathering was to identify Shakespeare as specifically British and so to complicate the capacity for Americans to recognize him as part of their cultural heritage. This may be why the commemorative speeches that have survived from these St George's Society celebrations tend to move so quickly away from Shakespeare's British birth to his universal, transcendent qualities, especially his capacity to cross class and national boundaries. The critical sentiments in play would have been familiar to anyone who had read their Johnson and Coleridge, but in the context of the American Civil War, the emphasis upon Shakespeare's depiction of a shared human nature, his capacity to accommodate opposites in a single, capacious myriad-mindedness, would have had an urgent, if implicit, political resonance.

The Chicago commemoration of Shakespeare's Tercentenary is a case in point, though it was somewhat more elaborate than other St George's Society celebrations of Shakespeare in 1864. In Chicago, the St George's Society commemoration took place in Bryan Hall, the city's largest gathering place, and it consisted of the usual dinner, speeches, toasts and songs.[18] Elias Colbert, then city editor of the *Chicago Tribune* and a noted polymath, gave the commemorative oration, produced, he tells us in the published version, in two days when organizers discovered that the gentleman assigned the task had not written it. Colbert's 'Eulogy on

[17] *Cleveland Morning Leader*, 27 April 1864, 3.
[18] Unlike most other St George's Society commemorations, however, this celebration also had a public component, for in the afternoon of 23 April a Shakespeare Oak was planted in Rosehill Cemetery, the city's primary graveyard. Sadly, newspaper reports suggest that this commemorative event was not well attended (see 'Shakspeare', *Chicago Tribune*, 25 April 1864, 4), and the tree seems not to have survived to the present.

Shakespeare' has two overarching themes. The first is that of Shakespeare's humble origins 'in an obscure village in the middle of England'. There as a young man he had boasted 'no honorable birth', 'no prodigies of intellect, of childish acquirement, no precocity of intellect' and 'no sign of future greatness, save ... the possession of that free, fearless spirit of adventure which is the true type of Nature's noblemen – he who disdains the petty conventionalities and repudiates the trammeling formulas of society'.[19] His British birth acknowledged, then almost immediately forgotten, Colbert's Shakespeare comes to resemble the plucky American frontiersman who strikes out for points West, or the mythic American colonist who rejects the tyranny of the hidebound motherland, the self-created solitary man of Nature not bound by the circumstances of his birth or education. To stress the implicit point, Colbert highlights Shakespeare's distinctively American rowdiness –'his boisterous sportings, his carousals' – and he likens the Bard to a 'young eagle', bringing into play all of that symbol's patriotic resonance.[20] Colbert's second theme is Shakespeare's capacity for transcendence and 'kaleidoscopic versatility', his ability to capture 'all the variations of human thought, and action' and to reconcile opposites.[21] He notes, for example, how 'the most unlettered boor' is instantaneously enthralled because Shakespeare offers 'a language of the heart which needs no learning to enable us to interpret', and yet Shakespeare also satisfies the learned reader who can appreciate 'the more exquisite touches'.[22] Noting that the occasion is St George's Day, Colbert observes that 'while Englishmen may feel justly proud of [Shakespeare's] fame, they are only his more immediate neighbours. The whole world claims kin.' The spirit of kinship that reconciles the divisions between classes, nationalities and educational strata, argues Colbert, a spirit that Shakespeare as 'the perfect cosmopolite' both embodies and engenders, has the power to 'bring about that for which all men pray – the good time coming'.[23] Colbert's final phrase alludes to Charles Mackay's popular poem 'There's a Good Time Coming', written in 1846 and set to music by Stephen Foster, a piece with special suggestiveness given the direction

---

[19] Elias Colbert, *Scoriae: Eulogy on Shakespeare* (Chicago: Fergus Print Co., 1883), 5–6. The address was delivered by Evelyn Evans, a professional orator, who also performed the 'seven ages' speech from *As You Like It* and selections from *Hamlet* and *King Lear*, interspersed between Shakespeare-themed musical selections.

[20] Colbert, *Scoriae*, 6.   [21] Colbert, *Scoriae*, 8.   [22] Colbert, *Scoriae*, 10.

[23] Colbert, *Scoriae*, 11–12.

of the war in the Union's favour in 1864. Colbert's oration navigates between the Scylla of Britishness and the Charybdis of American national conflict by presenting Shakespeare as a catalyst for and symbol of inclusive union and thus as a figure for the American nation itself.

In some other cities, tercentenary commemorations were arranged by literary or cultural clubs. Such was the case with the April 1864 meeting of the Shakspeare Society in Philadelphia.[24] Legend has it that it was in 1864 that the Shakspeare Society switched its annual banquet from December to April in honour of the Tercentenary, a change spearheaded by then dean of the society Henry Howard Furness. The decision was not without controversy, for it necessitated a change in the seasonal menu that irritated the former dean, Asa Israel Fish, and others.[25] The surviving programme suggests that the commemoration followed the Society's usual format of a lavish dinner (each course introduced by a Shakespeare quotation), followed by the presentation of members' scholarly papers ('literary exercises' on aspects of Shakespeare's life). In this case, the format was augmented by an elaborate sequence of toasts to, among other recipients, the Society's medical, legal and clerical brothers, a sequence marking not just Shakespeare's learning but also the professionalization of Shakespearean commentary and the cultural authority of the Society. The celebration was a decidedly private affair, a fact that becomes more apparent if one compares it to the Society's commemorative activities in 1916, when it organized a programme of public lectures and performances, and an ambitious public exhibition of Shakespeare memorabilia, and even planned to erect a public statue of Shakespeare in his honour.

In Cincinnati, the occasion was marked on 22 April by the local Shakespeare Club in their meeting rooms on Walnut Street. In this case, the commemoration had a striking theatrical flair, for it

---

[24] *The Philadelphia Inquirer*, 25 April 1864, 4, reports that a Shakespeare celebration at the Academy of Music was organized by German citizens; it included an original ode to Shakespeare by Mrs Gustavus Remak, orations in German and English, Shakespeare-themed music by German composers and magic lantern projections of Shakespeare illustrations by Wilhelm von Kaulbach. According to *The Press*, 25 April 1864, 1, the local Society of St George also marked the occasion with a banquet. The Chestnut Street Theatre offered Otto Nicolai's opera *The Merry Wives of Windsor* and the Walnut Street Theatre featured *Julius Caesar*; the New Arch Street Theatre touted a Shakespeare's birthday benefit for the American Dramatic Fund, but its play was not a Shakespearean one.

[25] Henry L. Savage, 'The Shakespeare Society of Philadelphia', *Shakespeare Quarterly* 3.4 (1952), 348.

revolved around the presentation of passages from *Henry IV*, *A Midsummer Night's Dream*, *Julius Caesar* and *Two Gentlemen of Verona*. Members responded to the obligatory toasts in the personae of Shakespearean characters, so that, the local newspaper reported, 'thus did Wolsey, Hotspur, Benedick, Portia, Hamlet, Dogberry, Falstaff, Juliet, Olivia, &c, &c, appear in person, to render tribute to Nature's favorite bard'. The commemoration also featured a touching ode to 'old Time', the 'relentless foe', who, despite laying millions low with a mocking laugh, is himself at last conquered by Shakespeare, the 'one at least [who] survives his brothers' fall'.[26] The reference to the war dead is unmistakable. This presentation of Shakespeare as a figure who transcends mortal civil strife is implicit in many American tercentenary orations and odes.

The fact that theatrical presentation was not a necessary feature of such commemorations is significant, for many of these celebrations maintain a distance from stage Shakespeare. In his oration at the tercentenary commemoration at Lowell, Massachusetts, William Bartlet identifies American Shakespeare with Shakespeare for readers. He notes that Americans 'are a reading people', and so claims that Shakespeare is more popular in the United States than in England because 'there are probably fifty readers of Shakspeare in the States for every one in England'.[27] Quoting Charles Lamb, Bartlet goes on to argue that Shakespeare is best experienced by the solitary reader, for 'some of the finest effects of Shakspeare's plays vanish when an attempt is made to represent those plays upon the stage'.[28] He also suggests that reading Shakespeare appeals to American individualism, for reading allows one to study the plays for oneself. This appeal to the Shakespeare of the page reflects a lingering Puritan suspicion of the stage, something particularly marked among Northeast cleric-scholars and not strongly felt in Southern culture, which, commentators agree, 'held a far more open attitude toward theater'.[29] The stress upon

---

[26] 'Shaksperian Festivals', *Cincinnati Daily Enquirer*, 25 April 1864, 3.
[27] *Lowell Shakespeare Memorial: Exercises on the Tercentenary Celebration of the Birth of William Shakespeare, April 23, 1864, by the Citizens of Lowell, Massachusetts* (Lowell, MA: Stone & Huse, 1864), 29 and 12.
[28] *Lowell Shakespeare Memorial*, 15.
[29] Michèle Vignaux, 'A Southern Shakespeare?' *Transatlantica: Review d'études américaines* 1 (2010), http://transatlantica.revues.org/4879, accessed 10 November 2014.

Shakespeare the book also reflects the interests of the reading clubs and scholarly fraternities sponsoring these small-scale commemorations, interested as they were in differentiating their apotheosized bard from Shakespeare the popular playmaker.

This is not to suggest that all American commemorations excluded theatrical performances from their celebrations. In Washington DC, the occasion was marked almost exclusively by theatrical benefits – one by the Washington Literary and Dramatic Association held at the Washington Theater, one at the Grover Theater featuring Leonard Grover's rendition of Shakespeare characters and one at Ford's Theater offering selections from *Romeo and Juliet*, *A Midsummer Night's Dream*, *As You Like It* and *The Taming of The Shrew*.[30] The only non-theatrical celebration was a commemorative dinner held at Star and Garter Hotel, about which little information is available other than that the guests were 'a few gentlemen, most of English and Scottish descent' and toasts were offered to Shakespeare (twice), Lincoln and Queen Victoria.[31] Certainly, throughout America acting companies embraced the opportunity to pack the house on 23 April. Nevertheless, Washington DC (and New York City) were exceptions to the place of theatre in East Coast commemorations of the Shakespeare Tercentenary. For the most part, these small-scale commemorations celebrated Shakespeare as script(ure) for readers and not Shakespeare as popular entertainment.

The second group of American tercentenary celebrations were public commemorations conceived as grand events open to the general public. The organizing groups for these celebrations varied markedly: in Chicago it was the St George's Society, in Detroit the Young Men's Society (an educational association), in St Louis the Western Sanitary Commission (a benevolent organization dedicated to the Union war effort), in Boston the New England Historic-Genealogical Society, in New York City a committee of actors, in Lowell, Massachusetts, a committee of local citizens. Notably, most of the commemorations in the Midwest were of this public variety, a fact that suggests that cities like Chicago, St Louis and Detroit regarded the Tercentenary as an opportunity to establish their civic sophistication. Typically, these

---

[30] 'Local News', *Evening Star*, 23 April 1864, 3. On 22 April, on the final night of Edwin Forrest's run of *Macbeth*, Ford's Theater was lit up in Shakespeare's honour.

[31] 'Shaksperian Celebration', *Evening Star*, 25 April 1864, 3.

celebrations featured the presence of prestigious local officials, public lectures, Shakespeare scenes or speeches and songs from Shakespeare or Shakespearean opera (Mendelssohn's overture to *A Midsummer Night's Dream* was a favourite), the performances typically provided by local amateurs. For example, the surviving programme bill from the St Louis tercentenary production, a benefit for the Mississippi Valley Sanitary Fair, resembles a theatrical extravaganza, with Shakespeare scenes interspersed with songs, all culminating in a performance of Locke's musical setting of *Macbeth*.[32] The scenes chosen for the programme's second half are noteworthy for their political resonances – Hotspur's description of Henry IV's foppish messenger, the downfall of Wolsey from *Henry VIII*, Hamlet's discussion of the death of great men with the gravediggers, Mark Antony's oration over Caesar's corpse, Falstaff's description of his rag-tag army and Macbeth's psychological struggle over the murder of Duncan. Taken together, these scenes obliquely register complex local sentiments towards the secessionists (though Missouri was a border state, St Louis was under Union control) and the toll taken by civil war casualties. This public gala was paired with a private commemorative dinner for gentlemen, where two original odes were read and toasts were offered to Shakespeare, 'Our Country', 'The Stage and Its Representatives', the city of St Louis, 'Woman', the press, Robert Burns and the presiding official at both gala and dinner, General William Rosecrans of the Western Sanitary Commission.[33]

The commemorative gala in Detroit was even more elaborate, combining the educational content of the public lecture with the entertainment value of stage performance. The first half of the afternoon was occupied by lectures on Shakespeare and the professions (Shakespeare as lawyer, doctor, cleric, orator) given by local dignitaries. These lectures stressed the breadth of Shakespeare's intellect, but, more important, by claiming Shakespeare as one of their own the lecturers recast Shakespeare as no longer a working-class man of the theatre, but as a symbolic member of the professional–intellectual class of Detroit, an object lesson in the cultural power of professionalization. The

[32] 'Three Hundredth Anniversary of the Birth of Shakspeare! Saturday Evening, April 23, 1864 at Mercantile Library, Large Hall, for the benefit of the Mississippi Valley Sanitary Fair!', in the Folger Library collection.

[33] 'Local News: The Shakspeare Celebration at Concert Hall', *The Daily Missouri Republican*, 24 April 1864, 3.

programme's second half, given in the evening, consisted of scenes performed by local amateurs (*A Midsummer Night's Dream, Romeo and Juliet, The Merchant of Venice, Hamlet, Henry VIII, I Henry IV*), each punctuated with a Shakespearean song or musical interlude; simpler tableaux (from *King Lear, King John, Merry Wives* and *Measure for Measure*) were performed in a 'Shakspeare Gallery'. The emphasis was on visual spectacle and the participation of local performers rather than on the political resonance or educational value of the scenes themselves. A contemporary account singles out the performance of the Morocco scene from *Merchant* 3.7 for its 'good taste, brilliancy of effect, and historic completeness and fidelity', claiming that 'no picture equal to this, we have no hesitation in asserting, has ever been produced in Detroit'. Notably, the account does not acknowledge the scene's racial content. The writer does, however, register the 'statues of white-robed Grief and Memory' in the performance of *The Mousetrap* from *Hamlet*, incongruous figures which clearly speak to the circumstance of civil war.[34] The Young Men's Society annual report for 1865 reveals that the event made a considerable profit.

Of the public celebrations discussed here, the commemoration in Lowell, Massachusetts, had its origins most directly in the community at large, for it was organized by a committee of local citizens (chaired by John A. Goodwin, ex-Speaker of the Massachusetts House of Representatives) after the Middlesex Mechanics Association turned down the opportunity for fear of failure. The programme included a speech by William Bartlet, a commemoration ode and songs sung by local schoolchildren and renditions of three speeches (Juliet's 'Wherefore art thou Romeo', Shylock's 'Hath not a Jew eyes?' and Constance's lament on the death of Arthur from *King John* 3.4) by Helen Eastman, a local townswoman. One theme of the presentation was the close kinship between New and Old England, a connection introduced in the opening 'Ode', the final stanza of which reads, 'So we here in dear New England, / Tribute to his greatness pay, / Joining with the far-off Homeland / Honoring the natal day'.[35] Though the phrasing leaves strategically ambiguous which celebration has priority, it unequivocally identifies England as New England's special 'Homeland'. The commemoration's centrepiece was the address by Bartlet, an Episcopalian minister from a

[34] 'Shakspeare: The Tercentenary', *Detroit Advertiser and Tribune*, 25 April 1864, 3.
[35] *Lowell Shakespeare Memorial*, 8.

prominent Boston family. In it, he traces the link between America and Shakespeare through Henry Wriothesley, third Earl of Southampton, 'an early and persevering friend of American colonization' who was 'one of [the colonies'] earliest benefactors'. Because Shakespeare, like New England, was a beneficiary of Southampton, *'this nobleman connects these States with the subject of this day's commemoration.* In honoring Shakspeare we may be said to honor his noble and virtuous friend.'[36] This odd logic allows Bartlet to shift attention away from Shakespeare himself to a more aristocratic, elite figure, one who, unlike Shakespeare, is not troubled by charges of indecency, unoriginality and especially association with the theatre, charges Bartlet feels at pains to answer in his oration. Only by stressing the need to read Shakespeare rather than see him performed can Bartlet purge Shakespeare of his latent vulgarity; though Shakespeare's works are in dramatic form, he argues, that is not of their essence. One wonders how he responded to Ms Eastman's performance immediately afterwards.

Like the celebrations in St Louis, the public commemoration in Lowell was followed by a more exclusive evening banquet during which toasts and responses were offered to the various classes of the city. Of interest is the third toast, to 'Our Country', which used passages from *Richard III* ('Now are our brows bound with victorious wreaths') and *2 Henry IV* ('There is not now a rebel sword') to express the desire for a close to the war, achieved by 'smit[ing] as with the sword of Gideon every traitorous hand and every traitorous tongue'.[37] Notably, Shakespeare is used to voice a transcendent hope for peace, whereas the Bible is invoked for partisan purposes. The Civil War intrudes again with the toast to 'Old England, the Home of Shakespeare', where respondent Reverend James Dean, an English expatriate, stresses the paired legacy inherited from England through Shakespeare: 'as sons of New England, possessing a common language and a common love of liberty, we cherish as our own this rich legacy bequeathed to our mother tongue by the immortal bard'. For that reason, it may be 'said of her, as of her fatherland, that New England never did, *nor never shall*, lie at the foot of a conqueror, until she shall have first wounded herself'.[38]

New York City's tercentenary commemoration had a rather different, more ambitious focus, which eventually provided America with its

---

[36] *Lowell Shakespeare Memorial*, 11.   [37] *Lowell Shakespeare Memorial*, 38.
[38] *Lowell Shakespeare Memorial*, 50.

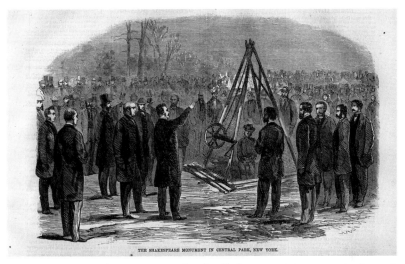

THE SHAKESPEARE MONUMENT IN CENTRAL PARK, NEW YORK.

Figure 7.2 Laying the cornerstone for the Shakespeare Monument in Central Park, New York City, 23 April 1864. *Harper's Weekly*, 7 May 1864.

most durable Shakespeare memorial from the 1864 Tercentenary.[39] The plan was to erect a statue of Shakespeare in Central Park, one to rival the Shakespeare statue then planned for the London Tercentenary. Originally spearheaded by the Century Club, an exclusive gathering of New York City's intelligentsia, preparations were taken over by three of America's most prominent Shakespearean actors, James Henry Hackett (renowned for his Falstaff), William Wheatley and Edwin Booth. (Edwin Forrest was asked to participate, but he declined.) The committee ran into difficulty financing the enterprise, and so the tercentennial celebration involved laying only the cornerstone of the proposed statue and conducting benefit performances in the evening to raise funds for the project. After the laying of the cornerstone, fund-raising efforts were extended nationwide, and the statue was

[39] Two other commemorative events in New York City should be noted. At Cooper Institute, the eccentric actor George Jones, who styled himself Count Joannes, gave a lecture on Shakespeare's life and offered 'histrionic illustrations' from *The Merchant of Venice, Romeo and Juliet, Othello, King Lear* and *Macbeth* ('Literary Notes', *The Round Table*, 23 April 1864, 297; 'Count Joannes on Shakspere', *New York Herald*, 24 April 1864, 5); his daughter Avonia Jones played Juliet to Booth's Romeo in his benefit performance at the Winter Garden. And a private celebratory dinner was held at the Century Club, at which toasts were offered and answered.

eventually erected in 1872. The ceremonial laying of the cornerstone, at noon on the 23rd, involved a relatively small gathering of New York City intellectuals, actors and dignitaries; the engraving of the ceremony published in *Harper's Weekly* seems to depict a larger crowd than contemporary accounts describe (see Figure 7.2).[40]

The *New York Times* characterized the proceedings as 'sober, we may almost say ... subdued', as befits 'this tragic epoch of our national history' and wondered whether the 'only moderately demonstrative' ceremony might indicate some lack of appreciation of or indifference towards Shakespeare.[41] The dedicatory orations of Judge Charles P. Daly and William Wheatley sounded two prominent themes. First was the need for America to provide a proper Shakespeare memorial as testament to the nation's cultural sophistication on the international stage. Were it not to do so, even at time of war, it 'would be a reflection upon us as an intellectual and cultivated people', for Shakespeare's statue would be 'alike commemorative of the event celebrated to-day, and of the state of the arts in this country'.[42] Daly's claim that Shakespeare is 'too universal to be the property of any one age or nation' and Wheatley's that Shakespeare speaks '*our* language' (my emphasis) thus underwrite the propriety of an *American* Shakespeare memorial. The second theme is Shakespeare's capacity for transcendence, his ability to address, in Daly's words, 'the varied tastes of men', 'the applause of the multitude' and 'the admiration of the profound': 'in him the greatest contrasts unite and the most opposite qualities'. For Wheatley the actor, this capacity explains why 'spectators of all classes and ages' find their sentiments awakened by the pathos of Shakespeare's characters, though when Wheatley turns to describing those responses in his dedicatory ode, he speaks of readers rather than spectators, asking 'who has not read his honeyed page'.[43] In any case, Shakespeare's capacity for uniting opposites did not extend to the divided political realm, for the ceremony ended with two songs of notably Unionist cast, 'Hail Columbia' and 'Yankee Doodle'. Many of New York City's major theatres offered matinee or evening benefits for the Shakespeare

---

[40] 'The Shakespeare Tercentenary', *Harper's Weekly*, 7 May 1864, 301.
[41] 'Shakespeare', *New York Times*, 24 April 1864, 4. The *Daily Picayune* of New Orleans (3 May 1864, 3) speculates that the relatively sparse attendance may have been due to New Yorkers' preoccupation with the New York Sanitary Fair.
[42] 'The Shakespeare Tercentenary', *New York Times*, 23 April 1864, 8.
[43] 'The Shakespeare Tercentenary', 8.

statue fund: Niblo's offered Wheatley and Hackett (the latter as Falstaff); the Winter Garden featured Booth as Romeo; the Academy of Music offered selections from Shakespeare operas under the baton of Max Maretzek; and even P. T. Barnum produced 'Katharine and Petrucio' along with various other curiosities at his American Museum.[44]

Befitting its reputation as 'the literary emporium, the Athens, of America', Boston's commemoration by the New England Historic-Genealogical Society was a predominantly scholarly affair.[45] Held at the State Capitol in the hall of the House of Representatives and chaired by the governor of Massachusetts, John Andrew, the commemoration consisted of a public lecture by Rev. James Freeman Clarke and an ode by John Sheppard, followed by a short speech by Rev. Frederick Holland. Clarke's address touches on familiar themes – 'the great family which speaks the English tongue'[46] that Shakespeare perfected, Shakespeare as a poet of nature and the imagination, Shakespeare as a moral writer and repository of wisdom. Towards the end of his lecture, however, Clarke turns specifically to the Civil War, noting that it provides a fine example of Shakespeare's timeless moral instruction. He argues that the South's secession finds an apt analogy in the Jack Cade rebellion in *2 Henry VI*, for Shakespeare's Cade, like the Southern rebels, tries to present himself as a gentleman when in fact he is of lower-class stock. Moreover, and even more damning, Southerners, like Cade, harbour a 'hatred of schools and learning', for theirs is 'the land where negroes were whipped for learning to read, and the schoolmistress who taught them was sent to prison'. Clarke concludes that 'the chief difference between the policy of the North and South is this, – that the North has determined to have all its laboring population educated, and the South has determined that theirs shall not be educated'.[47] The directness of Clarke's appropriation of Shakespeare for commentary on the war is unusual for tercentenary commemorations, and it serves in multiple ways. Beyond deploying Shakespeare's cultural authority to bolster

---

[44] 'Shakspere at the Theatres', *New York Herald*, 23 April 1864, 8. James Wallack, manager of Wallack's Theater, offered a cheque for $1000 to the fund in lieu of giving a benefit.

[45] *Tercentenary Celebration of the Birth of William Shakespeare by the New-England Historico-Genealogical Society* (Boston: George C. Rand & Avery, 1864), 6. Boston also marked the occasion with a concert at Music Hall, which featured Mendelssohn's *A Midsummer Night's Dream* and Beethoven's *Coriolan*, and a special tercentennial meeting of the Saturday Club (discussed below).

[46] *Tercentenary Celebration*, 11. [47] *Tercentenary Celebration*, 49–50.

Union stereotypes of the uncouth South and demonstrating Clarke's (and by extension the North's) learned facility with the Bard, these comments also loosen the bonds between England and Shakespeare, for, Clarke observes, the ruling classes of England have sided with the South, a position that puts them directly at odds with their own national poet. By making Shakespeare the voice of the Union and not of England, Clarke Americanizes him. Sheppard's ode followed Clarke's speech, and in it Shakespeare emerges both figuratively and literally as a figure of enlightenment, a familiar image in American tercentenary discourse: 'as the long, dark ages rolled away, / A light from heaven shone on SHAKSPEARE's face'.[48] After first locating Shakespeare and the reader in Stratford, 'the father-land of our New-England race', the poem quickly moves Shakespeare to 'the Rocky Mountains', 'the Golden Gate of fame', 'Schoodic's misty shores', and the Kennebec, via the imaginative resonances between the American and English landscapes: 'Nature herself proclaims each picture true / To Albion's echoing hills: nor there alone; / As e'en Niagara speaks in Prospero's thunder-tone'.[49] In the ode's penultimate stanza, Sheppard acknowledges the realities of the war in America, but in a move characteristic of tercentenary discourse of the day, Sheppard conceives of Shakespeare in transcendental terms, a figure outside rather than in history, one who guides 'Ambition's eye to aim far higher / Than light the flames of civil war with strange, unholy fire'.[50]

In this, Sheppard's ode resembles the most distinguished poem produced for the 1864 Tercentenary,[51] Oliver Wendell Holmes's 'Shakespeare', first given at the Saturday Club meeting on 23 April, and subsequently published in the *Boston Daily Advertiser* and the *Atlantic Monthly*.[52] The Saturday Club was an informal monthly meeting of

---

[48] *Tercentenary Celebration*, 61.   [49] *Tercentenary Celebration*, 61.
[50] *Tercentenary Celebration*, 61.
[51] The Tercentenary elicited a number of commemorative odes from American poets, many of which were reprinted in newspapers nationwide. Among these were Richard Henry Stoddard's 'William Shakespeare', Henry Ames Blood's 'Shakespeare, April 23, 1864', Miss Louisa Hawthorne's 'Ode on the Erection of a Statue to Shakespeare' and John A. Willis's 'The great die not!' The anonymous 'The Two Poets' (published in *Harper's Weekly*, 14 May 1864, 309) mocks Shakespeare's statue in Central Park by imagining Shakespeare confronting Schiller's bust, which had been erected in the park in 1859.
[52] Ralph Waldo Emerson writes of the gathering and of Holmes's ode in his journal for 24 April 1864; see Edward Waldo Emerson, *The Early Days of the Saturday Club, 1855–1870* (Boston: Houghton Mifflin, 1918), 337–42.

Boston's intellectual elite, and its modest tercentenary dinner was attended by thirty-two regulars and guests, a larger than average gathering for this otherwise intimate group. Holmes's ode, the only surviving oration from the evening, is, like Clarke's oration, concerned with America's claim to Shakespeare despite English sympathy for the South. It begins with the voice of the 'Old World', asking how America, 'that realm unknown' of 'warring aliens', can share the 'holy task' of honouring Shakespeare. Holmes's answer intensifies the impulse to transcendentalize Shakespeare that runs through so many American tercentenary celebrations. Civil war, he stresses, has not undermined the pride that Americans feel in 'every noble word [England's] sons bequeathed / The air our fathers breathed', a line which locates Shakespeare's legacy to America, as so many tercentenary speeches did, in England and America's shared language.[53] Echoing the words of King Henry at the opening of *I Henry IV*, Holmes argues that Shakespeare provides Americans with an imaginative, pastoral respite from the perpetual grind of war, turning funeral lilies into celebratory garlands:

> War-wasted, haggard, panting from the strife,
>   We turn to other days and far-off lands
> Live o'er in dreams the Poet's faded life,
>   Come with fresh lilies in our fevered hands
> To wreathe his bust, and scatter purple flowers,–
>   Not his need, but ours![54]

As Holmes progresses, his Shakespeare takes on an increasingly prophetic, even millennial quality. Shakespeare is among those 'who are first to mark / Through earth's dull mist the coming of the dawn', a poet for whom God 'the curtain rent / That veils the firmament', an author whose sublimity rivals that of the natural wonders of the American West. Ultimately, Holmes casts Shakespeare's work as a form of secular scripture – 'earth's clearest mirror of the light above' – and Shakespeare, though a player, as 'a prophet from on high, / Thine own elected'.[55] For this 'great gift', claims Holmes, God deserves our praise. His passing reference to 'Te Deum'–'therefore we bid our hearts' *Te Deum* rise'[56]– suggests that this poem traverses the distance between

---

[53] Oliver Wendell Holmes, 'Shakespeare', *Atlantic Monthly* (June 1864), 762.
[54] Holmes, 'Shakespeare', 762.   [55] Holmes, 'Shakespeare', 763.
[56] Holmes, 'Shakespeare', 763.

Henry IV's despair at endless war and Henry V's climactic triumph at Agincourt, after which he orders his soldiers to sing 'Te Deum' in recognition of divine blessing upon him. Like Agincourt for young King Henry V, Shakespeare's presence in America signifies God's ultimate favour upon the Union, the 'unstained drops of freshening dew' that 'keep us to every sweet remembrance true', memories of the cause for which 'our martyrs fall, our heroes bleed'. Shakespeare's very transcendence of history and his capacity for redemption and legitimation promises America a millennial future from which after the war will spring 'new-born / Our Nation's second morn'.[57]

Over the top though it may be, and harbinger of the 'highbrow' Shakespeare that would characterize America's version of the Bard in the century's second half, Holmes's ode nevertheless brings together many of the themes that ran through American celebrations of the 1864 Tercentenary. He articulates the need for America to participate in the Tercentenary in order to claim its place in the league of cultured nations, as well as America's need to defend its claim to Shakespeare, a claim which typically rested most firmly upon sharing of the English language rather than sharing a culture. He maps Shakespeare onto the American landscape by stressing his status as a poet of Nature and of the sublime. He emphasizes Shakespeare's status as a book ('we read, we reverence on this human soul … thy prophet's scroll … his page'[58]) rather than as stage performance, and he elevates Shakespeare to the status of scripture, purged of indecency and imbued with moral power. Most interestingly, Holmes reveals that the tendency in America to apotheosize Shakespeare during the Tercentenary has as one of its oft-unspoken catalysts the trauma of the Civil War. For all the obligation to locate Shakespeare's origin in a specific land and era (this was, after all, the Tercentenary of his birth), it is striking how much of the American commemoration strove to situate Shakespeare outside time and place, as a secure, sublime repository of universal value and wisdom untouched by the taint of America's recent history, and because it was universal, available for the nation to claim. Though the 1864 Tercentenary was not the source of Shakespeare's rise to the status of secular scripture within American cultural life, it provided, at least in the North, a moment in which that status was publicly consolidated, and so it contributed significantly to the making of a distinctively American Shakespeare.

---

[57] Holmes, 'Shakespeare', 763.   [58] Holmes, 'Shakespeare', 763.

8 | *Shakespeare's rising: Ireland and the 1916 Tercentenary*

ANDREW MURPHY

On 24 March 1916, the *Irish Times* (the longest-running newspaper in Ireland, closely associated with the anti-nationalist establishment) published a short article under the title 'Shakespeare in Dublin'. The writer worried that, with a month to go to the Tercentenary of Shakespeare's death, 'no hint has reached us that Dublin intends to take any formal part in it'. This was felt to be particularly depressing, given that it was 'quite probable that the Tercentenary of "*unser* Shakespeare" will be celebrated in Berlin'. 'At this time', the editorial notes, 'the whole Empire is fighting for ideals that Shakespeare, more than any other human being, helped to shape and glorify. Irish soldiers are bleeding and dying for those ideals.' Was it 'wholly impossible', the *Times* asked, 'that at such a time we in Dublin should render thanks to Shakespeare?'[1]

Three days later, the Dublin Branch of the British Empire Shakespeare Society – an organisation established 'to promote greater familiarity [with Shakespeare] among all classes throughout the British Empire', whose 'ominous motto' (as Richard Halpern has noted) was 'Using no other weapon but his name' – wrote to the editor of the *Irish Times* to assure him that his 'jeremiad' was unjustified.[2] The Society had organised performances of *Hamlet* at the Abbey Theatre for 7 and 8 April; arrangements had been made for 'Mr. Martin Harvey and his company [to] produce at the Gaiety Theatre the patriotic play, "Henry V"', and it was expected that Harvey would deliver 'some special afternoon lecture or entertainment in connection with the tercentenary'. The President of the Society, the Right Hon. Mr Justice Madden

---

[1] 'Shakespeare in Dublin', *Irish Times*, 24 March 1916, 4. Hereafter, *Irish Times* is given as *IT*.

[2] Richard Halpern, *Shakespeare Among the Moderns* (Cornell University Press, 1997), 20. Halpern notes that the Society had branches in British Guiana, Johannesburg and India, as well as Ireland.

would also deliver 'A very important paper'.[3] The Dublin branch had, in fact, been busy with preparations for the Tercentenary for some time. It had run an essay competition on the topic 'William Shakespeare, Patriot', with entries being judged by Professor Wilbraham Fitzjohn Trench of Trinity College Dublin.[4] In January of 1916, *The Winter's Tale* had been produced at the Abbey, under the auspices of the Society.[5] Other events were also being organised to celebrate the Tercentenary in Dublin: Trinity College placed its copies of the four folios on public display; the National Literary Society hosted a lecture by Professor William Magennis, entitled 'Shakespeare's Debt to Irishmen'; and, in a rather more specialist vein, a Mr Thomas Meally read a paper, at the Kingstown Gardeners' Society, on the topic 'Was Shakespeare a Gardener?'[6] The editorial writer at the *Irish Times* wished, however, for something more specific, something styled as 'really national', that would effect a 'linking together [of] the tribute to Shakespeare and the prosecution of the war in a way that should redound to the success of both our aims'. Speculating as to what this could be, he writes:

We can imagine nothing better calculated to stir the blood of the people than the recitation on Easter Monday, say, by skilled elocutionists of some of the many famous passages in which Shakespeare at once extols the past achievements of his countrymen and urges them to emulate the glories of their fathers.[7]

As it happens, on Easter Monday 1916, the enthusiastic Dublin playgoer Joseph Holloway wandered into the centre of the city from his home in the suburbs, seeking, precisely, a theatrical performance. His first port of call was the Empire, where he found the doors closed;

[3] 'Shakespeare in Dublin', *IT*, 27 March 1916, 9. For the dates and details of the *Hamlet* performances see 'Platform and Stage', *IT*, 25 March 1916, 7.
[4] Trench had been a student of the Trinity Shakespearean Edward Dowden, author of the highly influential *Shakespere: A Critical Study of His Mind and Art* (London: Henry S. King & Co., 1875). Trench succeeded Dowden as Professor of English at Trinity and his *Shakespeare's 'Hamlet': A New Commentary* was published 1913.
[5] On the competition and *Winter's Tale* performances see 'British Empire Shakespeare Society: Annual Meeting of Dublin Branch', *IT*, 11 January 1916, 9.
[6] See 'The Shakespeare Tercentenary', *IT*, 15 April 1916, 8; 'Coming Events', *IT*, 17 April 1916, 6; 'Coming Events', *IT*, 12 April 1916, 6.
[7] 'The Shakespeare Tercentenary', *IT*, 17 January 1917, 4.

he passed on to the Abbey, which was also closed. Running into the bell porter and pit-entrance keeper of the Abbey, he was told that 'the G.P.O. [General Post Office] had been captured early that morning and companies of Volunteers were entrenched in Stephen's Green and [that] Westland Row Railway Station was in their hands also'.[8] Holloway had, unwittingly, wandered into the heart of a separatist uprising against British rule in Ireland, which aimed to take advantage of the overstretching of Britain's military capacity as a result of the war. In his travels Holloway came across a poster declaring 'that Ireland was now under Republican Government'. He characterised the proclamation as 'a long and floridly worded document full of high hopes'.[9]

Those involved in the Easter Rising can be said to have rejected almost everything that the British Empire Shakespeare Society – and the institutions in its orbit in Ireland – stood for. Where the *Irish Times* referred quite bluntly to '[o]ur enemies, the Germans', the insurrectionists looked to Germany as an ally and hoped to receive German arms and officers to assist them in their campaign.[10] For nationalists, Trinity College was, as Jack White, a leading commander in the socialist Irish Citizen Army (which made up a part of the insurrectionary forces), put it 'the alma mater of the British connection'.[11] For one nationalist commentator, the *Irish Times* might as well have renamed itself the *English Times*, for all the positive contribution it made to Irish society and culture; another nationalist commentator, D. P. Moran, did rename it (in his own *Leader* newspaper), styling it *The Bigots' Dustbin*.[12]

---

[8] Robert Hogan and Michael J. O'Neill (eds.), *Joseph Holloway's Abbey Theatre: A Selection from his Unpublished Journal Impressions of a Dublin Playgoer* (Carbondale and Edwardsville: Southern Illinois University Press, 1967), 179.

[9] *Ibid.*, 178. The coincidence of the Rising with the Shakespeare Tercentenary resonates interestingly with the coincidence of the Tercentenary with Anzac Day, just a year after the Gallipoli landings – see Philip Mead's chapter in the present volume.

[10] 'The Literary World', *IT*, 26 March 1916, 6. The failure of the German ship the *Aud* to land its cargo of weapons on the southwest coast of Ireland in the days immediately preceding the Rising was significant for the outcome of the insurrection.

[11] See R. M. Fox, *The History of the Irish Citizen Army* (Dublin: James Duffy, 1944; originally issued 1943).

[12] See 'Literary Intelligence', *United Irishman*, 4:88, 3 November 1900, 7 and Patrick Maume, *D. P. Moran* (Dublin: Historical Association of Ireland, 1995), 23.

And yet, it is only *almost* everything associated with the culture of the British Empire Shakespeare Society that the insurrectionists rejected. Crucially, the one thing they emphatically did *not* reject was Shakespeare himself. In his overview history of Irish nationalism, Richard English has noted that, in terms specifically of their literary tastes, 'these were paradoxically very British rebels'.[13] Individual advanced nationalists in this period professed a love of Byron, Dickens, Scott, Browning, Shelley, Chaucer and – above all else – of Shakespeare.[14] Indeed, John O'Leary – one of the most senior figures in Irish nationalist circles at the time – once observed that 'If England had only Shakespeare and Milton and the rest, the Fenians would not be against her.'[15]

Irish nationalists' embracing of Shakespeare was, in fact, all of a piece with radical political appropriations of the playwright that had occurred on the other side of the Irish Sea during the course of the nineteenth century. At the time of the previous Tercentenary – of Shakespeare's birth, in 1864 – the London celebrations were lent a political edge as they were planned and executed by the Working Men's Shakespeare Committee, who organised a commemorative tree planting ceremony on Primrose Hill. The event segued into a frankly political protest, as, in the wake of the tree planting, a large section of the crowd reconfigured itself into a demonstration to object to the way in which the radical nationalist Giuseppe Garibaldi's visit to Britain had been cut short by the government authorities.

The commemorative and political events at Primrose Hill can be said to have had their roots in a tradition of radical autodidacticism stretching back to the early decades of the nineteenth century. Self-educated radicals – particularly those associated with the Chartist movement – tended to work their way through a relatively predictable canon of texts, with Shakespeare at its apex. Thomas Cooper (1805–92) serves as an emblematic instance here.[16] Cooper was a sometime cobbler,

---

[13] Richard English, *Irish Freedom: The History of Nationalism in Ireland* (London: Pan, 2007), 302.

[14] *Ibid.*, 302–3.

[15] Quoted in James Moran (ed.), *Four Irish Rebel Plays* (Dublin: Irish Academic Press, 2007), 5.

[16] For the details of Cooper's life see his autobiography, *The Life of Thomas Cooper* (Leicester University Press, 1971; originally published 1872). I have written about Cooper in *Shakespeare for the People: Working-class Readers 1800–1900* (Cambridge University Press, 2008), 144–9.

with minimal access to formal education, who taught himself Latin, Greek, Hebrew and French, and developed an extraordinary devotion to Shakespeare. He memorised all of *Hamlet* and much of *King Lear* and set up a Shakespearean Chartist Association in his native Leicester, staging a fund-raising performance of *Hamlet* with the group in 1842.

The devotion of early twentieth-century radical Irish nationalists to Shakespeare can be seen as dovetailing with this earlier British tradition. In the case of James Connolly – union leader, founder of the Irish Labour Party and Commandant in Chief of the Irish Citizen Army – the parallels are particularly striking. Born to an Irish family in Edinburgh, Connolly was the son of a night-soil man and he received very little formal education. He told his daughter, Nora, that his own parents 'couldn't afford lights' and that he 'used to lie down on the floor near the fire so that it would shine on my book'. 'I had no pencil to write with, either', he observed. 'I had to char bits of stick in the fire for a pencil, and for paper used whatever scraps I could find.'[17] Like Cooper, Connolly worked for a spell as a cobbler. As Samuel Levenson has observed, the 'Labour movement at the time seemed full of cobblers. It was the victimized man's retreat.'[18] Connolly was possessed of an 'obsessive desire for self-education'.[19] Describing him as 'the master-intellect of them all', Darrell Figgis – a fellow participant in the 1916 Rising (and himself author of a book on Shakespeare) – noted of Connolly that his 'reading [was] as deep as [it was] voluminous, including books and documents difficult to obtain. Even for a student of leisure the range of his reading would have been unexpected – for one who was, as he was, self-taught it was extraordinary.'[20] In many respects, then, Connolly feels like a 'belated' Chartist, following an

---

[17] Nora Connolly O'Brien, *James Connolly: Portrait of a Rebel Father* (Dublin: Four Masters, 1975; first published 1935), 91–2, 92.

[18] Samuel Levenson, *James Connolly: A Biography* (London: Martin Brian & O'Keefe, 1973), 39. Also in common with Cooper, Connolly had no talent for the trade: the Edinburgh suffragist Ana Munro recalled taking all her family's shoes to Connolly for repair and that 'Not a pair could be worn again' – see C. Desmond Greaves, *The Life and Times of James Connolly* (London: Lawrence and Wishart, 1961), 53.

[19] Ruth Dudley Edwards, *James Connolly* (Dublin: Gill & Macmillan, 1981), 2.

[20] Darrell Figgis, *Recollections of the Irish War* (London: Ernest Benn, 1927), 87. For Figgis' work on Shakespeare, see his *Shakespeare: A Study* (London: Dent, 1911).

educational, political and cultural track quite common among working-class British radicals in the nineteenth century.

Connolly was said to have 'devoured Shakespeare', but only in print form, as 'he had never been in a financial position to see a single performance'.[21] His love of the playwright was something he shared with fellow nationalist Patrick Pearse, with whom he led the 1916 uprising (Pearse served as President of the short-lived Provisional Republic). Pearse's father, James, was, like Connolly, an autodidact. He quit Sunday School 'in disgust at the inadequate answers to his acute questions' and received no further formal schooling.[22] Despite his limited education, James Pearse 'developed a strong passion for reading' and 'bought a lot of books mostly on English literature, art, architecture, history and religion'.[23] He passed his love of reading on to his children, particularly to his elder son (from his second marriage) Patrick.

Patrick Pearse recalled daydreaming himself into the world of the books that he read when he was young, including imagining himself as *Lear*'s Gloucester 'deprived of my sight with the good Kent'.[24] His sister, Mary Brigid, remembered home performances of Shakespeare mounted by Pearse and his siblings. Brothers Patrick and Willie, she writes, 'used to act the famous Quarrel Scene from *Julius Caesar*. Pat took the part of Brutus, and Willie that of the wily Cassius. Pat was fine in that scene – dignified, keen, and commanding; a splendid foil to Willie's equally good rendering of the tricky, affected Cassius.'[25] All of the children together had 'learned virtually the whole of' *Macbeth* and they staged a performance in the home. Subsequently, when Pearse acquired an early phonograph, they used the machine to make a

---

[21] Greaves, *Life*, 322. Greaves' source was the political activist and friend of Connolly, Jack Mullery, interviewed by Greaves when he was working on his biography. It is not entirely clear whether the comment about Connolly not being able to attend a performance of the plays is correct. He was certainly known to have attended the Abbey, at least after 1910 – see Nelson Ó Ceallaigh Ritschel, 'Under Which Flag, 1916', *New Hibernia Review*, 2:4 (1998), 54–68.

[22] Ruth Dudley Edwards, *Patrick Pearse: The Triumph of Failure* (London: Faber & Faber, 1979), 1.

[23] Joost Augusteijn, *Patrick Pearse: The Making of a Revolutionary* (Basingstoke: Palgrave Macmillan, 2010), 13.

[24] Patrick Pearse, 'My Childhood and Youth', in Mary Brigid Pearse (ed.), *The Home Life of Pádraig Pearse: As Told by Himself, His Family and Friends* (Dublin and Cork: Mercier, 1979; first published 1934), 22.

[25] *Ibid.*, 48.

recording of the first scene of the play.[26] After he left school, Pearse founded a debating group called 'The New Ireland Literary Society', for which he served as president. Social events organised for the Society often included Shakespearean recitals, with Pearse, on one occasion, acting out the opening scene of *Hamlet*, with a high degree of emotion and drama: at the end of the scene 'his anger died ... as the [ghost] beckoned him, and nothing but triumph and profound pity remained'.[27] In 1908, Pearse established his own school, St Enda's, and one of his students, Desmond Ryan (who, himself, was 'obsessed by Shakespeare'[28]), recalled of him that he 'was nearly as orthodox in his views on literature as in his views on religion'. He introduced his pupils to 'the classics of English and Irish literature', including Shakespeare, whom 'he read and re-read'.[29] The library at the school ran to hundreds of volumes, with 'choice editions of Shakespeare' among the collection.[30] Ryan's account of Pearse's acquisition of multiple copies of the playwright's works reveals a fetishistic bibliomania with a complex dynamic: 'He loved his books [especially] his many editions of Shakespeare, all of which he watched in the booksellers' windows, nobly renounced, entered, fingered, steeled himself, fled whole streets away, lingered, wavered, turned back and purchased, radiant and ashamed until he saw the next.'[31]

Ryan observed of Pearse that he 'learned much from Shakespeare', seeing the influence of the poet particularly in his oratory.[32] As much as anything else, however, we might say that what Pearse and Connolly both took from their intensive devotion to Shakespeare was a sense of the political value of theatre, and of the theatricality of politics. Long before the advent of Cultural Materialists and New Historicists, Pearse and Connolly came to understand that politics often operate partly through the public staging of power – and of resistance. This is, of

[26] *Ibid.*, 48, 84.   [27] See *ibid.*, 88–9.
[28] R. F. Foster, *Paddy and Mr Punch: Connections in Irish and English History* (London: Allen Lane, 1993), 305.
[29] Desmond Ryan, *The Man Called Pearse* (Dublin: Maunsel, 1919), 102, 84, 102. See also Augusteijn, who quotes (from private letters) Michael Dowling, whose children attended St Enda's: 'I spent a day there. I remember hearing him lecture on *Julius Caesar*. I knew the play well but was genuinely interested and noticed that the boys too were.' *Making of Revolutionary*, 177.
[30] Desmond Ryan, *Remembering Sion: A Chronicle of Storm and Quiet* (London: Arthur Barker, 1934), 116.
[31] *Ibid.*, 159.   [32] Ryan, *Remembering*, 92.

course, a signature theme of the history plays, and, indeed, of many other of Shakespeare's plays.

At the end of the nineteenth century, Victoria, as queen, together with her administration, also clearly understood the value of the public projection of power – as John Plunkett has traced in his study *Queen Victoria: First Media Monarch*.[33] This is particularly evident in the Diamond Jubilee festival of 1897, which, at the instigation of Victoria's Colonial Secretary, Joseph Chamberlain, became a celebration of British imperial power. In responding to the Jubilee, Connolly sought, effectively, to fight one form of theatricality with another. The Irish capital, like the other outposts of empire, had been exhorted to participate in the celebrations on Jubilee Day, 22 June, and, in the city, 'all the shops which relied on Unionist custom had decorations and electric lamps for night-display'.[34] Connolly linked up with the radical nationalist Maud Gonne – with whom, as Ruth Dudley Edwards puts it, he shared 'a penchant for the bold move and the flamboyant gesture' – and together they orchestrated a counter-spectacle on Jubilee Day itself.[35] Connolly had a black coffin fashioned, with 'British Empire' inscribed on the side, which he and a group of activists paraded through the streets on a handcart decorated as a hearse. The demonstrators carried black flags 'embroidered with facts on famines and evictions which had marked Victoria's reign, the fruits of Connolly's research'.[36] The police attempted to break up the demonstration but, as Gonne herself writes, 'Connolly was not a man to be easily stopped and the procession arrived in fair order at O'Connell Bridge.' By this point the police had been significantly reinforced and progress was halted, so Connolly heaved the coffin into the River Liffey, shouting 'Here goes the coffin of the British Empire. To hell with the British Empire!'[37]

Later that evening, a second phase of the demonstration was initiated. In a gesture striking in its modernity, Gonne had secured a window at the National Club in Parnell Square from which images

---

[33] John Plunkett, *Queen Victoria: First Media Monarch* (Oxford University Press, 2003).

[34] Maud Gonne MacBride, *A Servant of the Queen: Reminiscences*, ed. A. Norman Jeffares and Anna MacBride White (Gerrards Cross: Colin Smythe, 1994; first published 1938), 215.

[35] Edwards, *James Connolly*, 23.   [36] Levenson, *Connolly: A Biography*, 52.

[37] MacBride, *Servant*, 217 (both quotations).

could be projected onto a giant screen in the street outside. As Gonne observes, 'with the help of the Corporation workmen, we had arranged for the cutting of wires to prevent the display by the Unionist shops of their electric decorations' and to darken the streets to make the projected images more clearly visible. The slides displayed included 'Pat O'Brien's photos of ... Eviction scenes ... and photos of the men who, during Victoria's reign, had been executed or who had died in prison'.[38] The police baton-charged the spectators watching the magic lantern show, killing an old woman in the process. This prompted the crowd to smash the windows of those shops on Sackville Street (now O'Connell Street) that were displaying Jubilee decorations.

The anti-Jubilee demonstration was street theatre in the very most literal sense. But Connolly and Pearse – and many of the other nationalist activists – were also involved in more conventional forms of theatre, often with an explicitly Shakespearean underpinning. Thomas MacDonagh, for example, who served as a teacher at Pearse's St Enda's before taking up a lectureship in English at University College Dublin and who was the Dublin brigade commandant during the Rising (being executed with the other leaders after the insurrection) was the author, among other plays, of *When the Dawn is Come*, performed at the Abbey in 1908. MacDonagh was one of those Irish nationalists who were close admirers of English literature. His MA thesis, published as a book in 1913, was a study of the poetics of Shakespeare's contemporary Thomas Campion.

When the Dawn is Come is set 'Fifty years hence, in Ireland, in time of insurrection', though, in fact, there is nothing futuristic about the world of the play. The central character is Thurlough MacKiernan, a captain in the 'Irish Insurgent Army' and a member of the Council of Ireland.[39] MacKiernan is a national hero in the play, but he is also given to introspective intellectualisation, sometimes to the detriment of his immediate political project. At the end of the play, fatally wounded, he finds himself craving 'A perfect rest'. The *Hamlet* resonances are heavily accented here and elsewhere in the text, to the extent that, as James Moran nicely puts it, '*When the Dawn is Come* almost feels like the bad quarto of Shakespeare's play.'[40] In the final lines of the drama,

[38] *Ibid.*, 215.
[39] Thomas MacDonagh, *When the Dawn is Come*, in Moran (ed.), *Four Irish Rebel Plays*, 43.
[40] Moran, 'Introduction' to *Four Irish Rebel Plays*, 5.

Father John – as something like a composite of *Hamlet*'s Horatio and *Lear*'s Kent – commands the onstage audience: 'Hush! Hush! Our voices are vain in the ear of the world. Pray for his soul. Peace at last to his soul!'[41] Ultimately, however, Thurlough dies a hero, having led his troops in a battle that has 'won Ireland which else had remained unwon a further while, perhaps a weary while'.[42] By contrast with the Shakespearean original to which it is so indebted, then, at the end of MacDonagh's play no Fortinbras, we might say, stands waiting ominously in the wings.

Pearse, too, was a dramatist – indeed, his sister, Mary Brigid, reports in her memoir that 'when he was a mere child he began to write plays and to teach us how to act them'.[43] Pearse was a founding committee member of the Theatre of Ireland/Cluicheoirí na hÉireann group, which aimed to offer an alternative to the Abbey project (while often also working in collaboration with the Abbey group).[44] A number of Pearse's pieces were, in fact, performed at the Abbey, generally with pupils from his school serving as the cast; between 1908 and 1912, the St Enda's boys appeared in seven different pieces by Pearse staged at the theatre.[45] Róisín Ní Ghairbhí and Eugene McNulty have noted that 'at the time of their first performance Pearse's plays were viewed by a *who's who* of the Dublin literati and were reported on and discussed widely and positively in the press'.[46] In May of 1915, his play *The Master* was staged at the Irish Theatre in Hardwicke Street. The play draws indirectly on the historical shift in Ireland from paganism to Christianity, often conceptualised by Irish writers through an imagined encounter and debate between the Christianising St Patrick and the mythological figure Oisín (who belatedly returns to Ireland, having survived beyond his era, living in Tír na nÓg – the 'Land of Youth').[47] Pearse's play is set in an unspecified time, when Ciarán, a monk-like schoolteacher, clashes with Daire, holder of a local kingship. Daire is emblematic of an old world order, while Ciarán represents something

---

[41] MacDonagh *When the Dawn is Come*, 79.   [42] *Ibid.*, 76.
[43] Pearse, *Home Life*, 45.
[44] See *Patrick Pearse: Collected Plays*, ed. Róisín Ní Ghairbhí and Eugene McNulty (Sallins, Kildare, RoI: Irish Academic Press, 2013), 12.
[45] See Augusteijn, *Making of Revolutionary*, 174.
[46] *Collected Plays*, ed. Ní Ghairbhí and McNulty, 2.
[47] See, for example, W. B. Yeats, *The Wanderings of Oisin*, in Richard J. Finneran, *The Collected Poems of W. B. Yeats* (Basingstoke: Palgrave, 1983).

new and more spiritual. Daire's men surround Ciarán's school, and he revels in his power over the master: 'There is a watcher at every door of your house. There is a tracker on every path of the forest. The wild boar crouches in his lair for fear of the men that fill this wood.'[48] As Daire threatens him, Ciarán calls out, 'My God, my God, why has Thou forsaken me?', forging a clear identification with Christ. Ciarán is a heroic failure who becomes the victim of a clinical form of politics and power, and possibly we may see Pearse here drawing inspiration from Shakespeare's figuring of Richard II – overwhelmed in his encounter with the coldly efficient Bolingbroke – not least since Irish nationalists specifically figured Shakespeare's Richard as a clearly heroic figure (references in the play to his Irish military ventures notwithstanding).[49]

Ciarán is slain, but an invocation by one of his disciples causes the archangel Michael to appear and, when challenged by Daire to declare who he is, he replies (in language which might be said to owe more to the King James Bible than to any native Irish source):

I am he that waiteth at the portal. I am he that hasteneth. I am he that rideth before the squadron. I am he that holdeth a shield over the retreat of man's host when Satan cometh in war. I am he that turneth and smiteth. I am he that is a Captain of the Host of God.[50]

As Ní Ghairbhí and McNulty have noted, the play uses the traditional narrative of the shift from the pagan to the Christian to provide 'an analogue for nationalist resistance to the impositions of imperial power'.[51] Ciarán's transmutation into a Christ-like figure and the intercession of the archangel uses Christian iconography to suggest that self sacrifice in the face of superior power need not be read as failure – but, rather, that it can trigger a greater power which can ultimately enact an enduring triumph.[52] These ideas would, as we shall see, prove to be central to Pearse's conception of the Rising itself.

[48] *The Master* in *Collected Plays*, ed. Ní Ghairbhí and McNulty, 196.
[49] See, for instance, W. B. Yeats, 'At Stratford-on-Avon', in Richard J. Finneran and George Mills Harper (gen. eds.), *The Collected Works of W. B. Yeats, Volume IV: Early Essays*, ed. George Bornstein and Richard J. Finneran (New York: Scribner, 2007).
[50] *Collected Plays*, ed. Ní Ghairbhí and McNulty, 196.
[51] *Collected Plays*, ed. Ní Ghairbhí and McNulty, 40.
[52] I focus here on the use of Christian iconography. But for Pearse and many others it was, more narrowly, specifically *Catholic* iconography and doctrine that was central to their thinking.

Connolly, as we have seen in relation to the Jubilee protests, also had a keen appreciation of the value of theatrical spectacle in a political context. As leader (from 1914) of the Irish Transport and General Workers' Union, he controlled the union's Dublin headquarters building, Liberty Hall. The Front Room of the Hall had been used as a theatre space from the end of 1912 and various groups mounted theatrical and other performances there.[53] In September of 1915, for example, the Irish Women Workers' Union announced that '"Spreading the News," that favourite farce by Lady Gregory, will be performed, and will be followed by a high class Concert, New Songs in Irish and English will be heard, and we promise our Friends a Good programme.'[54] Early in 1916, the main hall itself was set up so that it could serve as a theatre, and Connolly officially opened the new facility on 20 February. The *Workers' Republic*, in announcing the inauguration of the new space, hailed it as 'Next to the Revolution the Greatest Event of 1916'.[55]

From February to March, regular performances were offered at the new theatre by the Irish Workers' Dramatic Company. At the end of March, a new play was advertised for the 26th, with the title *Under Which Flag?* It had been written by Connolly himself.[56] Connolly was a lifelong versifier and his biographer, Samuel Levenson, has observed of his poetry that 'he was addicted to the Victorian device of turning prose into poetry by reversing the usual word order; his idea of poetry was nothing more than rhymed exhortation to combat', and he likewise dismisses Connolly's dramatic output, concluding that 'his ignorance of the playwright's craft was as complete as that of the poet's'.[57] The judgement is a touch harsh: Connolly's poetry is no better or worse than the efforts of predecessor radical autodidacts such as Cooper (whose 9,000-stanza *Purgatory of Suicides* was published in 1845). *Under Which Flag?* has a certain real dramatic vigour and

---

[53] In this sense, Liberty Hall offers an odd parallel to the Shakespeare Hut set up in London during the First World War, where troops returning from the front were provided with theatrical entertainments – see Gordon McMullan's, Philip Mead's and Ailsa Grant Ferguson's chapters in the present volume.

[54] *Workers' Republic*, Vol. 1, no. 17, 18 September 1915, 8. Hereafter, *Workers' Republic* is given as WR.

[55] WR, Vol. 1, no. 39, 19 February 1916, 4.

[56] See WR, Vol. 1, no. 44, 25 March 1916, 7.

[57] Levenson, *Connolly: A Biography*, 106.

conviction to it, and Connolly demonstrates, in fact, quite a good ear for the nuances of everyday speech. The journalist and activist Francis Sheehy-Skeffington praised the play in a review in the *Workers' Republic*, observing that 'The dialogue is excellent, – entirely unforced, and in harmony with the characters depicted.' Ironically, the one aspect of the play that Sheehy-Skeffington disliked was the element that is most Shakespearean: Connolly's persistent use of soliloquy. Sheehy-Skeffington found this to be 'dramatically inartistic', though noting slyly, with a nod to '*unser* Shakespeare', that Connolly could 'plead the example of a great English Dramatist who is more honoured in Germany than in his own country'.[58]

As James Moran has indicated, Connolly set his play in close dialogue with Yeats' *Cathleen ni Houlihan*, which had first been performed in 1902, with Maud Gonne taking the title role.[59] Yeats' play quickly became a staple of the nationalist theatre. *Cathleen*'s simple plot offers a central character, Michael Gillane, who opts to reject domestic contentment and prosperity in favour of following Cathleen – an emblematic figure for Ireland – into battle in the 1798 United Irish uprising. In the process, he effectively turns his back on his fiancée, Delia Cahel. Connolly shifts the setting to March 1867 and the eve of the abortive Fenian uprising – a moment seen as foundational for the militant separatism of Connolly's own period. As with Yeats' play, *Under Which Flag?* is framed around a choice. In this instance, however, it is not the domestic that serves as a competing attraction to militant activism. In Connolly's play, the central couple are Frank O'Donnell and Mary O'Neill.[60] Both are politically naïve, but O'Neill is brought to embrace a nationalist standpoint by a neighbour, Dan McMahon, who has lost his sight in an earlier separatist campaign and who serves as a kind of symbolic 'seer' in the play. O'Donnell's naïveté is figured as a decision to join the British army, with high expectations of what this will mean for his future: 'I will see the world, be well taken care of, and after my time is done, retire on a pension, and come home

---

[58] F. S. S. [Francis Sheehy-Skeffington], '"Under Which Flag?": James Connolly's Patriotic Play', *WR*, Vol. 1, No. 46, 8 April 1916, 6.

[59] Moran, 'Introduction' to *Four Irish Rebel Plays*, 16–18.

[60] There is a historical resonance to the names here. In the early modern period, Ulster was a stronghold of native Irish power and the two most important family-based leadership groups were the O'Neills and the O'Donnells.

and spend my days in Ireland.'[61] In a significant revision of Yeats' narrative, it is O'Neill who compels her beloved to re-evaluate his position, so that his choice becomes a matter of whether he will fight for the British, under the Union flag, or for his own people under the Irish flag. Prompted by O'Neill, O'Donnell reverses his decision to join the British army and, as at the end of Yeats' play, he exits at the conclusion of the drama to join the other militants. O'Neill turns to McMahon and observes 'Now, Dan, the boys are *all* gone – and my boy with them.'[62]

Connolly's play was intricately bound in with the Rising itself in a way which illustrates very clearly the extent to which theatre and political action became, in a way, fused virtually to the point of indistinguishability in Ireland at the time. The issue of the *Workers' Republic* which carried Sheehy-Skeffington's review of *Under Which Flag?* included an announcement that 'The Council of the Irish Citizen Army has resolved after grave and earnest deliberation, to hoist the Green Flag of Ireland over Liberty Hall, as over a Fortress held for Ireland by the arms of Irishmen.'[63] The flag-raising ceremony was arranged for the afternoon of Sunday 16 April – Palm Sunday – and a second performance of Connolly's play was organised for that evening.[64] In the afternoon, the Irish Citizen Army (ICA) – the socialist separatist volunteer force, commanded by Connolly – mustered outside Liberty Hall. In his history of the ICA, R. M. Fox quotes a member of the Colour Guard present on the occasion: 'I noticed ... that some men, old and middle-aged, and a great number of women were crying, and I knew then that all this was not in vain and that they all realised what was meant by the hoisting of the flag.'[65] Fox himself characterises the flag-raising ceremony as 'the prologue to the play'.[66] He intends the phrase metaphorically, of course. But in a more literal sense the flag ceremony was also folded into an actual theatrical epilogue. In the performance of *Under Which Flag?* on the evening of the flag-raising ceremony, Seán Connolly (no relation to James Connolly), the Abbey

---

[61] James Connolly, *Under Which Flag?* in Moran (ed.), *Four Irish Rebel Plays*, 113.

[62] *Ibid.*, 129.   [63] WR, Vol. 1, No. 46, 8 April 1916, 1.

[64] Donal Nevin, *James Connolly: A Full Life* (Dublin: Gill & Macmillan, 2005), 625.

[65] Fox, *History of the Irish Citizen Army*, 127.   [66] *Ibid.*, 129.

actor who played the part of Dan McMahon, flourished the same flag from earlier in the day on the Liberty Hall stage, declaring, 'Under this flag only will I serve. Under this flag, if need be, will I die', the title of the play now effectively becoming literalised.[67]

The Rising as it unfolded continued to be overlaid with theatrical connections and consciously conceived elements of theatricality. During the course of the week leading up to Easter, Kathleen Lynn, an ICA medic, drove to Pearse's school, where volunteers 'loaded [the car] up with ammunition and put some theatrical stuff on top of it' to disguise the weaponry for the journey back across the city to Liberty Hall.[68] On Easter Saturday evening Constance Markievicz, a senior member of the ICA – who had, some years earlier, acted opposite Seán Connolly in the patriotic melodrama *The Memory of the Dead: A Romantic Drama of '98*, written by her husband Casimir – was busy with military preparations when a friend visited her at Liberty Hall. Assuming that the business in hand was theatrical, the friend commented 'Rehearsing, I suppose', before enquiring of the imagined play: 'Is it for children?' With a dry sense of irony, Markievicz responded 'No, it's for grown-ups.'[69]

Seán Connolly was also a member of the ICA and, on Easter Sunday night, he was told that in the morning he was to be given command of a group of Volunteers tasked with attacking Dublin Castle, the centre of British authority in Ireland. He embraced the assignment enthusiastically, telling a colleague 'I have been given a dandy job!'[70] Included in Connolly's small force was Helena Molony, Honorary Secretary of Inghiníde na hÉireann ('The Daughters of Ireland'), a militant nationalist women's group, founded by Maud Gonne. Molony had taken part in several dramatic performances staged by the group, including playing the part of Delia Cahill in a production of Yeats' *Cathleen ni*

[67] See Levenson, *Connolly: A Biography*, 625.
[68] Kathleen Lynn, Witness Statement 357, File no. S.166, 2, Bureau of Military History, Republic of Ireland; the insurrectionists had been manufacturing ammunitions (including primitive hand grenades) at St Enda's – see Eamonn Bulfin, Witness Statement 497, File no. S.1088, 2–3. Both documents available at: http://www.bureauofmilitaryhistory.ie/. Further documents from this archive are referenced by statement and file numbers only. All documents accessed 5 May 2014. Heartfelt thanks to Vanessa Gildea for pointing me in the direction of this material – and for discussing the general context of the Rising with me.
[69] Levenson, *Connolly: A Biography*, 294.   [70] Fox, *Irish Citizen Army*, 141.

Houlihan, and subsequently joining the Abbey company itself, where she had acted opposite Seán Connolly.[71]

As the leader of his small force, Connolly 'headed the march to the Castle, demanded admittance, and[,] when the policeman on duty slammed the gate to[,] shot him dead', thus inflicting the first casualty of the Rising.[72] Because the Castle complex was considered too difficult to defend with the severely limited number of insurgents available, Connolly's group retired to occupy positions in a series of nearby buildings, including City Hall. Connolly was wounded in the arm early in proceedings, but he made light of it, telling his younger brother (a fellow volunteer and a member of the City Hall group) that 'it was only a revolver shot and would be alright soon'.[73] A little while later, he ventured out on to the roof of the Hall, intending to raise the Irish flag there, quite possibly the same flag that he had, a little more than a week previously, flourished on stage at the end of James Connolly's play.[74] A sniper positioned in the clock tower of the Castle fired at him, killing him instantly.[75] Kathleen Lynn pronounced him dead and Helena Molony whispered a prayer in his ear, observing later: 'We were all very distressed at [his] death, I particularly, as I had known him for so long and acted with him.'[76] With a grimly neat symmetry, having inflicted the first casualty of

---

[71] See Helena Molony, W.S.391, File no. S.164, under the section heading 'Introduction to a Stage Career' (6ff) and *passim*. On theatrical performances staged by Inghiníde na hÉireann, see Mary Trotter, *Ireland's Theaters: Political Performance and the Origins of the Irish Dramatic Movement* (Syracuse University Press, 2001), chapter 3.

[72] Desmond Ryan, *The Rising: The Complete Story of Easter Week* (Dublin: Golden Eagle, [1949]), 117.

[73] Matthew Connolly, W.S.1746, File no. S.3045, 7.

[74] I say 'quite possibly' because there's an element of confusion in relation to the flag. Pearse's fellow militants adopted the green, white and orange tricolour (now the national flag of the Republic of Ireland). The Citizen Army, however, favoured a green flag, emblazoned with a harp without the surmounted crown that formed part of the official government insignia. Desmond Ryan, in *Rising*, indicates that this was the flag raised over Liberty Hall (76) and that what Connolly was attempting to raise over City Hall was a tricolour (119). Others, however, have suggested that the same flag was used in both instances (see, for example, Ritschel, '*Under Which Flag*, 1916', 67; Moran, 'Introduction', 123).

[75] See Fox, *Irish Citizen Army*, 150.

[76] Molony, 'Introduction to a Stage Career', 37.

the Rising on the British side, Connolly became himself the first casualty on the Irish side.[77]

Daniel Corkery nicely described the participants in the Rising as a 'league of bookworms and students at whom the politicians were wont to jeer'.[78] It might be as accurate to say that it was an uprising carried forward by a league of playwrights and actors, most of them heavily under the dramatic sway of Shakespeare. But the Rising can also be said to have been itself a kind of theatrical event – as Fox indicates in styling the Palm Sunday flag-raising ceremony as the prologue to a play. Connolly and Pearse both knew that they had no prospect of success and that their actions largely constituted a symbolic perform-ance.[79] As he left Liberty Hall on Easter Monday morning Connolly commented to a colleague, William O'Brien: 'We are going out to be slaughtered.' 'Is there no chance of success?' O'Brien asked. 'None whatever,' Connolly is said to have replied.[80] Likewise, on the same morning, as Seán Connolly was about to depart for Dublin Castle, James Connolly shook his hand and said 'Good luck, Seán.

---

[77] Yeats would later memorialise Seán Connolly in 'Three Songs to the One Burden':

> Who was the first man shot that day?
> The player Connolly,
> Close to the City Hall he died;
> Carriage and voice had he;
> He lacked those years that go with skill
> But later might have been
> A famous, brilliant figure
> Before the painted scene.

In Finneran (ed.), *Collected Poems*, 330.

[78] Daniel Corkery, *Synge and Anglo-Irish Literature* (Cork: Mercier, 1966; first published 1931), 50. In the wake of the executions of the central participants following the rising, the *Leader* newspaper, published in Dublin, observed: 'Anyone who would suggest a few years ago that P. H. Pearse, Thomas MacDonagh, and Joseph Plunkett, all men of considerable literary ability and intellectual powers, would be in the van of a revolution would be laughed at as crazy'. *The Leader*, vol. 32, no. 15, 20 May 1916, 296.

[79] The loss of the arms shipment on board the *Aud* (see note 10 above) was decisive. But even if the arms had been landed, it is unlikely that the Rising would have been a success, given the relatively small number of Volunteers fully committed to armed action. Conflicts within the leadership also meant that there was considerable confusion as to whether the Rising was going ahead or not.

[80] Levenson, *Connolly: A Biography*, 297.

We won't meet again.'[81] Pearse too knew that the action would be futile, militarily. Possessed by a form of what Joost Augusteijn has very usefully termed 'messianic nationalism', he clearly regarded the symbolism of the occasion as its dominant power.[82] A proponent at times of a crude blood and soil ideology, Pearse (in)famously had written in 1913 that 'bloodshed is a cleansing and a sanctifying thing, and the nation which regards it as the final horror has lost its manhood'.[83] Across the Irish Sea, the organisers of the Shakespeare tercentenary celebrations in London were keen to avoid even the faintest suggestion of blasphemy in celebrating Shakespeare on Easter Sunday, Shakespeare's birth/death day coinciding exactly, of course, with Easter in 1916.[84] By contrast, Pearse, a devout Catholic, leaned heavily precisely on the symbolism of blood sacrifice and renewal suggested by the launching of the Rising on the day immediately following Easter Sunday. Indeed, the very word 'rising' itself has a double potency in this context.

We have already seen the way in which Pearse invoked Christian mythology to serve a nationalist agenda in *The Master*. This invocation is even more pointed in his final play, *The Singer*. Pearse originally intended that the St Enda's boys should perform the drama in the week leading up to the Rising, but appears to have changed his mind, fearing that its politically explicit theme might be picked up by British intelligence sources.[85] The principal character in the play is MacDara, 'the Singer', who has been exiled from his home village because the 'songs he was making ... were setting the people's hearts on fire' with opposition to those in power. (Perhaps we hear something of an echo here of the anecdotal story of Shakespeare being banished from Stratford by Sir Thomas Lucy.) He returns to his home at a time of political unrest and takes upon himself the task of facing the enemy unarmed and

---

[81] Nevin, *Connolly: A Full Life* , 638.

[82] Augusteijn, *Making of Revolutionary*, 321.

[83] Patrick Pearse, 'The Coming Revolution', included in *The Coming Revolution: The Political Writings and Speeches of Patrick Pearse* (Cork: Mercier, 2012), 84.

[84] The Dean of Westminster, Herbert Ryle, wrote to the London *Times* specifically to make clear that there were no plans to commemorate Shakespeare at the Abbey on Easter Sunday: 'A statement in your columns on January 29 has unfortunately produced the impression that the Dean and Chapter of Westminster Abbey intend to commemorate Shakespeare on Easter Sunday, April 23. I need hardly say that we have no such intention.' *Times*, 29 February 1916, 7.

[85] See James Moran, *Staging the Easter Rising: 1916 as Theatre* (Cork University Press, 2005), 36–7, n. 31.

unprotected, declaring: 'One man can free a people as one Man redeemed the world. I will take no pike. I will go into the battle with bare hands. I will stand up before the Gall as Christ hung naked before men on the tree!'[86] It is a symbolic gesture which gambles certain immediate failure against longer term triumph: precisely the wager that Pearse made in launching the Rising itself.

* * *

The Rising lasted less than a week in the end. On the Thursday, the *Irish Times* reprinted the text of the 'Regulations to be observed under Martial Law', observing that by 'keeping these regulations with religious strictness we shall help the State, and we shall be doing a very valuable service to ourselves'. Under the terms of Martial Law, a curfew was imposed every evening, commencing at 7.30 p.m. The *Times* offered suggestions for how to fill the hours of confinement. The householder

might put his little garden into a state of decency that will hold promise of beauty. He can do some useful mending and painting about the house. Best of all, perhaps, he can acquire, or reacquire, the art of reading – that is to say, the study, with an active and receptive mind, of what the great writers of the past have said nobly and for all time. How many citizens of Dublin have any real knowledge of the works of Shakespeare? Could any better occasion for reading them be afforded than the coincidence of enforced domesticity with the poet's tercentenary?[87]

The question 'How many citizens of Dublin have any real knowledge of the works of Shakespeare?' might well, as we have seen, have been answered in a way that would probably have discomfited the editorial staff of the Dublin newspaper, the barbarians at the gates having proved themselves to be much better read than the *Irish Times* and its core constituency might have expected. But, in any event, the process of re-assimilating Shakespeare to the cosy certainties of imperial Dublin continued blithely in the weeks that followed, just as the clearing up of the debris left by the Rising got underway. In July, the Royal Hibernian Military School mounted a Shakespeare Festival. The programme patriotically included 'a pageant depicting the battle

---

[86] *The Singer* in *Collected Plays*, ed. Ní Ghairbhí and McNulty, 228.
[87] 'Martial Law', *IT*, 27 April 1916, 2.

of Agincourt'. The intention was that the performances should be held
in the grounds, 'but the weather partially upset the arrangements',
forcing the performers and spectators into the school's gymnasium,
where matters proceeded in a space 'devoid of theatrical trappings, and
simply with the Union Jack as a background'.[88] In the same month, the
British Empire Shakespeare Society was fully back in business, staging
an outdoor performance of *A Midsummer Night's Dream* at Lord
Iveagh's Gardens, near Stephen's Green.[89]

To regular readers of the *Irish Times*, it must have felt as if their
world was slowly righting itself after the turbulence of Easter week.
But, as James Moran has noted, the Rising very quickly generated its
own commemorative culture, becoming the subject of endless 'provincial memorial ceremonies, popular ballads, decorative tea towels, novelty mugs, and a bewildering array of other flotsam and jetsam' – and
all of this served, of course, in the immediate term, to maintain separatist momentum through to the Anglo-Irish war, and onward to the
founding of the independent state.[90] Contemplating this memorialising
activity, one might be reminded of the emergence of what Barbara
Hodgdon has styled 'the Shakespeare trade', particularly in Stratford-
upon-Avon in the wake of the act of national cultural memory that was
the 1864 Tercentenary.[91] That Tercentenary – particularly noted for its
own tide of 'decorative tea towels, novelty mugs, and … bewildering
array of other flotsam and jetsam' – served as a key stimulus to Shakespeare's rising centrality in the cultural field of Victorian Britain. Militant
Irish nationalists, for all their rejection of other aspects of British culture
and identity, were, as we have seen, heavily drawn to the cultural force of
a Shakespeare thereby elevated to the position of supreme – and, indeed,
effectively supranational – playwright. Ultimately, of course, they refash-
ioned Shakespeare, drawing on his work – and on the power of theatre
more generally – to stage actual plays of their own and also a public
spectacle of political resistance.[92] In their turn, these separatists – and

---

[88] 'Royal Hibernian Military School', *IT*, 3 July 1916, 7.
[89] For a review of the performance, see *IT*, 8 July 1916, 5.
[90] Moran, *Staging*, 3.
[91] Barbara Hodgdon, *The Shakespeare Trade: Performances and Appropriations* (Philadelphia: University of Pennsylvania Press, 1998).
[92] Just as Irish militants appropriated Shakespeare for nationalist ends, so some of the performers at the Shakespeare Hut in London brought a subtle suffragist mindset to their presentations at the facility – see Ailsa Grant Ferguson's chapter in the present volume.

their staged event – entered into national cultural memory, serving as an immediate spur to further militant action, but also persisting as a force in the Irish imaginary as the Rising entered Irish national(ist) mythology, serving, emotionally and psychologically, as the origin myth of the modern state. Commemoration and cultural memory intertwine in complex ways throughout this whole extended process. The mythologised Rising, theatricalised in its own historical moment, shadows the Tercentenary of the death of a Shakespeare seen as the supreme playwright, whose emergence *as* the supreme playwright is partly indebted to the cultural constructions effected during an earlier commemorative moment: the 1864 Tercentenary, which, in its turn, had been politicised by radical activists who appropriated Shakespeare for their own ends. The process presents, finally, something like an effect of cultural and political infinite regress.

In a nice observation, W. I. Thompson has noted that 'before Pearse fired a shot he rehearsed insurrection by writing a play about it' and, indeed, the remark might be extended to take in many of the other central participants in the Rising.[93] Reviewing the history of this theatrically saturated insurgency, led by an intellectual faction deeply indebted to Shakespeare, we can surely say that, for these Irish revolutionaries, the play was indeed very much the thing.

[93] W. I. Thompson, *The Imagination of an Insurrection* (New York: Oxford University Press, 1967), 118.

9 | Goblin's market: commemoration, anti-semitism and the invention of 'global Shakespeare' in 1916

GORDON MCMULLAN

Sir Israel Gollancz: medievalist, Shakespearean, professor of English at King's College London, editor of the *Temple Shakespeare*, founding member of the British Academy, director of the Early English Text Society, creator of both the Cervantes Chair in Spanish and the Camões Chair in Portuguese at the University of London, Honorary Secretary of the London Shakespeare League, the Shakespeare Tercentenary Committee and the Shakespeare Memorial National Theatre Committee – and 'Goblin' to his friends (to one of them, anyway: there is a letter in the Gollancz archive at Princeton written by his old university friend William Rouse on the occasion of his knighthood. 'Congratulations', he writes, 'on becoming Sir Goblin, + kind remembrance to Lady Goblin').[1] Gollancz was a quietly ubiquitous figure in the English culture of literary memorialisation during the first quarter of the twentieth century, an energetic initiator of ideas, sponsor of new institutions and negotiator of cultural capital, in so many ways the driving force of a commemorative process that led directly, if belatedly, to the building of the National Theatre in London. Yet, despite his lifelong engagement with what Ton Hoenselaars and Clara Calvo have called 'the cultures of commemoration', Gollancz's own memorialisation has been less than glowing.[2] For Geoffrey Whitworth, in his history of the National Theatre, Gollancz is a sort of proto-George

I am grateful to the Australian Research Council for providing the 'Discovery' grant that made this work possible, to my collaborator Philip Mead (Principal Investigator for the project) and to Ailsa Grant Ferguson, research associate for the project (2009–13), for her invaluable work in the Princeton, National Theatre and other archives.

[1] Sir Israel Gollancz correspondence, Special Collections, Princeton University Library, Series 1: Correspondence, 1890–1948, Box 3, letter from William Henry Denham Rouse to Gollancz, 29/4/1919.

[2] Ton Hoenselaars and Clara Calvo, 'Introduction: Shakespeare and the Cultures of Commemoration', *Critical Survey* 22 (2010), 1–10.

Smiley figure: 'Behind [the] kaleidoscopic maze of committees', reports Whitworth, 'flitting to and fro, one glimpses the mercurial figure of Israel Gollancz ... benign, discreet, master of innocent intrigue ... with every thread in his hands, and alone capable of unravelling the tangled skein when the right moment came'.[3] (I will come back to Whitworth's phrasing later.) Less flatteringly, Gollancz is, for Jonathan Bate, little more than a propagandist with 'an exalted sense of duty'.[4] He quotes Gollancz's paean to Shakespeare:

While all the world acclaims him, those who are privileged to be his fellow-countrymen owe to themselves the high duty of gratefully recalling, on this occasion of the Tercentenary of his death, some of the lessons he has left us, and, especially at the present time, how it behoves us as patriots to strive to play our part in war as in peace, and how best to maintain our faith in the ultimate triumph of a noble humanity.[5]

– and he notes that Gollancz

had a predictable taste in Shakespeare ... includ[ing] 'the never-to-be-forgotten words' which close *King John* ('This England never did, nor never shall, / Lie at the proud foot of a conqueror, / But when it first did help to wound itself'), the 'imperishable' praise of England from the lips of the dying John of Gaunt, and ... the Crispin's day oration from *Henry V*, the play in which 'Shakespeare gives us, in the person of the King, his ideal Patriot-Englishman'.[6]

Gollancz, then: the embarrassing patriot, the cliché-monger. A figure to forget. And it seems he was indeed quickly forgotten even as he was remembered: when J. R. R. Tolkien gave the Gollancz Memorial Lecture at the British Academy in 1936, he seems not to have bothered to acknowledge the fellow medievalist in whose name he was speaking.[7]

I want, in response, to rethink Gollancz's role in the memorialisation of Shakespeare at the time of the 1916 Tercentenary and thus in the ongoing phenomenon that is the national and international negotiation of the anniversaries of the canonical writers of the English literary

---

[3] Geoffrey Whitworth, *The Making of a National Theatre* (London: Faber, 1951), 44.
[4] Jonathan Bate, 'Shakespeare Nationalised, Shakespeare Privatised', *English* 42 (1993), 1–18 (4).
[5] Bate, 'Shakespeare Nationalised', 5–6.   [6] 'Bate, Shakespeare Nationalised', 6.
[7] J. R. R. Tolkien, '*Beowulf*: The Monsters and the Critics', Sir Israel Gollancz Memorial Lecture, British Academy, 1936, *Proceedings of the British Academy*, vol. 22 (London: Oxford University Press, 1937).

tradition, and I wish to argue that Gollancz's impact was more progressive and culturally complex than has been recognised. Focussing
on the reworking of the rhetoric of imperialism as cosmopolitanism or
globalism, I wish to consider the relationship between Gollancz's
commemorative entrepreneurship, his central place in the tercentenary
process, his complex identity as England's first Jewish professor of
English literature, and his place in the emergence of what has become
known as 'global Shakespeare'.

Why should we care about Gollancz? In part, because of his role
in locating Shakespeare at the heart of negotiations over national
identity in a period that marks the pivot of the imperial and the
postcolonial, one savagely foregrounded by the geographical spread
of the First World War. After all, the Shakespeare Tercentenary of
April and May 1916 took place in the same brief period as the Battle
of Verdun, the introduction of conscription and the Easter Rising
in Dublin, and just a few months before the Battle of the Somme, and
it fell almost exactly a year after the catastrophic Gallipoli campaign
and the birth of the Anzac story. Shakespeare is a defining distraction
at this historical moment, and Gollancz's sheer perseverance in making
this so deserves to be recognised and his underpinning premises
vindicated.

What were Gollancz's achievements? They were substantive, despite
circumstances of near-endless delay and deferral. The story of the
SMNT – the Shakespeare Memorial National Theatre committee, with
its urge to create a national theatre in Shakespeare's name – is one of
aspiration and, at least locally, failure: decades of wishful thinking
hardly ever matched by actual fundraising; tensions between those
who wanted to build a monument and those who argued for the
creation of a theatre. Yet tangibles did emerge – not only (eventually)
an actual National Theatre but also (more immediately) the
Shakespeare Hut, an extraordinary, oblique improvisation by Gollancz in the middle of the war. His committee had acquired a site in
Bloomsbury for the theatre they wished to build, and the question was
how best to use it, in Shakespeare's name, in time of war. They
addressed this by offering the site to the YMCA for that organisation's
programme of temporary buildings for troops, both at home and
overseas. The Shakespeare Hut was the result – temporary respite
accommodation for overseas troops too far from home to return when
on leave, designed to keep the soldiers away from London's less

wholesome opportunities. 'Hut' is a misleading word: this was a fairly substantial building with a solid brick chimney stack, which included dormitories, a restaurant, a lounge and – notably – a theatre or concert hall in which many of the leading Shakespeareans of the day performed exclusively for the soldiers.[8] The Hut is proof, if it is needed, of Gollancz's entrepreneurial ability and flexibility and his willingness to forge unlikely alliances. He had already moved seamlessly from his role as Hon. Sec. of the Memorial Committee (i.e. those who wanted to build a Shakespeare *monument*) to Hon. Sec. of the *Theatre* Committee, though membership of these camps had seemed mutually exclusive. The YMCA Hut offered both a form of Shakespearean commemoration with a theatrical element and a direct engagement with the war effort, providing accommodation primarily for the New Zealanders and, to a lesser extent, Australians, of the Anzac regiments in their lemon-squeezer and slouch hats, all invited to sit through performances of Shakespeare by famous actors they had mostly, presumably, never heard of.[9] The photographs are poignant, given that some may have been survivors of Gallipoli on their way to the Western Front – and there they were, because of Gollancz's ingenuity, sitting in the Hut's theatre watching improving scenes from Shakespeare.

A further, key achievement of Gollancz was to effect a shift in the geography of Shakespearean commemoration away from rural Stratford-upon-Avon and towards cosmopolitan London. Previous Shakespearean commemorations – Garrick's Jubilee of 1769, the Royal Gala of 1830, the 1864 Tercentenary and both the annual Birthday and

---

[8] On the Shakespeare Hut, see the following essays by Ailsa Grant Ferguson: 'Lady Forbes-Robertson's War Work: Gertrude Elliott and the Shakespeare Hut Performances, 1916–1919', in Gordon McMullan, Lena Cowen Orlin and Virginia Mason Vaughan (eds.), *Women Making Shakespeare: Text, Performance, Reception* (London: Bloomsbury Arden Shakespeare, 2014), 233–42; 'Entertaining the Anzacs: Performance for and by Australian and New Zealand Troops on Leave in London, 1916–1919', in Andrew Maunder (ed.), *British Theatre and the Great War* (London: Palgrave Macmillan, 2015), 234–50; and '"When Wasteful War Shall Statues Overturn": Forgetting the Shakespeare Hut', *Shakespeare* 10 (2014), 276–92.

[9] On the kinds of performance that took place at the Hut, see Ailsa Grant Ferguson's chapter in this volume; for the intersections of the Shakespeare Tercentenary and the emergence of the Anzac story, see Philip Mead's chapter in this volume.

Summer Festivals – had been held in Stratford, and the town would again play a leading role in the 1964 Quatercentenary of the birth. But between 1912 and 1916 London acquired the central role, not only because Stratford, as the locus of the revered Birthplace, tends to prefer 64s to 16s but also because of Gollancz's sheer perseverance. One of the early letters in the Princeton Gollancz archive is from the actor Johnston Forbes-Robertson (who later contributed to performances at the Hut). Writing of the proposed National Theatre and implicitly chiding Gollancz, Forbes-Robertson suggests that 'one of the governors of the Stratford-upon-Avon Memorial might be a governor', appearing to imply that Gollancz has ignored Stratford in his projected organisational structures for the National Theatre.[10] This seems to be not only because Gollancz lived and worked in London and thus had a vested interest in Shakespeare the urban Londoner rather than Shakespeare the rural Warwickshireman but also because of the 'world vision' he held for Shakespeare. Jonathan Bate is right to note the number of occasions when Gollancz's language is, to our eyes, embarrassingly patriotic; at the same time, this is by no means a consistent thread in Gollancz's communications, and certainly not in his private ones; in fact, it could be argued that Gollancz's official voice and private voice were quite far apart in this regard. Certainly, he never defended the Romantic vision of Shakespeare as the embodiment of English green space; on the contrary, his orientation was always outward, always centrifugal: Shakespeare and London as a combined access point to the world, and not only to the limited world of the British Empire.

This outward urge is at its most apparent, despite the constrictions of wartime publication, in *A Book of Homage to Shakespeare*, Gollancz's most immediate contribution to the tercentenary celebrations. The *Book of Homage* was, as Coppélia Kahn has noted, a remarkable volume:

a handsome folio bound in white leather and embossed with gold lettering and a version of Shakespeare's coat of arms with its motto, '*Non sanz droict.*' Its 557 pages contain 166 tributes to Shakespeare by scholars, novelists, poets, literati, and public figures from ... around the globe ... Tributes

---

[10] Sir Israel Gollancz correspondence, Special Collections, Princeton University Library, Series 1: Correspondence, 1890–1948, Box 1, letter from Johnston Forbes-Robertson to Gollancz, 21/12/1908.

written in twenty-three languages back up the idea of "a universal homage": in addition to the major European tongues (with the conspicuous omission, owing to the war, of German [– and, it should be added, Turkish]), one may read of Shakespeare in Chinese, Japanese, Armenian, Setswana, Hebrew, Sanskrit, Pali, Burmese, and Arabic.[11]

Kahn's is the key critical essay on the *Book of Homage* and on the complexities of imperial and English identity it expresses. 'On one level', she notes,

the originators of *Homage* would seem to have achieved their aim of creating a universal intellectual fraternity of those who know and love Shakespeare as the epitome of Englishness ... [T]he book effects the cultural performance of a community it presents as autochthonous, united under the sign of an 'English' Shakespeare. In this light, every tribute in a strange script or foreign language could be seen as a kind of imperial trophy, a sign of the successful interpellation of the colonial writer into the imagined community of Shakespeare's England.[12]

On another level, however, some contributors stand outside this inter-pellatory process, providing material for the *Homage* but declining to be part of its interpretative community. Kahn specifies the unnamed author (the only unnamed contributor in the volume) of 'A South African's Homage' (whom we now know to be Solomon Tshekisho Plaatje, an early African National Congress activist), the Burmese scholar Maung Tin, and the Irish contributor, and future president of the Irish Republic, Douglas Hyde. These contributors, Kahn argues, 'make Shakespeare their own, or make their own Shakespeare, employing him in a rearguard action on behalf of their own cultures in contradistinction to the Shakespeare who signifies England, empire, and Anglo-Saxon superiority for the British Academy'.[13] Kahn's essay has been important for subsequent work on the Tercentenary, and in picking up where she left off – quite literally so, in developing some of the possibilities in her final paragraph, where she notes Gollancz's complex identity as 'a hybrid in spades, and at the very core of the British intellectual establishment' – and in re-thinking some of her conclusions about Gollancz and the *Book of Homage*, I pay a little homage to her work too.[14] But I want, in reflecting on

---

[11] Coppélia Kahn, 'Remembering Shakespeare Imperially: The 1916 Tercentenary', *Shakespeare Quarterly* 52 (2001), 456–78, 457.
[12] Kahn, 'Remembering', 478.   [13] *Ibid.*   [14] *Ibid.*

certain aspects of Gollancz's relationship with the British Establishment, to read his attitude to Empire as other than has been assumed by critics to date.

Kahn, Bate and others are right to foreground the imperialist language Gollancz used in his quest for the SMNT. But the Gollancz story can be traced back further than this language seems to suggest, and it starts to be clear quite early on that his preferred language was that of the 'international', of the 'cosmopolitan'. Not that this should be especially surprising. He was, after all, of Polish heritage (the parts of Poland that have long been disputed with Germany); he was married to a German, Alide Goldschmidt; and one of his most significant relationships was his friendship with Frida Mond, a German-Jewish philanthropist whose many high-cultural sponsorships included the bequests that created the annual Gollancz Memorial lecture at the British Academy. (Mond may also have introduced Gollancz to Alide, who was the niece of one of her friends.) Many of Gollancz's social connections were German – German-Jewish, to be exact – and it seems to have pained him that the *Book of Homage* necessarily excluded German Shakespeareans, who, after all, had legitimate claim to be the leading promoters of Shakespeare's pre-eminence in literary history. The Deutsche Shakespeare-Gesellschaft (DSG) marked its 150th anniversary in 2014 as the oldest national Shakespeare association in the world, and it is apparent that Gollancz re-formed ties with the DSG as soon as the war ended. Remarkably, he spoke at the DSG's conference in Weimar in April 1919, just months after the end of hostilities – a gesture clearly appreciated by his German colleagues. There is a letter in the Princeton archive dated 29 April 1919 from Professor Alois Brandl, president of the DSG, lavish in its praise of Gollancz's recent assistance: 'Far have you travelled over land and sea in order to come to my help ... The Shakespeare Society and I thank you most warmly for all the trouble you have undergone on our behalf.'[15] Brandl's appreciation is underscored by the fact that he had given the Third Annual British Academy Shakespeare Lecture in 1913, presumably at Gollancz's invitation, and had stated in conclusion – poignantly, as it turned out – that he was looking forward to returning for the

---

[15] Sir Israel Gollancz correspondence, Special Collections, Princeton University Library, Series 1: Correspondence, 1890–1948, Box 1, letter from Alois Brandl to Gollancz, 29/4/19.

Tercentenary: '*Au revoir* till Shakespeare Day, in 1916!'[16] If Gollancz were the patriotic British jingo-monger he is claimed to be, it seems unlikely that he would have been quite so keen to work with German Shakespeareans so very soon after the end of the war and in such a public manner.

This connection offers a good instance of the differences in Gollancz's rhetoric from private occasions to public ones. A year later, in 1920, he wrote a foreword to a 'Shakespeare Day Festival Matinée at the New Theatre' in which he promotes the cause both of the Shakespeare Association he founded for the Tercentenary – one of whose aims is 'to further the appreciation of Shakespeare in the life of the nation and the English-speaking peoples, and in other countries' – and of the idea of a worldwide 'Shakespeare Day'.[17] 'The Shakespeare Day movement, which is being more and more recognised throughout the Empire and America', he notes, 'will, it is hoped … emphasize in the era of peace the common ideals for the welfare of humanity uniting English-speaking peoples.' And he adds that

> it has been urged from many quarters that an effort should be made to establish a Shakespeare Society for the advancement of Shakespearean studies and research and for the publication of investigations. Before the war the only available organ for publications of this kind was 'The German Shakespeare Society's Year-Book'. It is, perhaps, hardly necessary further to urge the claims of the Shakespeare Association, which hopes to satisfy the undoubted need in this respect.[18]

The jingoism of the phrasing here, the implication that if the Germans can do it surely the British must too, is tangibly different from Gollancz's private exchanges.

Gollancz looked beyond the empire to the whole world. Right back in 1906, in his Mansion House statement announcing the competition for the design of a Shakespeare Memorial, he had emphasised that

---

[16] Alois Brandl, *Shakespeare and Germany: The British Academy Third Annual Shakespeare Lecture* (London: Humphrey Milford for Oxford University Press, 1913), 15. I am grateful to Clara Calvo for pointing me to Brandl's comment: see Calvo, 'Fighting over Shakespeare: Commemorating the 1916 Tercentenary in Wartime', *Critical Survey* 24 (2012), 48–72 (54).

[17] Israel Gollancz, 'Foreword', *Shakespeare Day Festival Matinee at the New Theatre* (under the Auspices of the Shakespeare Association), Friday 23 April 1920 (London: George W. Jones, 1920).

[18] Gollancz, 'Foreword'.

what was sought was a 'movement' that 'will be truly international', 'for', as he added, 'there is good reason to believe that the various municipalities will readily join in what should ultimately prove to be world-wide commemoration', and he describes 'the movement' as 'an endeavour to link the world by the one common enthusiasm, ever-increasing, for the great World-Poet of modern times'.[19] Oddly, perhaps, he lists Venice, France and China as locations or nations especially keen on the memorial – places not marked in pink, as part of the British Empire, on any of Gollancz's maps. In his peroration, he claims that 'it may reasonably be expected that organisations will be formed throughout the world, "from China to Peru", to help the carrying out of the idea of a World Monument to Shakespeare', which 'should be an accomplished fact by the year 1916, the Tercentenary of the Poet's death, when there will assuredly be a universal Festival, commemorating the world's debt to the greatest of Englishmen' (3). And again, in 1911, in his 'Epilogue' to the *Souvenir* of the Shakespeare Memorial National Theatre Ball, he waxes lyrical about the world's Shakespeare: 'Transcending all divisions of race, nationality, and speech, so Shakespeare himself . . . links together all peoples of the world as the world-poet'.[20] It is this vision that Gollancz seeks to sustain five years later by way of the *Book of Homage*.

His efforts, however, have been a little misunderstood and certainly a little understated. Kahn describes the *Book of Homage* as the outcome of work by Lord Bryce and others on the Tercentenary Committee. 'A few weeks before Britain declared war on the Central Powers', she writes, 'a group of distinguished men met to plan a celebration of Shakespeare commemorating the three-hundredth anniversary of his death, two years in the future.'[21] 'They were convened', she continues, 'by Lord Bryce, president of the British Academy[, and they] gathered to create "some fitting memorial to symbolize the intellectual fraternity of mankind in the universal homage accorded to the genius of the

---

[19] Statement by 'Professor I. Gollancz, Hon. Sec. of the Memorial Committee, Mansion House, May 9th. 1906', 2. The emphatic 'truly' and 'good reason to' are added to the typescript in Gollancz's hand.

[20] Israel Gollancz, 'Epilogue', in Mrs George Cornwallis-West (ed.), *Souvenir of the Shakespeare Ball held at the Albert Hall, June 20, 1911, in Support of the Shakespeare Memorial Fund* (London: Shakespeare Ball Committee, [1912?]).

[21] Kahn, 'Remembering', 456. Subsequent page references to this article are given in parentheses in the text.

greatest Englishman"' (456). And she adds simply that 'the memorial they produced was a volume titled *A Book of Homage to Shakespeare*, edited by Sir Israel Gollancz' (456). Beginning by referring to the Committee members as 'the originators' (457) of the volume, she then transfers agency to the book itself in phrases such as 'by commemorating Shakespeare, the book aims …' (459) and '*Homage* insists on identifying Shakespeare with England…' (461). I would like to suggest that this attribution of agency first to committee and then, synecdochically, to object is something of a misrepresentation, since the *Homage* was to all intents and purposes Gollancz's own work. He may only have been 'Hon. Sec.' but, to use Whitworth's words, he seems to have held 'every thread in his hands'.

This tendency to disperse or objectify agency unintentionally echoes some less-than-generous contemporary writing about the Tercentenary process that foregrounds the composition of a Committee that seems to have been nominal at best. The best-known instance of this is G. K. Chesterton's mildly amusing poem 'The Shakespeare Memorial', which relates to the earlier committee set up in 1906 with the intention, as I have mentioned, of building a monument – an architect's drawing in the National Theatre archive makes it look like a cross between the Albert Memorial and the Scott Monument, with Shakespeare seated at its heart – and the committee membership seems to have been distinctly transient, as Chesterton implies:

> Lord Lilac thought it rather rotten
> That Shakespeare should be quite forgotten,
> And therefore got on a Committee
> With several chaps out of the City,
> And Shorter and Sir Herbert Tree,
> Lord Rothschild and Lord Rosebery,
> And F.C.G and Comyns Carr
> Two dukes and a dramatic star,
> Also a clergy man now dead;
> And while the vain world careless sped
> Unheeding the heroic name –
> The souls most fed with Shakespeare's flame
> Still sat unconquered in a ring,
> Remembering him like anything.
> Lord Lilac did not long remain,
> Lord Lilac did not come again.

He softly lit a cigarette
And sought some other social set...[22]

This particular committee was not, it seems, brimful with commemorative agency.

A far less savoury account of the Tercentenary Committee – the later, wartime committee, that is – can be found in thirty-three lines of handwriting, now at the Folger, graced with the title 'Shakespeare's Tercentenary: A Masque', by Lord Alfred Douglas ('Bosie'), best known as Oscar Wilde's former lover, whose venom ranges far and wide. In his brief satire, he imagines a 'vast theatre packed with people' where 'Mr. Robert Ross, Sir George Lewis and Sir F. E. Smith occupy the Royal Box'. This is a resonant, if unlikely, conjunction of individuals. Ross, who had preceded Douglas as Wilde's lover, later became his literary executor, and was harried fiercely by Douglas until his death in 1918, was mentor to a group of gay or bisexual war poets such as Siegfried Sassoon and Wilfred Owen; Sir George Lewis was a lawyer and patron of the arts who, like Gollancz, was Jewish and had a German wife; F. E. Smith, Lord Birkenhead, was a lawyer and Conservative politician in Asquith's wartime government with no known Shakespearean interests. It is, in sum, a fictional list – not least because Lewis had died in 1911 – a sense reinforced when Douglas proceeds to describe the imaginary occasion:

The curtain / Rises and reveals the Shakespeare Tercentenary Committee / Consisting of a few gentlemen with German-Jewish names, headed / By Mr. Asquith (the President) who carries a large laurel wreath, / Lord Plymouth, Sir George Alexander and Mr. Mackail. The /Committee is grouped around a colossal paper mâché statue of / Shakespeare.

By this point the focus of the Tercentenary Committee had in fact long turned away from a monument and towards a theatre, Douglas's *papier mâché* Shakespeare notwithstanding. Then: 'Sennet: Enter Prologue, who speaks as follows', and the 'text' of the 'masque' begins:

This is great Shakespeare's tercentenary,
And consequently lo! The German Jew
(As is most meet) supported by a few

---

[22] G. K. Chesterton, 'The Shakespeare Memorial', in George J. Marlin, Richard P. Rabatin and John L. Swan (eds.), *G. K. Chesterton: The Collected Works*, vol. X: *Collected Poetry, Part 1* (San Francisco, CA: Ignatius, 1994), 519.

Distinguished gentlemen. They needs must be
Culled from the Ross-admiring galaxy
Who lately gave to that sweet soul his due…

He continues with more swipes at the people he calls 'Rossites', finishing with a flourish as Asquith, 'interposing', says

> Wait a bit, what fun
> Lets give the wreath instead to Oscar Wilde.

(Loud applause from the Royal Box. Mr. Asquith / thereupon hands the / Wreath to Oscar Wilde's "literary executor" Mr. Robert Ross, who / returns thanks in a voice choked with emotion. Frantic cheers from the / audience (I don't think)–Curtain. …).

Douglas was a notorious Jew-hater who in 1920 founded an anti-semitic journal, *Plain English*, and maintained belief in the claims of the *Protocols of the Elders of Zion* even after it was exposed as a forgery – and, unedifying as his 'satire' is, it is nonetheless helpful in demonstrating at least one establishment view of Gollancz, as a 'gentleman with [a] German-Jewish name' or, more simply, as 'The German Jew', underlining the anti-semitism with which Gollancz had to contend even as he worked assiduously to promote the primary cultural icon of the Anglo-Saxon world.

Douglas's unpleasant 'masque' requires us to review Gollancz's role as editor, originator and promoter not only of the *Homage* but of the tercentenary celebrations in general and to consider the *Homage* not as the collective endeavour of Bryce's committee but as Gollancz's own creation – all the evidence of the Folger *Homage* archive and of the correspondence suggests that he was sole commissioning editor – and to see what difference this adjustment of perspective makes.[23] This might logically prompt us to look at Gollancz's own contribution to the *Book of Homage* – so it is odd that nobody to date has done so, given that there have been several studies of the *Homage* since Kahn's. Not least among these is Andrew Murphy's engaging account of the inclusion in the volume of Douglas Hyde's poem in Gaelic and Gollancz's embarrassed censorship of adjectives in the English translation of a passage describing England – 'Albion' – as 'deceitful sinful guileful / Hypocritical destructive lying slippery' (all a little awkward

---

[23] See, e.g., Folger MS W.a. 79 and Y.d. 85 for the Gollancz–Hyde correspondence.

for the projected readership in wartime and – though of course Gollancz wasn't yet to know this – at the moment of the Easter Rising).[24]
Murphy makes the usual critical assumption that Gollancz sought to
create a thoroughly patriotic English collection. Commenting on Gollancz's request of the Irish writer George Russell that he offer something for the *Homage* – a request that was declined – he simply notes
that Russell 'was a somewhat unusual choice, but Gollancz was casting
his net pretty wide'.[25] Again, of Gollancz's request to Hyde, Murphy
notes that 'in some respects Hyde seems rather an odd person for
Gollancz to have approached in connection with the book', given his
'prominent public role … as founder and President of the Gaelic
League, established to promote the Irish language and native Irish
culture more generally', the programme for which, 'as summarised in
the title of a speech delivered [by Hyde] at the National Literary
Society in Dublin in 1892', was 'The Necessity for De-Anglicising
Ireland'.[26] It is possible, however, to view these choices differently, as
something other than anomalous.

Kahn's analysis of the *Homage* glances at the acentric contributions
of Israel Zangwill, author of *Children of the Ghetto* and *The Melting
Pot*, of Tin and Plaatje and Hyde – but no critic has looked to date
at the contribution of Gollancz himself. Certainly, at first glance,
the article is not promising. 'Bits of Timber', it is called, 'Some Observations on Shakespearian Names – "Shylock", "Polonius", "Malvolio"'. Surely if you were editing a vast *Homage to Shakespeare* and you
had delivered major speeches about Shakespeare and Empire, you
would aim to wax lyrical about the role of the Bard as national
landmark and address the three hundred years of increasing fame since
the playwright's death – especially if, in Bate's words, you 'had a
predictable taste in Shakespeare'. Yet instead it is the apparently bath-
etic 'Bits of Timber', focussing on plays quite other than the 'patriotic'
King John, *Richard II* or *Henry V*. A failure of nerve, perhaps? Closer
inspection suggests another possibility.

---

[24] Andrew Murphy, 'Bhíos ag Stratford ar an abhainn: Shakespeare, Douglas
Hyde, 1916', in Janet Clare and Stephen O'Neill (eds.), *Shakespeare and the Irish
Writer* (Dublin: University College Dublin Press, 2010), 51–63. On the
interrelations of the Shakespeare Tercentenary and the Easter Rising, see
Murphy's chapter in this volume.
[25] Murphy, 'Bhios', 2.   [26] Murphy, 'Bhios', 4.

Gollancz begins his brief essay with an account of *The Merchant of Venice*, tracing the possible origins of the names of Shylock and Antonio to the book that, he claims, 'was read by Elizabethans for everything relating to the later Jewish history, and which went through edition after edition, [namely] Peter Morwyng's translation of the pseudo-Josephus, "A compendious and most marveylous History of the latter Times of the Jewes Commune Weale"'. Near the beginning of this volume, he notes, is a passage about a battle between Jews and Romans: '"They sent therefore ... *Schiloch the Babylonian* ... with a power of the common people... Within the town was a Roman cap-taine called *Antonius*, a valiant man, and a good warrior"', and he argues that 'this passage may well account for [the name] "Shylock"; and possibly also for "Antonio"'.[27] And he continues to gloss the name Shylock, opening up further possibilities. 'I am strongly inclined', he notes, 'to explain the use of the name as due to the quite erroneous association of "Shiloch" with "Shallach", the Biblical Hebrew for "cormorant", the bird that "swoops", or dives after its prey', and he adds that 'in Elizabethan England "cormorant" was an expressive synonym for "usurer"' (172). Thus Shakespeare, Gollancz argues, 'created almost a special English idiom for Shylock' and he 'evidently knew the peculiar force of the words "to bait fish withal", uttered by his Cormorant Usurer ... a legendary monstrosity fraught with all the greater possibilities inasmuch as at that time Jews were not yet permitted to reside in England, and there was still the popular prejudice' (172).

Gollancz insists that Shakespeare's intentions for Shylock were *not* to let him succumb to this 'popular prejudice' but rather to present him as a kind of tragic hero: 'Shakespeare's humanity and understanding saved Shylock from being the mere Cormorant-monster', he argues. 'Despised, maddened by the sense of wrong, obsessed by the fixed idea of claiming his due at all costs', Shylock 'has kinship with the type of tragic character best represented by Hieronimo, the wronged and demented father, who in *The Spanish Tragedy* madly achieves, at the cost of his very life, the vengeance on which he has set his whole jangled mind' (172). At which point, he abruptly moves on to *Hamlet* and a discussion of the origin of the name 'Polonius', so markedly

---

[27] Gollancz, *Homage*, 171. Subsequent page references are given in parentheses in the text.

changed from Q1's 'Corambis', noting the revised name's likely emergence from a recently translated Polish work, *De Optimo Senatore* by Laurentius Goslicius, Bishop of Posen (now Poznan, in the disputed territory on the borders of Germany and Poland from which Gollancz's father had emigrated to England) and thus foregrounding the extent to which the Elizabethans were conscious of Poland and Polish culture.

I cannot help but sense what I'll call a *signature* here – Gollancz quietly, humorously even, marking his hybrid identity as a Jewish Briton of Polish extraction in an ostensibly straitlaced philological analysis of Shakespearean names. Moreover, this was by no means the only outlet for Gollancz's material about the association of cormorants and Jews; the topic seems to have been something of an obsession for him. In the Princeton archive, there are two bulky, heavily overscored and amended typescripts of lectures on the topic that he gave across a span of many years. In the principal lecture – entitled 'The Shylock of Shakespeare' – given a couple of weeks after the Tercentenary (on 22 May 1916) at University College London to the Jewish Historical Society (of which, as Kahn notes, he was a founding member, as of so many other organisations), he expanded substantially on the material condensed so enigmatically into the *Homage* entry. He makes it clear in the lecture – unlike in the entry, where he simply notes the 'traditional popular prejudice' that was 'still' in place in Shakespeare's day – that the anti-semitism represented in *The Merchant of Venice* persists, that the 'prejudice and hatred' Shylock faces 'can still be understood'.[28] Moreover, he is fascinated by his sense that Shylock the character 'speaks a very beautiful English' yet at the same time has what he calls a 'twang', which he defines, curiously, as 'a special idiom torn almost from the Bible that [Shakespeare] tries to put into the lips of Shylock' (14). He is much clearer, too, to this audience than he is in the *Homage* entry both that the name Shylock draws on the Hebrew word for cormorant – 'Now most of you in this room know more and better than I do that the Hebrew for Cormorant, one of the forbidden beasts, is Shaloch, and I have not the least doubt

---

[28] Typescript, '"The Shylock of Shakespeare", Lecture delivered by Professor Gollancz before the Jewish Historical Society at University College, Gower Street, W.C. on Monday, 22nd May, 1916', 7, in Sir Israel Gollancz correspondence file, Special Collections, Princeton University Library. Subsequent page references to this lecture are given in parentheses in the text.

that Shakespeare converted the Schilloch from the book (already referred to) with that of Shaloch the cormorant' (15) – and that Shylock is, as a result, a strange and resonant convergence of types: 'the hero personifying the usurer' (14–15).

There is an interesting element of risk-taking in this. Focussing on Shylock – on Shylock's Hebrew 'Englishness', no less – and connecting the Elizabethan association of cormorants and usury with Shakespeare opens up a potentially uncomfortable nexus of England, Judaism, capital and Shakespeare in the context of a volume designed to extend Shakespeare's reach from poet of Empire to 'world-poet'.[29] Moreover, it prompts a glance at Gollancz's own relationship to this nexus: he is on every committee, has a finger in every pie; he is a cultural broker with Shakespeare as his currency. The problem, of course, is that this makes him available for precisely the kind of anti-semitism championed by Douglas and the malign hoaxers of the *Protocols of the Elders of Zion*, who deployed terms such as 'global' and 'cosmopolitan' as shorthand for the 'world Jewish conspiracy' they claimed was in progress. In this context, a glance back at Whitworth's phrasing in his history of the National Theatre becomes just a little unsettling. 'Behind [the] kaleidoscopic maze of committees, flitting to and fro', he comments, 'one glimpses the mercurial figure of Israel Gollancz ... benign, discreet, master of innocent intrigue ... with every thread in his hands, and alone capable of unravelling the tangled skein when the right moment came.' I am not accusing Whitworth of anti-semitism; in context, however, his phrasing is a little unfortunate, implying as it does that Gollancz was the focal point of a vast (if 'innocent') intrigue, manipulator of an efficient and unstoppable process. Given the delays, the failures and the inability to raise funds that dogged Gollancz's activities as commemorative entrepreneur, this would seem a little wide of the mark. But the characterisation – or caricature – is uncomfortable nonetheless.

The underlying twist, moreover, is the hint in the cormorant–Shylock material that Gollancz is aware of what he is doing, that he is mimicking (and parodying) the role he will be assigned anyway by the dominant culture – and thus that in his hands the language of

---

[29] On the 'Englishness' of the name Shylock, see Stephen Orgel, 'Shylock's Tribe', in Tom Clayton, Susan Brock and Vicente Forés (eds.), *Shakespeare and the Mediterranean* (Cranbury, NJ: Associated University Presses, 2004), 38–53, 44.

nationalism/patriotism becomes pure rhetoric, designed to distract from the primary purpose, which is the precise opposite of the role attributed to Shakespeare in bringing the empire together under the sign of Britain and that Gollancz is held to have maintained in celebrating the Tercentenary by way of the *Book of Homage*. Rather, Shakespeare becomes not so much an emblem of patriotism but the fluid currency for a global cultural market, appropriable to national identities beyond the British. On these grounds, Kahn is entirely right when, in the final paragraph of her 2001 essay, she notes that Gollancz was 'a hybrid in spades'. I suggest, moreover, that Gollancz was *aware* of his hybridity, that the apparent arbitrarinesses of his work – the odd topic for his own *Homage* contribution, the choice of contributors unlikely simply to toe the imperial-Shakespeare line – suggest a higher degree of consciousness on his part than is usually assumed by critics. After all, he could easily have selected only obliging members of the establishment or the Empire to contribute to the *Homage* – yet he chose Russell and Hyde and Plaatje and Tin.

I do not wish to credit him with a master-plot, since that would involve speaking the questionable language of some of the less appealing characters in this story, but I would at least like to give him the benefit of the doubt, intellectually speaking, and to see in his work for the *Homage* a degree of playfulness paired with an emerging ideology of globalisation that recognises the beginnings of the end of empire (for Britain, at least) and the possibility of an international story on a broader stage. By way of the *Book of Homage*, the Shakespeare Hut, the SMNT and his role in redirecting the geography of Shakespearean commemoration away from provincial Stratford and towards cosmopolitan London, Gollancz can be seen quietly, assiduously, to have effected a shift in the relationship between Shakespeare and national culture, between Shakespeare and global culture, the effects of which arguably began to become apparent only at the latter end of the twentieth and beginning of the twenty-first centuries. Gollancz, I wish to suggest, set out not to create the imperial propaganda with which he has repeatedly been associated, but to try, in his quietly insistent way – by reversing the cultural impact of 'cosmopolitanism' as anti-semitic shorthand, by quietly renegotiating the imperial into the global – to adapt Shakespeare to a post-imperial world, moving him from the local green spaces of Stratford to cosmopolitan London and from there to the world – and not only to the shrinking world of the British Empire. What, then, if those ostensibly odd choices of contributor to the *Homage* – those who would, for Kahn, have made Gollancz 'pause, perhaps even blink' – were not so accidental, not made by someone wholly unaware of what they would write, of the extent to which their contributions would stretch the ostensible imperial premise of the collection? In this light, perhaps the longest-lasting legacy of Gollancz's 'commemorative entrepreneurship' (itself a highly problematic identity, as has become clear) is not only the concrete – the undeniably concrete – materiality of the National Theatre, the belated outcome of the SMNT debates, but also, and still more resonantly, the invention of the much less tangible, but far more culturally powerful, idea of 'global Shakespeare'.

* * *

A postscript, in which I return to the British Academy's Gollancz Memorial lecturer for 1926, J. R. R. Tolkien. One of the favourite practices of *Lord of the Rings* devotees is the work of derivation: where do the names of Tolkien's characters and places come from, and what do they mean or imply? One of the more uncomfortable suggestions over time has been that the language of the orcs (that is, goblins) stems in part from Hebrew, a suggestion that Tolkien scholars tend understandably to reject, along with its implications of anti-semitism. A further uncomfortable suggestion is that the name 'Gollum' – the malign Nibelung figure who begins as the hobbit Sméagol but, under the influence of the ring, is transmuted into a kind of amphibian with a preference for water and dark places – might in part derive from the Hebrew 'golem' (in Jewish mythology, a humanoid figure created by magic from inanimate matter). Tolkien enthusiasts rightly point out that Tolkien is on record vehemently opposing anti-semitism. When the German publisher just about to release a translation of *The Hobbit* in 1938 wrote to him to check that he was 'of Aryan origin', he reacted by writing as follows:

If I am to understand that you are enquiring whether I am of *Jewish* origin, I can only reply that I regret that I appear to have *no* ancestors of that gifted people ... I have been accustomed ... to regard my German name with pride, and continued to do so throughout the period of the late regrettable war, in which I served in the English army. I cannot, however, forbear to comment that if impertinent and irrelevant inquiries of this sort are to become the rule ... then the time is not far distant when a German name will no longer be a source of pride.[30]

This is both eloquent and impressive, and I wish to stress that I am not accusing Tolkien of anti-semitism (he was no Alfred Douglas). Yet Tolkien is likely to have been aware of the implicit anti-semitism of Wagner's portrayal of Alberich, the Nibelung who has the ring in his possession at the beginning of *Das Rheingold* and who, obsessed with gold and living beneath the waters of the Rhine, is so obviously the working model for Sméagol/Gollum.[31] Moreover, Tolkien knew Gollancz's work as a medievalist, his editing of *Pearl* and *Gawain*, and he did not like it. Derek Brewer, in the introduction to his *Companion to the Gawain-Poet*, reminisces briefly about his undergraduate years in Oxford just after the Second World War. 'Tolkien himself', he notes, 'lectured on [*Gawain*] to a small group of devotees, confining himself entirely to textual cruces (often forgetting to tell us which line he was discussing), and doing obscure (to me) battle with some mysterious entity, prophetically as it may now seem, called something like "Gollancz"'.[32]

And he adds a footnote. 'Even I eventually discovered', he writes, 'that the reference was to the admirably ingenious Early English Text Society edition by Sir Israel Gollancz, *no relation to Gollum*' (my italics). 'No relation to Gollum'. But I wonder if Brewer is in fact wrong, if Gollum *might be* a relation. I can only sketch the possibility – that Tolkien, who was twenty-eight years his junior and was in the trenches being shot at when Gollancz was creating the *Book of Homage* and the Shakespeare Hut, might have known the senior medievalist's work on Shylock and the cormorant, not just in the *Homage* but also on the lecture circuit, and might just possibly have been tempted to make a wry, tacit association (an unfortunate one, in hindsight) between

---

[30] *The Letters of J. R. R. Tolkien*, ed. Humphrey Carpenter and Christopher Tolkien (London: George Allen & Unwin, 1981), Letter 30.

[31] I am grateful to Peter Holland for discussion of the Alberich/Gollum connection. On Alberich as Jewish stereotype, see Theodor W. Adorno, *In Search of Wagner*, trans. Rodney Livingstone (London: Verso, 1981), 1–17; Paul Rose, *Wagner: Race and Revolution* (New Haven, CT: Yale University Press, 1996), 69–70; and Mark Weiner, *Richard Wagner and the Anti-semitic Imagination* (Lincoln: University of Nebraska Press, 1997), 135–43.

[32] Derek Brewer, 'Introduction', in Brewer and Jonathan Gibson (eds.), *A Companion to the Gawain-Poet* (Cambridge: D. S. Brewer, 1997), 2. I am very grateful to Andrew Johnston for directing me to Brewer's comments about Tolkien and Gollancz.

'Goblin' Gollancz the writer about cormorants that are also Jews and usurers and the figure of Gollum, who dives underwater and catches both fish and gold and is thus both cormorant-like and a hoarder of gold and of power, a kind of negative, slippery entrepreneur with a name quite unlike that of a normal hobbit. This is not, in the end, demonstrable, but the possibility serves as a reminder of the discomfort that has at times been caused by Israel Gollancz's remarkable tercentenary legacy, his global vision and his hybridity-in-spades.

10 Performing commemoration in wartime: Shakespeare galas in London, 1916–19

AILSA GRANT FERGUSON

London celebrations for Shakespeare's Tercentenary in 1916 were barely to resemble those discussed before the outbreak of war. Proposals for commemorating Shakespeare would be completely reassessed in a wartime context; the new plans should be frugal and patriotic, selective and pertinent, 'a very simple observance of the Tercentenary in a manner consonant with the mood of the nation under present conditions'.[1] As a result, the gala revue format, selecting as it could the smallest of textual fragments or the stylised 'Shakespeares' expressed in sketches, extracts, songs and pageants, was bound to flourish. On 2 May 1916, a flamboyant, yet tactfully inexpensive, Shakespeare Tercentenary commemorative gala, 'A Tribute to the Genius of Shakespeare', took place at Drury Lane. In August 1916, the commemorative Shakespeare Hut, a YMCA respite Hut for Anzac troops on leave, was erected. In its purpose-built performance space, this Hut held modest gala commemorations, for audiences of servicemen, annually from 1917 to 1919.[2] The fragmented Shakespeare at the Hut and, by contrast, the elaborate spectacle presented at Drury Lane offer two very different versions of Shakespearean commemoration in wartime. Yet a recursive pattern of commemoration emerges in both, in which commemoration reflects commemoration and public memory of Shakespeare interacts with both public and private memories of war and its losses. In these productions, too, can be found varying attitudes

---

[1] Israel Gollancz, *The Times*, 'The Shakespeare Tercentenary', 23 November 1915, 9.

[2] See Ailsa Grant Ferguson '"When Wasteful War Shall Statues Overturn": Forgetting the Shakespeare Hut', in *Shakespeare*, 10 (2014), 276–92 and 'Lady Forbes-Robertson's War Work: Gertrude Elliott and the Shakespeare Hut Performances, 1916–1919', in Gordon McMullan, Lena Cowen Orlin and Virginia Mason Vaughan (eds.), *Women Making Shakespeare: Text, Performance, Reception* (London: Bloomsbury Arden Shakespeare, 2013), 233–42.

to cultural value and the treatment of Shakespeare on stage in wartime. Legitimate and popular modes are transgressed. Gender roles are challenged. The two cases present a contrast between the disappearing spectacle of late-Victorian Shakespeare at Drury Lane and the new, minimalist style represented, through both necessity and design, at the Hut.

The Shakespeare being 'remembered' in London in 1916 was a deconstructed one, often fragmented to fit wartime agendas and sensibilities. Recruitment posters featured Shakespearean quotations, morale-boosting postcards boasted Shakespearean phrases, plays were performed to bolster injured soldiers. In this context, the fragmented revue format of the Shakespeare Hut performances would not have seemed out of place; the pageant of Drury Lane, too, would have fitted within both this context and a longer tradition of Shakespearean pageantry and tableaux, especially of the late-Victorian and Edwardian period.[3] Yet, critically, the fragmentation of Shakespeare tends to be viewed as forming a definitive aspect of modernist treatments of his texts after the First World War. As Julia Briggs articulates,

The modernist project of demythologising Shakespeare has continued to the present day with occasional pauses or backlashes, moments when a more dignified or a more patriotic version was called for. Oppressed by ancestral voices (among which Shakespeare's was the most pervasive), modernism had to confront the too-familiar words it had inherited.[4]

Critical views of Shakespeare's relationship to the Modernist project after the Great War centre around a notion of deconstruction, on the act of fragmenting Shakespeare representing either a conversation or a struggle (Bloom's 'anxiety of influence'[5]) with that ancestral Shakespearean voice. Yet the deconstruction and fragmentation of Shakespeare's texts was the pervasive treatment of Shakespeare during both the War and the preliminary tercentenary commemoration debates, especially after the turn of the century. The Shakespeare inherited by modernists – woven, for example, into Woolf's *Mrs*

---

[3] Michael Dobson, 'The Pageant of History: Nostalgia, the Tudors, and the Community Play', *SEDERI* 20 (2010), 5–25, 20.

[4] Julia Briggs, *Reading Virginia Woolf* (Edinburgh University Press, 2006), 11–12.

[5] Harold Bloom, *The Anxiety of Influence: A Theory of Poetry*, 2nd edn (Oxford University Press, 1997) 13–16.

Dalloway or Eliot's *The Wasteland* – was already widely fragmented. The version of Shakespeare experienced by wartime audiences, especially those in military service, was more often than not fragmented and reconstructed into a suitable 'whole' for wartime consumption. While Briggs characterises those post-modernist lapses of the more interrogative 'demythologising' of Shakespeare as 'moments when a more dignified or a more patriotic version was called for', one of these moments came *before* the emergence of some of the most definitive modernist appropriations of Shakespeare.

In these unique circumstances, how best to mark the Tercentenary in wartime conditions was debated and agreed by a new Tercentenary Committee, whose leading light, Sir George Alexander (acting star and, later in 1916, member of the Shakespeare Hut Committee), was to organise the main theatrical event: a lavish gala performance at Drury Lane on 2 May 1916.[6] Meanwhile, Sir Israel Gollancz,[7] Honorary Secretary of the Shakespeare Memorial National Theatre (SMNT) Committee and a Shakespearean academic, mooted a plan to use land in Bloomsbury bought for the erection of a new National Theatre to construct, instead, a temporary memorial to Shakespeare in the form of a mock-Tudor style YMCA hut for active soldiers on leave from the front (Figure 10.1).[8] The Shakespeare Hut would provide, above all the usual conveniences of the YMCA huts elsewhere in the capital, a dedicated performance space and a programme of education to include Shakespeare's works.

To commemorate the commemoration, as it were, a lavish Souvenir Programme for the Drury Lane gala was produced in the form of a large hardback book, featuring sixty diverse illustrations.[9] Sir George Alexander's[10] annotated copy of this

---

[6] The Tercentenary would have fallen on 23 April but was, in 1916, measured by exact reference to the Old Style date of his death (thus conveniently avoiding the Easter weekend).

[7] Gollancz's involvement in the Tercentenary is explored by Gordon McMullan in Chapter 9 of this volume.

[8] Grant Ferguson, '"When Wasteful War Shall Statues Overturn"'.

[9] *A Tribute to the Genius of William Shakespeare* (London: Macmillan, 1916).

[10] Annotations are assumed to be written by Sir George Alexander based on the following evidence: (a) inscription is initialled "G.A."; (b) the formal hand used in the annotations correlates with the informal hand in a letter from Sir George Alexander to Sir Israel Gollancz, dated 18 November 1916 (National Theatre Archive SMNT/2/1/12); (c) depth of organizational knowledge displayed in lists of volunteers and players, consistent with Sir George Alexander's Tercentenary Committee leadership.

Figure 10.1 The Shakespeare Hut. By permission of the YMCA.

volume[11] provides an insight into this performance both as a moment in theatre history and for its own commemorative purposes. In the pages of his copy, Alexander undertook the completion of all the missing lists of performers and volunteers involved in this huge production, an omission for which the printed copy carries an earnest apology. The book also contains handwritten Shakespearean quotes and an inscription expressing Alexander's thoughts on war losses and Shakespeare in wartime (which appeared in print in a less expensive incarnation of the programme). By contrast to the Drury Lane tome, programmes for the Hut galas were ephemeral. Nevertheless, a few rare copies do still survive and, through these simple one-sheet programmes, we can learn much about the Shakespeare Hut performances.[12] The Hut's modest annual Shakespeare galas configured Shakespearean fragments into a production which would ostensibly build morale, showcase the war work of theatrical superstars (Ellen Terry, Martin Harvey, Johnston Forbes Robertson, his wife, Gertrude Elliott, Mary Anderson and more) and revive, each year, the tercentenary 'spirit' that the Hut was built to represent. It would also become a stage on which modes and expectations of Shakespearean transmission were quietly transgressed.

The Drury Lane gala comprised a full performance of *Julius Caesar*, followed by a Shakespeare-themed musical programme, itself no small affair, performed by the London Symphony Orchestra. Finally, there was an ambitious pageant of 'all the characters'[13] from *Much Ado About Nothing* (directed by Sir George Alexander), *The Merry Wives of Windsor, As You Like It, Romeo and Juliet, The Winter's Tale, Coriolanus, Macbeth* (planned but not performed),[14] *Twelfth Night* and *The Merchant of Venice*. Despite wartime austerity, the Drury Lane gala was genuinely spectacular, with a cast of hundreds. Scenery and costumes were borrowed from the tsar of spectacularism, Sir Herbert Tree;[15] the Drury Lane gala was the acting profession's

---

[11] At the time of writing, this copy of *A Tribute to the Genius of Shakespeare* has been newly acquired and is not yet entered in the catalogue but is being held at the National Theatre Archive, London.

[12] E.g. Programme for entertainments at the Shakespeare Hut, Ellen Terry & Edith Craig Archive, National Trust, held at British Library: BL/125/25/2/Ellen Terry Archive/ET/D439.

[13] 'The Shakespeare Celebration', *The Observer*, 16 April 1916, 13.

[14] Alexander has crossed through the listing for *Macbeth* with the annotation '(not performed)'.

[15] 'Dramatis Personae', in *The Observer*, 9 April 1916, 7.

extravaganza of bardolatry. Alexander's annotations reveal that, in addition to the several hundred listed players in the printed programme, nearly 150 more were onstage in *Julius Caesar* as 'Senators, Patricians, Citizens, Guards, Attendants'. In contrast to the spectacular sets and costumes – and the grand venue – of the Drury Lane gala, the Shakespeare Hut stage had no sets and was comparatively tiny; its very existence was based on impermanence, transience and liminality. A YMCA image (Figure 10.2) shows the Hut's little stage, with its black and white timber and plaster background. The black and white stripes function paradoxically, in a way: they simultaneously draw attention to both the pseudo-historical, mock-Tudor – commemorative – design of the Hut's exterior and, contradictorily, to the temporary, transient substance of the Hut's wooden and plaster structure. As the picture illustrates, at any moment this purpose-built performance space would need to be transformed into a functional dormitory. The impact of this transience on the relationship between commemoration, memory and performance evades definition. The prospect of the Hut's always imminent destruction was, tragically, shared by its audience. The performers' space is separated from the audience not only by that layer of imagination required of the spectator but by the relative safety and normality of their lives, a luxury not shared by the men who looked on. The tragic was thus ever-present in the Hut's entertainments.

The delineation of this whole building as a manifest commemoration of Shakespeare had a range of impacts on its performance function. On the most literal level, a Shakespearean bias is abundantly clear in the Hut's general weekly programme of entertainments and concept of 'recreative education'.[16] Ill-suited as its tiny stage was to the demands of full-length Shakespearean drama, the Hut's performance hall was still utilised as the Shakespearean focus for this place delineated for commemoration. Although 'complete' Shakespearean plays were never attempted, the Hut presented gala or revue-style entertainments, often consisting of a series of Shakespearean scenes interspersed with music, readings, talks and speeches. The Hut's fragmentary and diverse productions made playful use of Shakespeare's perceived 'value'.

---

[16] 'New Shakespeare Movement: A Notable Alliance in London and Stratford', *The Observer*, 27 April 1919, 3. Assumed author, Gollancz ('the great Shakespeare hut, which it was my privilege to found', 3).

Figure 10.2 Concert Hall, The Shakespeare Hut. By permission of the YMCA.

A surviving programme for one of the Hut's annual Shakespeare galas documents the format of this annual event. Co-directed by Gertrude Elliott and Edith Craig, it included Johnston Forbes Robertson performing a soliloquy from *Hamlet* and Jacques' 'Seven Ages' speech, 'Shakespeare Songs' (Lady Maud Warrender), an address by Gollancz,

Ellen Terry as Portia (the same role reprised in the Drury Lane gala's pageant),[17] scenes from *Henry V* (performed by the all-female, teenage troupe, the Junior Players) and a range of other songs and extracts, including scenes from *King John*.[18] The choice of extracts serves as a representative 'revue' of those individual plays that were particularly often used in wartime in the form of postcards and broadsheets to bolster morale, commemorate those lost,[19] and even recruit troops. Posters featuring Shakespearean quotes such as 'Stand not upon the order of your going, / But go at once' (*Macbeth* III.4) were widely displayed to encourage volunteer recruits, even after conscription began in 1916.[20]

However, to find only naked patriotism or imperialism in the Shakespeare Hut performances would be highly reductive. Other themes emerge from the fragmented version of Shakespeare that its stage presented. By piecing together parts of Shakespeare, the Hut performances did not necessarily create synecdochic representations of the plays from which the extracts were drawn, nor simply present a patriotic message. Instead, fragments pieced together to make a whole performance that suited the new cultural and entertainment space offered by the Hut. These fragmentary presentations of Shakespeare toy with the role of memory in how the audience experiences these most famous texts. Marvin Carlson's notion of 'ghosting' is helpful in theorising the process of recognition that may have affected Shakespearean transmission and reception at the Hut and, to a certain extent, in the pageant and songs of Drury Lane. Carlson writes:

Theatre ... is the repository of cultural memory, but, like the memory of each individual, it is also subject to continual adjustment and modification as the memory is recalled in new circumstances and contexts. The present experience is always ghosted by previous experiences and associations while these ghosts are simultaneously shifted and modified by the processes of recycling and recollection.[21]

---

[17] 'The Shakespeare Celebration', 13.

[18] Programme for entertainments at the Shakespeare Hut, BL/125/25/2/Ellen Terry Archive/ET/D439.

[19] E.g. *The Welwyn and Woolmer Green Book of Remembrance*, Old Woolmer, UK quotes 'There's rosemary, that's for remembrance' (*Hamlet* IV.5). Imperial War Museums (IWM) War Memorials Database, 20015.

[20] Poster (1915) Parliamentary Recruiting Committee, IWM PST 5154.

[21] Marvin Carlson, *The Haunted Stage: The Theatre as Memory Machine* (Ann Arbor: University of Michigan Press, 2001), 2.

Where Shakespearean fragments are performed, the re-iteration of a 'familiar' text is subverted from its usual course into one where the memory of the audience might reconstruct the 'whole' text around each synecdochic fragment, or associate each fragment with an external context (such as a recruitment poster or morale-boosting postcard) and/or receive the entire production as a new text, a sum of its parts.

In the case, for example, of *King John* at the Hut, this text may have been unknown to many young soldiers. Russell Thorndike, as King John, and several other members of this cast had performed in the Old Vic production of the same year (1917). The Hut's Anzac audience would not have known of this overlap. However, Faulconbridge's patriotic, if historically inaccurate, lines 'England never did nor never shall / Lie at the proud foot of a conqueror' and 'Nought shall make us rue, / If England to itself to rest but true' (V.7) were both used prolifically in morale-boosting and patriotic materials such as postcards and memorial plaques.[22] Such quotations being the only links to the play familiar to many in the Hut's audience, assumptions of the play's 'message' on war and patriotism are likely to be not remembered but rather constructed around the smallest of fragments. In the Old Vic production, audiences were apt to find wartime allusions in the text and performance. They would have 'thought the line about "Austria's head" to be a topical interpolation ... Falconbridge's final speech ... "brought the house down", and the lines were inscribed over the proscenium arch for the remainder of the war.'[23] However, at the Hut, the 'ghost' of *King John* that shadows the Hut's fragments must also have been affected by the Hut's particularly limited demographic of young soldiers, again showing the recursive mode of commemoration in these memorial performances.[24]

Julius Caesar was chosen for Drury Lane's main feature, to display the talents of its star, Frank Benson (knighted by the king after his

---

[22] Such as the inscription on a memorial bench in Warwickshire: 'The men whose names are inscribed on the neighbouring monument gave their lives for that England which never did, and never shall lie at the proud foot of a conqueror.' IWM War Memorials Database 38528.

[23] Gordon Williams, *British Theatre in the Great War* (London: Bloomsbury, 2003), 248–9.

[24] Surviving poster images show that only Allied servicemen were admitted to Shakespeare Hut performances. For example, see poster for *Macbeth* (Hoover Institution Political Poster Database Ref 3943).

performance), and to provide a multitude of male roles, rather than to reflect the wartime environment. Big names were engaged, such as Oscar Asche, H. B. Irving and Arthur Bourchier. However, the play may have held some resonances intended to strike a chord during wartime. In his audacious exercise in Shakespearean fragmentation and exploitation, *Shakespeare in Time of War*, Francis Colmer compiled an extensive collection of extracts, taken entirely out of context and reordered thematically to form wartime messages, resonances and commentary. He named the Kaiser 'Imperious Caesar' and pieced together some strange 'poems' from a number of plays, including *Julius Caesar*, to create a picture of a megalomaniac Kaiser.[25] Possibly, such pejorative cultural references resonated with the audience. Nevertheless, the obvious choice would have been *Henry V* and its total absence from the production as a whole is striking, as it 'was just the play to draw all the soldiers in London'.[26] On 22 April 1916, *The Times* carried a long editorial, in which the writer waxes lyrical on the immediate relevance of the play to the times in which Shakespeare is to be commemorated:

> It is with thoughts of Henry the Fifth rather than any other Shakespearean hero that the nation at large will prefer now to commemorate Shakespeare … If the time is not propitious to such a celebration of Shakespeare's death as we could wish, if the toasts and the fanfaronade have to be curtailed, Shakespeare at least left behind him an eloquence which burns all the brighter for the smoke and dust of battle.[27]

The planned gala at Drury Lane had also been announced in the national papers during April, yet it is conspicuous in its absence from this editorial on the upcoming Tercentenary, despite being patronised by the King himself. Nevertheless, the gala received much positive press after the event, not least due to its having raised funds for the Red Cross and to the curiosity of Benson's public knighting at the end of the play.

However, while *Henry V* was absent from the stage at Drury Lane that day, King Henry, or at least Prince Hal, does feature briefly in the

[25] Francis Colmer, *Shakespeare in Time of War: Excerpts from the Plays Arranged with Topical Allusions* (New York: E. P. Dutton & Company, 1916), 47–57.
[26] Sybil and Russell Thorndike, *Lilian Baylis* (London: Chapman & Hall, 1938), 125.
[27] 'Once More Unto the Breach', *The Times*, 22 April 1916, 5.

Souvenir Programme. An illustration by Byam Shaw shows Prince Hal in full heraldic armour gazing, somewhat quizzically, at Edward, Prince of Wales, who is standing to attention in modern military uniform. The modern Prince is tipping Hal a salute and casually holding a smoking cigarette, implying a more 'modern' and fashionable future for monarchy (lent tremendous irony with hindsight, given Edward VIII's abdication in 1936). The illustration is inscribed '"It is the Prince of Wales" *1 Henry IV*, Act V, scene iv' and, above the two figures, the feather insignia of the Prince of Wales appears with his motto, 'Ich Dien', German for 'I serve'.[28] Its use here is perhaps surprising, drawing as it does so much attention to that German monarchic link that, a year later, the Royal family did their best to obliterate, changing the dynasty's name permanently from the very German Saxe-Coburg-Gotha to the very English, Windsor. The image lightheartedly posits the Drury Lane gala event, the Souvenir programme and Shakespeare's most popular King in a wartime moment and appears incongruous with the romanticised illustrations and personal portraits filling the rest of the volume. The two Princes of Wales coming face to face in war attire and the nonchalance of the smoking Prince Edward present a humorous image of modern England meeting Shakespeare's portrayal of an adventurous medieval past. The illustration emphasises glory and confidence in war, rather than Shakespeare or war commemoration.

Drury Lane's male-dominated *Julius Caesar*, Benson's knighting, the patriotic foreword to the Souvenir, its spectacular pageantry and the notable absence of *Henry V* all reveal commemoration with a patriotic agenda while yet attempting to escape from the war outside. The Shakespeare Hut's immersion in the war and its status as a physical memorial to Shakespeare allowed its performances to blur the boundaries between Shakespearean commemoration and the wartime environment, with a uniquely recursive effect. While the Drury Lane gala performance may have avoided being overtaken by wartime themes by omitting *Henry V*, Alexander redressed the balance in his annotations. Among his Souvenir Programme marginalia is a

---

[28] See Figure 10, 'It is the Prince of Wales', by Byam Shaw, in Richard Foulkes, *Performing Shakespeare in the Age of Empire* (Cambridge University Press, 2002), 201. The double portrait of the two Princes of Wales is reproduced from the *A Tribute to the Genius of William Shakespeare*.

fascinating inscription that serves to conflate the Shakespearean commemorative purpose of the book – and the gala itself – with commemoration of war dead and support for the fighting soldier-actors:

The number of actors and actresses assembled within these historic walls, in order to do honour to the memory of their immortal brother-player, approaches four hundred. Even that number would have been exceeded but for the war, which has denuded our ranks very greatly, particularly in regard to our younger men. It has been computed that some two thousand members of the theatrical calling had voluntarily – long before compulsory service was mooted – joined His Majesty's Forces. Many are now in the trenches, while some – over forty for certain, perhaps more for identification is impossible, several actors having enlisted under their real names – have died for King and Country. To those who are still serving, it is intended to send a copy of the programme as a souvenir of this memorable occasion. For we are all –

'We few, we happy few, we band of brothers'
 – United in love and gratitude for the man who, above all others, has enriched the stage and ennobled our calling.[29]

Henry V is deployed as if a mouthpiece for Shakespeare's own patriotism, a cliché of the Great War years. Alexander flits from solidarity within the acting profession, to grief at the loss of so many actors, affording honour to their deaths, to bardolatry within the shortest of passages. He takes up the anaphoric fragment, 'We few, we happy few, we band of brothers' (*Henry V* IV.3), Henry's perfect rhetoric of persuasion and call to arms, to describe instead fraternity within the acting profession in wartime. He conflates male wartime solidarity with male professional solidarity; he makes those stage words to acting soldiers into a message for – or in support of – actors-turned-soldiers. Alexander's inscription in the Souvenir Programme transforms it into a very different artefact of commemoration to its unannotated equivalents and provides a different view of the dual commemorative function of both book and performance. However, Alexander's inscription made it into print on the less opulent standard programmes for the event. The two programmes, if viewed unannotated, represent different approaches to commemorating Shakespeare in wartime.

---

[29] *A Tribute to the Genius of William Shakespeare*, annotation (see notes 6 and 7), No page numbers.

Furthermore, the plan to send copies of the large, delicate and opulent souvenir version to serving soldiers 'in the trenches' suggests a highly romanticised notion of active service in the trenches and of commemoration.

While the Drury Lane production was primarily for a (predominantly local) civilian audience, the Hut performances were, almost exclusively, for (predominantly Australian and New Zealander) servicemen. Unsurprisingly, then, at the Shakespeare Hut, too, lines between commemorating Shakespeare and commemorating war dead would become blurred. The Hut's main lounge was known as the Leslie Tweedie Memorial Lounge (Figure 10.3). It had been dedicated in memory of a young officer killed in 1915 and sponsored by his mother, the prolific travel writer Mrs Alec Tweedie (occasionally wrongly credited with founding the Shakespeare Hut[30]). This part of the Hut became a memorial within a memorial while the adjacent performance space was dedicated to providing Shakespearean entertainments to an exclusive audience of active servicemen. At the Hut, Shakespeare was 'remembered' via an eponymous building in which Shakespeare was performed, where an individual soldier was commemorated and in which many more servicemen remembered their lost friends: a recursive commemorative effect. The process of Shakespearean commemoration reflected the act of commemoration of war dead in a *mise-en-abîme* of acts of remembrance.

A similarly recursive process can be read in Alexander's sombre inscription which seems to interweave – even conflate – the act of commemorating Shakespeare with the acts of commemorating war dead. 'Some [actors]... have died for King and Country... we are all – "We few, we happy few, we band of brothers" – united in love and gratitude for the man who . . . ennobled our calling.' Shakespeare's Tercentenary also becomes an occasion to merge notions of commemoration with those of the 'lost' actors who have already died 'for King and Country'. Shakespeare is part of that nationhood for which the men are dying and the sense of pride in the actors' sacrifice in particular is clear. Alexander indicates many actors joined up

---

[30] For example, Mrs Tweedie is described as the 'Prime mover', in the Shakespeare Hut project in H. H., 'The Shakespeare Hut', *The British Journal of Nursing*, 57 (16 September 1916), 234. See also Ailsa Grant Ferguson, '"When Wasteful War Shall Statues Overturn"'.

Figure 10.3 The Leslie Tweedie Memorial Lounge, The Shakespeare Hut. By permission of the YMCA.

'voluntarily – long before compulsory service was mooted', suggesting that the acting profession is one of particular patriotism (the less sentimental view being that it is a profession of notoriously variable income, making military service more appealing). While this passage renders this particular copy of the Souvenir Programme a fascinating intersection of commemorations, it did not appear in other copies, even though the inscription did appear in print on the more functional event programme. Unlike the Shakespeare Hut, the Drury Lane gala ostensibly functioned purely as a commemoration of Shakespeare in its content and audience (though it did raise funds for the Red Cross). It is Alexander's words alone that impart the recursive commemorative function at least of the book, if not the performance too.

However, elements in the Souvenir Programme hint at a dualism in the commemorative function of both the event and the volume. The Foreword by W. L. Courtney, the event's Literary Advisor, is as much a piece of patriotic fervour as a dedication to Shakespeare's work. Shakespeare, the 'Great Englishman', is represented as a paragon of English cultural identity. However, Courtney also views this commemoration, in its wartime context, in terms of Shakespeare's work and art itself as an immortal, transcendental force: 'For all his countrymen alike the deathless art of Shakespeare – especially at a time like this, so unpropitious to the higher levels of imaginative creation – is at once a vindication and a pledge that Art itself is immortal.'[31] Courtney sees the war as a barrier to 'imaginative creation', while Shakespeare is something like an antidote, clearly on the side of 'all his countrymen'. Mixing notions of art as transcendental, even defying death, with a very tangible jingoism has a jarring result but one arguably typical of the use of Shakespeare in England during the Great War.

While the debates surrounding Shakespeare's tercentenary commemorations divided bardolators, enthusiasts, practitioners and academics, the onset of war meant that Shakespearean performance adopted new agendas, in which both practicalities and sensitivities contributed to a shift in production styles and performance modes. Both the Drury Lane and Shakespeare Hut galas purported to function as commemorations of Shakespeare. Yet neither could possibly offer

---

[31] W. L. Courtney, 'Foreword', *A Tribute to the Genius of William Shakespeare*, no page numbers.

such a 'celebration' in wartime without tacitly functioning as war commemorations, patriotic expressions or in other senses becoming part of the English wartime performance – and commemorative – landscape. This new environment was troubled by opposing notions of the validity of theatre in times of conspicuous austerity, especially in the capital. When a new Entertainment tax (1916) suddenly increased theatre and cinema ticket prices and an increasingly vocal puritanical rhetoric on the frivolity of theatre in wartime began to take hold, perceived categories of entertainment and cultural value became less defined. So-called legitimate theatre struggled to cater for the wartime need for escapism, while popular performance and cinema was criticised for its lack of respect for the austere times.[32]

In the textual choices and editorial interventions of these two very different venues' presentations of Shakespeare as 'gala', boundaries between legitimate and popular theatres of the early twentieth century are blurred. The Shakespeare Hut revues and galas are unequivocally transgressive, while the Drury Lane production flouts tradition less decisively. The 'complete' performance of *Julius Caesar*, mixed with a programme of music and Shakespearean pageant, recalled pre-war SMNT fundraising events such as the extravagant Shakespeare Costume Ball of 1911. Plans for the staging of the pageant are described in *The Observer* on 16 April 1916:

All the characters will enter the stage at the top of a great staircase. They will walk downstairs and group themselves at the foot …

Celebrated artists will be seen in the various groups, notably Miss Mary Anderson as Hermione, the part she played in her production of 'The Winter's Tale' at the Lyceum many years ago, and Miss Ellen Terry as Portia.[33]

Devoid of text, these representations are pure spectacle and their stars remind the audience of those old days at the height of Victorian spectacular Shakespeare.

Embedded as it had become in high-class social entertainments, the pageant is less modally transgressive than that of the Shakespeare Hut revue, which clearly overlapped with music hall modes characterised

[32] Andrew Shail, *Cinema and the Origins of Literary Modernism* (London and New York: Routledge, 2012), 178.
[33] 'The Shakespeare Celebration', 13.

by short dramatic sketches interspersed with music. However, in the early twentieth century, Shakespeare's status in performance as either legitimate or populist was becoming increasingly vexed. In late Victorian and Edwardian critical debates on the relationship between popular performance, especially music hall versus 'legitimate' theatre, Shakespeare's weight is thrown around a great deal. Exponents of the validity of music hall as a timeless, populist expression, such as Elizabeth Robins Pennell, argued that 'variety' performance such as music hall arose from ancient popular desire,[34] and was itself a legitimate cultural form not to be demoted below the 'classical'. Pennell's notion of 'variety' performance leads to the argument for music hall – and broader variety entertainments – as itself a legitimate form of cultural expression not to be demoted 'below' the classical or legitimate.

The merging of Shakespeare and variety at the Shakespeare Hut moves further into a transgression of the legitimate and the popular than does the pageant of the Drury Lane gala. The Hut's audience of servicemen, at a time when 'public preference was for bright and informal entertainment',[35] was perhaps perceived as requiring a popularised Shakespeare, which provided a compromise between lighter amusement and a perceived need for 'quality' entertainment for the troops.[36] Essentially, the commemorative galas and indeed regular, smaller productions at the Hut, respond to the debate on Shakespeare's popularism at a time when the austerity and patriotism brought by the war collide with aficionados' compulsion to commemorate Shakespeare. While pre-war Shakespeare memorial debates touted Shakespeare as 'of the people', the ill-conceived extravagance of events such as the Shakespeare Ball (1911) and Exhibition (1912) had branded the campaign as very much for the upper class and arguably led to its failure. With the onset of war, the need to present Shakespeare as both popular *and* culturally 'elite' was exploited as much by recruitment agencies as by tercentenary memorial supporters.

The Hut's challenging approach to acceptable modes of Shakespearean transmission was influenced by its female direction.[37] Its Chair of

[34] Pennell, Elizabeth Robins, 'The Pedigree of the Music Hall', *Contemporary Review*, 63 (1893), 575–83, 583.
[35] Williams, *British Theatre*, 148.   [36] Williams, *British Theatre*, 151.
[37] Grant Ferguson, 'Lady Forbes-Robertson's War Work'.

Entertainments, Gertrude Elliott (Lady Forbes-Robertson), had been President of the Actresses Franchise League (AFL), while the Hut's main director, Edith Craig, also a prominent AFL member, had directed the pro-suffrage Pioneer Players. Meanwhile, though the pageant format at Drury Lane recalls fundraising pageants organised by female socialites rather than pro-suffrage agitprop, several 'arrang [ers]' of these pageant pieces were, like the Shakespeare Hut's core directors, AFL leading lights: Lillah MacCarthy, Violet Vanbrugh and, again, Edith Craig. The recent pro-suffrage activism of these women, especially the Hut's leading creative directors, may have brought with it the challenge to legitimacy that had characterised pro-suffrage agit-prop productions of the immediate pre-war period. These perform-ances were distinct in their 'refusal to distinguish between . . . the value of a play or a sketch, a raffle and a recitation',[38] presenting the transgression of 'high' and 'low' cultural modes. The levelling of 'value' onstage in pro-suffrage plays came to represent the concept of universal franchise and, to an extent, burgeoning ideals of popular 'equality'.

In wartime, the franchise agenda had been tactfully (by pro-suffrage groups) sidelined, and the female dominance of the Hut stage, while offering an opportunity to women directors, also reflected the absence of young male actors. In Alexander's inscription, he estimates that some two thousand actors were away in active service, while at least forty were already dead by the time of his writing. Cross-dressed young actresses regularly appeared on the Hut's stage as part of the Shake-speare Day commemorative galas, which carnivalistically reverses ori-ginal practice but could also be viewed as a poignant near-necessity in the absence of all those young male actors away at war or already lost. Yet, while tactfully sidestepping any overt feminist agenda (in the absence of so many young men) by performing 'war work', the Hut performances took a similar creative approach to that of the suffrage performances via female-led direction of Shakespeare. Remembering Shakespeare in the Hut's performances became inextricable from its charitable, 'war work' agenda and, more subtly, its engagement with progress in women's theatre. A democratic Shakespeare might be fragmented and interspersed with songs, talks and skits, and still be

---

[38] Katherine Cockin, *Edith Craig: Dramatic Lives* (London: Cassell, 1998), 93.

presented as 'legitimate', just as, in the Hut, the war work of the female directors also legitimised female theatrical leadership without the political stigma of suffragism in wartime.

Women, who outnumbered men onstage at the Hut, were also changing Shakespeare commemoration. A most fascinating example is the Hut's Junior Players, led by Edith Craig. By contrast to Drury Lane's avoidance of *Henry V*, the Shakespeare Hut presented an all-female representation of extracts from the play for its soldier-audience. In all surviving programmes from the 1917–19 Shakespeare memorial galas, we find a group of young girls, the Junior Players, listed as performing extracts from the play. In her 1978 autobiography, Fabia Drake, who would become a well-known British actress and director, recalls playing Henry V on the Hut Stage when she was just fifteen years old:

> as ... we would be playing to soldiers, it was decided that the scene we would enact should be from *Henry V* ... We had no extras, we had no army, but we had an audience of four hundred soldiers and Edy Craig had the inspiration that I should come out in front of the curtain and speak the Agincourt speech to my Army on the floor.
>
> ... Four hundred war-weary men rallied to the cry of 'God for Harry, England and Saint George', springing to their feet and cheering to the rafters.[39]

She spells out the rationale for using these 'magnificent speeches' as she calls them, citing their 'urgency and a rallying force that can be incandescent'.[40] The approach to performing a stripped-down Shakespeare, with 'no extras ... no army', strikes a contrast with the hundreds onstage at the Drury Lane gala, and the notion of the 'army on the floor' conjures a picture of an inclusive, interactive, even immersive exchange between performer and audience at the Hut. The youthful player and audience are both, it seems, whipped into a frenzy by Shakespeare's stirring words. Drake appears proud of the contribution she perceives herself to have made to the morale of the troops she entertained as a diminutive, cross-dressed, Henry V. A female *Henry V* in wartime, a 'rallying' cry from a young woman dressed as a King, reminds the audience of the absence of young men, of the war

---

[39] Fabia Drake, *Blind Fortune* (London: William Kimber & Co, 1978), 36–7.
[40] Drake, *Blind Fortune*, 37.

contribution of women and even of women's political and rhetorical potential.

Such Shakespearean male impersonation was another way in which the Hut performances transgressed the boundaries between the classical or legitimate and populist music hall traditions. The male impersonator had become a popular and regular fixture in the Edwardian and wartime music halls.[41] Certainly, in music hall tradition, cross-dressing was a norm. As Alison Oram articulates, 'the gender-crossing woman came from the world of entertainment, comedy, and marvellous happenings. What is fascinating about women's gender-crossing is how strongly it continued to carry this playful and humorous tone, and how late it was in the twentieth century before it was reinterpreted as sexual deviance.'[42] So Drake's Henry would not have been perceived to be politically, socially or sexually challenging in the context of a 'variety' stage format. However, with hindsight, this female Henry V hints at a more significant moment in female theatre history. Directed by openly gay, pro-suffrage Edith Craig and AFL president Gertrude Elliott, Henry's magnetism and leadership, the very fact he is a soldier-king embodied in the form of a young woman amounts to a significant theatrical and socio-political moment.[43] While Drury Lane's tribute to Shakespeare had a male-dominated centrepiece and stopped short of a real foray into the variety stage, the Hut's fluid transgression of theatrical modes allowed a female-led Shakespeare to flourish.

These onstage transgressions, though, also present a major question of how to commemorate Shakespeare in 1916. Even before the outbreak of war, the question of whether to commemorate Shakespeare with some functional memorial, such as a theatre, library, or even almshouse, or with a statue, was vexed. Most prominent in the debate was the proposal of a Shakespeare Memorial National Theatre

---

[41] See J. K. S. Bratton, "Beating the Bounds: Gender Play and Role Reversal in the Edwardian Music Hall', in Michael R. Booth and Joel H. Kaplan (eds.), *The Edwardian Theatre: Essays on Performance and the Stage* (Cambridge University Press, 1996), 86–111.

[42] Alison Oram, *Her Husband was a Woman!: Women's Gender-Crossing in Modern British Popular Culture* (London and New York: Routledge, 2013), 4.

[43] Shakespeare had been used by suffragists in the pre-war years, including arguments that his work shows a proto-suffragist outlook (for example, 'Shakespeare as Suffragist', *The Vote*, 29 July 1911).

and it was on land purchased for this purpose that the Shakespeare Hut was built. The notion of a Shakespeare 'for the people' who should be commemorated in some way that is usable by 'all' was in contrast to the idea of a statue, which some viewed as conspicuously expensive and without practical function.[44] As one newspaper article commented, 'from one point of view the War seems to have done real good in regard to the Shakespeare Tercentenary ... At least, there is now withdrawn all temptation to waste any money on statues and marble shrines.'[45] The statue would have presented Shakespeare literally as a monolith, aloof from the public, despite being constructed among them. This was a proposition many were beginning to consider expensive, outmoded, and untenable in a wartime London where virtually every new monument commemorated war dead.

In the context of broader debates about the cultural value of theatre, it was perhaps inevitable that the notion of an Elizabethan 'golden age' would figure significantly. In his 1911 essay 'The Music-Hall', G. H. Mair proclaims the 'pur[ity]' of the music hall by referring to this perceived past. 'The music hall is our one pure-blooded native amusement. It has a pedigree that is clear and undoubted, through the tavern, that great agent of social continuity, back to Elizabethan days – to the days when the theatre did really represent and embody the soul of the nation.'[46] As Barry J. Faulk articulates, Mair 'assimilat[es] the unique figure of Shakespeare, a fountainhead of legitimate culture, into the broad inclusive stream of the popular'.[47] However, Mair's eugenic discourse of 'native[ness]', 'pure-blooded[ness]' and purity draws the popular music hall into line with a specific notion of pure English heritage, belonging to the same tradition and 'pure' cultural line as Shakespeare, hinted at in the reference back to some Elizabethan utopia. Such a version of England that would seem so very much 'worth fighting for' intensified within Shakespeare tercentenary rhetoric during the war. Returning to the Souvenir Programme's Foreword, 'to all

[44] For an excellent study of the notion of a 'people's Shakespeare' see Andrew Murphy, *Shakespeare for the People: Working Class Readers, 1800–1900* (Cambridge University Press, 2008).
[45] Unidentifiable newspaper clipping in Sir Israel Gollancz's papers, NT Archive [uncatalogued to item level] SMNT1. Handwritten '6th February 1916'.
[46] G. H. Mair, 'The Music Hall', *The English Review* (1911), 122-9, 124.
[47] Barry J. Faulk, *Music Hall and Modernity: The Late-Victorian Discovery of Popular Culture* (Athens, OH: Ohio University Press, 2009), 42.

artists', writes Courtney, 'the memory of the Great Englishman is as dear to those who recall with gratitude his patriotic love of his native land'. His rhetoric is punctuated, like Mair's, with a racialised notion of Shakespeare's 'value', his language – 'native land', 'master intellect' – reminiscent of eugenic discourses. Here, as became the norm during the war, the assertion of Shakespeare as a paragon of Englishness overwhelms the single commemorative function of 'remembering' an individual and becomes a celebration of English patriotism.

Both Drury Lane and the Shakespeare Hut might be read as presenting Shakespeare as inherent to Englishness itself. However, the Hut, by virtue of its very existence as a space for Dominion soldiers to experience 'merry old England', explicitly situates Shakespeare as central to the motherland myth. Its commemorative function becomes more than a monument to Shakespeare, closer to a monument to a particular notion of Englishness. Its environmentally incongruous mock-Tudor architectural style (see Figure 10.1) was deliberately designed to represent 'Shakespeare's England'. This new way of constructing a cultural 'memory' of Shakespeare's age was far more successful than the pre-war attempts to capture public support of the commemoration of Shakespeare via ['re']construction. In a letter to Sir Israel Gollancz in March 1916, YMCA Chairman Basil Yeaxlee compliments the Hut's architect, Charles Waymouth, for the Elizabethan references in his design concept, his 'Tudor touches'.[48] Waymouth's contrivance of 'Elizabethan' style renders the Shakespeare Hut as a stage set of the past, rather than just as the functional space provided by other YMCA huts. In this way, it presented its transient Anzac residents with a unique package of English 'heritage'.

An editorial ruminating on the Tercentenary appeared in *The Times* on 22 April 1916. 'Perhaps only a soldier can best pay worthy honour to Shakespeare now', the writer ponders. 'Perhaps the truest way of celebrating his fame is not so much by remembrance as by decision, and by decision converted into deeds.'[49] In this climate of an inextricable blend of patriotic duty with cultural memory, the idea of commemoration through performance produced, at Drury Lane in 1916 and at the Shakespeare Hut for the next three years, differing results. While

---

[48] Letter: Basil Yeaxlee to Sir Israel Gollancz, 3 March 1916, National Theatre Archive, SMNT/2/2/55.
[49] 'Once More Unto the Breech', *The Times*, 22 April 1916, 5.

the Drury Lane gala was, in many ways, a last hurrah for the spectacular Shakespeare of the pre-war decades, the limitations of the performance facilities at the Shakespeare Hut gave rise to a stripped-down Shakespeare that bridged the gap between the avant-garde and the austere, the 'original' and the modern. Nevertheless, these galas, commemorating as they did a civilian in wartime, both produced a recursive commemorative effect, whereby the act of 'remembering' Shakespeare reflects the wartime environment of commemoration and loss in which the events took place.

Infinitely reflexive, these acts of public remembrance beget each other and become inextricable. Drury Lane's spectacle and the Shakespeare Hut's modesty both aspired to represent a version of Shakespeare that honoured a nation's 'memory' of a figure bound so tightly to English national identity as to have become almost synonymous with England. In wartime, this would inevitably lead to commemorations becoming as much expressions of national identity. Yet those Anzac troops that Fabia Drake claimed 'raised the rafters' at her cross-dressed delivery of the Agincourt speeches, or the suffragists who directed elements of the Drury Lane gala and dominated the creative direction at the Hut, provide a glimpse of changes to come in the redefinition of what it meant to be English and 'remembering' Shakespeare. Challenging the hierarchy of elite and popular entertainment, gender roles in theatre and traditional modes of performing Shakespeare, all under the guise of YMCA-approved 'quality' entertainments, the Shakespeare Hut performances were certainly more transgressive than could ever be claimed for the more conservative Drury Lane gala. Nevertheless, in all these gala performances, de- and re-constructions of Shakespeare mark a unique intersection, even amalgamation, of commemoration and performance, as they 'remember' Shakespeare in wartime.

11 Lest we forget: Shakespeare tercentenary commemoration in Sydney and London, 1916

PHILIP MEAD

In 1916 Shakespeare commemoration became, for the first time, a trans-national phenomenon, but it was by no means culturally equivalent across the sites where it was performed. The discrete, diplomatic investments of national cultures in Shakespearean heritage that existed at the beginning of the era of modernity were radically disrupted by war, and remembering (and forgetting) Shakespeare became subject to new global, trans-Atlantic and antipodal changes in Shakespearean institutions. This chapter considers some of the relations and differences between two constellations of tercentenary commemoration in April and May 1916: in Sydney, where Shakespeare and commemoration of the first Anzac Day intersect; and in London, where Shakespeare commemoration is variously unsettled by the proximity of war, Anzac commemoration and accidents of the calendar, including Easter Sunday. These commemorations were related to each other by more than just a desire to remember Shakespeare. In London there was unease about tercentenary commemoration in time of war that produced a kind of absence of Shakespeare, spatially and temporally, from the calendrical centre of the Tercentenary on 23–5 April.[1] Important figures at the core of tercentenary commemoration, like Herbert

Every effort has been made to secure necessary permissions to reproduce copyright material in this work, though in some cases it has proved impossible to trace copyright holders. If any omissions are brought to our notice, we will be happy to include appropriate acknowledgements on reprinting in any subsequent edition.

I am very grateful to the Australian Research Council for a Discovery Project grant, 'Monumental Shakespeare', which supported the research for this chapter, and to my collaborative investigator on that project, Gordon McMullan. I would also like to acknowledge the invaluable research assistance of Olivia Murphy, Ailsa Grant Ferguson, Anna Kamaralli and Sally Barnden.

[1] Easter Sunday in 1916 fell on 23 April, traditionally the anniversary of Shakespeare's death. The first Anzac Day anniversary fell on the 25th, the following Tuesday. The traditional date of Shakespeare's death, old style, was 3 May 1616. See Samuel Schoenbaum, *Shakespeare's Lives* (Oxford: Clarendon, 1970), xv.

Beerbohm Tree, Johnston Forbes-Robertson and Frederick Warde were in fact displaced to New York, where a partially transported tercentenary was able to be conducted in celebratory, festival mode, which it couldn't easily be in London. In Sydney, as well, Shakespeare remembrance is displaced from its traditional anniversary dates and incorporated into the first commemoration of the Anzac Cove landing, a disastrous First World War campaign that immediately became an event of national definition. The coincidence of anniversary dates means that this Shakespeare Tercentenary, initially displaced by Easter Sunday and Monday (23 and 24 April), then by the first Anzac Day (25 April) to 3 May, is 'synchronised' with the celebrations in England (*Sydney Morning Herald*, 'Homage to Shakespeare', 22 April 1916, 14). However much Shakespeare is present in these commemorations, they are all variously theatrical and their contradictions belong to the history of the complex processes of Shakespeare memorialisation in the twentieth century, and also to the history of cultural memory more generally. They are originary performative moments in a collective but heterogeneous desire for memorialisation, with very different social trajectories, but that never achieves, in the present, a permanent or immovable site of public or social memory. In this sense, Shakespeare commemoration, after 1916, never recovers from the disruptions of the Tercentenary. The prehistory of the Sydney Shakespeare monument and England's National Theatre, for example, clearly demonstrate the ways in which the origins of a particular memorialisation – contradictory, prolonged and disjunctive in place, time, form and cultural memory – shape the belated materialisations they eventually produce. Remembering Shakespeare is never free of the history of the present, while at the same time the actual contingencies of that remembrance are always subject to cultural forgetting.

1

In Australia plans to commemorate the 300th anniversary of Shakespeare's death began in the early years of the twentieth century. The New South Wales Shakespeare Society was established in 1900; the Melbourne society had been going since 1884. On 22 April 1909 at the 'conversaziones' held in celebration of Shakespeare's birthday by the Sydney society, the (third) President Henry Gullett's lecture included the observation that in recent years there had been:

a somewhat sluggish, self-reproachful impulse on the part of a portion of the English people towards national commemoration in some permanent form of the work of England's greatest poet. It cannot be said that much, so far has come of it, though we had the cabled announcement the other day that, some anonymous donor had given the sum of £70,000 to found a national theatre as a memorial to the poet. But since this movement, if it can be called so, first showed itself, anniversary after anniversary of the poet's birth has been celebrated, and the matter remains much the same as when the question why Shakespeare had not a monument was asked a few years after his death, when it was answered by Milton in his famous sonnet, practically to the effect that Shakespeare's work and its impression on the minds of his readers were his best monument. How far this is an adequate answer to the question may be left for each to determine for himself.[2]

Gullett's ambitions for Shakespeare memorialisation are already evident here and the opportunity for an antipodal 'monument' to Shakespeare – in contrast to a London-based national theatre – is clearly already exercising his mind, as is how to deal with Milton's point about Shakespeare's plays being best thought of as intangible heritage. By January 1912 the *Sydney Morning Herald* was reporting on English plans for a tercentenary memorial theatre and in May the Sydney Shakespeare Society decided to contribute to the London Shakespeare Memorial fund (*Sydney Morning Herald*, 11 May 1912, 8), in the spirit of what it referred to as an 'imperial' memorialisation movement (*Sydney Morning Herald*, 4 February 1914, 5). As in London, there were public meetings, press commentary and citizens' and executive committees contributing to the conversation about what form the Sydney memorial should take.[3]

Initially, the debates were similar to those in London and the work of the London Shakespeare Memorial Committee was regularly reported in the Australian papers, including its purchase in 1914 of the Bloomsbury National Memorial Theatre (later Shakespeare Hut)

---

[2] 'Shakespeare's Place in Poetry', *Sydney Morning Herald*, 23 April 1909, 10. Gullett had been President of the New South Wales Shakespeare Society since 1904 and in 1905 had published a collection of his papers, *The Making of Shakespeare*.

[3] In August 1912, in response to the request by a number of citizens, including the poet Chris Brennan, the Lord Mayor of Sydney, George Clarke, convened a public meeting for the purpose of forming a committee to devise a scheme for celebrating the Tercentenary in April 1916 of the death of Shakespeare.

site.[4] Should the Sydney memorial take the form of a statue, a bas relief, a memorial hall, a library or library wing, a museum, a picture gallery (by analogy with the Stratford Memorial theatre), a festival, a theatre, funds or prizes for the study of Shakespeare in schools, or university research scholarships?[5] These exchanges were all inflected by the discourses then in circulation about Shakespeare and race (Anglo-Saxon triumphalism) and, closely related, Shakespeare and empire (Carlyle's 'King Shakespeare' being the frequent reference for Australians, with its mention of the Sydney satellite town Parramatta), Shakespeare and the perfectibility of man, Shakespeare as a possible name for Australia's as yet unnamed Federal capital (courtesy of the enthusiasm of the colourful Minister for Home Affairs in the Federal government, King O'Malley) and the idea (from Milton) of Shakespeare's works themselves as an imperishable monument.[6] By February 1913 the Sydney citizens' committee of the Shakespeare

[4] See 'The Shakespeare Memorial', *Sydney Morning Herald*, 4 February 1914, 5. Later, the opening of the YMCA Shakespeare Hut was also reported in the *Sydney Morning Herald* for 30 August 1916, 7.

[5] It was the idea of a 'memorial hall' that seemed to offend Gullett most and which was the catalyst for his commissioning Mackennal: 'Mr. Gullett was an ardent Shakespearean, and for some years was President of the Sydney Shakespeare Society. When a proposal was made to establish a memorial hall in honour of the poet in Sydney, Mr. Gullett opposed that form of memorial, on the ground that the hall would be used for other purposes, and that its main purpose would be obscured. After the proposal had been dropped Mr. Gullett decided to present a memorial of Shakespeare to Sydney on his own account, and he wrote to Sir Bertram Mackennal, commissioning him to execute the work. *Sydney Morning Herald*, 5 December 1922, 9.

[6] M. Lyons, 'Literary Anniversaries: Commemorating Shakespeare and Others, 1900–1940', in M. Lyons and J. Arnold (eds.), *A History of the Book in Australia 1891–1945: A National Culture in a Colonised Market* (St Lucia: University of Queensland Press, 2001), 394. For a comprehensive set of perspectives on the Australianisation of Shakespeare see J. Golder and R. Madelaine (eds.), *O Brave New World: Two Centuries of Shakespeare on the Australian Stage* (Sydney: Currency, 2001). O'Malley on Shakespeare was reported on in the *Sydney Morning Herald* for 24 February 1913: 'The Shakespeare Tercentenary Memorial Fund Committee ought to engage Mr. King O'Malley to put in his spare time lecturing on Shakespeare. He may not be the greatest Shakespearian scholar in the Commonwealth, but he is certainly the greatest enthusiast. "To my mind, there's only one name big enough for the Federal Capital," he said to a "Herald" representative yesterday, "and that is Shakespeare. That was my first choice. My second choice was Robbie Burns, and my third choice Longfellow. But the Cabinet has decided against me, and it is to be a native name. What that name is to be will be settled on the 28th of this month"' (8).

Tercentenary Memorial Fund, established in August of the previous year, had decided on a set of proposals for commemoration. The committee aimed to raise £25,000

for the purpose of establishing a Shakespeare wing at the New South Wales National Library, to include Shakespearean and Elizabethan literature generally, together with a statue, bust, or other form of sculpture as may be decided later, and provision for a suitable hall for lectures and dramatic representations: a financial provision to be made for prizes for the study of Shakespeare among the young. (*Sydney Morning Herald*, 4 February 1913, 10)

Significantly, these debates and proposals included persistent voices arguing that the commemoration of Shakespeare should also involve the study of Australian literature. W. Farmer Whyte, for example, a member of the Fund's committee and executive member of the Shakespeare Society, managed to get the Fund to agree to his motion that 'one-fifth of the money raised (not exceeding £3000) be devoted to the encouragement of Australian literature and dramatic art, either by means of an annual prize, or in such other way as may hereafter be determined' (*Sydney Morning Herald*, 4 February 1913, 10). The committee launched the fundraising for these proposals with a Shakespeare Ball, with sets, costumes and a pageant, delayed until 22 May 1913, and which raised £480.[7] The Sydney Shakespeare Balls, which ran until at least 1929, were major social events. By 1913, also, every school in New South Wales was participating in an annual Shakespeare Day (23 April) (*Sydney Morning Herald*, 28 April 1913, 11). The height of this pre-war fundraising and celebration was the four-day Shakespeare Festival in April 1914, which altogether raised £256 for the Fund. All these funds were eventually handed over to the New South Wales Public Library in 1923 for the establishment of a Shakespeare library. More than a decade later Shakespeare memorialisation in Sydney would represent a kind of spatio-temporal reversal of these proposals with, not a bust, but a large statue featuring Shakespeare and five of his dramatic characters outside the entrance to the Mitchell Library, and a Shakespeare Room within the library, rather than the proposed Shakespeare wing.

With the outbreak of war only a few months after the Shakespeare Festival and Australia's involvement in the Gallipoli campaign in the

---

[7] See Lyons, 'Literary Anniversaries', 393.

following year, the social mentality of tercentenary Shakespeare and the timetable for commemoration in 1916 were seriously disrupted. In fact, the whole remembering of Shakespeare in Australia suddenly became entangled in the contingencies of the war, just as it did in England and the United States, although differently in each case. The crucial historical conjunction in Australia was a result of the fact that the invasion of the Gallipoli Peninsula by a joint Australian and New Zealand Army Corps (ANZAC), part of an allied force sent to open the Dardanelles and neutralise Turkey's role in the war, began on 25 April 1915 and from 1916 this date became the anniversary of the landing, or Anzac Day.

On 22 April 1916 in an article headed 'Homage to Shakespeare', the *Sydney Morning Herald* reported that

it was originally decided by the Shakespeare Society of NSW and the Sha-kespeare Tercentenary Fund ... to hold a patriotic demonstration in the Town Hall to mark the occasion of the evening of the 25th instant. That was before there was any mention of the commemoration of Anzac Day by the Returned Soldiers' Association, and in view of the fact that the tercenten-ary falls on a Sunday. When, however, it was pointed out that the Returned Soldiers' Association contemplated the celebration of Anzac Day, and making a special feature of recruiting rallies, [it] was decided to hand over the Town Hall, which had been engaged for this date by the Shakespeare Society, to that association; and the local commemoration of the tercenten-ary [was] postponed until May 3, synchronizing with the celebrations in England. Mr Allan Wilkie, of the Shakespearian company, at present playing in the city, has agreed to organise a special matinee for May 3, including scenes from Hamlet, the Twelfth Night, and Romeo and Juliet. (*Sydney Morning Herald*, 'Homage to Shakespeare' 22 April 1916, 14)

This first Sydney Anzac Day commemoration was held on (Tuesday) 25 April 1916 in the Town Hall, under the patronage of the Governor General Sir Ronald Ferguson, the Governor of New South Wales Sir George Strickland and the Anzac Day Executive, whose President was the New South Wales Premier, W. A. Holman. This evening event (8–10.30 p.m.) beginning with a 'Grand Paraphrase of Patriotic Airs' also involved Shakespeare in the form of 'Excerpts from Shakespeare' performed by Allan Wilkie, as well as other musical and dramatic items. Gladys Moncrieff sang and the 'Royal Belgian Orchestra' 'spe-cially brought over from Melbourne' played. One of the performers was 'Miss Vera Pearce', who sang Marsh Little's popular 1915 song

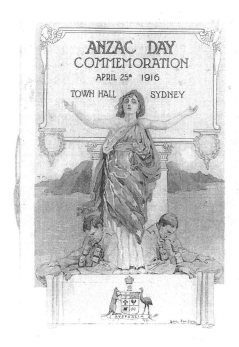

Figure 11.1 Anzac Day Matinee programme, Sydney, 25 April, 1916. Australian War Memorial.

'Boys of the Dardanelles' in the first part of the programme. Pearce, billed as 'The Australian Venus', was born in Broken Hill in 1895 and by this time had starred in two silent films. She would appear in another sixteen films over her long career before she died in 1966. Pearce was also the star of the second to last item of the commemoration, just before the finale of national anthems, a 'Tableau – Brittania [sic] welcoming the Anzacs', 'assisted by Returned Soldiers'. The front of the programme for this event is illustrated with what is probably an artist's impression of this tableau (Figure 11.1).[8]

The use of tableau in this commemorative event is significant and is related to the history of memorialisation. As a genre of performance, tableau represents 'the action at some stage in a play (esp. a critical one) [that is frozen], created by the actors suddenly holding their

---

[8] *Anzac Day Commemoration April 25th 1916 Town Hall Sydney*. Australian War Memorial Museum, Souvenirs 1 1/1/1.

positions' (*OED*). Sometimes referred to as *tableau vivant*, or a living picture, it is a kind of chiasmus of the rhetoric of painting that refers to the representation of inanimate objects as 'still life'; *tableau vivant* is the depiction by apparently inanimate (dead) actors of painterly or statuary scenes – both a freeze and a frieze.[9] A still. Tableau has a long history within the theatrical traditions – sometimes as a stage direction – as well as in pageantry and parades. It also has a domestic and community history: 'In Victorian England … *tableaux vivant* [were used as] parlour games to amuse guests and engage them in a deeper appreciation of art'.[10] The audience in Sydney on Anzac Day 1916 would have been familiar with the varieties of ways in which tableaux work within theatrical performance, historical pageantry and popular entertainment. They may also have had a peripheral awareness of their frequent deployment by activist women, as a mode of protest, in the trans-Atlantic and Irish republican suffrage movements. Vera Pearce's tableau, 'Brittania welcoming the Anzacs', combined the female allegorical figure, Britannia, draped in an Australian flag, and the dead Dardanelles boys gripping a scroll with the new Federation's coat of arms, played, with what complexities of irony we can only guess at, by 'returned soldiers'.

This programme is a souvenir – a small memorial itself of an event that started with patriotic music and Shakespeare – of the conjunction of a tableau of war and empire and the sense of memorialising duty. Significantly, the text on the page following the 'programme' of theatrical performances is explicit about the impulse to memorialisation:

Anzac Day calls for a lasting memorial, some outstanding legacy that shall quicken the blood of future generations, and in honoured memory of those who won for Australia its place amongst the Nations.

Failure on our part to materialise such a lasting memorial would be to deprive ourselves of a singular and coveted privilege.

If we can raise to the glorious and everlasting memory of Anzac Day a dignified architectural memorial, and can in so doing make tolerably assured the comfort and well-being of those who won for us the right to raise it,

---

[9] P. Pavis, *Dictionary of the Theatre: Terms, Concepts, and Analysis* (University of Toronto Press, 1999).

[10] See S. Murphy, 'Tableaux Vivant: History and Practice'. Art Museum Teaching: a forum for reflecting on practice. 6 December 2012.http://artmuseumteaching. com/2012/12/06/tableaux-vivant-history-and-practice.

then we shall accept our privileges and do something towards paying our debt at the same time.

London is to celebrate befittingly the first Anniversary of Anzac Day; every town and village in the Home-land is to honor on that day – Australian valor and the kinship of Empire that binds us all in Anglo-Saxon brotherhood.

Can Australia do less? Shall New South Wales be found wanting? Are we to forget our promises? [11]

This call for a lasting, architectural memorial to Australians in war was read by an audience who were present at the theatrical event of that first Anzac Day matinee and who experienced its primary impulse, the enactment of memorialisation. The last page of the programme read simply 'Lest We Forget'. Designed to produce the lasting impression of a tableau that prefigured an Anzac war memorial, it provided a visual reinforcement of the experience in the theatre: a living war memorial to the absent dead, motionless as a statue.

The 'Historic Shakespeare Tercentenary Matinee', produced by George Marlow and directed by Allan Wilkie, which had been displaced by the Anzac memorial occasion, took place not that far across town at the New Adelphi Theatre, the week following the Anzac Day commemoration on 3 May.[12] This event was under the auspices of the Shakespeare Society of New South Wales and was to 'commemorate the 300th Anniversary of the death of William Shakespeare'. It was also 'in aid of the Anzac Day Fund'.[13] The fact of death hovers behind both these commemorative gestures, but incommensurately: as an

---

[11] The 1916 London Anzac Day matinee was held at His Majesty's Theatre, 'lent by the courtesy of Sir Herbert Beerbohm Tree', 'given to the Australian Imperial Forces in Great Britain on Anzac Day under the auspices of the High Commissioner for Australia and the Agents-General of the States of the Commonwealth of Australia' and was addressed by Andrew Fisher, High Commissioner and formerly Prime Minister. *Anzac Day Matinee*.

[12] The appropriateness of the May dates was asserted by the anonymous report in the *Sydney Morning Herald* for 5 May 1916: 'Yesterday was the actual tercentenary of Shakespeare's death corresponding to April 23 Old Style. It was celebrated in the primary schools, the morning being devoted to lectures on Shakespeare's works and special national prayers. There was a holiday in the afternoon. The celebrations occupy considerable space in the newspapers, but the grave national events are distracting the public attention' (8).

[13] *Historic Shakespeare Tercentenary Matinee*. New Adelphi Theatre, Wednesday, 3 May 1916. Souvenir Programme. Sydney: State Library of New South Wales, 'Shakespeare Society of New South Wales records, 1900–1958, being minute books, correspondence, and newscuttings'. MLMSS 3096.

anniversary of Shakespeare's death the Tercentenary has no trace of solemnity; the Anzac anniversary, though, as the Town Hall souvenir programme reminds us, was a schizoid gesture of pride in Australia's winning its 'place amongst the nations' and the awareness of the devastating fact of thousands of Australian and New Zealand deaths. This ambivalence, as we shall see, is echoed in Beerbohm Tree's speeches in New York during the 1916 Shakespeare Festival week.

The matinee began with scenes from *Twelfth Night*, followed by George Darrell's declamation of 'his poetic description of the Australians' heroism 'Around the Dardanelles' (the Anzac connection once again), followed by a song and scenes from *As You Like It* and *Romeo and Juliet*. There was then an address by Henri Verbrugghen, Director of the Conservatorium of Music, on 'Shakespeare and Music', followed by scenes from *Othello* and *Hamlet*. The matinee concluded with a 'special finale' written for the occasion by the Sydney poet Dulcie Deamer, originally a New Zealander, and in the 1920s, the 'Queen of [Sydney] Bohemia'.[14] For her performance of the poem in the 'Tableau Effect' mentioned in the programme, Deamer appeared 'in classic robes', 'with Britannia enthroned', Anzac soldiers at her feet, all the artists on the stage, and an actor to represent Shakespeare. Deamer's poem, which is printed on the programme, doesn't appear in any of her published volumes or anywhere else, and was obviously written for the matinee event. The newspaper report of the next day describes it as 'illustrating the spirit of the British race as displayed by the pen of Shakespeare and the sword of the Anzac':

THE PEN AND THE SWORD

Shakespeare! No sun shall ever set on thine undying day –
Thou art the soul of England – in her crown the gem of purest ray.

The soul of England! Yes, her soul indeed,
Speaking clear-voiced down the long centuries,
The birth-right of all men of British breed,
From pole to pole, and on the seven seas,
Where'er the British flag, unconquered, undefiled, floats on the taintless breeze.

---

[14] P. Kirkpatrick, *The Sea Coast of Bohemia: Literary Life in Sydney's Roaring Twenties* (St Lucia: University of Queensland Press, 1992), 165–86.

Thou art our heritage, and thou hast been,
Our inspiration still from age to age,
Thy golden, wondrous pen was deadly keen
As any sword, and on the world's broad stage
The sons of England's sons, touched by thy fire, have carved their names
with swords
on Fame's immortal page.

Spirit of Genius that shall never die,
In all our hero-deeds thou hast thy share,
Trafalgar, Waterloo, Gallipoli.
Oh surely thou invisible, were there,
When Anzac's deathless heights showed all the world what sons of
England's sons could do and dare.

Thy words were in each claimant bugle cry,
When winged with death the Turkish shrapnel flew,
And that wild charge swept up to the pale sky,
Thy ringing words that thrill us through and through;
'Come the four corners of the world in arms, but we shall meet
them, nought shall make us rue if England to herself do stand but true.'[15]

The enlistment of Shakespeare here in the patriotic rhetoric of English-ness, 'British breed', is familiar enough, but a noticeable move of Deamer's within this discourse is her reversal of the rhetoric of stalwart English defence in the final lines from *The Life and Death of King John* into a retrospective rallying cry for the Anzac invasion of Turkey in April 1915. When Deamer declaimed the final lines of the poem, and of *King John*, the Shakespeare figure 'clasped hands with a wounded Anzac warrior in khaki; and the audience cheered. The matinee closed with "Rule Britannia" … and the "National Anthem" in general chorus'.[16] This staging of unabashed imperial patriotism enlists the figure of Shakespeare in the tragedy of Gallipoli, drawing a complex and confused analogy between pens and swords. Shakespeare's pen, the implement that had created English heritage in its writing for the stage, now inspires Anzac troops to write their names 'with swords/ on Fame's immortal page'. There is the uncomfortable equation, here, of pens and swords as weapons as much as writing implements,

[15] *Historic Shakespeare Tercentenary Matinee.*
[16] *Sydney Morning Herald*, 4 May 1916, 'The Tercentenary Shakespearian Festival', 6. Lyons notes this matinee event in 'Literary Anniversaries', 395.

underlined by the title of the poem, and against the adage about the pen being mightier than the sword, of writing being more effective than violence. Shakespeare's pen is 'deadly keen,' as sharp and menacing as the soldier's bayonet. The reader wonders what role Shakespeare's pen, as an instrument equivalent to the weapon of the Anzac soldier, played in the creation of English heritage. Deamer's poem also rewrites the history of English military heroism to include Gallipoli in the roll of legendary victories, 'Trafalgar, Waterloo, Gallipoli', occluding what had been, in fact, a shambolic military defeat and subsequent withdrawal, completed only three months previously at the beginning of 1916.

At the centre of this theatrical finale is the tableau of Deamer with Britannia – a reprise of Vera Pearce's Britannia the week before – Shakespeare, and the wounded Anzac, a conjunction of a personified England, the spirit of English 'genius,' and the Australian/New Zealand soldier who has fought and died in the imperial cause. (Whether the Anzac soldier was wounded in 'tableau effect', or in reality, isn't clear.) In this way the 1916 Sydney commemoration of Shakespeare's death enabled Shakespeare to be brought to life, a fact strangely enacted in the tableau: a theatrical spectacle staged by living actors and yet representing abstract, allegorical entities or dead individuals. Before Gallipoli, the Tercentenary was an anniversary that presented different and competing claims to commemoration. As it turned out, the arbitrary historical near-conjunction of Anzac Day and the Tercentenary allowed Shakespeare to be incorporated into a jingoistic tableau of a memorialising impulse that was already well under way, that had shaped the tableau at the Town Hall only the week before and that, as the Australian historian of war memorials Ken Inglis has documented, would be contentious in deeper and more fraught ways than Shakespeare commemoration. Not the least economy of affect at work in First World War commemoration and no doubt in the Sydney audiences at the Town Hall and the New Adelphi is the fact that the war dead would always be un-repatriated, with no graves or individual monuments.[17] First World War memorials, cenotaphs and monuments have that particular poignancy in Australia and New Zealand: the war dead are always absent, a hemisphere away. Perhaps this explains why this theatrical performance was designed to bring them half to life.

---

[17] K. S. Inglis, assisted by J. Brazier, *Sacred Places: War Memorials in the Australian Landscape* (Carlton South: Miegunyah, 1999), 101.

2

The simultaneous events in London were also shaped by the same coincidence of a war anniversary and the Tercentenary. There the theatrical element of the first Anzac Day commemoration was held at His Majesty's Theatre on 25 April. This was part of a full day of commemorative proceedings of great significance to the war effort and imperial relations. On the eve of the 25th, the King had sent a message to the Governor-General of Australia and the Governor of New Zealand, announcing that he would be 'joining with their fellow countrymen in paying solemn tribute to the memory of the dead heroes' (*Daily Mirror*, 25 April 1916, 2). This event, the first public holiday of the war, took over central London, beginning with a memorial service at Westminster Abbey, attended by the King and Queen, and followed by parades of some 2,000 Australian and New Zealand troops along the Strand and back to the Haymarket, a luncheon at the Hotel Cecil, which included addresses by the Australian Prime Minister W. M. Hughes and General Birdwood, and afterwards a matinee at His Majesty's Theatre (*Daily Express*, 26 April 1916, 5; *Daily Mirror*, 26 April 1916, 2). This matinee, as the programme notes, was under the auspices of the High Commissioner, former Prime Minister Andrew Fisher. Fisher spoke briefly at the matinee and handed out medals to some wounded Anzac soldiers. As the programme and newspaper reports recorded, it was a theatrical experience of musical, operatic and sentimental songs but also included an Australian major giving a 'display of dexterity with a long-stockrider's whip ... flicking the ash off a cigar with the tip of a fifteen-foot long lash' (*Manchester Guardian*, 26 April 1916, 4). The printed programme included four photographs of Anzac Cove, Anzac Pier, Second Division Headquarters at Anzac Cove and Turkish prisoners. The programme also states that His Majesty's Theatre was 'lent by the courtesy of Sir Herbert Beerbohm Tree'.

Tree, though, was in New York, where he'd been since 7 March. There he was centrally involved in the vast and variegated programme of American Shakespeare week festivities for 1916. He went to performances of *Henry VIII* and *The Merchant of Venice*, read at a church service at St John the Divine Cathedral (with Forbes-Robertson and Frederick Warde), attended a screening of his film version of *Macbeth*, went to actors' fund benefits, appeared in a Red Cross fund-raising matinee at the New Amsterdam Theatre as Macbeth, Falstaff, Richard the Second and Malvolio, gave an after-dinner speech to the Shakespeare Club, joined a wreath-laying at the Shakespeare statue in Central Park (an 1864 memorial), delivered a lecture on 'Shakespeare and the Actors', attended the black Lafayette Theatre's performance of *Othello* (and addressed the audience at the end of the play) and on 25 April attended an evening commemoration for the Tercentenary at Carnegie Hall.[18] The *New York Times* reported that

Sir Herbert Tree who will begin his Shakespearean season at the New Amsterdam Tuesday, March 14, has written the following formal announcement of this, his first appearance in New York since 1896: 'During the last ten years I have given an annual Shakespeare Festival at His Majesty's Theatre in London. Owing to the conditions prevailing at home, I have decided to celebrate this year's festival in New York. In this project, I have already met with encouragement on every side, and, this year being the 300th anniversary of Shakespeare's death, I have reason to hope that the New York public will consider this effort to celebrate a date of so much significance to our language, to our two great nations and to humanity at large, deserving of their support. (*New York Times*, 27 February 1916, 8)

'Just now', Tree is quoted as saying, '[the English] have enough that is serious to think about without going to the theatre for it. That is why I am here' (*New York Times*, 12 March 1916, 15). For Tree, celebration of the Tercentenary in London was not possible, it seems, at a time when 'civilization was bleeding, [and it was] a mourning world' (*New York Times*, 24 April 1916, 7). This sentiment was also recognised around the English-speaking globe, even reported on in the *Sydney Morning Herald* for 29 April 1916: '[Shakespeare] may be "all men's Shakespeare," as Coleridge says, but he is ours first: and nowhere, not even in England itself, is greater homage being paid to his memory than in America. In that great English-speaking country peace still reigns, and the conditions allow of celebrations on a scale that cannot be thought of in England' (16). Tree's rhetoric of mourning, however, doesn't precisely match the reality: there was in fact a London Shakespeare Tercentenary Festival, produced by Martin Harvey and 'by Arrangement with Sir Herbert Tree', at Tree's His Majesty's Theatre,

---

[18] H. B. Tree, *Diary (of engagements), 1916*. Mander and Mitchenson Collection Bristol Theatre Collection, HBT/000268/1/.

but starting on 8 May, opportunistically (one suspects) alluding to the alternate 'proper' date of Shakespeare's death via the 'old style' or Julian calendar, as 3 May.[19] This festival included performances of *The Taming of the Shrew*, *Richard III* and *Henry V* and ended up running until 17 June. Martin Harvey had also presented a condensed forty-minute version of *The Taming of the Shrew*, described by *The Times* as a 'contribution to the Shakespeare Tercentenary performances', at Oswald Stoll's Coliseum in the week leading up to the Anzac matinee (*The Times*, 18 April 1916, 11). Tree was also the Honorary President, in absentia, of the Actors' Committee for the Drury Lane Shakespeare Pageant of 2 May 1916, attended by the King and Queen because it was a fund-raiser for the Red Cross (*A Tribute*). So in London at the calendric epicentre of the Tercentenary on the 23–4 April 1916 – and anniversaries and commemorations are always fetishisations of dates – there is a trans-Atlantic displacement of Shakespeare celebration to New York, and from the traditional date of Shakespeare's anniversary on 24 April to the week before and after, allowing space for the serious commemoration of Australian and New Zealand contributions to the war effort on 25 April.[20] This emptying out and modification of tercentenary celebration in central London included the refashioning of Shakespeare in the interests of the Imperial war alliance. Israel Gollancz and the Australian-born theatre impresario Oswald Stoll were both responsible for raising funds to have the National Theatre Memorial site in Bloomsbury dedicated to the building of the 'Shakespeare Hut', under construction at the time of the

---

[19] The change from the Julian to the Gregorian calendar occurred in England in 1752.

[20] There is an exception to this aspect of tercentenary displacement in London, which is a 'Special Matinee' on 25 April at the Old Vic Theatre at exactly the same time as the His Majesty's matinee. This matinee was 'Given by Friends of the Vic' and included Ellen Terry as Queen Katherine in *Henry VIII* as well as Edith Craig, Ben Greet, Viola Tree and Sybil Thorndike in various roles in excerpts and songs from Shakespeare. More curiously, given King George's involvement in Anzac commemoration on the morning of the same day at Westminster Abbey, this matinee seems to have been heavily patriotic in tone, ending with 'The King's Prayer' and 'God Save the King'. It also included an item by a musical trio, 'Orpheus and his Lute', in German. Given the location of the Old Vic and the fact that the Anzac troops are described in newspaper reports as all returning to barracks via Waterloo station after the matinee at His Majesty's, it's hard not to imagine that they would have intermingled with the audience coming out of the Old Vic at the same time of the afternoon.

tercentenary weekend and to be opened in August that year. This respite facility, an initiative of Gollancz, as chairman of the Shakespeare National Memorial Theatre committee, and the YMCA, was built for Anzac, specifically New Zealand, troops on leave from the front and throughout the war would provide Shakespeare and Shakespeare-related performance for the support and entertainment of Anzac troops in London.[21] As Basil Yeaxlee, Editorial Secretary at YMCA Headquarters in London, wrote to Gollancz at the beginning of March 1916, in relation to the fund-raising for the hut:

The [National Memorial] Theatre cannot be built and is unlikely to be built for some considerable time, while the Prime Minister and others in high places have deprecated the adoption of any festive kind of celebration. Your proposal is that the site should be used for a practical and National service in the spirit of Shakespeare, who would certainly desire that those who are maintaining the traditions of his England should be sustained and inspired, not only during the war but afterwards.[22]

The war, then, more proximate in London than in Sydney obviously, had displaced tercentenary Shakespeare commemoration both spatially and temporally. At the same time, as Yeaxlee's letter makes plain, Shakespeare memorialisation in London, in the form of the Bloomsbury Hut, needed to be shorn of any festiveness and adapted to the cause of imperial alliance with its underpinning 'traditions' of Shakespeare's England. In Sydney the contingencies of dates had created a coincidence of Shakespeare tercentenary and more theatrically patriotic war commemoration. The cross-currents in this complexly layered historical and trans-national moment are emblematised, in many ways, in the figure of Israel Gollancz, Shakespeare scholar

[21] For a history of the Shakespeare Hut and its role in the war effort see Ailsa Grant Ferguson, 'Entertaining the Anzacs: Performance for and by Australian and New Zealand Troops on Leave in London, 1916–1919', in Andrew Maunder (ed.), *British Theatre and the Great War* (London: Palgrave Macmillan, 2015), 234–50; '"When Wasteful War Shall Statues Overturn": Forgetting the Shakespeare Hut', *Shakespeare: the Journal of the British Shakespeare Association* 10.3 (2014), 276–92; 'Lady Forbes-Robertson's War Work: Gertrude Elliott and the Shakespeare Hut Performances, 1916–1919', in Gordon McMullan, Lena Cowen Orlin and Virginia Mason Vaughan (eds.), *Women Making Shakespeare: Text, Performance, Reception* (London: Bloomsbury Arden Shakespeare, 2014), 233–42; and her chapter in this volume.
[22] Basil Yeaxlee, Letter to Professor I. Gollancz, 3 March 1916. National Theatre Archive, SMNT/2/2/55.

and instigator of the first global Shakespeare in the tercentenary *A Book of Homage to Shakespeare* project. Gollancz was centrally involved in most Shakespeare tercentenary commemoration in London, including the establishment and running of the Shakespeare Hut. Gollancz's knighthood in 1919 was for services to the war effort, in reality for adjusting the institutions of Shakespeare to the support of Anzac soldiers as part of an imperial army.[23] In London in 1916, then, the Tercentenary is a time of practical and national memorialisation and international homage, but not local festivity or commemoration.

3

Back in Sydney, one person who was not present at the Anzac Day commemoration or the tercentenary matinee was Henry Gullett, former President of the New South Wales Shakespeare Society and the man who had commissioned the tercentenary statue of Shakespeare and his characters from Sir Bertram Mackennal, the expatriate Australian sculptor living and working in London. Overriding the various proposals of the Shakespeare Memorial Trust, and eventually accomplished by Gullett's widow and daughters, the statue was to be the lasting outcome of the Shakespeare Tercentenary, and remains to this day the most visible instance of Shakespeare memorialisation in Australia (Figure 11.2). Gullett had died on 4 August 1914, the day Britain declared war on Germany, so he never saw the way in which Shakespeare was enlisted in the patriotic cause of the war, before becoming a statue in his own right. In ways specific to Sydney, and because of Gullett's commission, the conjunction of Shakespeare and First World War commemoration is extended in the city's Cenotaph, because that monument, also a Mackennal commission, is a near relative of the Shakespeare statue in terms of commemorative design.

The contention about what form an Anzac Memorial should take, foreshadowed in the Anzac matinee programme, was symptomatic of the post-war discourse of commemoration and the concerns about 'when memory vanished' and the purpose of monuments was

---

[23] For an account of Gollancz's ubiquity in tercentenary commemoration, see Gordon McMullan's chapter in this volume.

Figure 11.2 Sydney Shakespeare Monument, Shakespeare Place.
By permission of Peter F. Williams, Monument Australia.

forgotten – sacredness or amenity; obelisk or fountain?[24] The memorialising impulse behind the first Anzac Day, as well as funds raised, eventually led to the Sydney Anzac memorial in Hyde Park, but that still unfinished memorial wasn't opened until November 1934 and was the subject of considerable uncertainty and debate. By 1934, of course, all the recruiting theatrics of 1916 had been forgotten. And the long equivocation about what form an Anzac memorial should take, together with an opportunistic political alliance between the patriotic entrepreneur Hugh D. McIntosh and the Premier J. T. Lang, led to Bertram Mackennal, in Australia in 1925 for the raising of the

---

[24] Inglis, *Sacred Places*, 140, 138 and 303. Inglis notes the differences between men's and women's ideals of war commemoration and therefore the design and purpose of monuments.

Shakespeare statue, being commissioned to design the city's Cenotaph. This monument, consisting of two bronze sentinel figures, a soldier and a sailor, has become the central war memorial of the city, while the Anzac memorial remains a curiously displaced site of public memory and commemoration. In the minds of politicians, Mackennal was the sculptor of Shakespeare and of statues of Queen Victoria, Edward VII, the allegorical 'Glory' of the Boer War, and of 'imperial coins and postage stamps for the reign of King George V'.[25] Back in England, Mackennal made the two bronze figures for the Cenotaph in his St John's Wood studio where he had also designed and made the Shakespeare bronzes. After these were transported to Sydney the Cenotaph was able to be unveiled in February 1929, three years after the raising of the Shakespeare statue.[26]

The Shakespeare statue had been shipped to Sydney in 1925. By the time Shakespeare Place, between the Mitchell Library and the Botanical Gardens, and with the statue as its centrepiece, was completed in 1926 it represented a backward-looking gesture of late-Victorian–Edwardian memorialisation. As Inglis notes 'the number of statues (apart from soldiers) in public places almost doubled between 1900 and 1914'.[27] Mackennal's style of commemorative sculpture belonged to a pre-war and late-imperial mentality of civic remembering, along with equestrian statues of monarchs. In this sense, the Sydney Shakespeare statue is a kind of zombie memorial: it comes to life, as a *tableau vivant* at least, twelve years after its commissioner's death, and a decade after the Tercentenary itself, made possible by Gullett's personal wealth and the memorialising dedication of his widow and daughters.[28] Now Mackennal's edifice of Shakespearean

---

[25] Inglis, *Sacred Places*, 38, 299.   [26] Inglis, *Sacred Places*, 302.
[27] Inglis, *Sacred Places*, 69.
[28] In one way the Sydney Shakespeare monument is as much a memorial to Gullett as it is to Shakespeare. In addition to an inscription of lines from *The Tempest*, the statue also includes the inscription:

> SHAKESPEARE,
> 1564–1616.
> Presented to the City of Sydney by
> Henry Gullett.
> August, 1914.

The inclusion of the date 'August, 1914', makes this a memorial to Gullett as well, given that this is the date of his death, not of the Tercentenary or the installation of the monument.

remembrance seems silently oblivious to what had been the enlistment and demobilisation of Shakespeare in the Great War, as much as his own tercentenary, and to the fact that it is no coincidence that its artistic DNA is almost identical to the Cenotaph's. It took until the Second World War for the curtain of history to be drawn across the tableau effects of 1916 that lived on in Sydney's popular pageants and anniversaries celebrating Shakespeare, often alongside Anzac commemoration.[29] But the origins of those effects in the forgotten role of Shakespeare in the commemorations around the first Anzac Day remind us of the temporal and spatial disjunctions that characterise the history, as well as the pre-history, of memorialisation.

Similarly, in London, the temporal chain of Shakespeare memorialisation after 1916 is a history of forgetting and displacements. Owing to the emergency of war, the property between Gower and Keppel Streets, Bloomsbury, purchased originally by the Shakespeare Memorial Theatre committee as the site of a proposed National Theatre, was given over to the temporary memorial of the Shakespeare Hut. By 1924 the Hut was demolished and this application of Shakespeare to war-work almost entirely forgotten. And the long history of tercentenary commemoration in London is hardly remembered in the eventual opening of the National Theatre, on South Bank, in 1976. Remembering Shakespeare, then, as these two stories of tercentenary commemoration, hemispheres apart but antipodally related, suggest, is hardly as simple as remembering a date and time.

---

[29] After the war the 'Shakespeare fetish', as Martyn Lyons describes it, was the main driver of a commemoration mania that ran up to the start of the Second World War: 'In 1938 ... an "Anzac Festival" was held at the Sydney Conservatorium. It included a "Pageant of April", which simultaneously commemorated St George's Day, Shakespeare Day, Anzac Day and Cook's discovery of Australia. Such a combination implied that Englishness and Australian national consciousness were mutually complementary, and this implication was reinforced by reports in the *Sydney Morning Herald*, which frequently juxtaposed articles and photographs of Shakespeare Day and Anzac Day on the same page. Shakespeare himself was to become an Anzac'. Lyons, 'Literary Anniversaries', 390. As this chapter argues, Shakespeare was an Anzac from the first Anzac Day in 1916.

12 Brought up to date: Shakespeare in cartoons

CLARA CALVO

Memorials and acts of commemoration often mediate between identity and memory. As identity and memory are not tangible realities with a material body but representational constructs, memorials and sites of remembrance provide a physical space that helps to shape, however provisionally or temporarily, both individual and group identity.[1] For a long time, tombs, monuments and statues, together with the celebrations in honour of the memory of national heroes or national bards, have been central to the cultures of commemoration of many nations and societies. Cartoons, instead, have remained marginal to the official sites of memory and commemoration; their nature as vehicles for satire somehow renders them slightly incompatible with the established rhetoric of sorrow or celebration that suits collective acts of public remembrance. Cultures of commemoration could be thus regarded as partly perpetuating the divide between high and popular culture.

The Tercentenary of Shakespeare's death in 1916 offered multiple opportunities for commemoration in different media. The official 'Shakespeare Week' in London, the homage of scholars and actors in speeches and plays and the worldwide scope of the celebrations were often punctuated by the less reverential attention paid to Shakespeare in the popular press. Instead of celebrating the universal genius and the Bard of the English language unproblematically, cartoons in newspapers and weeklies questioned Shakespeare's popularity and cultural capital. In 1916, the American magazine *Life* chose the cartoon as one

Research for this article has been financed by Research Project 12014/PHCS/09, 'Great War Shakespeare II: Myths, Social Agent and Global Culture' (Fundación Séneca) and by Research Project FFI2011-24347 'Cultures of Commemoration II: Remembering Shakespeare' (Spanish Plan Nacional de I+D+i 2008–2011).
[1] John R. Gillis, 'Memory and Identity: The History of a Relationship', in *Commemorations: The Politics of National Identity* (Princeton University Press, 1996), 3; J. Wolschke-Bulmahn, 'Introduction', in *Places of Commemoration: Search for Identity and Landscape Design* (Washington, DC: Dumbarton Oaks, 2001).

of the main means of memorialising and celebrating, but also challenging Shakespeare's presence as high-culture icon. In the same year, a British newspaper, the *Daily Mirror*, published a series of cartoons suggesting that Shakespeare's tragedies were more of an age than for all time, that they were regarded as relics of a past at odds with Edwardian theatre experience and that they required a facelift. During the year the world honoured the Tercentenary of the death of Shakespeare, cartoons blurred the dividing line between high and popular culture, and provided an ambivalent *lieu de mémoire*, a site of both memory and conflict for Shakespeare the man and Shakespeare the body of works. Cartoons published on both sides of the Atlantic show how in the midst of the Great War, and in the so-called 'Year of the Battles', Shakespeare was seen to be under fire from a variety of cultural practices. Music-hall, the craving for light comedy, the fame of individual actors and actresses, the Bacon controversy, the relation between drama authors and theatre managers, and the technical advantages of the cinematograph over the limitations of the stage were all called upon to represent the diminished stature of Shakespeare.

The celebrations of the 1916 Tercentenary of Shakespeare offer an opportunity to study the relation between death, commemoration, identity and memory. The commemoration of the dead favours remembrance of personal history and commemoration rituals contribute to the fixing and maintaining of identities. Identity – 'a sense of sameness over time and space sustained by remembering'[2] – is subject to change, but commemorative practices often help to single out features, establish prototypes and delimit what we remember of an individual or an event. The Shakespeare cartoons that proliferated around the 300th anniversary of Shakespeare's death function as memorial and sites of commemoration that preserve his memory but also help to fix his identity in popular culture. Cartoons often reproduce crucial features that illustrate how cultural icons are processed by popular culture, and they often carry it out from a self-conscious perspective. Thus, cartoons constitute one of the channels that popular culture avails itself of to comment on itself. The 1916 Shakespeare cartoons show how Shakespeare was constructed and remembered in the popular imagination around the First World War and, indirectly, they also show how the mechanisms of popular culture work. From many of these

---

[2] Gillis, 'Memory and Identity', 3.

cartoons, Shakespeare emerges as both a popular celebrity and a playwright past his best – the result is a case of 'multiphrenia', a Bard with conflicting selves and a plurality of identities.[3]

As sites of commemoration, the Shakespeare cartoons published in 1916 are ambivalent constructs that also invite a plurality of readings. Memorials do not always trigger the same common response in all beholders and they do not always stimulate the awareness and memory of past events originally intended. Like other memorials and sites of remembrance, the 1916 tercentenary cartoons are anchored in time and space and they are subject to precise ideological constraints. As products of the early twentieth-century culture of commemoration, they perhaps tell us just as much about the 1910s in London and New York as about Shakespeare or his works.

In 1916, the magazine *Life* contributed to the memorialising of Shakespeare with a special tercentenary issue published on 20 April. Although the primary targets of the many cartoons and articles that fill this issue are humour and contemporary social satire, Shakespeare's identity as playwright and his cultural capital are often questioned. From its very cover, the commemorative *Life* issue questions Shakespeare's success as writer and husband by showing the writer at his desk with Anne Hathaway appearing in the background (See Figure 12.1). Shakespeare's wife defiantly scolds him as the caption makes clear: 'WHAT! SCRIBBLING AGAIN, WILLIAM?' The habitual nature of the action, conveyed by 'again', points to repeated marital conflict. Shakespeare looks at the reader almost pleadingly, with a clenched fist barely disguising frustration and annoyance, and a body pose that betrays the pleasant but anxious pangs of creation.

The memorialising of Shakespeare in his daily activity as a writer is recurrent in the tercentenary issue of *Life*. In some cartoons, Shakespeare's identity as both universal bard and true-born Englishman is replaced with the image of a contemporary American author, who has to conform his writing to the demands of the theatre industry. He is no longer the shareholder of his company or the writer who according to his friends 'never blotted a line'. Figure 12.2 shows Shakespeare in his study, frantically hitting his typewriter, his floor carpeted with

---

[3] Kenneth J. Gergen, *The Saturated Self: Dilemmas of Identity in Contemporary Life* (New York: Basic Books, 1991); quoted in Gillis, 'Memory and Identity', 4.

Figure 12.1 'WHAT! SCRIBBLING AGAIN WILLIAM?' *Life*, Shakespeare Number, 20 April 1916.

discarded copy; in Figure 12.3, Shakespeare tensely awaits the verdict of a theatre manager on *Hamlet*.

'If Shakespeare wrote to-day' torpedoes a myth about Shakespeare the writer – that he never had second thoughts or hesitations about his work. In the other cartoon, the playwright, actor and manager of early

IF SHAKESPEARE WROTE TO-DAY

Figure 12.2 'IF SHAKESPEARE WROTE TO-DAY'. *Life*, Shakespeare Number, 20 April 1916.

modern England is rewritten as a twentieth-century drama author who depends on the approval of a market-oriented manager. Both cartoons rely on contemporary settings, décor and atmosphere – everyone is in modern dress except Shakespeare himself, anachronistically – but iconically – clad in doublet and hose. Past and present are conflicting but

Manager: WHAT—THE—HELL!

Figure 12.3 '*Manager:* WHAT – THE – HELL!' *Life*, Shakespeare Number, 20 April 1916.

simultaneous drives in the representation of Shakespeare as author of plays. These cartoons clearly present the Bard as 'not our contemporary' and yet both toy with the idea of what he would be like if he were alive today. A conflict between the past and the present is enacted through a clash between what the visual image and the verbal message convey – what we see (Shakespeare in early modern dress) is at odds with the contemporary bourgeois *habitus* in which he is placed.

To most cultures of commemoration, identity is as indispensable as history or memory. As John R. Gillis reminds us, any nation, community, group or individual requires both an identity and a history for commemorative practices to take place. Remembrance also demands 'access to mementos, images, and physical sites' so that those who do the remembering can 'objectify their memory'.[4] Identity and memory

---

[4] Gillis, 'Memory and Identity', 17.

then require a material projection of some sort. Shakespeare's identity as popular cultural icon partly rests on his doublet and hose but an angular face above a ruff is also semiotically linked to both popular and high-culture representations of the Bard.

Two other central features of Shakespeare's visual identity, his receding hairline and his ample brow, are often construed as the unmistakable sign of his genius. This indispensable trait of Shakespeare the visual icon is an integral feature of representations of Shakespeare even as young man – in a 1916 cartoon that commemorates Shakespeare's 'First Play', an athletic Shakespeare who leaps with an acceptance letter in his hand is already endowed with a visibly balding pate (Figure 12.4). The same iconic element is picked out in a cartoon by W. K. Haselden (Figure 12.5) several years after the Tercentenary to signal Shakespeare's cultural circulation as a Great Man.

The iconic relation between baldness and wisdom is also behind a rare, propagandistic cartoon in *Life* that makes unexpected political use of Shakespeare to disparage the German Kaiser (Figure 12.6). This unusual cartoon stands out as the only openly commemorative cartoon in *Life* that praises Shakespeare without questioning his capital value.

As William Shakespeare and the German Emperor shared their first name, the wordplay on 'bill' and 'Bill' would have been obvious to 1916 readers. Although the Bard is noticeably balding and Wilhelm II has a generous tuft of hair, they embody here countries rather than selves. Shakespeare's individual identity gives way here to national identity – Shakespeare stands in for England in the same way that the Kaiser stands in for Germany. In 1916, this American cartoon conveys an unexpected political message, as in the tercentenary year America was still a neutral country in the Great War. The unambiguous political message emerges from the opposition good bill/bad bill and from the quotations from *Hamlet* associated with each 'Bill'. Polonius's words to Laertes ('To thine own self be true, thou canst not then be false to any man', *Hamlet*, 1.3.77) are signed by W.S. and illustrate Shakespeare's wisdom. The Kaiser is equated with a serial killer, Claudius, and given his words ('Oh my offence is rank, it smells to Heaven', *Hamlet*, 3.3.36).[5] The 'greenback' design and the clear value judgement

---

[5] William Shakespeare, *Hamlet*, ed. Ann Thompson and Neil Taylor (London: The Arden Shakespeare, 2006).

HIS FIRST PLAY
" ACCEPTED "

Figure 12.4 H. MacDonald, 'His first play "Accepted"'. *Life*, Shakespeare Number, 20 April 1916.

combine to articulate an American voice that, in 1916, cannot be neutral at all, as it equates the US with the UK and WS. Through Shakespeare's cultural value in the popular imagination, the American dollar bill clearly sides with the Triple Entente against the Triple Alliance.

The past, Lowenthal suggests, is 'integral to our sense of identity' and 'Rousseau's *Confessions* and Wordsworth's lyrics have taught us to view our identity in terms of our cumulated lives.'[6] In 1916, *Life* construed Shakespeare's identity as composed of significant moments: his childhood, first play accepted, his marriage and speeches at banquets in his honour. As a child (Figure 12.7) Shakespeare is a pedantic

[6] David Lowenthal, *The Past is a Foreign Country* (Cambridge University Press, 1985), 41.

Figure 12.5 W. K. Haselden, 'The mystery of baldness'. *Daily Mirror*, 6 November 1924. By permission of Mirrorpix.

Figure 12.6 'A Good Bill – a Bad Bill', *Life*, Shakespeare Number, 20 April 1916.

Figure 12.7 P. Goold, 'The boyhood of William Shakespeare'. *Life*, Shakespeare Number, 20 April 1916.

whiz-kid who cries in pentameters; his wedding today would be a celebrity show and a windfall for the Shakespeare industry (Figure 12.8); the acceptance of his first play by a theatre manager would make him leap with happiness (see above Figure 12.4) and his speeches as an honoured guest would either bore or shock those attending, some of whom would giggle, and some would unceremoniously leave (Figure 12.9). All these cartoons show the genius as a common man, who got thrashed as a toddler, had to pose for his photograph at his wedding, had a very understandable reaction when he got his first play accepted and, like anyone else, could lose his audience.

Figure 12.7 shows a cartoon in which Shakespeare as a child – already wearing his iconic doublet, hose and ruff, with his angular face and ample forehead faintly suggested too – displays a precocious poetic talent. While memorialising the Bard's words from *As You Like It* ('Sweet are the uses of adversity', 2.1.12),[7] the cartoon also ridicules them – they are meant to be enjoyed as incongruous with the non-poetic scene depicted (a child being spanked) and they promote a conflict between the verbal and the visual. If the quoted words kindle

---

[7] William Shakespeare, *As You Like It*, ed. Juliet Dusinberre (London: The Arden Shakespeare, 2006).

Figure 12.8 'Had Shakespeare married today'. *Life*, Shakespeare Number, 20 April 1916.

the memory of Shakespeare and commemorate his work, they do so by reminding us that Shakespearean language can be old-fashioned, difficult, pedantic and archaic.

'Had Shakespeare Married To-day' (Figure 12.8) participates in the same desire to see Shakespeare as one of us – to blend the past and the

THE HONORED GUEST TELLS A FEW STORIES

Figure 12.9 'The honored guest tells a few stories'. *Life*, Shakespeare Number, 20 April 1916.

present, to dissolve historical difference. As in the cartoon 'If Shakespeare Wrote To-day' (Figure 12.2), the old and the contemporary anachronistically mix here – it is the privilege of cartoons that they are not subject to conventionally realistic forms of representation. As cartoons are not bound by the laws of temporal coherence, Shakespeare can retain his iconic early modern ruff, and wear it along with his bridegroom's nineteenth-century tail coat, in a twentieth-century Stratford taken over by the Shakespeare tourist industry and film camera crews (Figure 12.8). As a commemorative site, this cartoon is particularly metadiscursive – it lavishly shows how Shakespeare, Stratford and Anne Hathaway's cottage can be visited, filmed, photographed, painted and therefore memorialised.

As Lowenthal notes, 'Heroes are often memorialized in garb reflecting a retrospective ideal.'[8] In the commemorative practices of high culture, George Washington is draped in a Roman toga and Pakistan's founding father Jinnah, well-known for his Westernised attire, is memorialised in the national dress or *sherwani*. Popular culture often inverts the *modus operandi* of high culture and here Shakespeare is not memorialised as a bay-wreathed classical poet but as a contemporary great man – a Hollywood celebrity (with his own film-making company, by the look of it). Most memorials, as Lowenthal also notes, 'simply reflect the iconographic fashions of their own days'.[9] Shakespeare's wedding day cartoon is both a Shakespeare memorial and a satire on contemporary mores: cinema, advertising, tourism, the souvenir craze and evening lectures – and, above all, the obsessive recording of today for tomorrow. It is also a debunking memorial of sorts – if he were alive in 1916, the Bard would have his own wedding filmed and turned into a movie by his own producing company.

The clash between contemporary setting and iconic representation in early modern dress reappears in 'The Honored Guest Tells a Few Stories' (Figure 12.9). The proud lady in the background who arrogantly leaves the banquet room and the shocked expression of the male guest in the foreground suggest that Shakespeare's stories are not always to everybody's liking. Although the cartoon's satire is mostly directed

---

[8] Lowenthal, *The Past is a Foreign Country*, 321.
[9] Lowenthal, *The Past is a Foreign Country*, 321.

towards upper-middle-class prudery, bourgeois narrow-mindedness and Edwardian affectation, it is also clear that the Bard's sense of humour is not for all ages and all times.

Popular memory, unlike elite memory, is not consecutive and linear and makes 'no effort to fill in all the blanks'.[10] For Gillis, elite history 'marches' while popular time 'dances' and 'leaps'. Popular time is local and episodic, 'measured not from beginnings but from centers' and it perpetuates the celebration of 'Great Days'.[11] *Life*'s cartoons compress Shakespeare's life into the glossy life of a tabloid celebrity – there is no trace of his property investments or legal entanglements, and no sights of his daughters. These commemorative cartoons offer snap-shots of days in the life of a bard meant to satisfy popular curiosity: what he was like as a child, his wedding photo, what he did the day his first play was accepted and what kind of speech he gave at a banquet. Behind this there is an awareness of historical difference and a drive to turn the past into something resembling the present. Shakespeare's life can be readily remembered and commemorated – and laughed at – if it reminds us of our own. The commemorative cartoons in *Life*'s Shakespeare Number, like altered antiquities, con-tribute to what Lowenthal has called 'the proliferation of new and altered pasts' – what is peculiar to these cartoons is the deliberate or conscious changing of the past.[12]

Cartoons in *Life* also commemorate the 1916 Tercentenary by dip-ping into the authorship controversy. In Figure 12.10, the Shade of Sir Francis Bacon looks aghast at a poster that announces *Life*'s special Shakespeare tercentenary issue and exclaims: 'What! A special number for that impostor – and none for me?' Even if this cartoon pokes more fun at Bacon than at Shakespeare, it also questions the authority of Shakespeare, casting doubts on his authorship of the plays and fore-grounding him as – at least for some – an impostor. Shakespeare is here simultaneously celebrated and questioned and this cartoon becomes a place for ambivalent commemoration and conflict.

The same light-hearted tone inspires, at first sight, another *Life* cartoon, apparently suggesting that the only way to end the Bacon controversy is through a Shakespearean séance (Figure 12.11).

---

[10] Gillis, 'Memory and Identity', 6.   [11] Gillis, 'Memory and Identity', 6.
[12] Lowenthal, *The Past is a Foreign Country*, 324.

Figure 12.10 *'Shade of Sir Francis Bacon:* What!—a special number for that impostor—and none for me?' *Life*, Shakespeare Number, 20 April 1916.

Figure 12.11 *'Boston Lady:* Are you Shakespeare, or Bacon, or aren't you? *Shakespeare's Ghost*: Hanged if I know'. *Life*, Shakespeare Number, 20 April 1916.

Shakespeare's reply to the Lady from Boston ('Hanged if I know') leaves the identity of the author and the authorship of the plays hopelessly unresolved, undermining to some extent the celebratory and commemorative festivities of April 1916. In fact, the Bacon–Shakespeare

Figure 12.12 David Low, 'Shakespeare–Bacon in the Box'. *The Spectator* [New Zealand], 8 October 1909, p. 6. By permission of Associate Newspapers Ltd/ Solo Syndication and British Cartoon Archive, University of Kent, www. cartoons.ac.uk, LSE0225.

controversy seems to have been a favourite topic for cartoonists.[13] In 1909, the New Zealand *Spectator* published a cartoon by David Low in which a bust of 'Shakespeare–Bacon' is sentenced to six months of hard labour for refusing to plead guilty or not guilty (Figure 12.12). The primary jibe is directed at the court of justice but the cartoon leaves the authorship of the plays unresolved – both Shakespeare and Bacon remain in the accused box.[14]

The Bacon question posed a threat to the pride – and flourishing tourist industry – of those places that could boast 'Shakespeare was here'. The 1916 Tercentenary, in fact, triggered innumerable acts of

---

[13] For a taste of early Bacon–Shakespeare cartoons, see 'Egging on Bacon', in Bruce R. Smith, *Roasting the Swan of Avon: Shakespeare's Redoubtable Enemies and Dubious Friends* (Washington, DC: Folger Shakespeare Library, 1994). Smith describes an 1874 cartoon kept in one of the Folger Library scrapbooks 'that shows the distraught ghost of Shakespeare observing laurel wreaths being laid on a bust of Bacon' (56).

[14] For an account of the attempt to settle the Bacon controversy in the literary court devised by a Boston monthly, see Smith, *Roasting the Swan of Avon*, 60.

appropriation. London and Stratford laid their claims to Shakespeare with exhibitions designed to prove that Shakespeare the man existed.[15] Southwark also wanted its blue plaque. In *Shakespeare and Southwark*, a pamphlet published in May 1916 by Robert Woodger Bowers, with a preface by the mayor of Southwark, the Bacon question reappears with a cartoon in which Ben Jonson and 'Master' Bowers shake hands to signal their agreement and Ben Jonson exclaims: 'Then we both agree Master Bowers that Bacon is not Shakespeare'.[16] Ben Jonson is here portrayed as the anti-Baconian *par excellence*, given his love of Shakespeare this side idolatry, one presumes, and Bowers is surprisingly dressed not in Edwardian but in Renaissance garb. Unlike Shakespeare, who wore his doublet and hose sitting at his typewriter, Bowers leaps over centuries and lands in the Elizabethan past. The effect is not dissimilar to 'creative anachronism' – one of the earliest uses of the past was 'to validate the present'.[17] Ben Jonson is invited to appear in this commemorative cartoon as a friend of Shakespeare's and as a knowledgeable person, but it is precisely Jonson's dictum that Shakespeare is not for an age but for all time that the cartoons in the commemorative Shakespeare issue of *Life* often undermine and question.

The conflict between Shakespeare and the theatre industry is a recurrent topic in the *Life* cartoons. In one of these (Figure 12.13), Shakespeare's ghost stands next to a list of the major New York theatres, named after actors and managers. In the caption, the 'Shade' of Shakespeare, with a tinge of sadness, exclaims: 'I wonder how great a fellow must be before they name a theatre after him?'

For those acquainted with the history of the National Theatre in London, this cartoon has telling resonances.[18] With the onset of the

[15] Sidney Lee, *Shakespeare Tercentenary Commemoration, 1616–1916: Shakespeare Birthplace. Catalogue of an Exhibition of Original Documents of the XVth & XVIIth Centuries Preserved in Stratford-upon-Avon, Illustrating Shakespeare's Life in the Town* (Stratford-upon-Avon: Edward Fox and Sons, 1916); *Shakespeare Exhibition, 1916: A Catalogue* (Victoria and Albert Museum, London, 1916).

[16] Robert Woodger Bowers, *A Paper on Shakespeare and Southwark. By … Robt. W. Bowers … With a catalogue of the Exhibition held in connexion with the dedication to Shakespeare of a bay in the Reference Department of the Central Library, etc.*, (London, 1916).

[17] Lowenthal, *The Past is a Foreign Country*, 369.

[18] For the history of the Shakespeare Memorial National Theatre Committee, see Geoffrey Whitworth, *The Making of a National Theatre* (London: Faber, 1951).

Figure 12.13 '*Shade of Shakespeare*: I wonder how great a fellow must be before they name a theatre after him?' *Life*, Shakespeare Number, April 1916.

Great War the plan to erect a Shakespeare Memorial National Theatre in London fell through, and the site acquired to this effect was leased to the YMCA for the provisional erection of a 'Shakespeare Hut' (see Ailsa Grant Ferguson's and Gordon McMullan's chapters in this volume). So in the year of the Shakespeare 1916 Tercentenary the projected memorial for Shakespeare had not been built. The caption clearly encodes a certain anxiety on Shakespeare's part regarding his present fame and suggesting that he himself has doubts about his current 'greatness'.

George Bernard Shaw was amongst those Edwardians who, in the early 1910s, prominently campaigned against the erection of another statue to Shakespeare in London and in favour of a subsidised National Theatre. In an article published in *The Theatre* in April 1916, Lawrence Street discussed 'The Enemies of Shakespeare' and the

From *Punch*
Shakespeare completely eclipsed by the
superior genius of Shaw.

Figure 12.14 E. Reed, 'Man and Superman. All The World's A Stage-Society. Shakespeare completely eclipsed by the superior genius of Shaw'. Reproduced from *Punch* in *The Theatre*, April 1916, 223.

article's title was festooned with the faces and names of Leo Tolstoy, Francis Bacon and G. B. Shaw.[19] On the same page, *The Theatre* reproduced a cartoon by Edward Reed previously published in *Punch* (Figure 12.14): a giant, superhuman Shaw bends over a dwarfed Shakespeare, who leans on a plinth bearing the inscription 'Man and Superman' – Shaw, like Master Bowers, has been cast into anachronistically Elizabethan doublet and hose. The pose of Shakespeare and Shaw mocks the statue in William Kent and Peter Scheemakers' 1741 Shakespeare Memorial in Westminster Abbey. The inscription on the plinth in the cartoon proudly displays the title of a play by Shaw, *Man and Superman*, which replaces the text on the scroll coming out loose from under the books on which Shakespeare's elbow rests. Shaw's words have displaced the Bard's misquoted words from *The Tempest*: 'The Cloud capt' Towers / The Gorgeous Palaces / The Solemn Temples, / The Great Globe itself / Yea, all which it Inherit / Shall Dissolve / and like the baseless Fabrick of Vision / Leave not a wreck behind' (4.1). As Michael Dobson has told us, this misquotation constitutes a

---

[19] L. Street, 'The Enemies of Shakespeare', *The Theatre*, Shakespeare Number, vol. 23, April 1916.

latter-day addition, filling an embarrassing blank space that gave offence as soon as the memorial was unveiled.[20] The botched-up quote infuriated Alexander Pope, who referred to it as 'that Specimen of an Edition'.[21] In the cartoon, Shaw's words are used to emend the Bard's. Prospero's words had previously been sentenced to oblivion in Giovanni Fontana's replica (1874) in Leicester Square. Fontana's marble statue closely follows Scheemakers' design for Shakespeare's statue in Westminster Abbey but replaces the words Shakespeare's index finger points to with Feste's words to Malvolio: 'There is no darkness but ignorance' (*Twelfth Night* 4.2). The inscription on the plinth is fluid and replaceable, like much paratext in editions of early modern plays.

From Prospero to Feste to Shaw, the memorial provides a site for remembering and forgetting where the visual interacts with the verbal in subtle ways. With each subsequent replacement and displacement, the words on the pillar bear less and less relation to *The Tempest*'s evocation of the implacable flow of time, the victory of decay and the impossibility of memory: even the greatest things will vanish without a trace. Prospero's (and Shakespeare's) words have been prey to the fate they announce, wrecked by time, modern playwrights and popular culture. At the same time, the cartoon's iconographical programme makes it clear who is the 'man' and who the 'superman', so Shaw's play is turned against him. The cartoon enshrines an anti-Shaw reading: Shaw thinks himself superhuman when he is in fact leaning on Shakespeare. The caption and the inscription added at the bottom of the plinth are equally ambivalent if taken at face value: Shaw's genius completely eclipses Shakespeare's, says the caption – but the inscription on the plinth pokes fun at Shaw's socialist activism ('All the world's a stage-society') and, possibly, at the turn of the century craze for cultural societies, drama leagues and Shakespeare clubs. The cartoon works in opposing directions and its commemorative value, when reproduced in the tercentenary issue of *The Theatre*, is clearly

[20] For a detailed description of the history of the memorial's inscription, see Michael Dobson, *The Making of the National Poet: Shakespeare, Adaptation and Authorship, 1660–1769* (Oxford: Clarendon Press, 1992), 143–6.
[21] Pope's reference to the words on the scroll is to be found in the notes to the 1743 revision of *The Dunciad*. Quoted in Dobson, *The Making of the National Poet*, 146.

LOVERS ONCE BUT STRANGERS NOW

Figure 12.15 'Lovers once but strangers now'. *Life*, Shakespeare Number, 20 April 1916.

diminished – the cartoon is more a taunt of Shaw than a site of memory for Shakespeare, possibly because of Shaw's pro-German sympathies.

Shakespeare's troubles with the theatre industry in 1916 are the topic of another cartoon in *Life* depicting Shakespeare one evening at the stage door of a theatre. He fondles his goatee beard and looks nostalgically at 'The Drama', embodied by a pretty, young, fashionable actress who ignores him as she comes out of the building dressed in a fur-trimmed coat and sophisticated headgear. The caption reads: 'Lovers once but strangers now' (Figure 12.15). This *Life* cartoon shares much with a David Low cartoon published in the New Zealand *Spectator* in 1909: Shakespeare, in doublet and hose, his ample forehead prominently in sight, pushes a young female dancer out of the limelight. The caption reads: SHAKESPEARE REDIVIVUS. BILL THE BARD: 'Get out of this now, my dear, and let me have a show!' (Figure 12.16).

The gendered nature of these cartoons is alarming – 'The Drama' and 'Musical Comedy' are both allegorically represented by pretty young women. In processes of commemoration, women are often

SHAKESPEARE REDIVIVUS.

Bill the Bard : ' Get out of this now, my dear, and let me
have a show ! "

Figure 12.16 David Low, 'Shakespeare Redivivus', *The Spectator* [New Zealand],
4 March 1909. By permission of Associate Newspapers Ltd/ Solo Syndication and
British Cartoon Archive, University of Kent, www.cartoons.ac.uk, LSE3850.

relegated to personifying abstract notions such as Liberty or the
Empire, partly through iconographical association with the classical
representation of moral virtues, such as Justice, or intellectual pursuits
like Poetry or Grammar. Here, neither 'The Drama' nor 'Musical
Comedy' can benefit much from these precedents – they are both
demonised and cast as the real 'enemies' of Shakespeare. Both cartoons
rest on an implicit breach between high culture and popular entertainment. It is not Tolstoy or Shaw so much as the vitality of popular culture
that poses a threat to Shakespeare. The *Life* cartoon, like previous ones,
creates a more complex relation between the visual and the verbal,
as it pokes fun at Shakespeare's diminished circumstances in his

tercentenary year but it also lavishes satire on the contemporary theatre scene. The posters by the theatre stage door suggest that what passes as 'The Drama' now is a 'pretty', 'giggly girl' who brings in costly furs and commercial success. The threat from new theatrical genres and modern popular taste leaves Shakespeare out of a job and we find him sitting alone in a bench at what looks like Washington Square, staring vacantly at the ground, unaware of the policeman standing next to him, who, hand on chin, wonders whether this strange figure in doublet and hose is another poet or just another homeless person (Figure 12.17).

Once again, in his tercentenary year, Shakespeare's presence is memorialised and questioned simultaneously. Three hundred years after his death, his plays are not the thing and Shakespeare is not the successful playwright, the national poet or the wealthy grain merchant, but a poor homeless poet, wearing unusual clothing and standing out from his surroundings: a misfit. According to *Life*, in 1916, modern drama and musical comedy were only some of the enemies of Shakespeare. The cinematograph constituted an even greater threat. The 1916 Shakespeare issue contains another ambivalent tercentenary site of memory: a sequence of three so-called 'Motion Picture Sonnets', signed by Wallace Irwin and addressed to Shakespeare. Irwin tells Shakespeare that his plays are a waste of time, as audiences now prefer Mary Pickford and Charlie Chaplin. Shakespeare is out, according to this fourteen-line sonnet because language is out – what counts is the moving image. Words, according to the second sonnet, are no longer needed to summon ghosts; one needs only a camera, some actors and some 'spot out West' – presumably Hollywood. Shakespeare is then told that he should have written filmscripts, not plays. In the third and final sonnet, Shakespeare is taken to the motion picture palace ('Come, Poet, to the movies! Here's a seat'). He has to learn how life can be expressed without words – or as Irwin puts it 'by hands and feet'. In these three sonnets, Shakespeare's gift of words is presented as inferior to the capacity of silent film to represent reality through the moving image.

The threat posed by the cinematograph is also mixed in with commemoration of the celebrity playwright in an imaginary, comic letter from 'Mrs. Shakespeare to Mrs. Bacon' also published in *Life*'s Shakespeare Number. This letter encodes gender trouble and anxiety about authorship as well as the tacit acceptance of the replacement of drama by cinema. Most of the letter is taken up by Anne Hathaway's

"WONDER IF THAT'S ONE OF THESE HERE POETS OR JUST A BUM?"

Figure 12.17 'Wonder if that's one of these here poets or just a bum?' *Life*, Shakespeare Number, 20 April 1916.

bitter complaint to Bacon's wife. Since Shakespeare began to sell his rights to the motion pictures, she says, her husband has given up writing plays, has nothing to do, and spends his time flirting with Mary Pickford. This letter clearly rewrites Shakespeare as a thing of the past, as an author who no longer writes. Far from being a global bard and universal genius, Shakespeare is a retired gentleman who lives off royalties, someone who makes a living out of the capital generated by disposing of the control over his plays.

In October 1916, the *Daily Mirror* ran a series of four cartoons on Shakespearean tragedies by W. K. Haselden (1872–1953). All four cartoons, published on 20, 24, 25 and 26 October, followed the same pattern: a two-frame cartoon with the top frame depicting a conventional production of *Hamlet, Romeo and Juliet, Othello* or *Julius Caesar* and the bottom one showing how these plays could be 'brought up to date' in contemporary stages or, presumably, filmed adaptations. Haselden's cartoons are unique for their creative and innovative shape – a cross between the single frame of the traditional political cartoon and the multiple frame of the comic strip. Although his trademark was the six-framed cartoon (see Figure 12.5, above), he experimented with four-framed and, as here, two-framed cartoons (Figure 12.18). Occasionally, Haselden combined the cartoon's usual caption with the balloons found in comic strips, as in the *Julius Caesar* and *Romeo and Juliet* cartoons (Figures 12.18c and d).

The original artwork for these cartoons shows that Haselden conceived them as a series and gave them a unifying title – 'Shakespeare Brought up to Date'. On the top margin of the first cartoon, Haselden wrote: 'One of our correspondents complains (this morning's 'Mirror') that Shakespeare is out of date and dull – Shakespeare brought up to date and enlivened.'[22] Haselden's gift for satirical commentary on theatre trends makes these cartoons ambiguous – traditional Shakespearean *mise-en-scène* may be the first target but, in the process, comedy, music hall, cinema and celebrity actors also come under attack. The 'Hamlet Brought up to Date' cartoon mocks Sir Johnston Forbes-Robertson's *Hamlet* – the resemblance with the Ghost scene in Hay Plumb's 1913 film adaptation of *Hamlet* is striking. The cartoon's top frame mocks the set, *mise-en-scène*, costume and the performance style of Forbes-Robertson (Hamlet) and Percy Rhodes (the Ghost).

[22] British Cartoon Archive, WH1513.

Figure 12.18 W. K. Haselden, 'Shakespeare brought up to date', *Daily Mirror*, 20–5 October 1916. By permission of Mirrorpix.

The *Julius Caesar* cartoon singles out the most famous scene in Herbert Beerbohm Tree's famous – and long-lasting – production of the play and echoes the *mise-en-scène* of Max Reinhardt's *Oedipus Rex* (1912), with Martin Harvey in the title role.

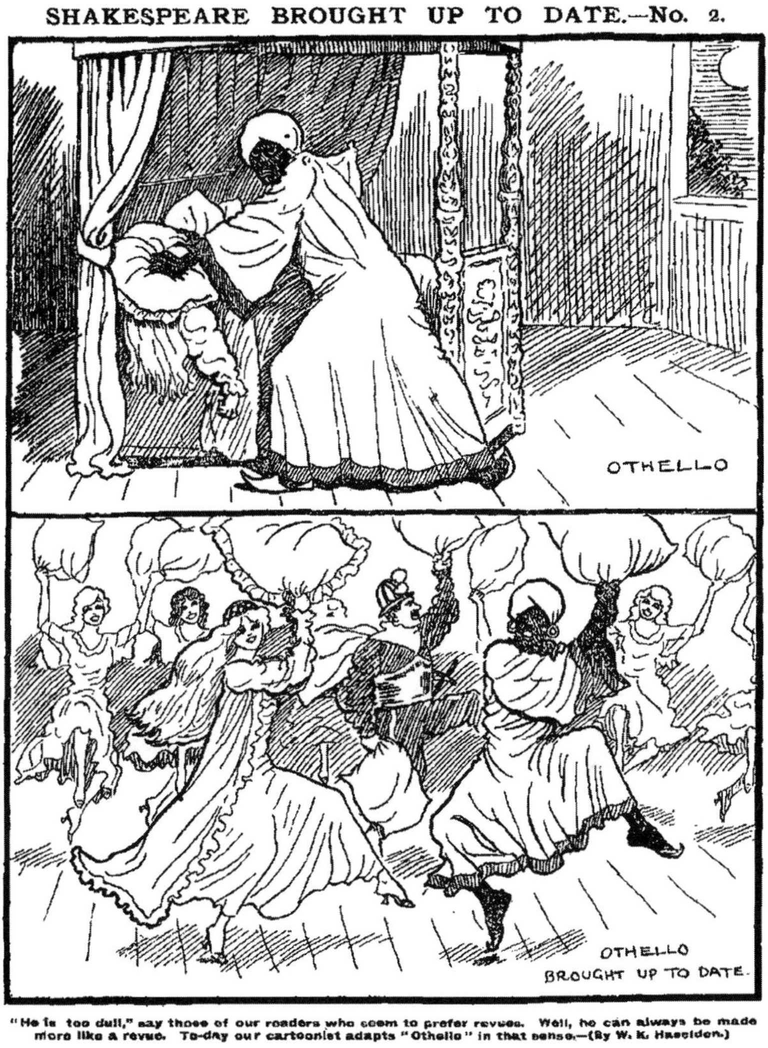
SHAKESPEARE BROUGHT UP TO DATE.—No. 2.
OTHELLO
OTHELLO BROUGHT UP TO DATE.
"He is too dull," say those of our readers who seem to prefer revues. Well, he can always be made more like a revue. To-day our cartoonist adapts "Othello" in that sense.—(By W. K. Haselden.)

Figure 12.18b (*cont.*)

Haselden's Shakespeare, unlike the Bard in *Life*, is not antagonistically related to new forms of drama. In Haselden's cartoons, Shakespeare only needs to be 'brought up to date' and adjusted to current theatrical trends. The plays can easily be adapted to or integrated into

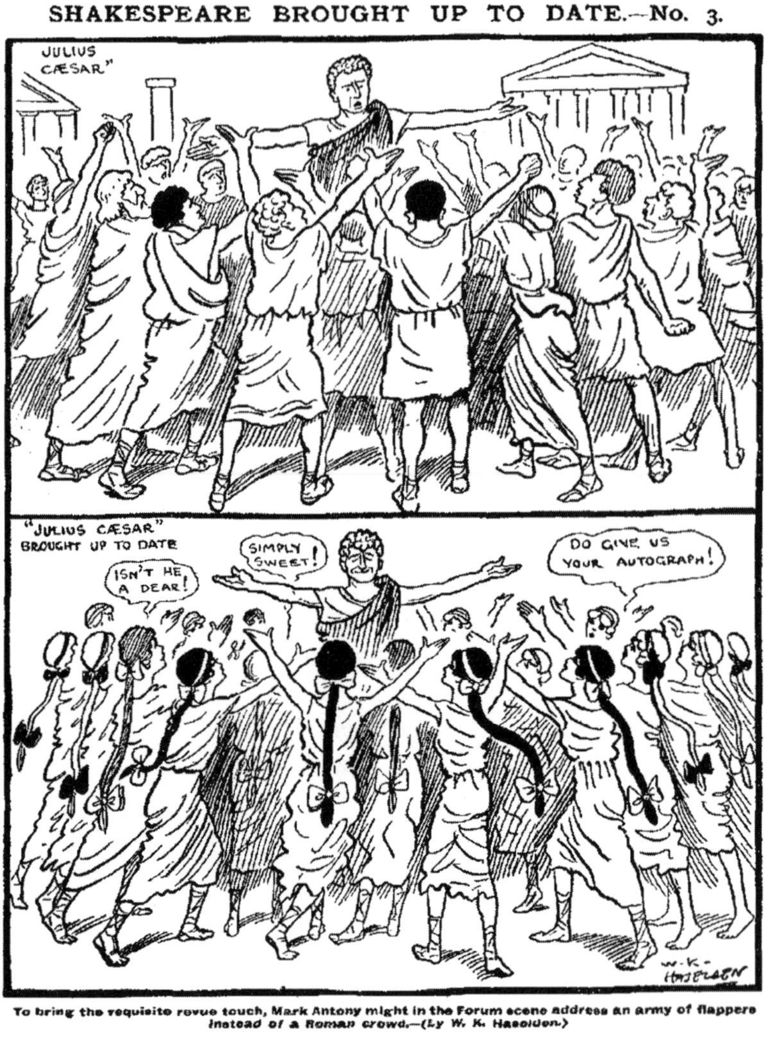

SHAKESPEARE BROUGHT UP TO DATE.—No. 3.

To bring the requisite revue touch, Mark Antony might in the Forum scene address an army of flappers instead of a Roman crowd.—(By W. K. Haselden.)

Figure 12.18c (*cont.*)

musicals or, alternatively, they can import the tricks of motion pictures and update the dialogues. Shakespeare will no longer need to wait at the stage door or push Musical Comedy out of the limelight so that he can step in. All it takes is for the stage managers to make some quick

SHAKESPEARE BROUGHT UP TO DATE.—No. 4.

Obviously modern managers have utterly failed to realise the revue possibilities of "Romeo and Juliet."—(By W. K. Haselden.)

Figure 12.18d (*cont.*)

changes: the Ghost and Hamlet could join the chorus line and jig about with the young female dancers; Desdemona and Othello could recycle the pillow into a useful comic prop for a musical number. The dialogue in *Romeo and Juliet* can be easily updated from 'How cam'st thou hither...? With love's light wings...' to 'You clever boy!' and Romeo can avail himself of the latest mechanical inventions. For *Julius Caesar* to be a success all that is needed is a good-looking celebrity actor.

Haselden's cartoons constitute a response to 'the urge to commemorate' that rises from a 'desire to break with the past, to construct as great a distance as possible between the new age and the old';[23] they jokingly suggest that this is how Shakespeare's plays have been performed till now, but this is how they are likely to be performed from now on. The top frames of his cartoons show how the plays are construed by the collective memory of his time and the lower frames contain his individual response to the effects of the Great War on the theatre scene of London's West End.

In the tercentenary year, when Shakespeare was widely commemorated as a universal genius, the cartoons in *Life* and the *Daily Mirror* added a discordant note to the harmonious, concerted praise of the official celebrations, showing that Shakespeare is not for all times and all ages. His plays had been replaced by music hall and contemporary drama and, to survive in new media such as the cinema, his works had to be adapted and transformed, leaving him practically out of the process. When Shakespeare was enjoying one of his highest points of popularity, being celebrated as global bard and national hero, his plays were felt to be deficient. The memorialising and commemorating of Shakespeare in 1916 also brought to the fore the conflict between Shakespearean drama and the present. In the tercentenary year, both 'blighters' and soldiers on leave wanted revue and movies, not plays by Shakespeare. The greatest threat to Shakespeare in 1916 comes from the growing cultural presence of film and the film industry.

'We speak so much of memory', says Pierre Nora, 'because there is so little of it left'.[24] Memory sites emerge when and where there is an 'acceleration of history',[25] 'a perceived or constructed break with the past'.[26] The 1916 Shakespeare Tercentenary was such a time. The effects of the mechanised war being fought in Europe had already begun to alter collective remembrance of the past – even in neutral countries. Shakespeare was also caught in this acceleration of history, in which Walter Benjamin's angel of history could be said to be moving

---

[23] Gillis, 'Memory and Identity', 8.
[24] Pierre Nora, 'Between Memory and History: *Les Lieux de Mémoire*', *Representations* 26 (1989), 7–24; 7.
[25] Nora, 'Between Memory and History', 7.
[26] Gillis, 'Memory and Identity', 8.

faster in the direction of the future, propelled by the storm blowing from the Western Front, rather than Paradise, but always looking backwards to a past increasingly recreated through commemoration.[27] The Tercentenary generated a specific cluster of commemorative practices and memory sites in which cartoons play a special role. Between the collective and the individual, astride memory and history, these cartoons enshrine how Shakespeare was perceived in popular culture and how a sophisticated observer of culture comments on Shakespeare's cultural presence through the refraction provided by commemoration practice. 'There are *lieux de mémoire*, sites of memory, because there are no longer *milieux de mémoire*, real environments of memory.'[28] Nora's distinction between *lieux* and *milieux de mémoire* explains the ambivalent nature of the tercentenary cartoons – modern replacements for oral memory – which simultaneously commemorate and deride, crystallising collective memory of Shakespeare and questioning the cultural value of the Bard and the plays.

In 1925, Haselden published two other Shakespeare cartoons in the *Daily Mirror* (Figures 12.19 and 12.20). The first cartoon shows that modern-dress performances, which had increasingly attracted attention since H. K. Ayliff's modern-dress *Cymbeline* (1923) for the Birmingham Rep, gave Shakespeare a new lease on life as successful playwright.[29] Ayliff's *Hamlet*, premièred in London at the Kingsway on 25 August 1925, probably triggered Haselden's cartoon. If during the 1910s Shakespeare's star as commercial and popular West End playwright declined, since the 1920s his plays have become an attractive space for experimentalism and the theatrical avant-garde. The other 1925 cartoon (Figure 12.20) shows how the authorship question may never be settled. 'Who wrote Shakespeare's plays?' will always be a question with multiple answers for the popular imagination.

The recently celebrated tercentenary of the publication of the *First Folio* (1923) and the Oxford authorship question – recently raised by

---

[27] Walter Benjamin, 'Theses on the Philosophy of History', in *Illuminations* (London: Pimlico, 1999), 249.

[28] Nora, 'Between Memory and History', 7.

[29] For a discussion of the modern dress productions of the Birmingham Rep in the 1920s, see C. Cochrane, *Shakespeare and the Birmingham Repertory Theatre 1913–1929* (London: Society for Theatre Research, 1993). *Cymbeline* (1923), the first play to be produced in modern dress, was a commemorative event: for the tercentenary of the publication of the First Folio and mostly for the tenth anniversary of the founding of the Birmingham Rep itself.

Figure 12.19 W. K. Haselden, 'Dressing Shakespeare up to date'. *Daily Mirror*, 27 July 1925. By permission of Mirrorpix.

J. Thomas Looney in *'Shakespeare' Identified* (1920) – are perhaps behind this other 1925 cartoon. Here, Shakespeare is once more iconically memorialised through his pointed chin and receding hairline, together with his doublet and hose. The Kent and Scheemakers

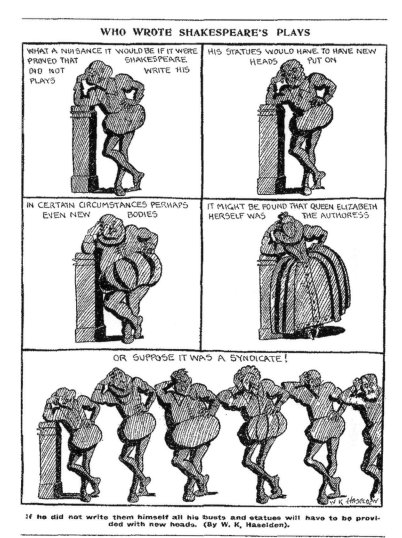

Figure 12.20 W. K. Haselden, 'Who wrote Shakespeare's plays' *Daily Mirror*, 28 September 1925. By permission of Mirrorpix.

memorial once again provides the extra iconic support the Shakespeare figure needs to be unmistakably Shakespeare. The scroll has disappeared, the pile of books seems to have diminished, and there is no inscription on the pedestal. Shakespeare's finger no longer points at

words of any sort. Once again, the iconicity of the Kent and Scheemakers memorial is used to simultaneously question the authorship of
the plays and poke fun at the authorship question.

The construction of Shakespeare and his plays as a site of conflict
during the 1916 Tercentenary reveals not only the complexity of the
mechanisms that infuse the cultures of commemoration but also the
contradictory drives propelling commemorative practices. The reception of Shakespeare in America, as Bruce Smith has argued, often
revolves around a certain indecision about 'what to do with Shakespeare – worship him as a cultural hero or treat him as "one of us"'.[30]
The cartoons in *Life*, uncharacteristically perhaps, show no hesitation –
for them, there is no choosing. During the 1916 Tercentenary, Shakespeare is both a cultural hero and an American citizen who has to earn
his living in the whimsical showbiz.

As these cartoons show, memorialising Shakespeare in popular
media implies a paradoxical desire to preserve the past and to alter
it. The cultural past is simultaneously commemorated and discarded
as ancient, memorialised and changed to resemble the present – and so
is Shakespeare. Like the past it belongs to, Shakespeare is contradictorily treasured and seen to be in need of *aggiornamento*. The Haselden
cartoons signal a breach between two different types of Shakespearean
cultural identity that would be consolidated throughout the twentieth-
century. From the 1916 Tercentenary onwards, the cultural life of
Shakespeare's plays will oscillate between the two extreme poles of the
cultural continuum, popular culture and avant-garde experimentation.

The 1916 Tercentenary thus provided an opportunity for cartoons
to construe Shakespeare as a site of memory but also as a site of
conflict. In the course of questioning Shakespeare's cultural value,
cartoons also problematise the notion of authorship and present new
technologies – and the moving image in particular – as a threat to the
survival of drama. The construction of Shakespeare and his plays as a
site of conflict during the 1916 Tercentenary reveals not only the
complexity of the mechanisms that infuse the cultures of commemoration but also the contradictory impulses behind commemorative
practices – such as, for instance, a desire to appropriate the past and
an urge to see the present and the future as distinct from the same past
that is being simultaneously commemorated and rejected.

---

[30] Smith, *Roasting the Swan of Avon*, 50.

13 | Sculpted Shakespeare

TON HOENSELAARS

The statues and busts of Shakespeare that we encounter worldwide provide access to a number of rare histories that comprise many of the commemorative fortunes of the playwright's life, his work and the afterlives of both. Each sculpted object has a rich story of its design, production, erection and maintenance that enhances our appreciation of Shakespeare's cultural position in the world. In order to reveal some of these riches, the first part of this chapter focuses on the cultural history of Shakespearean busts and statues as three-dimensional, visual images in bronze or stone, but also images of these images as represented in other media, such as paintings or literary texts. The second part of the chapter focuses on the ways in which Shakespearean busts and statues will only yield their full story if we take into consideration their specific geographical contexts. It does this by exploring in greater detail the phenomenon of nineteenth-century statuemania with specific reference to the cultural history of the Paris Shakespeare statues by both Pierre Fournier and Paul Landowski between the 1880s and the middle of the twentieth century. The final part of this chapter looks at the evolving history of the statue as a specific genre, and explores the ways in which a change of perception with regard to the medium of expression that statues and monuments represent has engendered new modes of commemorating Shakespeare in Europe, the United States and Australia.

This story of sculpted Shakespeare is not an obvious one. Shakespeare himself expressed the belief that statues and monuments do not guarantee the lasting remembrance of a writer. In Sonnet 55 we read of the speaker's conviction that 'Not marble nor the gilded monuments / Of princes shall outlive [the poet's] powerful rhyme.' The poem argues that whereas 'wasteful war shall statues overturn' the beloved will 'live' in the

Research for this article has been financed by Research Project 12014/PHCS/09, 'Great War Shakespeare II: Myths, Social Agent and Global Culture' (Fundación Séneca) and by Research Project FFI2011-24347 'Cultures of Commemoration II: Remembering Shakespeare' (Spanish Plan Nacional de I+D+i 2008–2011).

279

sonnet that we are reading.[1] The written or the printed word celebrating love will be read and remembered until the Last Judgement, but statues will perish because of neglect, adverse weather conditions or wars.

Some early readers, like John Milton in his dedicatory poem to the Second Folio (1632), were inclined to take Shakespeare at his word, and argued:

> What need my Shakespeare for his honoured bones
> The labour of an age in pilèd stones,
> Or that his hallowed relics should be hid
> Under a star-ypointing pyramid?[2]

Rather than funeral statuary or another form of commemorative edifice, the argument continued, Shakespeare's writings should be recognized as a monument in their own right, with us, as readers, petrified in awe of him, metaphorically positioned like pensive and attentive statues on its periphery:

> Thou in our wonder and astonishment
> Hast built thyself a lasting monument,
> . . .
>
> [and] thou, our fancy of herself bereaving,
> Dost make us marble with too much conceiving,
> And so sepulchered in such pomp dost lie
> That kings for such a tomb would wish to die.[3]

Milton – sounding rather like Ben Jonson, who called Shakespeare 'a monument without a tomb'[4] – was to be echoed by many who, in the course of the centuries, preferred to commemorate Shakespeare, privately or in public, without recourse to statuary.

Shakespeare's Sonnet 55, with its imagery denigrating monuments, supported by Milton and Jonson, began a history of commemorative practice that is pervasively ironic, because the same poet who expressed such scepticism about statues and monuments was to have readers and admirers who doggedly tried to honour him in marble or

---

[1] Stanley Wells and Gary Taylor (eds.), *The Oxford Shakespeare*, 2nd edn (Oxford: Clarendon Press, 2005), 785.
[2] Wells and Taylor, *Oxford Shakespeare*, lxxiii.
[3] Wells and Taylor, *Oxford Shakespeare*, lxxiii.
[4] Wells and Taylor, *Oxford Shakespeare*, lxxi, line 22.

brass. Such efforts remained largely unchanged, as we shall see, when statues and monuments even seemed to confirm the poet's vision and disappeared off the face of the earth, unlike Shakespeare's own verse. As the developing story reveals, however, in the course of the centuries after Shakespeare's death, the admirers, too, slowly came to acknowledge the ephemeral nature of statuary of which the poet spoke, including the statue's tendency to become 'invisible'. Such new insights have changed the way in which Shakespeare is commemorated: the monuments and statues that we still have are made visible again by creative means, and when Shakespeare inspires aficionados to construct new effigies, there is an attempt to stress the very objects' ephemeral nature, as he himself did. However, there is a difference too. We also tend to turn this vice into a virtue, arguing that the lasting value of such commemoration is our actual practice of it.

Statues, busts, icons

Despite the various reservations in the work of Shakespeare, Jonson and Milton, the making of monuments dedicated to Shakespeare began shortly after the poet's death. Soon after the burial of Shakespeare in Holy Trinity Church, Stratford-upon-Avon, a painted bust was installed in the chancel to the left of his grave (c.1616–23). Few admirers of Shakespeare are convinced that this rather plain individual represents the author of *Romeo and Juliet* or *The Sonnets*. The Victorians were inclined to believe that it was based on the so-called Darmstadt mask which had been 'rediscovered' in Germany in 1849. This also explains why, in 1857, Henry Wallis depicted sculptor Gheerart Janssen working on his famous monument with that mask as his model (Figure 13.1). Few still believe that the Darmstadt mask is authentic or reliable as a guide to the appearance of Shakespeare, so the bust in Holy Trinity Church remains shrouded in mystery.[5]

During the early eighteenth century the first attempts were undertaken to produce new effigies of Shakespeare. An early bust of Shakespeare appeared in Richard Temple, Viscount Cobham's Temple of British Worthies in The Elysian Fields at Stowe.[6] Curiously, on this

---

[5] Samuel Schoenbaum, *Shakespeare's Lives*, new edn (Oxford University Press, 1993), 338–9.

[6] See David R. Coffin, *The English Garden: Meditation and Memorial* (Princeton University Press, 1994).

Figure 13.1 Henry Wallis (1830–1916), *A Sculptor's Workshop, Stratford-upon-Avon, 1617* (oil on canvas). Royal Shakespeare Company Collection, Stratford-upon-Avon, Warwickshire, Bridgeman Images.

early occasion installing the sculpted bust of the man from Stratford represented a decidedly oppositional, anti-establishment gesture.[7] Yet, Shakespeare soon became the national poet with the creation, in the course of the 1730s, of the now famous statue at Poets' Corner in Westminster Abbey, designed by William Kent and executed by the Flemish sculptor Peter Scheemakers. The statue represents a cross-legged Shakespeare leaning on a pedestal with books. He seems to be pointing at a scroll with (slightly rewritten) lines from *The Tempest* (which had not been part of the statue's original design). The same statue was to go through many changes, as copies were made of it, some effected by the sculptor himself. Star actor David Garrick ordered a lead copy of a later version as a gift to the Stratford Corporation. This rough mirror image of Scheemakers' statue is now at the Town Hall. For his own Shakespeare Temple at Hampton, however, Garrick commissioned the French sculptor Louis-François Roubiliac to produce a new statue (see Peter Holland's chapter in this volume). Completed in 1758, Roubiliac's Shakespeare, as Michael Dobson has described it, 'metamorphoses the portentous scroll at which the Abbey figure points, and the ponderous volumes on which it rests a glum elbow, into an immense Bard-sized blank page of infinite possibility, over which the writer leans; with an unconscious lifting of the left forefinger to the chin he is swiftly turning his head away, in a spontaneous movement of inspiration.'[8] The Roubiliac statue is no longer at Garrick's Shakespeare Temple, but graces the hall of the new British Library, welcoming readers as they mount the stairs.

Over the centuries, the Roubiliac and Scheemakers statues, as much as the Janssen effigy, have become canonical worldwide, determining the appearance of many representations of Shakespeare produced since, including other statues, busts and related effigies for both public and private spaces (parks and squares, facades, public libraries, private studies), but also often smaller versions to decorate such everyday objects as bookends, Christmas trees, tobacco stoppers and key rings. Effigies of Shakespeare also make good stage props, like the bust of the Bard that featured in the *Batman* television series; tilting back the

---

[7] Michel Dobson, *The Making of the National Poet: Shakespeare, Adaptation and Authorship, 1660–1769* (Oxford: Clarendon Press, 1992), 135–7.
[8] Dobson, *The Making of the National Poet*, 180.

venerable head of the man from Stratford would disclose the button that operated the motorized door to the Batcave.

As symbols of acknowledged fame, statues and busts have entered the field of advertising with some ease, in attempts to sell Flowers Bitter, Gordon's Gin, Waterman's Fountain Pen and numerous other products. As iconic symbols *par excellence* Shakespearean statues and busts represent sizeable cultural capital. This explains why the funeral monument furnished forth the idea for the golden mosaic over the entrance to The Old Bank in Stratford-upon-Avon, and how, between 1899 and 1926, it graced the one-shilling Shakespeare Stamp sold in support of the Holy Trinity Church in Shakespeare's place of birth. Undoubtedly, the cultural-cum-commercial capital of Shakespeare statuary is best evidenced by the fact that from 9 July 1970 until 19 March 1993 the Scheemakers statue graced the twenty-pound banknote in Britain.[9]

Perhaps the oldest and most intriguing form of statue appropriation is that of individuals depicted in its presence. In 1762, Adrien Carpentiers painted a portrait of Roubiliac putting the finishing touches to his Shakespeare statue, begging the question of who the great creator was on this occasion. Similarly, in 1784, David Garrick had himself painted, reciting his 'Ode to Shakespeare' by the Scheemakers statue. The implicit rivalry between one poet and another here also underlies the 1892 cartoon of Oscar Wilde posing as a rival playwright to Shakespeare by adopting the famous carriage of the Scheemakers statue.[10] This practice continues, and there are numerous photo series of actors and singers portrayed with the Bard's bust in an attempt to legitimate their own achievement. In a tradition that started around the time of the Stratford Jubilee of 1769, when David Garrick (again) had himself represented with his right arm around the Shakespeare bust by Thomas Gainsborough, we find a remarkable photo series of Orson Welles with the Shakespeare bust taken by Cecil Beaton in New York in 1942.[11] During a photoshoot after the release of Baz Luhrmann's

---

[9] Graham Holderness (ed.), *The Shakespeare Myth* (Manchester University Press, 1988), xi–xx.

[10] Clara Calvo, 'Shakespeare, *lieu de mémoire*', in Christophe Hausermann (ed.), *Shakespeare et la mémoire*. http://shakespeare.revues.org/1961.

[11] Christian Deelman, *The Great Shakespeare Jubilee* (London: Michael Joseph, 1964), 68–75; and Ian McIntyre, *Garrick* (Harmondsworth: Penguin Books, 1999), 413–14. See also http://patriciadamiano.blogspot.nl/2011/04/orson-welles-shakespeare-y-cecil-beaton.html.

Romeo + Juliet, Leonardo DiCaprio and Clare Danes were photographed with a bust of the Bard.[12] The cover of Cleo Laine's *Shakespeare and All that Jazz* album of 1964 also unmistakably belongs to this tradition, but the singer clearly presents a challenge to the sacrosanct status of the playwright and poet.

Some of the most intriguing as well as neglected recreations of Shakespeare statues may be found in literature, from the earliest period onwards, as in Elizabeth Boyd's *Don Sancho or, the Students Whim* (1739), which marks a vital stage in the development of Shakespeare as a ghost to Shakespeare as a stage character.[13] During the early twentieth century, a musical comedy entitled *The Merry-Go-Round* was popular in Europe and the United States. It depicted the life of a man-about-town who passes through the 'Seven Ages' of Jacques in his dream, accompanied by a statue of Shakespeare come to life.[14] In George Bernard Shaw's short story entitled 'A Dressing Room Secret' (1910), Shakespeare intriguingly confesses how in the course of his life 'conscience' always tended to make him paint thoroughly unethical characters like Iago, Lady Macbeth and Prince Hal as more likeable humans. Unfortunately, a current of air in the dressing room causes the Shakespeare bust to sneeze, and with its consequent crash to the floor, its much-desired revelations cease forever.[15]

One of the most remarkable and extensive literary texts devoted to statuefying Shakespeare is Charles Kelsall's *The First Sitting of the Committee on the Proposed Monument to Shakespeare* (1823), written as part of an early statue craze during the 1820s. *The First Sitting* features the fictional midnight meeting of a venerable company, seated around a bust of Shakespeare in a green room in London, to discuss the erection of a public monument to the 'the main bulwark of the British stage' and, as the native Chairman puts it, 'the pride of our isles'.[16]

---

[12] www.fanpop.com/clubs/leonardo-dicaprio.

[13] Dobson, *The Making of the National Poet*, 161.

[14] Meyer Lutz, Seymour Hicks and Aubrey Hopwood, *The Merry-Go-Round: Musical Comedy* (London: F. Day & Hunter, 1910).

[15] George Bernard Shaw, 'A Dressing Room Secret', in Maurice J. O'Sullivan, Jr. (ed.), *Shakespeare's Other Lives: An Anthology of Fictional Depictions of the Bard* (Jefferson, NC: McFarland and Co., 1997), 104–8.

[16] Anon. [= Charles Kelsall], *The First Sitting of the Committee on the Proposed Monument to Shakespeare. Carefully taken in Short-Hand by Zachary Craft, Amanuensis to the Chairman* (Cheltenham: printed for G. A. Williams, 1823), resp. 48, 9.

Present at this extended conversation are many representatives from all over Britain and the rest of the world, and from across the entire social spectrum. In addition to members representing the clergy and the acting profession, students are present, landowners, farmers, architects and builders, shopkeepers, schoolmasters, merchants and tourists. In the course of the lively discussion, we become privy also to the outspoken views of international philosophers and writers, present and past, whose representatives include British poets such as John Milton and John Dryden, Alexander Pope, Francis Thomson and Thomas Gray, as well as David Garrick. Editors of Shakespeare, too, are present, including George Warburton, Dr Johnson, Edmund Malone and George Steevens. And from beyond the British Isles originate the many ghosts of classical philosophers, poets and playwrights – Aristotle, Longinus, Aeschylus, Euripides, Aristophanes, Plautus and Terence – while more recent European writers who participate in the discussion include Lope de Vega, Molière, Voltaire, Diderot and D'Alembert, as well as Vittorio Alfieri. There is no space here to do justice to the richness and the subtlety of *The First Sitting*, but several examples may suggest the complexity of erecting a statue, and the multiple issues that are at play.

The First Sitting begins by evoking the ancient classical tradition of which Shakespeare is an heir, as the Homer of the North. The ghost of Aristotle is in favour of a monument, but dislikes Shakespeare's sometimes 'ill-digested stuff', work that shows no respect for the Aristotelian unities and is written in a dialect inferior to Ancient Greek.[17] Classical and Neo-classical poetics are deftly juxtaposed with the early-Romantic vision of Longinus, who finds that Shakespeare is sublime at illustrating his theories.[18]

Poetical concerns such as these easily shift into a political gear. The ghost of Aeschylus wants a monument but cannot stay because he is needed in Greece to help deliver the country 'from the yoke of barbarians'.[19] Kelsall's branding of Aeschylus as a Greek national poet may seem traditional, but matters are complicated when a Greek merchant from Patras named Pelagio Dimitri also seeks to involve 'Shakespeare' in the Greek drive for independence, like a second Byron. Pelagio Dimitri will vote in favour of a statue, but only in return for political

---

[17] Kelsall, *The First Sitting*, 11.   [18] Kelsall, *The First Sitting*, 12–13.
[19] Kelsall, *The First Sitting*, 14.

and military support: 'If you will help Athenians and Albanians in heart good, to drive barbarous and infidel *Tourkoi* to Asia-side, I will answer on head mine, that New-Greece government will grant bit of ground on Parnassus mountain.'[20]

Next to political opportunism there is the commercial interest of the Stratford butcher Frank Crib, who owns the birthplace, and, considering it to be a fine monument in its own right, is ready to sell it for 2,000 pounds.[21] Completing this cameo of pre-Victorian business acumen is Crib's preparedness in future to maintain the monument and to combat the graffiti from visitors who were indeed to be an increasing source of income as well as disquiet in the course of the century ahead.[22]

Finally, personal reasons play a role. A Jew named Mechisedech Levi refuses to pay for a statue devoted to the creator of Shylock and Jessica.[23] However, Lancelot Blood, a cardiac specialist from Edinburgh, holds a different opinion. With both a scientific interest in Shylock's 'pound of flesh' and his admiration of Shakespeare's knowledge of the emotions, Lancelot Blood believes the playwright ought to be represented 'holding in his right hand a human heart turned inside out, and pointing with his left, to all its naked deformity and wretchedness'.[24] It no longer comes as a surprise that midshipman John Alworthy wants a boat-like statue of oak in Stratford.

Clearly, every participant at the meeting projects his own life and experience onto Shakespeare and, by extension, seeks to erect a monument not in Shakespeare's but in his own image.[25] *The First Sitting* demonstrates how the idea of a public statue for Shakespeare tends to create more problems than it solves. For poetical, political, commercial as well as personal reasons, Kelsall suggests, a project of this kind seems doomed to fail.

Perhaps the greatest problem, however, is that interest in the statue brings so many different nations together. By itself, this international traffic is not new: in the seventeenth and eighteenth centuries the great busts and statues of Shakespeare had all been created by foreigners to

---

[20] Kelsall, *The First Sitting*, 67. [21] Kelsall, *The First Sitting*, 49.
[22] Stratford in the 1820s is not discussed by Julia Thomas in *Shakespeare's Shrine: The Bard's Birthplace and the Invention of Stratford-upon-Avon* (Philadelphia, PA: University of Pennsylvania Press, 2012).
[23] Kelsall, *The First Sitting*, 64–5. [24] Kelsall, *The First Sitting*, 77–8.
[25] Kelsall, *The First Sitting*, 81.

English culture: the Dutchman Gheerart Janssen, the Fleming Peter Scheemakers, the Frenchman Louis-François Roubiliac. The participation of these continental others had been largely unproblematic during an age that was decidedly cosmopolitan in attitude. In the nineteenth century, however, the question as to who was to sculpt the national poet became a divisive issue on many occasions.

In Kelsall's *First Sitting*, Shakespeare emerges as a universal playwright and poet by Neo-classical standards, but he does so at a time when national interests have come to prevail over any ideal of a transnational or cross-border philosophy. Interestingly, the most salient friction in the *First Sitting* takes place between England and the United States, in an encounter that also reflects the social unrest at the time between English intellectuals (including William Hazlitt) and Washington Irving who, in 1822, had been appointed to the committee planning the construction of the Shakespeare monument. The English press argued that 'a *national* monument' could have been raised to Shakespeare without selecting on the committee 'a member of a republic which ha[d] denationalized itself', whereas the American press replied that it was precisely the universal character of Shakespeare that justified Washington Irving's membership on the committee and, with it, the United States' claim to the Bard.[26]

Kelsall's *First Sitting* and the events of the 1820s foreshadowed some of the debates that were to rage across Britain in the course of the nineteenth century, particularly around the time of the century's commemorative year par excellence, 1864. Across England, there were many initiatives and attempts to erect a statue of Shakespeare as the national poet, symbolically financed by public subscription, but all plans failed dismally, and this was not only because a number of them were in competition with each other.[27] As a consequence, the major British statues of the period that we know – the Shakespeare statue and monument in London's Leicester Square, erected in 1874, and

---

[26] Richard V. McLamore, 'The Dutchman in the Attic: Claiming an Inheritance in *The Sketch Book of Geoffrey Crayon*', *American Literature* 72:1 (2000), 31–57.
[27] Sidney Lee, 'The Commemoration of Shakespeare in London', in his *Shakespeare and the Modern Stage, and Other Essays* (London: John Murray, 1906), 214–42. See also Richard Foulkes, *The Shakespeare Tercentenary of 1864*, with a foreword by J. C. Trewin (London: Society for Theatre Research, 1984).

the Ronald Gower monument, unveiled in Stratford on 10 October 1888 – were personal gifts.[28] The Stratford monument was a gift from the sculptor himself.[29] The monument in London – a copy of the Scheemakers statue, integrated into a new monument by James Knowles – was a personal gift to the city from Albert Grant, MP.[30] It remains ironic that England's national poet should not have obtained a national statue in his own country, particularly when such initiatives did prove successful abroad, as in the United States, where John Quincy Adams Ward's statue was inaugurated in Central Park, New York, in 1872.

Statuemania

The long nineteenth century – from the French Revolution to the First World War – has been justly diagnosed with the cultural fever known as statuemania. Amidst the political ebb and flow in this age of revolution and restoration, the newly empowered citizen began to adopt a decisive role in the production of statuary. Monuments, he believed, should no longer commemorate simply the nation's political and military leaders, as had been customary until 1789, but be dedicated also to its laudable citizens, its 'great men', including playwrights like Shakespeare.[31]

It is during this period – which coincided with the apogee of bardolatry – that Shakespeare statues mushroomed across the globe. The statue by John Quincy Adams Ward, commissioned during the commemoration year 1864, and completed in 1870, was unveiled in New York's Central Park in 1872. In 1878 Ferdinand von Mueller's was unveiled in Tower Grove Park, St Louis. In 1888 three new statues were inaugurated during the same year: William Ordway Partridge's statue of Shakespeare in Lincoln Park, Chicago; Lord Ronald

---

[28] Unique is the bust of Shakespeare as part of the 'Memorial to John Heminge and Henry Condell' at Aldermanbury. See Philip Ward-Jackson, *Public Sculpture of the City of London* (Liverpool University Press, 2003), 2; and Graham Holderness, 'Shakespeare Remembered', *Critical Survey* 22:2 (2010), 39–61.

[29] Michael Kimberley, *Lord Ronald Gower's Monument to Shakespeare* (Stratford-upon-Avon Society, 1989).

[30] See also Helke Rausch, *Kulturfigur und Nation: Öffentliche Denkmäler in Paris, Berlin und London, 1848–1914* (Munich: R. Oldenbourg Verlag, 2006), 627–41.

[31] June Hargrove, 'Les Statues de Paris', in Pierre Nora (ed.), *Les Lieux de mémoire* (Paris: Éditions Gallimard, 1997), vol. II, 1855–6; and her *Les Statues de Paris: La Répresentation des grands hommes dans les rues et sur les places de Paris* (Antwerp: Fons Mercator, and Paris: Albin Michel, 1989).

Gower's memorial to Shakespeare in Stratford-upon-Avon; and, inaugurated no more than one week after the unveiling ceremony at the Memorial Theatre, the Pierre Fournier statue on the Boulevard Haussmann in Paris.[32] In 1896 the Shakespeare statue by Frederick William MacMonnies came to grace the Library of Congress in Washington. Otto Lessing was responsible for Germany's statuary tribute unveiled in Weimar in 1904, and, commissioned in 1914 but delayed by the outbreak of the Great War, Sir Bertram Mac-Kennal's memorial to Shakespeare in Sydney entered the public space in 1926.

No well-documented account, coherent cultural history or even a reliable catalogue of these statues exists, or of the hundreds of less canonical effigies worldwide.[33] Statues and busts are the most neglected part of Shakespeare's afterlife.[34] This is surprising, if we realize how much such commemorative material and practice may reveal about the way in which the playwright has become iconic across the globe in the course of the centuries. A particularly intriguing cultural history is that of the Shakespeare statue in Paris.

The statue was a gift to the city of Paris from the wealthy Scotsman William Knighton, who himself owned an apartment overlooking the place where the statue was to be erected. The city council gladly accepted the offer, since doing so represented a form of rapprochement between two historical enemies, England and France, at a time when the memory of the disastrous 1870–1 war with Prussia induced the French to explore new international alliances. A poem, read at its inauguration, spoke of the Shakespeare statue as the recycled bronze of wartime cannons (like those used by the opposing English and the French armies at Waterloo) to boost the canon of the international Republic of Letters that France and England now shared.[35] Such irenic

---

[32] Kimberley, *Lord Ronald Gower's Monument to Shakespeare*, 28–34.

[33] For a discussion of the Sydney memorial, however, see Philip Mead's chapter in this volume, pp. 00–00.

[34] Manfred Pfister, '"In States Unborn and Accents Yet Unknown": Shakespeare and the European Canon', in Ladina Bezzola Lambert and Balz Engler (eds.), *Shifting the Scene: Shakespeare in European Culture* (Newark, NJ: University of Delaware Press, 2004), 41–63.

[35] Ton Hoenselaars, 'The Pierre Fournier Shakespeare Statue in the City of Paris, 1888–1941: Reflections on Commemoration, Cosmopolitanism, and Urban Development during the Third Republic', *Shakespeare-Jahrbuch*, 147 (2011), 105–23.

idealism existed alongside age-old reservations about the English, and this explains why the popular press developed the theory that William Knighton had given the statue to the city in order to prevent the place outside his apartment from being used for a noisy merry-go-round each year on 14 July, disturbing his night's rest. This obviously potent myth of King Shakespeare preventing Parisians from celebrating Bastille Day was to persist well into the twentieth century, when it had also come to be used by city planners (combating traffic congestion) to remove a number of statues around the city, and Shakespeare's was included: 'What is Shakespeare doing on the Boulevard Haussmann ...? Let all the statues that are out of place in Paris be transferred to the new gardens, ranged in intelligent order, and thus accomplish their purpose.'[36] In the end, the Shakespeare statue did not make it to any garden. In 1941, a committee, inaugurated by the Vichy government and headed by Paul Landowski (the sculptor of Rio de Janeiro's iconic 'Christ the Redeemer'), drew up lists of bronze statues that had to be melted down for the war industry. As part of an operation that later became known as 'La Mort des statues', canonical Shakespeare was removed on 13 December 1941, and served as bronze for cannons once again.[37]

The story of the Paris Shakespeare statue makes up a vital chapter in the playwright's afterlife as shaped by the unusually complex Anglo-French relations of the Third Republic. It is also a contribution to the broader history of urbanization and city noise, because William Knighton was not the only citizen on Boulevard Haussmann who tried to negotiate the noise of the capital of the nineteenth century. In 1906, it was Marcel Proust, who moved into the second-storey apartment a few houses down from 134, Boulevard Haussmann – at 102, to be precise – and famously proceeded to line the bedroom with cork tiles 'to reduce the noise from his neighbours and the boulevard'.[38]

But the Paris Shakespeare statue is also the exemplary story of the rise and fall of statuemania, and here its post-Second World War

---

[36] *The New York Times*, 14 August 1910.

[37] Kirrily Freeman, *Bronzes to Bullets: Vichy and the Destruction of French Public Statuary, 1941–1944* (Stanford University Press, 2009), 148.

[38] Diana Fuss, *The Sense of an Interior: Four Writers and the Rooms that Shaped Them* (New York and London: Routledge, 2004), 70; and Jon Kear, 'Une chambre mentale: Proust's Solitude', in Harald Hendrix (ed.), *Writers' Houses and the Making of Memory* (New York and London: Routledge, 2008), 221–33, 222.

history is telling. In 1944, Paul Landowski agreed to replace the Pierre Fournier statue with one of his own making.[39] Landowski had many plans: he worked on Shakespeare as Moses, Shakespeare reading *Hamlet*, Shakespeare addressing the actors and Shakespeare as Prospero.[40] Some of the models he produced were more abstract than others, but ultimately all of them were distinctly representational, with their planned pedestals containing numerous figures evoking the characters of Shakespeare.[41] In 1951, however, seven years after getting the commission, and after many reminders, Landowski abandoned the project, and the Paris authorities decided not to have a new statue. Instead they supported plans for an alternative site of memory for Shakespeare, the Théâtre Shakespeare in the Jardin du Pré Catelan in the Bois de Boulogne.[42]

The moral of the Paris Shakespeare statue or statues seems to be that in the course of some six decades, ideas about public sculpture and the practice of commemoration had changed. As Sergiusz Michalsky has demonstrated, nineteenth century statue fever abated during the early years of the twentieth century and roughly came to an end with the First World War.[43] In the course of the War the need to glorify the meritorious citizen gradually ceded to a desire for statues and monuments that could rehearse grief over public loss, in abstract rather than realist terms. This change of direction continued after the Holocaust, as traditional, representational statuary came to be seen increasingly as doubtful instances of glorification and heroism, associated with an excessive degree of public exhibitionism. In the process, abstract monuments developed as sites for meditation and self-reflection. The

---

[39] Georges Poisson, 'Le Sort des statues de bronze parisiennes sous l'occupation allemande, 1940–1944', *Paris et Île-de-France – Mémoires* 47:2 (1996), 165–309.

[40] Michèle Lefrançois, *Paul Landowski: L'Oeuvre sculpté* (Grâne: CREAPHIS Éditions, 2009), 382–4.

[41] Lefrançois, *Paul Landowski*, 382–4.

[42] Kirrily Freeman, '"Pedestals Dedicated to Absence": The Symbolic Impact of the Wartime Destruction of French Bronze Statuary', in Patricia M. E. Lorcin and Daniel Brewer (eds.), *France and Its Spaces of War: Experience, Memory, Image* (Houndmills: Palgrave Macmillan, 2009), 163–77 (168). On the 'Jardin Shakespeare', see Ron Engle, Felicia Hardison Londré and Daniel J. Water Meier (eds.), *Shakespeare Companies and Festivals: An International Guide*. (Westport, CT: Greenwood Press, 1995), 414–17.

[43] Sergiusz Michalski, *Public Monuments: Art in Political Bondage, 1870–1997* (London: Reaktion Books, 1998), 171–84.

criticism of representational statuary as being extroverted engendered a tradition that favoured the statue or monument as a void, as something invisible, a site inviting the observer to reflect on emptiness, disintegration and decay. Against the background of these developments, we may begin to appreciate that the attempt of Paul Landowski – who, as Lefrançois puts it, was neither an 'avant garde' sculptor, nor an 'indépendant' but an 'académique'[44] – to sculpt a new, highly representational statue of a deserving world citizen as a role model after the Second World War, was perhaps bound to fail from the beginning in 1944.

Changing statuary, changing Shakespeare

The potent concept that has evolved of the statue or monument as an absent presence, as a present void, a space not for praise but for meditation, where one does not honour heroes but engages in self-reflection instead, exists alongside a decidedly more popular perception of the statue's 'visibility'. This popular view derives from a short essay by the twentieth-century German novelist Robert Musil (1880–1942). Musil famously observed that the most remarkable thing about statues is that one does not notice them ('das Auffallendste an Denkmälern ist ... daß man sie nicht bemerkt').[45] According to Musil, one cannot simply argue that we do not observe statues well enough. There is a quality intrinsic to the genre of the statue that makes it escape our notice. How unlike traffic signs, he reasons, which use bright colours to attract our attention! How unlike locomotives, which blow their whistle each time they approach! Even our public mailboxes are painted so you cannot miss them! But, admittedly, it was not only in the nature of the statue's genre that commemoration paradoxically produced neglect and oblivion. By the 1920s, Musil argued, the same statue that had just profited from a worldwide mania lasting almost a century had entered a new age, and had become 'backward' (*rückständig*). In our age of noise and movement, Musil wrote, in our modern world of traffic signs and advertising (where manikins – the advertising industry's alternative to the static statue – may rivet

---

[44] Lefrançois, *Paul Landowski*, 8.
[45] Robert Musil, 'Denkmale', in Robert Musil, *Gesammelte Werke 7: Kleine Prosa. Aphorismen. Autobiographisches* (Hamburg: Rowohlt Verlag, 1978), 506–9 (506).

pedestrians' attention at seeing them move like automatons in shop windows), the traditional statue should find a way to draw attention to itself once again.[46]

Musil's views about the invisibility of statues – and the need to make them visible again – also shed interesting light on the way in which statues of Shakespeare have come to be used in a creative manner during the twentieth and twenty-first centuries. Mead Schaeffer's front-cover artwork for the *Saturday Evening Post* of 28 April 1945 captures the problem of visibility in an exceptional fashion and offers a solution.[47] The cover drawing, entitled 'Romance under Shakespeare's Shadow', shows John Quincy Adams Ward's statue of Shakespeare in Central Park on a spring day in wartime New York (Figure 13.2). Shakespeare is surrounded by children innocently chasing one another, or queuing up for ice-cream; a boy in a striped shirt is flying a kite brandishing a star; a woman is walking her dog; GIs amorously engage with their partners; a lone sailor is eying a lone nurse pushing a pram; and another man seated on a bench at Shakespeare's feet is watching it all. No one among this considerable crowd of innocent New Yorkers seems to show any interest in the Shakespeare statue. To them, Shakespeare is invisible. The exception here is a group of pigeons, one of which, coloured white and bearing a rather obvious resemblance to the popular icon of the Holy Spirit, is about to touch down at Shakespeare's feet. Both by direction and by indirection, Mead Schaeffer directs our gaze to the invisible statue, and suggests the unrecognized merit that deserves recognition. The cover of the *Saturday Evening Post* confirms the truism about the invisibility of statues, but it also effectively realizes Musil's hope that 'in our contemporary world of signs, in our age of noise and movement, the statue might find a way to draw attention to itself'.[48]

Schaeffer was not the only artist at the time to make this point with reference to the Shakespeare statue in Central Park. In 1935, Edward Hopper completed his highly evocative painting entitled 'Shakespeare at Dusk'. In an urban park environment, devoid of humans, and hauntingly lit by the setting sun, Hopper depicts Ward's Shakespeare statue from the rear. Shakespeare is sunk in solitary reflection, like

---

[46] Musil, 'Denkmale', 507–8.
[47] www.saturdayeveningpost.com/artists-gallery/saturday-evening-post-cover-artists/mead-schaeffer-art-gallery.
[48] Musil, 'Denkmale', 507–8.

Figure 13.2 Mead Schaeffer, 'Romance under Shakespeare's Statue', *Saturday Evening Post*, 28 April 1945. By permission of Curtis Publishing.

many of the individuals that Hopper painted, also in night scenes. Soon, however, as we grow accustomed to the indistinctness of the twilight, we become aware that the Shakespeare statue is not alone. As Hopper's sketches make clearer than the eventual painting, or the painting's official title that directs our gaze to the man from

Stratford – the Shakespeare statue (1872) is facing Gaetano Russo's statue of Christopher Columbus, erected there in 1892, on the occasion of the quatercentenary of his arrival in the New World.[49] No specific rapport or communication between these two men is suggested, and their pairing in the park seems as puzzling as the relationship between the visitors in Hopper's *Nighthawks* (1942) or between the characters in Hopper's New York nocturnes.[50]

Yet, there is no coincidence about the meeting of these remarkable men in the painting, not on Hopper's part, despite the painting's selective title. Here, the notes in Hopper's ledger help: '2 statues on high pedestals. L. Shakespeare – green, R. Columbus not distinct', as do the accompanying sketches for the painting in the same notebook.[51] Interestingly, though, employing the method that Musil suggested to make statues visible again, Hopper uses advertising signs available in the public space to make this clear. The neon on the high-rise beyond the park reads 'US'. It underpins the viewer's thinking of the painting in terms of two statues. But it also introduces the question what it might be that they share as 'US'. Since, by way of a pun, the word 'US' raises the issue of togetherness as well as that of location or nation, the painting invites the question of what these two Europeans, alone by themselves in the twilit park, mean for the US or what the US has with them. Using the signs of the public, urban space, Hopper makes visible two poorly visible, and in a sense also abandoned, statues erected to commemorate 1564 and 1492, and in this way poses rather than answers some of the most vital questions about America's sense of cultural self-identity at the time.[52]

---

[49] Edward Hopper, 'Artist's ledger – Book II, 9 Shakespeare at Dusk' under 'Hopper and Shakespeare' at www.davidrumsey.com/amica/.

[50] William Chapman Sharpe, *New York Nocturne: The City after Dark in Literature, Painting, and Photography, 1850–1950* (Oxford University Press, 2008), esp. 277–91. Sharpe, however, does not discuss the Shakespeare painting.

[51] Edward Hopper, 'Artist's ledger – Book II, 9 Shakespeare at Dusk'. Columbus is larger and more conspicuous than Shakespeare in 'Drawing for painting "Shakespeare at Dusk"' at The AMICA Library (Art Museum Images from Cartography Associates), at www.davidrumsey.com/amica/.

[52] See Douglas Bruster, *Quoting Shakespeare: Form and Culture in Early Modern Drama* (Lincoln, NE, and London: University of Nebraska Press, 2000), 171–208. In *Columbus, Shakespeare and the Interpretation of the New World* (New York and Houndmills: Palgrave Macmillan, 2003), Jonathan Hart mentions the statue of Columbus, but neither the Ward statue of Shakespeare, nor Hopper.

In recent years, creative and captivating encounters of this kind with statues have become customary. A different investigation of American and European values took place when Columbia Pictures released *Anonymous* in 2011, Roland Emmerich's movie arguing that Shakespeare was 'a fraud' and that the true author of the plays and poems was Edward de Vere, Seventeenth Earl of Oxford. The movie revived the authorship debate across the world, but nowhere was the response managed as deftly as in Shakespeare's own Warwickshire. Here 'the Bard's name was temporarily removed from pub and street signs in a campaign against the movie' and the Shakespeare Birthplace Trust actually draped a white sheet over the famous Gower statue in Bancroft Gardens.[53] In order to combat the anti-Stratfordians in an appropriately ludic fashion, the Birthplace Trust drew attention to the true face of Shakespeare by making the Gower statue temporarily invisible.

Along similar lines of conflict between traditional British values and the values of Hollywood, the Gower statue plays an important role in Walt Disney Studios' *Gnomeo and Juliet* (directed by Kelley Asbury, 2011). It is made very visible this time, however, since, like Pygmalion's Galatea statue (as narrated by Ovid in his *Metamorphoses*), it comes to life, and speaks. In *Gnomeo and Juliet*, the Gower statue towers high above a host of red and blue garden gnomes who are engaged in a social reenactment of what we recognize to be Shakespeare's greatest love tragedy. The difference in size between Shakespeare and these garden statues curiously informs the culture clash between them, which particularly manifests itself when one of the gnomes, sitting on top of Shakespeare's head, tells him the story of the lovers, and asks him, as a fellow statue, if he thinks the separated lover-gnomes will ever get back together again. The Gower statue – voiced by Sir Patrick Stewart – unsympathetically claims that he likes 'the whole death part better'. This Shakespeare is pedantic, patronizing, self-obsessed, uninterested in other beings (including the gnome trying to keep his balance on top of the Bard's head) and preoccupied with death, not life. At the same time, the Blue Gnome is immodest to call the classical tragic ending of *Romeo and Juliet* 'rubbish' simply because he wants the amorous protagonists, in true Hollywood fashion, to live happily ever after. The friction that we witness here, it would appear, is that of an ambivalent popular

---

[53] David Bentley, http://blogs.coventrytelegraph.net/thegeekfiles/2011/10/roland-emmerichs-anonymous-spa.html.

culture snub (though mild) at the very high culture 'author, author' who
provided the movie with a story, and without whose 'bravo, bravo'
reputation Walt Disney Studios might never have seen any return on their
investments. Yet, this twenty-first-century movie's Bard-bashing also
teaches us something about the typical nineteenth-century statue: its
perceived *hauteur* (both in terms of physical height and of his mental
prowess), the sedate obsession with its own achievements and its focus
on death rather than life. Modern encounters with Shakespeare statues
renegotiate features like these almost predictably.

Thus, in 2010, in order to counter the sedate quality of public
statues, creative director of the *Sydney Statues: Project!* Michelle
McCosker felt it was time for a special effort to bring the public
artworks in the city to the attention of the inhabitants. In addition
to the statues of Captain Cook, Queen Victoria and King Edward VII,
she selected Sir Bertram MacKennal's Shakespeare Memorial (1926)
currently near the Australian capital's State Library. To 'wake up'
the Shakespeare monument, as she put it, and with it, of course, also
the inhabitants of the Australian capital who daily rode or walked
by without paying attention, the statue of Shakespeare and his characters that make up the Sydney monument were clothed in bold and
flamboyant dress.[54] Only a handful of photographs posted on a rarely
visited website now remind us of the event. Yet, it is the event, the
ritual, that counted and that counts today.

Commemorative ritual such as this is both sincere and ludic, and
may indeed take many other forms, like that involving the Shakespeare
statue crafted at the Somerset Sand Sculpture Festival at Weston-super-
Mare in 2010. As a sand structure, with its more than merely latent
emphasis on the ephemeral, it revived Renaissance views of art and
evanescence, as discussed by James Fenton, who draws attention to
elaborately sculpted foods served and consumed at Renaissance
banquets.[55] In terms of its emphasis on ephemerality, sand sculpture
may recall the opening stanzas of Edmund Spenser's Sonnet 75:

> One day I wrote her name vpon the strand,
> but came the waues and washed it away:
> agayne I wrote it with a second hand,

---

[54] http://sydneystatues.wordpress.com/statues/shakespeare.
[55] James Fenton, 'On Statues', in his *Leonard's Nephew: Essays on Art and Artists* (Harmondsworth: Penguin Books, 1998).

but came the tyde, and made my paynes his pray.
Vayne man, sayd she, that doest in vaine assay,
a mortall thing so to immortalize,
for I my selue shall lyke to this decay,
and eek my name bee wyped out lykewise.

However, Spenser's sonnet also brings into focus an important historical difference of perspective. For, in the event, contemporary sand
sculpture creatively embraces the option that Spenser rejects in the
sonnet's sestet, where he counters the ephemerality of monumental fame
with the sonnet and the beloved's claim to lasting literary renown:

My verse your vertues rare shall eternize,
and in the heuens wryte your glorious name,
Where whenas death shall all the world subdew,
our loue shall liue, and later life renew.[56]

One last form of alternative statuary art that has emerged over the past
few decades is that of 'living statues'.[57] It may be read in the tradition
of Musil as an attempt of the proverbially invisible statue to rivet
the attention of the incredulous passer-by. It may also be read in
the older tradition of Pygmalion and Galatea that Shakespeare drama-
tizes in the final act of *The Winter's Tale* around the statue of Hermione, allegedly created by the real-life Renaissance artist Giulio
Romano. On the level of the play's plot, the point is that the statue,
like Galatea in the Ovidian myth, may come to life under the gaze
of the repentant and loving male.[58] On the level of the theatrical
event, however, the challenge is that the actor playing Hermione
must convincingly represent an inanimate and immobile object.
The modern tradition of performance art known as 'living statues'
fascinates the observer precisely through its emphasis on the latter

---

[56] Kenneth J. Larsen, *Edmund Spenser's 'Amoretti' and 'Epithalamion': A Critical Edition* (Tempe, AZ: Medieval and Renaissance Texts and Studies, 1997), 98.

[57] This use of the phrase 'living statues' is not discussed by Kenneth Gross in *The Dream of the Moving Statue* (Ithaca, NJ, and London: Cornell University Press, 1992).

[58] This is the interpretation that Princess Caroline – 'the exiled and estranged consort of the Prince Regent' – adhered to when she chose incognito to act out the statue scene of *The Winter's Tale* as a less than subtle hint to her own husband. See David Worrall, *Theatric Revolution: Drama, Censorship, and Romantic Period Subcultures, 1773–1832* (Oxford University Press, 2006), 197.

theatrical tradition, and this may also explain why attempts at being a Shakespeare statue have proved popular at venues including Stratford-upon-Avon and the Oregon Shakespeare Festival. This new form of street theatre with its own annual World Living Statues Festival can no longer be ignored as a medium for commemorating Shakespeare, also because (as in traditional, nineteenth-century statuary) after the author, his stage characters too have now started to be represented.[59]

In Sonnet 55, Shakespeare may well have acknowledged the Augustan poet Horace, who famously described the difference between poetry and sculpture as follows:

> I have achieved a monument more
> permanent than bronze and higher than the royal
> Pyramids, which no devouring rain,
> no raging North Wind can destroy or years
> in endless series or the flight of time.[60]

The very survival of Shakespeare's Sonnet 55 might seem to confirm the message that also Horace conveys. Yet, more recent processes of cultural redefinition, like those discussed above, also strongly suggest that although commemorative practice will continue to include statues and monuments, thus turning cultural heritage into current custom with considerable gain, those who are going to commemorate Shakespeare will do so in the joint awareness that monuments and statues are ephemeral by nature, and that it is continuing the cultural tradition that counts.

---

[59] www.alamy.com/stock-photo-B7FCXE/Living-statue-street-entertainer-performs-as-William-Shakespeare-outside.html; www.flickr.com/photos/14336807@N05/10688741993/galleries/; www.pinterest.com/pin/319544536031375698/.

[60] Jeremy H. Kaimowitz (trans.), *The Odes of Horace*, with an introduction by Ronnie Ancona (Baltimore, MD: The Johns Hopkins University Press, 2008), III: 30 (142).

14 | *Gardening with Shakespeare*

NICOLA J. WATSON

In the grounds of Northwestern University, situated in Evanston north of Chicago, there is a smallish formal garden, bounded by high hedges and furnished with stone seats, a sundial and a wall-fountain. It is usually deserted; the odd elderly lady, or sometimes a student, might pass through, although to judge by the green-blue shininess of the nose on the bronze bas-relief portrait of Shakespeare that presides over the fountain by the stone seats, it must be regularly visited. As a faculty member twenty years ago, I used to take my grading there without giving very much thought to the oddity of this garden, anomalous to the local garden aesthetic and clearly made in the teeth of Chicago's magnificently inhospitable winter and summer climate. On further investigation years later, rather than being merely a picturesque oddity on the side of the campus away from Lake Michigan and the athletics facilities, this garden turned out to be famous in its own right as a 'Shakespeare garden', made to commemorate the Tercentenary of Shakespeare's death in 1916. In what follows, I explore and explain the existence of the Northwestern garden by placing it within the long history of imagining Shakespeare in cultivated space. That habit begins within English landscape-gardening, moves to smaller scale English gardens, public and private, and is then propagated across the globe, most notably into North American soil in the early years of the twentieth century. What were the roots of this idea, what forced it into flower, and how come it was transplanted across the world?

Roots

There had been a history of celebrating Shakespeare within the English landscape long before the genre of the Shakespeare garden proper emerged. Shakespeare's own garden at New Place, complete with the famous mulberry tree said to have been planted by his own hand, was already a tourist attraction by the 1740s when it was shown to the young and admiring David Garrick (who made a point of sitting under the tree), and, famously, the house and garden had become enough of a tourist draw by the 1750s to inconvenience the then-owner the Rev. Francis Gastrell to the extent that he demolished the house and cut down the tree.[1] David Garrick's Jubilee of 1769 expanded the sense of Shakespeare within the landscape to include the whole of Stratford-upon-Avon, generalising the Shakespearean out from the Birthplace and the grave to the banks of the Avon, ornamented for the occasion with a handsome temporary pavilion in the shape of a classically styled rotunda. In this, he was invoking the aesthetic of contemporary land-scape gardening. In fact, Shakespeare had already made a guest appearance in the English landscape garden from the first half of the eighteenth century onwards, featuring as a cameo-bust in the Temple of British Worthies at Stowe designed by William Kent in 1734. David Garrick himself had already, in 1756, erected a Temple to Shakespeare as an ornamental garden folly in the grounds of his villa at Hampton (see Figure 1.1). Not only had Shakespeare there grown in scale to the life-size statue he commissioned from Roubiliac (based on the Chandos portrait), but the Temple boasted Garrick's increasingly extensive collection of Shakespeare relics, including a chair designed for Garrick by William Hogarth and made of mulberry wood from Shakespeare's celebrated tree (see Figure 1.2).[2] The Temple focussed a landscape setting for Garrick's various self-dramatisations as Shakespearean celebrity (here he entertained the Twickenham set including Horace Walpole, Samuel Johnson, William Hogarth and Mrs Delaney, report-edly making them write verses of homage to Shakespeare and lay them at the foot of the statue), family man (it was lavishly illuminated for a fête champêtre to celebrate twenty-five years of marriage) and local

[1] For a survey of the history of Stratford as a tourist attraction, see Nicola J. Watson, 'Shakespeare on the Tourist Trail', in Robert Shaughnessy (ed.), *The Cambridge Companion to Shakespeare and Popular Culture* (Cambridge University Press, 2007), 199–226.

[2] Items supposedly made from this mulberry tree were a staple of the Stratford souvenir trade from early on; a friend of William Shenstone seems to have acquired a mulberry wood tobacco-stopper, together with an authenticating letter, in 1759 or thereabouts, and the letter in which he records this also notes his efforts to acquire more wood to have carved to his own design. Garrick's chair, however, took an unusually princely slice of the tree. Walpole to Shenstone, 13 February 1759, *Select Letters between the Late Duchess of Somerset, Lady Luxborough, Mr Whistler, Miss Dolman, Mr R. Dodsley, William Shenstone and others* (London: J. Dodsley, 1778), I: 251–3.

patron (he would sit in 'Shakespeare's chair' on May Day to dispense largesse to locals).[3] Others would be inspired in their turn to ornament their garden landscapes with Shakespearean follies; a hundred years later, Charles Letts, owner of Southview House on the south coast of the Isle of Wight, installed a Shakespeare fountain and a prominent temple-like rotunda to celebrate the Tercentenary of Shakespeare's birth in 1864.[4]

Enabled in part by Garrick's Shakespeareanisation of Stratford, much travel-writing about visiting Stratford, such as Samuel Ireland's *Picturesque Views on the Upper, or Warwickshire Avon* (1795), expended considerable effort imagining the Bard inspired by his native Avon. The idea of Shakespeare as part of a classicised landscape gave way patchily to a national Shakespeare part classical, part historical and part topobiographical. Ireland's frontispiece, for instance, shows a Tudor-costumed Shakespeare reclining with a classical lyre on the banks of the Avon against a backdrop of Holy Trinity Church. He is depicted in the throes of inspiration attended by appropriate Muses and a swan, and captioned with a line from Charles Churchill: 'Here NATURE list'ning stood, whilst Shakespear play'd / And wonder'd at the Work herself had made!'[5] The high Victorian version of this had become more prosaically realist and educational: C. Roach Smith was entirely conventional in recommending a visit to Stratford because 'Those who have read Shakespeare ... may yet learn much of him in the fields, in the meadows, and, indeed, in the general kingdom of nature', given that Shakespeare was both a countryman and in all probability a gardener.[6] The romantic sense of the presence of Shakespeare within the landscape, the idea that native genius could be accessed or evoked by touching native soil and anything that grew

---

[3] See G. W. Stone and G. M. Kahrl, *David Garrick: A Critical Biography* (Carbondale, IL: Southern Illinois University Press, 1979), 4, 10, 451–2.

[4] http://jsbookreader.blogspot.co.uk/2012/03/ursula-and-blackgang.html (last accessed 5 August 2014); www.thisbeautifulisle.co.uk/southview/ (last accessed 5 August 2014).

[5] Samuel Ireland, *Picturesque Views on the Upper, or Warwickshire Avon, From its Source at Naseby to its Junction with the Severn at Tewkesbury: With Observations on the Public Buildings, and Other Works of Art in its Vicinity*, (London: Faulder and Egerton, 1795), frontispiece.

[6] C. Roach Smith, *Remarks on Shakespeare, his Birthplace etc., suggested by a visit to Stratford-upon-Avon, in the autumn of 1868* (London: privately printed, 1868–9), 7. See also, for example, J. R. Wise, *Shakspere: His Birthplace and its Neighbourhood* (London: Smith, Elder & Co, 1861), 7.

out of it, gave rise to the tourist habit of collecting leaves and flowers from Shakespearean sites, a sort of economy version of the early lucrative trade in things made from Shakespeare's mulberry, and subsequently from 'Shakespeare's crab-apple' at Bidford (under which the Bard was supposed to have lain dead drunk), which was said to have been destroyed by 'American curio-hunters'.[7] So important was this idea of an organic continuity between land and poet mediated by flora, that it gave rise to the replanting of both the mulberry (in 1862) and the crab-apple (some time towards the very end of the nineteenth century).[8] Later visitors were mostly forced to content themselves with plucking leaves or flowers from the locality of Shakespeare's grave or birthplace for pressing into albums. Julia Thomas notes one letter sent back to America on 6 September 1858 which 'still shows the stitching where [the sender] attached an ivy leaf from the wall of the church'.[9] Similarly, the Folgers sent back seeds from New Place to a friend in America.[10] It was a fashion that would persist through to the 1920s; a college English teacher from North Dakota, Emma Shay, collected for her friends' albums no fewer than forty daisies from Holy Trinity churchyard, forty leaves from the garden at New Place, forty specimens of flowers from the banks of 'Shakespeare's river', grass, pansies and rosemary from the environs of Anne Hathaway's cottage and clover leaves from the garden of what was then thought to be Mary Arden's house.[11]

This practice points to a sense that a love for Shakespeare could be appropriately described through plants and flowers. By the Tercentenary of 1916, there had already been some half a century of interest in depicting and identifying 'Shakespeare's flowers'. Early books on the subject were expensively produced to lie about on drawing-room tables to beguile an idle moment; they matched attractive and expensively produced chromolithographs depicting flowers with suitable

[7] F. G. Savage, *The Flora and Folk Lore of Shakespeare* (London: E. J. Burrow, 1923), 202.
[8] See *Illustrated London News*, 12 April 1862; Savage, *The Flora*, 202.
[9] Julia Thomas, *Shakespeare's Shrine: The Bard's Birthplace and the Invention of Stratford-Upon-Avon* (Philadelphia, PA: University of Pennsylvania Press, 2012), 154.
[10] S. H. Grant, *Collecting Shakespeare: The Story of Henry and Emily Folger* (Baltimore: Johns Hopkins University Press, 2014), 39.
[11] G. Abrahamson, *Mrs Shay Did It!* (Wessington Springs: A. L. Webb, 1976), 28–31.

quotations from the plays lettered in gold, and were designed as the basis for a little lightweight cultured conversation amongst women as much interested in art and botany as in Shakespeare per se. Perhaps, indeed, that is a little over-condescending; it might be truer to say that this was part of how women individually and collectively appropriated Shakespeare to the domestic, amateur sphere. These books included the expensive lithographs of Jane Giraud's *The Flowers of Shakespeare* (1846) and Paul Jerrard's *Flowers from Stratford-on-Avon* (1852), which last dressed its equally 'costly and novel' illustrations of flowers 'still growing on the very spots where they may have first inspired the boy Shakespeare' with graceful sentiment: 'the specimen was drawn from a most luxuriant spray in a hedgerow that Shakespeare may often have passed in his visits to Anne Hathaway'.[12] Or there was *Shakespeare's Bouquet: The Flowers and Plants of Shakespeare* (1872), Bessie Mayou's *Natural History of Shakespeare, being selections of Flowers, Fruits and Animals* (1877), or Leo Grindon's illustrated volume *The Shakespeare Flora* (1883), which sought to combine natural history with a compilation of poetic 'beauties'. The genre was still going strong in the 1900s with Leonard Holmesworthe's *Shakespeare's Garden; with reference to over a hundred plants* (1906), and would reach a height of feminised whimsy in Walter Crane's *Flowers from Shakespeare's Garden: A Posy from the Plays* (1906), which depicted a succession of 'flowers in human garb, or … human beings garbed as flowers' glossed by quotation from the plays.[13] These volumes brought Shakespeare into domestic space – capitalising on an extant feminocentric culture of album-making and flower-gardening.

Besides books to beguile wet days in the drawing room, there were scholarly monographs by horticultural enthusiasts caught up in the late Victorian revival of interest in flower-gardening, and especially in the 'old English garden'. This was a counter-response to urbanisation and industrialisation as much as to the boom in exotic plant collection from imperial territories indulged in by the Rothschilds amongst others. The first such book, it seems, was associated with the Tercentenary, Sidney Beisly's *Shakspeare's Garden, or the Plants and Flowers named in his Works Described and Defined* (1864). Most prominent amongst these

---

[12] Paul Jerrard, *Flowers from Stratford-on-Avon* (London; Paul Jerrard, 1852), caption to plate X.
[13] Walter Crane, *Flowers from Shakespeare's Garden: A Posy from the Plays* (London: Cassell, 1906), preface.

books was Henry N. Ellacombe's effort at a comprehensive survey and identification of all the plants mentioned by Shakespeare, *The Plant-lore and Garden-craft of Shakespeare* (1878). Originally published as a series of articles in the periodical *The Garden* during 1877, this book is composed equally of literary notes, botanical identifications, practical advice on how to grow the flowers mentioned, and descriptions of Elizabethan garden practice and design drawn from the works of Shakespeare and his contemporaries. Republished in 1884 and again in 1896, Ellacombe's book would become a classic. Along with the book subsequently derived from it by the American Esther Singleton, tellingly entitled *The Shakespeare Garden* (1922; republished 1932), it laid the practical groundwork for actually making a Shakespeare garden. Helpfully, it also hints at the late Victorian ideological groundwork for such gardens. Ellacombe celebrates, for example, 'one especial pleasure' in writing the book, which derives 'from the thoroughly English character of Shakespeare's descriptions' of 'thoroughly English plants'.[14] The sheer length of the list of 'Shakespeare's flowers' is cited as proof

that the love of flowers is no new thing in England, still less a foreign fashion, but that it is innate in us, a real instinct, that showed itself as strongly in our forefathers as in ourselves; and when we find that such men as Shakespeare ... were almost proud to show their knowledge of plants and love of flowers, we can say that such love and knowledge is thoroughly manly and English.[15]

Here 'Shakespeare's flowers' are hoicked out of the drawing room and into the realm of the 'thoroughly manly and English'; knowing them will be a way, too, of asserting genetic continuity of national identity with 'our forefathers'. By the 1890s and early 1900s, therefore, it was possible within England to conceive of actually making a 'Shakespeare garden', whether in feminine, private and sentimental mode or as something patriotic, public and manly.

Flowers

A 'Shakespeare garden' had certain fixed formal characteristics. First and foremost, ideologically, such gardens celebrated 'Englishness'.

---

[14] Henry N. Ellacombe, *The Plant-lore and Garden-Craft of Shakespeare* (Exeter: privately printed, 1878), 2.

[15] Ellacombe, *The Plant-lore*, 263–4.

This sort of Englishness had nothing to do with the English style of landscape gardening invoked by Garrick and imitated in 'English gardens' across northern Europe in the late eighteenth century and early nineteenth century (there are examples still extant in Berlin and Munich, for instance). As in Garrick's Hampton grounds, that sort of Englishness connoted a self-consciously natural landscaping with meandering pathways, naturalistic tree-planting, contrived views and eye-catching follies. The Shakespeare garden's 'Englishness' had rather more to do with the nativism, nationalism and localism evidenced by the 1864 planting of the Shakespeare oak (ceremonially transferred from Windsor in honour of *The Merry Wives of Windsor*) on Primrose Hill in London, watered in with Avon water, to celebrate the Tercentenary.[16] This may be glossed by the inclusion of a paper entitled 'Wild Flowers of Shakespeare' in the official tercentenary programme, and by the design of the Shakespeare tercentenary medal which encircled the poet's head with 'a wreath of wild flowers', lovingly detailed and partially referenced to the plays.[17] The now conventional idea that Shakespeare derived 'his lofty inspirations' in the meadows among the wild flowers by the side of the 'soft-flowing Avon' developed into the deliberate cultivation of Shakespeare's flora;[18] it seems from one casual mention by Robert Hunter in his description of the tercentenary celebrations that the garden of the Birthplace may have been planted up with 'Shakespeare's flowers'.[19] By the late nineteenth century, however, the Shakespeare garden had

---

[16] On the involvement of the actor-manager Samuel Phelps and the coverage of this event in the *Illustrated London News* see Richard Foulkes, *The Shakespeare Tercentenary of 1864* (Bath: Society for Theatre Research, 1984), 20–1, 42–3; Andrew Murphy, *Shakespeare for the People* (Cambridge University Press, 2008), 3. I am indebted to Clara Calvo for drawing my attention to the fact that this oak subsequently died and the replacement tree, planted in 1964, was also watered in with Avon water. See *The Guardian*, 24 April 1964. It too died.

[17] Foulkes, *The Shakespeare Tercentenary*, 7, 43, 48; *The Official Programme of the Tercentenary Festival of the Birth of Shakespeare, to be held at Stratford-upon-Avon, commencing on Saturday, April 23, 1864 ...* (London: Cassell, Petter and Galpin, 1864), 75. The description of the Shakespeare medal, along with other ephemera, is bound into the copy held in the Bodleian Library.

[18] J. Cox, *The Tercentenary: A Retrospect* (London: Cassell, Petter and Galpin, 1865), 4.

[19] R. E. Hunter, *Shakespeare and Stratford-upon-Avon, A 'Chronicle of the Time': comprising the salient Facts and Traditions, Biographical, Topographical, and historical, connected with the Poet and his Birth-Place; Together with A Full Record of the Tercentenary Celebration* (London: Whitaker & Co, 1864), 68.

become consciously historicist, typically designed in reference to current notions of the Elizabethan as the quintessential moment of merrie England. Elizabethan Englishness was realised principally through nativist planting, which aspired to include only plants and trees mentioned in Shakespeare's *Works*. These plants were implicitly or explicitly captioned with the relevant Shakespearean quotations. How they were organised within a ground-plan was much more variable, ranging from Victorian-style border planting of specimens, through scholarly reconstruction of the Elizabethan knot garden, to more impressionistic and generalised formal gardens composed of formal beds intersected with paths and enclosed by walls or hedges. Frequently, but not invariably, some sort of representation of the Bard himself would preside over the whole. A sundial proved an all-but essential component of this sort of garden, connoting as it did escape from urban modernity ruled by railway- and factory-induced clock-time.

Probably the earliest version of a 'Shakespeare garden' in this sense was made by the Countess of Warwick, the celebrated beauty and heiress 'Daisy' Greville, in the gardens of her home at Easton Lodge in Essex. Here she designed the planting of a four-acre 'plaisaunce' around Stone Hall, an old 'cottage' within the estate. By 1898, the Countess had installed a collection of Victorian-style themed gardens including a garden constructed as a living sundial, a rockery, a fernery, The Garden of Friendship, The Border of Sentiment, The Rosarie, The Scripture Garden and the Shakespeare Border. Her expensively produced and illustrated book about this project, revealingly entitled *An Old English Garden* (1898), begins by explaining the rationale for constructing the 'plaisaunce' as an antidote to the febrile thinness of contemporary urban socialite life. Referencing the garden of Lady Corisande in Benjamin D'Israeli's novel *Lothair* (1870) as her inspiration ('in the pleasure ground are the remains of an ancient garden of the ancient house that had long been pulled down'), the gardens were designed as a retreat into the medieval and Elizabethan past of the estate, which had been the honeymoon destination of Edward and Elizabeth Woodville, and a hunting resort of the Virgin Queen. The garden in *Lothair* is specifically described as a feminine idyll referencing a kinder past and gives a strong sense of what the romance and appeal of the Shakespeare garden was supposed to be:

When the modern pleasure grounds were planned and created ... the father of the present duke would not allow this ancient garden to be entirely destroyed, and you came upon its quaint appearance in the dissimilar world in which it was placed, as you might in some festival of romantic costume upon a person habited in the courtly dress of the last century ... The duke had given this garden to Lady Corisande, in order that she might practise her theory, that flower-gardens should be sweet and luxuriant, not hard and scentless imitations of works of art.[20]

Stone Hall, ivy-draped and elaborately leaded on the outside, Jacobethan within, provided the central folly in which charming lunch picnics of 'high revelry' were provided. The building also included the Countess's 'Garden Librairie' with a substantial collection of old garden books, including the Elizabethan John Gerard's famous and influential *Herball, or General Historie of Plantes* (1597), and the many photographic illustrations dwell lovingly upon 'Elizabethan' details such as the window-seat. The building is of a piece with the language of the essay, which offers a tour in the style of high Edwardian whimsy derived at distance from Charles Lamb, heavily laced with echoes of Shakespeare, Wordsworth, Keats, Ruskin; building and language are also of a piece with the associative and affective gardens captioned with labels providing quotation from poets, philosophers and Scripture. Foremost amongst these gardens she places her 'Shakespeare Border', which she describes as 'the greatest interest of my garden':

It represents the work of many a winter's evening spent in hunting for quotations, and in reducing them, when found, to these label limits – delightful pottery butterflies 'twixt green and brown, on each wing of which is the text, with the reference to the play from which it comes.[21]

The Countess had no thought of recreating the ground-plan of Tudor gardening; the border is laid out so that 'all the trees stand back in rows, while in front of them are grouped the flowers and herbs that the immortal bard loved so well'. Her plant list reveals how ambitious the border was, aiming at comprehensiveness of wild and garden plants.[22] In 1906, the garden was famous enough to encourage Walter Crane to

---

[20] Benjamin Disraeli, *Lothair* (New York: D. Appleton, 1881), 368.
[21] D. Greville, Countess of Warwick, *An Old English Garden* (London: Arthur L. Humphreys, 1898), 8.
[22] Greville, *Old English Garden*, 8; see also www.eastonlodge.co.uk (last accessed 5 August 2014).

dedicate his *Flowers from Shakespeare's Garden* 'to the Countess of Warwick, whose delightful Old English Garden at Easton Lodge suggested this book of fancies'. His frontispiece depicts her kneeling at the foot of a bust of Shakespeare and presenting it with flowers.[23]

Daisy Greville's 'plaisaunce' clearly shows Victorian sentimental planting shading into the Edwardian fantasy of an unalienated Elizabethan idyll that would eventually produce the Arts and Crafts houses and gardens of the Cotswolds – such as that at Rodmarton. Thirty years or so later, the Shakespeare garden had become something of a cliché. In 1931, E. F. Benson, brother of the Stratford-upon-Avon actor-manager Sir Frank, satirised 'Perdita's garden' as made by the inimitable Lucia, posturing heroine of his series of comic novels. Lucia ornaments her stockbroker mock-Tudor house in Surrey with a garden to match: cut down to suit a middle-class budget and space, a Shakespeare garden now consists of

a charming little square plot in front of the timbered facade of The Hurst, surrounded by yew hedges and intersected with paths of crazy pavement, carefully covered in stone crop, which led to the Elizabethan sundial from Wardour Street in the center [sic]. It was gay in spring with those flowers (and no others) on which Perdita doted.[24]

Benson's sly digs at his heroine's suburban pretension focus on the craftedness of the garden's olde Englisheness – the carefulness with which the crazy paving is made to seem artlessly overgrown, the clever urbanite purchase of the bargain antique sundial (discovered in a London street famed since Charles Lamb's time for bookstalls, curiosity shops, bric-a-brac and perhaps most pertinently theatrical props) relocated to authenticate a spurious Elizabethan manor, and the pseudo-scholarliness and nativism of the planting, which excludes all English imperialist plant collection since the time of Elizabeth. Behind the fiction of 'Perdita's garden' may well have lain the garden belonging to the woman who had immediately inspired E. F. Benson's satire, the best-selling novelist Marie Corelli, another social climber. Corelli's garden at Mason Croft in Stratford-upon-Avon was (and is) embellished with an eighteenth-century garden building which Corelli persisted in claiming as Tudor and which she accordingly refurbished

[23] Crane, *Flowers from Shakespeare's Garden*, frontispiece.
[24] E. F. Benson, *Mapp and Lucia* [1931] (New York, Cambridge, Philadelphia *et al.*: Perennial Library, 1986), 4.

with diamond leaded panes 'in the windows and "Jacobean" wood' panelled interior when she purchased the property in 1899.[25] A more sophisticated and scholarly version of Shakespearean gardening of the 1930s is provided by Eleanour Sinclair Rohde's 'Suggestions for the making of a Shakespeare Garden' in her *Shakespeare's Wild Flowers, Fairy Lore, Gardens, Herbs, Gatherers of Simples and Bee Lore* (1935). Rohde dismisses merely planting the flowers and herbs Shakespeare mentions as 'incredibly dull!' and recommends instead making 'a small garden characteristic of Elizabethan times' on the formal plan of a Tudor winter knot garden. She supplies a detailed plan (featuring 'A Fairy Entrance' embowered with musk-roses), succession planting, footnotes all relevant quotations, supplies botanical names, suggests an arbour and strongly recommends the inclusion of a sundial, providing a list of suitable Shakespearean mottoes for one (see Figure 14.1).[26]

Benson might laugh at 'Perdita's garden', but this enterprise was of a piece with the contemporary Shakespeareanisation of Stratford through its gardens. F. G. Savage's series of articles published in the *Stratford upon Avon Herald* between 1909 and 1916 captures the mood. He harps on the need to make a fully Elizabethan space at the Birthplace:

> If there is one garden more than another that should be set apart for the cultivation of the exact plants as mentioned by the poet, surely it should be this. At present there are several he could not have known, while others he well knew are entirely missing ... may I venture to suggest the planting of old-fashioned flowers such as those the poet would be likely to have known in place of the modern varieties.[27]

Modernity is to be rolled back in favour of authenticity; tellingly, he adds, 'I think even colour might be sacrificed for correctness', sounding a new, anti-Victorian note. Sidney Lee seems indeed to have planted the garden at the Birthplace with Elizabethan flowers before the war,

---

[25] See T. C. Coates and R. S. Well, *Marie Corelli: The Writer and the Woman* (London: Hutchinson, 1903), 319; M. Bell, 'A Brief History of Mason Croft', www.birmingham.ac.uk/schools/edacs/departments/shakespeare/about/mason-croft-history.aspx (last accessed 29 August 2012).

[26] Eleanour Sinclair Rohde, *Shakespeare's Wild Flowers, Fairy Lore, Gardens, Herbs, Gatherers of Simples and Bee Lore* (London: The Medici Society, [1935]), 216–27.

[27] Savage, *The Flora*, 235–6.

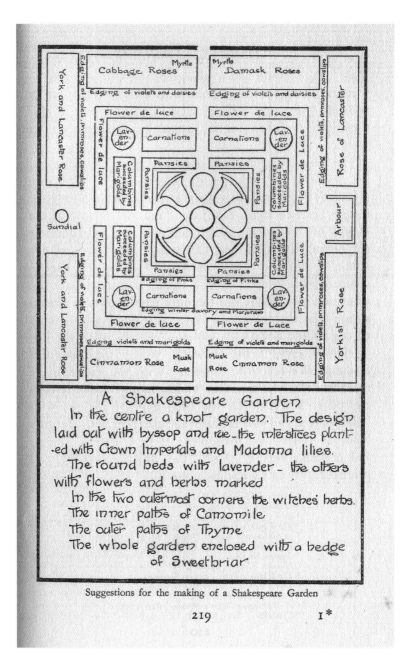

Suggestions for the making of a Shakespeare Garden

219   I*

Figure 14.1 E. Rohde, 'A Shakespeare Garden', *Shakespeare's Wild Flowers, Fairy Lore, Gardens, Herbs, Gatherers of Simples and Bee Lore* (London: The Medici Society, 1935), 219.

and in the early 1900s the gardens of the Shakespeare properties were indeed being Shakespeareanised. Together they made a series of localist arguments for Shakespeare's nativism, attempting to restore or realise the imaginary biographicised spaces conjured up by the aptly named J. Harvey Bloom in his book *Shakespeare's Garden* (1903) – 'such was the garden in which the poet may have spent some at least of his summer hours half-buried in his arbours of woodbine and sweetbriar'.[28] The style of planting would be at once modern and yet 'Shakespearean' in its naturalness and abundance. Like Ellacombe, who abominated bedding-out, Bloom, a latterday Perdita, promoted 'the cultivation of flowers in Nature's methods, their native elegance unrestrained and unfettered by man':

The leading idea is to copy Nature as near as may be and discard the tiring, gaudy colouring and set lines of bedding plants, the straight rectangular walks and plots, and to have everywhere constant change of shape and colour, an orderly wilderness of bloom against a background of ever-changing green.[29]

In practice, the gardens ranged from the 1870s so-called 'cottage-garden' style planting still substantially in place at Anne Hathaway's Cottage and put in place by Miss Wilmott, through to the antiquarianism of Ernest Law's 'curious-knotted' garden and the deliberate 'wildness' of the 'Wild Bank', both laid out at New Place in 1920 (Figures 14.2 and 14.3).[30] Between them, they described the spectrum of the Shakespearean cultivated landscape as envisioned within Edwardian and post-Edwardian culture.[31] They encompassed the charming, feminised, and native domesticity of Anne Hathaway's Cottage, the nativism of the Birthplace, the historicist sense of the Elizabethan at New Place and (also at New Place) a version of Shakespeare

---

[28] J. H. Bloom, *Shakespeare's Garden; Being a Compendium of Quotations and References from the Bard to all Manner of Flower, Tree, Bush, Vine, and Herb, Arranged According to the Month in Which They are Seen to Flourish* (London: Methuen, 1903), 6.

[29] Bloom, *Shakespeare's Garden*, 8.

[30] On Ernest Law's 1922 garden at New Place, see 'Shakespeare's 'curious-knotted' garden' remade at Stratford; a feature of the 358th birthday festival', *Illustrated London News* (29 April 1922), 622–3. Also Ernest Law, *Shakespeare's Garden, Stratford-upon-Avon, with Illustrations* (London: Selwyn and Blount Ltd, 1922). More recent exercises in the Shakespeareanisation of Stratford through its gardens have included the garden of Hall's Croft, which features herbs associated with his son-in-law's medical profession.

[31] See Savage, *The Flora*, 202.

THE "KNOTT GARDEN.

From a drawing by A. Forestier, by kind permission of the "Illustrated London News."

pp. 18 and 19.

Figure 14.2 'Knot-garden at New Place', from F. G. Savage, *The Flora and Folk Lore of Shakespeare* (London: E. J. Burrow, 1923).

314

THE WILD BANK.
Planted according to Bacon's suggestions. (*See* p. 25.)

(*Facing p.* 3)

Figure 14.3 'The Wild Bank', from Savage, *The Flora and Folk Lore of Shakespeare*.

as a 'countryman' which expressed a feeling of Shakespeare as so bound to his native soil that he might best be described in terms of wild rather than garden flowers, in Titania's flowers rather than Perdita's. What all these constructions have in common, though, is a sense that the truly Shakespearean garden preserved an English past. The Englishness that Law achieved in his redevelopment of New Place was composed of the past of the site, textual evidence for Shakespeare's knowledge of and love of gardening, plants from the gardens of royal palaces and historic houses associated with the Bard's life and works, genetic homage (roses sent by the royal family were planted by 'the direct lineal descendant of Sir Thomas Lucy') and Elizabethan groundplans.[32] More recent versions of Shakespeare gardens around the properties, from the orchard filled with sculptures at Anne Hathaway's cottage (1988) and latterly the enchanted wood hung with quotations, or the sculptures in the Great Garden at New Place (2003–4), extend and inflect these models – they continue to argue that Shakespeare's works grew out of English ground and are appropriately thought of on and in relation to that ground.[33]

In 1916, however, the gardens of Stratford were more than places to dream of Shakespeare's life and works; they were places of escape into Shakespeare's England from the anxieties of war. Marie Corelli's 'invitation to the summer festival at Stratford-on-Avon from July 29 to August 26, 1916', for instance, was entitled 'With Shakespeare in His Garden' and expressed the hope that Shakespearean Stratford might offer imaginative refuge:

In the midst of war and war's alarms, how many there are who would gladly escape, if only for a brief interval, from the hard strain of constant worry and suspense, and take something of a holiday, if they knew of any ideal spot where peace and beauty conjoined could give the weary heart and brain a spell of sorely needed rest.[34]

A sense of Shakespearean England as a metaphorical walled garden also suffuses the pageant conceived and performed in the garden at Wadham College, Oxford, in September 1916. Bernice de Bergerac's *In Shakespeare's Garden* was composed of a great number of garden scenes extracted from the plays, including one or two that only happen offstage, bound together by a series of ballets and masques featuring

---

[32] Law, *Shakespeare's Garden*, 24.
[33] On the sculptures in the Great Garden at New Place, see www.cotswolds.info/places/stratford-upon-avon/sculptures.shtml (last accessed 31 July 2014).
[34] M. Corelli, *With Shakespeare in his Garden: An Invitation to the Summer Festival at Stratford-upon-Avon, 1916* (Stratford-upon-Avon: n.p.,1916), 3; see also 5, 6.

a cast that included the Spirit of Nature, eighty-one flower fairies, seven bees, three butterflies, one moth, Puck and Shakespeare himself, the whole rendered bearable by teas provided by the local Boy Scouts in the interval. Like Corelli, Bergerac describes 'Shakespeare's garden' as a consolatory place of escape at once real, theatrical, and imaginary:

> If you would wander an hour or so
> In the garden that Shakespeare knew
> Where the night-wind waved the nodding rose,
> And the purple pansies grew,
> You have not to find some elfin sprite
> To speed you on your way,
> For that magic garden of Long Ago
> Is open to all today
>
> . . .
>
> And you shall forget for a little while
> The Banners of War unfurl'd,
> As you gaze at the kindly and gentle Shapes
> That people the Poet's world;
> And it may seem that the Dawn is nigh,
> And the darkness fled away,
> As you walk in the garden that Shakespeare made,
> That is open to all today.[35]

Like the de Bergerac pageant, the Shakespeare garden made beyond Stratford was instigated by the desire to celebrate the Shakespeare Tercentenary of 1916. Birmingham, for example, set about producing its own Shakespeare garden at Lightwoods Park in 1915, conceived equally as a matter of civic pride and of mass education. 'Birmingham citizens will thus be able to see at a glance, and study on the spot, another phase of our Warwickshire poet's glorious work, and I trust it will be a shrine at which many of his admirers will obtain still more knowledge in ideal surroundings', wrote the chairman of the City of Birmingham Parks Committee.[36] On a smaller scale, the Tercentenary Committee suggested that schoolchildren might make up their own

[35] Bernice de Bergerac, *Tercentenary Shakespeare Festival. 'In Shakespeare's Garden'.* (Oxford, n.p., 1916), n.p.

[36] G. Johnson, *A Complete List of Shakespeare's Plants for Use in the Shakespeare Garden at Lightwoods Park, Birmingham* (Birmingham Parks Committee, 1915), preface.

Shakespeare gardens 'containing plants and flowers mentioned in his works' as 'permanent memorials'.[37] More generally, the fashion for playing Shakespeare outdoors, especially in gardens, from 1884 onwards discussed by Michael Dobson might be related to this need to celebrate and commemorate deep England.[38] But although the *idea* of the Shakespeare garden was strong in the Britain of 1916, the exigencies of wartime meant that it was rarely realised until after the war. It was only in 1919, in keeping with Corelli's rhapsodic version of the town, that New Place was improved by the addition of several gardens including 'the wild bank' and 'the knot garden' to match the planting already in place at the Birthplace.[39] By that time, such gardens were functioning as a poignant memorial to a lost England – they expressed nostalgia for pre-war England enfolded within an already established structural nostalgia for Elizabethan England. W. Foxton's preface to the 1934 reprint of his book *Shakespeare Garden and Wayside Flowers*, originally published in 1914, tellingly identifies them as such when he remarks that 'In England a Shakespeare garden is now a familiar memorial'.[40] And, perhaps because Stratford proper was already (in Corelli's words) 'Shakespeare's garden', and because otherwise Shakespeare's garden was all but lost, it was not primarily in Britain that the tercentenary Shakespeare garden took root, but across the Atlantic in the United States.

Transplantation

If, in England, gardens invoking Shakespeare might stake claims to professional or social territory (like Garrick's or Corelli's), or might re-create an older lost England (as in Stratford) or might more simply celebrate civic and national pride (as in Birmingham), in the United States the making of Shakespeare gardens whether private or public was generally motivated by a desire to claim the Bard as a true

---

[37] See *Shakespeare Tercentenary Observance in the Schools and Other Institutions* (London: for the Shakespeare Tercentenary Committee, 1916), 30.

[38] Michael Dobson, *Shakespeare and Amateur Performance: A Cultural History* (Cambridge University Press, 2011), 164–5, 167–172, 188–9.

[39] Law, *Shakespeare's Garden*, 14.

[40] W. Foxton, *Shakespeare Garden and Wayside Flowers. With Appropriate Quotations for Every Flower. A Complete and Authentic Pocket Guide to Shakespeare Flora.* [1914] (London: n.p., 1934), foreword.

American and Americans as the true heirs to a Shakespearean England. The effort to make Shakespeare adequately American had already had a long history: the American poet and sage William Cullen Bryant, dedicating the statue to Shakespeare in Central Park on the occasion of Shakespeare's birthday on 23 April 1870, remarked that 'Shakespeare, though he cannot be called an American poet, as he was not born here and never saw our continent, is yet a poet of the Americans' arguing for continuity on the basis of shared language and shared bloodlines.[41] The idea of asserting another sort of organic continuity had already taken hold before the outbreak of the First World War: in Los Angeles a replica Birthplace was built in 1901, which included a garden filled with Shakespeare's flowers; and Wilhelm Miller had promoted the Shakespeare garden as one of 'Sixty Suggestions for New Gardens' in an article of the same name published in 1912 in *The Garden Magazine*.[42] But it received new impetus from the spectacle of an England in the throes of world war. Making a garden in honour of the Tercentenary was a shortish step from collecting seeds in Stratford and sending them back home, and not that far removed from the American habit of installing memorials in Stratford itself, from the American fountain in the marketplace to the two American windows in the church.

Monika Smialkowska notes that, preparing for the Tercentenary in 1915 'the Drama League of America put forward suggestions for the appropriate kinds of celebratory activities'. These suggestions included 'plays, masques, festivals, pageants, music, dancing, chorus, lectures, sermons, art and craft exhibitions, club programs, library exhibits, study courses, story telling, tableaux, planting of trees, and developing of Shakespeare gardens'.[43] In America, although the Shakespeare garden was not conceived of as a refuge from war, it was still inflected by a sense that English culture was under strong threat and was in need of urgent conservation. What that intervention might be was

---

[41] See P. Rawlings, *Americans on Shakespeare* (Aldershot: Ashgate, 1999), 278–9.

[42] See Katherine W. Scheil, *She Hath been Reading: Women and Shakespeare Clubs in America* (Ithaca: Cornell University Press, 2012), 28; R. E. Gresee, *Jens Jensen: Maker of Natural Parks and Gardens* (Baltimore: Johns Hopkins University Press, 1992), 110–11.

[43] Monika Smialkowska, '"A Democratic Art at a Democratic Price": The American Celebrations of the Shakespeare Tercentenary, 1916', *Transatlantica* 1 (2010), accessed online.

exemplified by a one-act play devised for an amateur company of
Junior Leaguers, written, performed and published just after the war
had ended, in 1919. *The Shakespeare Garden Club* by Mabel Moran
enjoyed a long success thereafter across the States, being performed by
women's clubs, Shakespearean societies and garden clubs in a variety
of venues, including outdoors in gardens.[44] The scene is set in
Anne Hathaway's Cottage in Shottery, where Anne Hathaway and
her colleagues – busily American-sounding versions of Mistress Page,
Mistress Ford, Perdita, Desdemona, Cordelia, Katherine, Jessica,
Rosalind, Portia, Juliet, Titania, Ophelia, Rosaline and Cleopatra –
have convened for a club meeting, with Lady Macbeth in the chair.
The business in hand is to decide on action to conserve the banks
of the Avon following a previous meeting at which Shakespeare
had requested the ladies to tidy up and replant the riverside area,
currently disfigured by 'defunct felines'. Their discussions consider at
length the flowers they might plant, each lady contributing quotations
from her own play, and the meeting is wrapped up by Lady Macbeth
with this closing statement: 'Ladies, let me prophesy, that when
our members have died, and worms have eaten them and Master
Shakespeare himself hath become but ancient history – clubs in times
to come will remember fair Avon's shores made lovely by your sweet
suggestions.'[45]

What this play proposed imaginatively – the conservation by
American amateurs of the English landscape for posterity, in the name
of Shakespeare, others were already literalising on American soil.
There seem to have been, for instance, many temporary evocations of
Shakespeare country associated with tercentenary pageants. Orie
Latham Hatcher's handbook, *Shakespeare Plays and Pageants*, not
only suggests how a pageant-master might Elizabethanise the landscape with a fair ('any available stream may serve as the Avon and
furnish pleasure boats for the people') and how to build a replica
Birthplace, but how to embellish a replica of Anne Hathaway's
Cottage with a suitable garden: 'with proper forethought there might
even be some of the old English garden flowers popular in Shakespeare's time, growing outside the door'. A helpful list of such plants

---

[44] Mabel M. Moran, *The Shakespeare Garden Club. Comedy/Fantasy in One Act*
(New York: Dramatists Play Service, *c*.1938), preface.
[45] Moran, *Shakespeare Garden Club*, 17.

is provided in an appendix.[46] Hatcher notes that 'the ideal for every pageant is that it shall represent a community' and that the rationale for the evocation of the ground of Stratford within such a pageant is educational – 'knowing Shakespeare and his plays better is the natural motive behind such a festival, and the advantage of suggesting the environment in which he and his work developed is too obvious to need argument'.[47] Putting these two statements together, a Shakespeare tercentenary pageant thus naturalised Shakespeare within American communities and on American soil.

On a much larger scale, between 1913 and 1916, five important permanent 'Shakespeare gardens' were dedicated or celebrated: in Central Park, New York City; in Cleveland, Ohio; at Northwestern University in Evanston, Illinois; at Vassar College in New York state; and at Wellesley College in Massachusetts.[48] What Mark Tebeau says of Cleveland's 1916 garden – that it 'referenced broader attitudes about the ascendancy of Anglo-Saxon racial identity, an outpouring of sympathy for Britain's entry into World War 1, and the resurgence of centenary celebrations as vehicles for asserting collective identity' – holds true for all five 1916 gardens.[49] But their strategies for evoking 'Shakespeare' were rather different. Was 'Shakespeare', for example, primarily to be described as a real biographical subject who was best

---

[46] Orie Latham Hatcher, *A Book for Shakespeare Plays and Pageants: A Treasury of Elizabethan and Shakespearean Detail for Producers, Stage Managers, Actors, Artists and Students* (Westport, CT: Greenwood Press, 1916), 242–4, 312.

[47] Hatcher, *Shakespeare Plays and Pageants*, 207.

[48] There are still books being published which celebrate Shakespeare gardens and facilitate the making of them, e.g. M. Hales, *Shakespeare in the Garden: A Selection of Gardens and an Illustrated Alphabet of Plants* (New York: Abrams, 2006), which lists Shakespeare or Tudor gardens in Britain (in Stratford, Hatfield House, Cranborne Manor and the museum of garden history in Lambeth, London) alongside North American versions (Central Park, Vassar, Northwestern, Stratford Ontario, Stanley Park in Vancouver, amongst them). See also J. Kerr, *Shakespeare's Flowers* (London: Longman, 1969); D. Hunt, *The Flowers of Shakespeare* (Exeter: Webb & Bower, 1980); L. de Bray, *Fantastic Garlands: An Anthology of Flowers and Plants from Shakespeare* (Poole: Blandford Press, 1982); E. Clarke and C. Nichols, *Herb Garden Design* (London: Francis Lincoln, 1995), which includes a design for a Shakespeare garden, as does J. Lowe, *Herbs! Creative Herb Garden Themes and Projects* (Brentwood, TN: Cool Springs Press, 2010.). See also Mrs S. W. Blood, *Making a Shakespeare Garden with his Fragrant Flowers* (New York?: n.p., n.d.).

[49] Mark Tebeau, 'Sculpted Landscapes: Art and Place in Cleveland's Cultural Gardens 1916–2000' http://teaching.clevelandhistory.org/files/2009/08/ sculpted_gardens_Tebeau_June2009.pdf. (last accessed June 2012; this link broken as of 5 August 2014).

referenced by reiterating his own gestures of rootedness and ownership? That seems to have been the impulse behind the dedication in
1913 of a pre-existing garden of botanical specimens in Central Park to
Shakespeare, through the inclusion of a graft taken allegedly from the
original mulberry tree supposedly planted by Shakespeare in 1602.[50]
Central Park, of course, already had a statue of Shakespeare, erected in
1864, which, according to William Cullen Bryant, who gave the oration, would have already been sufficient to attract to the spot quantities
of fairies by moonlight.[51] Or was Shakespeare more appropriately transplanted in the shape of the flora mentioned in his works and native to his
Warwickshire? Central Park hedged its bets here by taking delivery of a
Stratford oak sent by the Mayor of Stratford-upon-Avon.[52] This strategy
of botanic quotation was also adopted by Vassar College. Their garden
opened on 24 April 1916 with a ceremony of the planting of pansies and
flower seeds from Shakespeare's gardens in Stratford-upon-Avon. Laid
out on the site of the old botanical gardens by the combined efforts of the
Shakespeare and Botany classes, it was meant to be a scholarly and
comprehensive library of Elizabethan plants.[53]

Or there again, was it more that a Shakespeare garden was designed to
evoke a more generalised Elizabethan Englishness understood as American prehistory? Cleveland, for instance, was 'Elizabethan in mood and
pattern. At the entrance are gateposts of English design and the garden
boundaries are defined with hedges.'[54] The garden was designed as a riot
of colour and scent, converging on a bust of Shakespeare. Cleveland, in
fact, was especially imaginative and energetic, for this garden boasted a

---

[50] See www.centralparknyc.org/things-to-see-and-do/attractions/shakespeare-
garden.html (last accessed 10 October 2014).

[51] See Rawlings, *Americans on Shakespeare*, 287–8.

[52] *New York Times*, 30 June 1916, 11.

[53] Redesigned and re-planted in the 1920s and 1970s, it retained the ambition of
including only plants appearing in the Works. In the remodelling of the 1980s,
this ambition was diluted, the plant-list expanding to include plants which were
grown in England in the seventeenth century, not just those mentioned by
Shakespeare. 'The original purpose of the garden was not forgotten, however:
the renovation included two special beds created for the display of medicinal
and culinary herbs, identified with tags bearing quotations from Shakespeare.'
http://vcencyclopedia.vassar.edu/buildings-grounds/grounds/shakespeare-
garden.html (last accessed 5 August 2014).

[54] http://clevelandmemory.org/ebooks/tpap/pg39.html (last accessed
5 August 2014).

multiplicity of Shakespearean authentications – biographical (a mulberry tree from a cutting made at New Place), botanic (it was planted with hawthorn, daffodils, violets, fleurs-de-lis, daisies, pansies and columbine – 'the flowers given immortality in the poetry of Shakespeare'), critical (the mulberry cutting was sent by the Shakespearean critic Sir Sidney Lee), bardic (the garden is adorned with oaks planted by Yeats and by the great great granddaughter of Shelley), theatrical (more trees were planted by Phyllis Neilson Terry, niece of Ellen Terry) and literary-topographic (a circular bed of roses – supposedly Shakespeare's 'favourite flower' – plus some ivy, was sent by the Mayor of Verona, from the monastery garden associated with the alleged tomb of Juliet, and saplings from Birnam Wood seem to have been sent to Cleveland as well). Other features included the Byzantine sundial presented by the distinguished actor Robert Mantell and jars planted with ivy and flowers by Sarah Bernhardt, Sir Herbert Beerbohm Tree and Rabindranath Tagore – the 'Shakespeare of India'. Cleveland in this respect was unusual in admitting a touch of global Shakespeare into this form of commemoration – a faint whisper here of Israel Gollancz's cosmopolitan *Book of Homage* (1916). Equal verve was demonstrated by the Shakespeare Garden inaugural exercises, which took place on 14 April 1916, on the upper boulevard near the garden entrance. Speeches of civic welcome were succeeded by selections from Mendelssohn's *Midsummer Night's Dream*, and the Normal School Glee Club performed 'Hark, Hark, the Lark' and 'Who Is Sylvia?' A group of high-school pupils in Elizabethan costume escorted the guests to the garden entrance and stood guard during the planting of the dedicatory elms. According to the *Cleveland Times*, 'Miss Marlowe climaxed the proceedings by her readings of Perdita's flower scene from "Winter's Tale," the 54th Sonnet of Shakespeare, and verses from the Star Spangled Banner. Her leading of all present in the singing of the National Anthem brought the impressive event to a close.'[55] In contrast, a Shakespeare garden, even one made in 1916, might remain remarkably feminocentric and sentimental. According to the *Wellesley College News* for 18 May 1916, the dedication ceremony of the Shakespeare garden at Wellesley College was characterised by the extensive and sentimental presentation of Shakespeare's flowers between various women faculty

[55] http://clevelandmemory.org/ebooks/tpap/pg39.html. See also Leo Weidenthal, *From Dis's Waggon ... a sentimental survey of a poet's corner, the Shakespeare garden of Cleveland* (Cleveland: the Weidenthal Company, 1926).

and students, together with ceremonial plantings enlivened with singing and the recitation of suitable quotations.[56]

And so, finally, to return to the Shakespeare garden in Evanston (see Figure 14.4). Designed in 1915 by the Danish–American landscape architect and conservationist Jens Jensen (1860–1951), it must have been cutting-edge for its time, for it was inspired by Bacon's 'Essay on Gardens' and claimed to take the form of an Elizabethan knot-garden.[57] It therefore predated Law's redevelopment of the garden at New Place, also inspired by Bacon. The planting, carried out by the Evanston Garden Club, was more of a Shakespearean quotation-quiz than an exercise in botanic comprehensiveness: 'The flowers, shrubs, trees and herbs in the garden are mentioned in Shakespeare's plays and are varieties best suited to the garden's location and Midwestern climate.' According to the current website, 'the more than 50 plants that can be planted' include 'rosemary, lavender, thyme, hyssop, rue, lemon balm, columbine, old roses, oxeye daisy, anemone, daffodil, pansy, poppy, nasturtium and marigolds. Parsley, holly, ivy, mint and peonies are also allowed.'[58] (This explains the otherwise inexplicable nasturtiums I noticed in the early 1990s, although it does not precisely justify them.) The Elizabethan-style stone bench and the fountain, featuring a bronze relief of Shakespeare's head and suitable quotations from *As You Like It*, *A Midsummer Night's Dream* and *The Winter's Tale*, were relatively late additions, eventually dedicated in 1930 (see Figure 14.5). In taking refuge in the only garden in Evanston, I discovered to my amusement, I had unconsciously chosen to be transported home to England.

These American gardens are divergent in their expressions of Shakespeare and Shakespearean authenticity, and divergent too in their modes – ranging from the grandly public and patriotic through to the markedly feminine and sentimental. All, however, claim authenticity by twinning transplantation and quotation. This was a habit of mind that extended beyond these particular gardens. As Katherine West Scheil has noted, in 1937 the Avon Bard Club laid out a Shakespeare garden in New Rochelle, NY, which included (as ever) 'a sun dial inscribed with a quotation from *The Merchant of Venice*' and 'a luxuriant bed of English ivy, grown from cuttings brought directly

---

[56] http://repository.wellesley.edu/news/498 (last accessed 31 July 2014).

[57] See Jens Jensen, 'A Shakespeare garden-plan', *Garden Magazine* 3 (April 1916), 168 (photo and groundplan).

[58] www.thegardencluboofevanston.org/html/gardens.php (last accessed 31 July 2014).

Figure 14.4 View of Shakespeare garden, Northwestern University, Evanston Illinois.

(a)

Figure 14.5(a) and (b) Shakespeare bench, bas-relief and quotations, Shakespeare garden, Northwestern University, Evanston Illinois.

from Stratford-upon-Avon'.[59] The dedication ceremony for the replica Globe Theatre in Dallas Texas in 1936 was also thought to require such gestures; Graham Holderness quotes a telegram requesting English aid: 'Please send earth Shakespeare's garden water River Avon ...' to sprinkle on the stage.[60] (Ivor Brown and George Fearon note that selling Avon water to Americans had been characteristic of the twenties.)[61] To what extent these gestures were acts of cultural self-fertilisation and to what extent compassionate conservation of the real thing, old England, is not entirely clear, but they find a satirical commentary in Angela Carter's fantasia *Wise Children* (1991), which tells of the Chance twins and their efforts to import Stratford earth (packed in a ceramic head of

[59] http://wikimapia.org/10873213/Davenport-Park; Scheil, *She Hath been Reading*, 27.

[60] Graham Holderness, *The Shakespeare Myth* (Manchester University Press, 1988), 2; see for more detail Kim Sturgess, *Shakespeare and the American Nation* (Cambridge University Press, 2004), 202–7.

[61] I. Brown and G. Fearon, *Amazing Monument: A Short History of the Shakespeare Industry* (London, Toronto: Heinemann, 1939), 6.

(b)

Figure 14.5 (*cont.*)

Shakespeare) onto the Hollywood filmset of *A Midsummer Night's Dream*. In this fiction, Stratford does not travel well; the soil has been used by a filmstar's pet Persian cat in default of a litter-tray on the long rail journey across the continent. The Chance sisters replace the soil with the most authentic available, dug out of a facsimile Shakespearean knot-garden at an Olde English motel called the Forest of Arden, consisting of multiple replicas of Anne Hathaway's Cottage set in grounds garnished with 'Warwickshire apple-trees, imported oaks, you name it'.[62] But though it is sprinkled onto the set by Melchior Hazard, proponent of global Shakespeare, this soil, perhaps because it is ersatz, fails to save the *Dream* from being a turkey. Nonetheless, Carter's comedy picks up on a continuing impulse within American culture. A hundred years on from the making of these tercentenary gardens there are still in existence some twenty-seven Shakespeare gardens across the States, of which sixteen are located in public parks or function as botanical gardens, eleven are attached to universities or colleges and four are associated with Shakespeare Festivals.[63] (For the sake of academic respectability,

---

[62] Angela Carter, *Wise Children* (London: Chatto & Windus, 1991), 120–1, 128–9, 134–6.

[63] Wikipedia currently lists twenty-nine gardens (excluding inadvertent duplicates), and for the sake of convenience I will repeat the list here:

> **Originally private gardens** include Huntington Library, CA (established 1959); Wessington Springs, South Dakota (1932); Vienna, Austria (2005); Herzogspark, Regensburg, Germany (n.d.)
>
> **Public/civic/botanic gardens** include Bethel Public Library, CT; Shakespeare's garden, Brookfield, CT; Brooklyn Botanical Gardens, Brooklyn NY; Cleveland, OH; Johannesburg Botanic Garden, South Africa; Central Park, NY; Golden Gate Park (1928), San Francisco, CA; the Elizabethan herb garden, Mellon Park, Pittsburgh, PA; Cedarbrook Park, Plainfield NJ
>
> **University gardens** include Misericordia University; Northwestern, Evanston, IL; Illinois State University, IL; Kilgore College; St Norbert College; Purdue University; University College of Fraser Valley, BC; University of Massachusetts; University of South Dakota; Vassar College; University of Tennessee at Chattanooga; Folger Shakespeare Library (1989)
>
> **Festival gardens** include International Festival Garden, Portland, Oregon (1945); Alabama Shakespeare Festival (Blount Cultural Park); Colorado Shakespeare Festival; Illinois Shakespeare Festival.

> To this may be added the College of St Elizabeth; the Texas Festival gardens; the garden at the Mayflower Inn, Washington CT; Cedar Rapids, Iowa; the botanical gardens in Wichita, Kansas, which contain a formal Shakespeare garden; Hiram College; and one in San Jose, CA. There is also a 'Jardin Shakespeare' in the Bois de Boulogne, Paris. There are almost certainly more.

I am not counting the garden attached to the Disneyland replica of Anne Hathaway's Cottage 'in which you are sure to meet Pooh Bear' as a Shakespeare garden.)[64]

The longevity of the Shakespeare garden in America suggests how successfully it has solved the problem of the relation between the native soil of genius and the trans-global portability of genius's printed works. It naturalises through transplantation, by botanic quotation. It brings Shakespeare home to somewhere he never knew. Nowhere is this power more clearly suggested than in the Shakespeare garden in Wessington Springs, North Dakota. This garden was made by the Mrs Shay who diligently collected leaves and flowers on her tour of Stratford for her friends in 1926. On her return, she not only conscientiously made up the albums she had promised her friends, but created a Shakespeare garden complete with quotations, setting at its centre a replica of Anne Hathaway's Cottage to which she and her husband in due course retired.

[64] www.wdwinfo.com/wdwinfo/guides/epcot/epws-uk.htm (last accessed 18 May 2015).

15 Anne Hathaway's Cottage: myth, tourism, diplomacy

KATHERINE WEST SCHEIL

In 1793, engraver Samuel Ireland travelled to Stratford-upon-Avon with his son, William, in search of materials related to Shakespeare. As part of his trip, he paid a visit to the nearby village of Shottery, where he made the first illustration of what is now known as Anne Hathaway's Cottage, under the title 'House at Shotery [sic], in which Ann Hathaway the wife of Shakspere resided' (Figure 15.1).

Until Samuel Ireland's drawing of the Hathaway homestead, it remained 'utterly unknown in Stratford'.[1] Today, Anne Hathaway's Cottage hosts thousands of visitors each year, and is one of the centre-piece properties owned by the Shakespeare Birthplace Trust (SBT). This chapter considers how the 'House at Shotery' was transformed into Anne Hathaway's Cottage, and then adapted in a number of locales worldwide as sites of commemoration, perpetuating romantic myths about Shakespeare and linking these material spaces to local and global issues, from world wars to local tourism. The story of how the 'House at Shotery' became 'Anne Hathaway's Cottage' comple-ments Julia Thomas's argument about how Shakespeare's birthplace functions as a *lieu de mémoire*, a 'site of cultural memory that is invested with the meanings of the heritage of the community'. As Harald Hendrix points out, 'the existence of a house facilitates the rise of a cult and favors its subsistence', but this only happens 'if the interpretation of what the house expresses agrees with the dominant opinions on what their dwellers and their literary works stand for'.[2]

---

[1] Edwin Reed, *The Truth Concerning Stratford-Upon-Avon and Shaksper* (Boston: Coburn Publishing, 1907), 46; Samuel Ireland, *Picturesque Views on the Upper, or Warwickshire Avon* (London, 1795).

[2] Julia Thomas, *Shakespeare's Shrine: The Bard's Birthplace and the Invention of Stratford-upon-Avon* (Philadelphia: University of Pennsylvania Press, 2012), 28; Harald Hendrix, 'Writers' Houses as Media of Expression and Remembrance: From Self-Fashioning to Cultural Memory', in Harald Hendrix (ed.), *Writers' Houses and the Making of Memory* (London: Routledge, 2008), 6.

Figure 15.1 Samuel Ireland, 'The House at Shotery'. By permission of the Folger Shakespeare Library.

In addition to the Warwickshire original, Anne Hathaway Cottages can be found in Asheville, North Carolina; Ashland, Oregon; Green Lake, Wisconsin; Staunton, Virginia; Perth, Australia; Victoria, British Columbia; and Wessington Springs, South Dakota – thus, the practices associated with these cottages extend their commemorative roles to several national identities and cultures. While some Cottages (like the one in Asheville, North Carolina) functioned as specific wartime commemorative sites connecting Shakespeare's family story to a larger political canvas, others have contributed to forge a romantic myth of Shakespeare through destinations for weddings, bed and breakfast lodgings, or other tourist sites. The wide range of commemorative practices associated with these various Cottages around the world, and the ways this space has been adapted and reshaped, circulate both local and global myths about Shakespeare, often in response to issues connected with tourism, economics, and industry well beyond the borders of the original Shottery property.

Unlike adaptations of Shakespeare's plays, which have some connection to a text that is then adapted and reshaped, the Hathaway Cottage is bound by three nontextual factors that determine how it has been given meaning – its rural locale, its association with the Hathaway family from the time of Shakespeare until its purchase by the SBT in 1892, and its adaptability to fulfil desirable romantic narratives about Shakespeare. First, the geographical location of the Anne Hathaway Cottage, in rural Shottery just outside Stratford, and even today still a somewhat remote walk away, has encouraged the proliferation of narratives about Shakespeare's pastoral love life that commemorate and enshrine a particular version of Shakespeare. As Nicola J. Watson argues, sites like birthplaces are produced by 'superimposing [a] narrative upon a surviving house'.[3] Had Shakespeare married a woman from the heart of the market town of Stratford, whose family lived in Sheep Street, for example, a pastoral narrative would not be as feasible. Charles Dickens's 1892 essay on the sale of Anne Hathaway's Cottage in Shottery captures this sentiment: 'If Stratford speaks to us of the poet's birth and education, of his years as a prosperous man of business, of the material side, which is yet so

---

[3] Nicola J. Watson, *The Literary Tourist: Readers and Places in Romantic and Victorian Britain* (Basingstoke: Palgrave Macmillan, 2006), 58. Julia Thomas suggests that since the Cottage was 'surrounded by beautiful English countryside', it encouraged 'a connection between Shakespeare and the natural world'. *Shakespeare's Shrine*, 132.

necessary a side even to the man of genius, Shottery speaks to us of the ideal side, of the time of youth's opening love, and of manhood's sweet communing with the peaceful sights and sounds of country life.'[4]

Second, the fact that the Hathaway Cottage has survived in roughly the same configuration as it was in Shakespeare's day has further secured the bucolic associations between Shakespeare's wife and his Stratford life. The Cottage's domestic and maternal associations were further linked by the longevity of the Hathaway family, particularly the last caretaker, Mary Baker, who, until her death in 1899, served tea to visitors and recounted stories of the Bard's romantic life and of his courting of her distant relative Anne.[5]

Third, the physical space of Anne Hathaway's Cottage – its location in the countryside and its survival virtually intact – have conditioned the type of commemorative narratives produced about Shakespeare's wife and family, even though there is no concrete evidence that Shakespeare ever spent any time there, despite popular belief. The other Warwickshire properties where it is more certain that Shakespeare resided (the birthplace on Henley Street and New Place) are both centrally located in the heart of the town. It would be difficult to associate Dickens's 'peaceful sights and sounds of country life' with the birthplace on Henley Street, or with New Place, and even more so today. The Cottage, however, maintains its idyllic character and allows for perpetuation of the 'country life' narrative associated with Shakespeare as a Warwickshire poet. Today, various commemorative practices and rituals maintain the cultural memory of Shakespeare the rural lover, both at the original Cottage and at several replicas in Anglo-speaking countries worldwide.

Romantic myth

Even though Anne Hathaway's Cottage was not a tourist destination in the eighteenth century (it played no significant part in David Garrick's

---

[4] Charles Dickens, 'Anne Hathaway's Cottage', *All the Year Round* (30 April 1892), 420.

[5] Anne Hathaway's brother Bartholomew is the one responsible for minor additions in the early seventeenth century. Mark Eccles, *Shakespeare in Warwickshire* (Madison: University of Wisconsin Press, 1961), 63. For the history of ownership of the cottage, see Robert Bearman, 'Anne Hathaway's Cottage', in Michael Dobson and Stanley Wells (eds.), *The Oxford Companion to Shakespeare* (Oxford University Press, 2001), 205.

1769 Stratford Jubilee), the earliest recorded visitors to the Cottage responded to its Hathaway family lineage and to its bucolic setting, putting in place the narratives of domesticity and pastoral romance that the Cottage still memorializes today.[6] The appearance of Shakespeare's will in 1747, with its infamous bequest of the 'second best bed' to his wife, may have inspired the need for a counter-narrative based on a romantic version of Shakespeare and Anne Hathaway, and linked to the Hathaway family farm. Samuel Ireland and his son, William Henry Ireland, were partly responsible for the shift from the 'House at Shotery' to what is now Anne Hathaway's Cottage, and with the construction of a quaint love story between Shakespeare and Anne Hathaway that preoccupied writers throughout the nineteenth century. In 1793, when the Irelands travelled to Stratford in search of any relics or papers connected with Shakespeare, they were taken around by local Stratfordian and Shakespeare aficionado John Jordan. As part of Jordan's tour of Stratford, he took them to Hewlands, the Hathaway farm, where Ireland bought from the Hathaway family a bugle purse 'said to have been a present from our great poet to the object of his choice', and Shakespeare's courting chair, 'wherein it was stated our bard was used to sit, during his courtship with his Anne upon his knee', now owned by the Shakespeare Birthplace Trust and displayed in the Cottage.[7] Ireland had his eye on a bed there as well, but, as it was still in use by the Hathaway family, they refused to sell it.[8]

After their largely unsuccessful trip to Stratford, in order to appease his disappointed father, son William Henry Ireland announced that a 'Mr. H' had given him a trunk of Shakespeare-related documents, including a profession of Shakespeare's Protestant faith, a letter from Queen Elizabeth to Shakespeare, playhouse documents, and a love letter and love poem from Shakespeare to Anne Hathaway, complete

---

[6] The Cottage regularly hosts domestic and romantic events, particularly for Mothering Sunday and Valentine's Day.

[7] William Henry Ireland, *The Confessions of William Henry Ireland* (London, 1895). Mary Hornby, tenant of the Birthplace in 1793, reportedly kept a letter from Shakespeare to his wife, as well as his wife's shoe. W. T. Moncrieff, *Excursion to Stratford upon Avon* (Leamington: Elliston, 1824), 15–16 and Henry C. Shelley, *Shakespeare and Stratford* (London: Simpkin, Marshall Hamilton, Kent, 1913), 151.

[8] See Samuel Schoenbaum, *Shakespeare's Lives* (Oxford: Clarendon Press, 1970), 131, 133.

with a lock of Shakespeare's hair.[9] Though the love poem is far from impressive in its poetic quality, represented by the couplet 'Is there on earth a man more true / Than Willy Shakespear is to you', it nevertheless speaks to the desire for evidence of Shakespeare the lover which captured the imagination of the nineteenth century, in numerous reproductions of Anne Hathaway's Cottage and fanciful love stories about the Shakespeares. As Nicola J. Watson points out, the Cottage provided 'an idealized pastoral love of the sort that is conspicuously absent' from Shakespeare's texts and from his documented biography.[10] In spite of the notorious history of the Ireland forgeries, exposed by Edmund Malone in 1796, Samuel Ireland's depiction of the Cottage, and his son William's construction of Shakespeare the lover in his forged love letter, stimulated the many imaginative works that commemorate a romantic, pastoral, and domestic version of Shakespeare.

The conversion of the 'House at Shotery' into 'Anne Hathaway's Cottage' involved a more substantial deployment of what Charles Dickens described as 'youth's opening love' and 'the peaceful sights and sounds of country life.' Exactly a hundred years after Ireland's first illustration of the Shottery House, Mathilde Blind's 1895 collection of 'Shakespeare Sonnets' exemplifies the full-blown commemorative potential of the Cottage to enshrine a story of Shakespeare's courtship. Blind describes the Cottage as 'ivy-girt and crowned' with a 'path down which our Shakespeare ran' to meet an Anne who 'made all his mighty pulses throb and bound'. The addition of a Shakespeare-centred narrative to the Hathaway home 'turned this plot to holy ground', in Blind's words. As Gail Marshall has pointed out, Blind's poems are a 'vicarious romantic memory' about a Shakespeare who is 'embedded fundamentally in the land in which he was born'.[11]

[9] Jeffrey Kahan, *Reforging Shakespeare: The Story of a Theatrical Scandal* (Bethlehem, PA: Lehigh University Press, 1998), 41. As Kahan points out, in order for a forgery to succeed, it must 'respond to contemporary tastes' (20).

[10] Nicola J. Watson, 'Shakespeare on the Tourist Trail', in Robert Shaughnessy (ed.), *The Cambridge Companion to Shakespeare and Popular Culture* (Cambridge University Press, 2007), 212. Anne Hathaway cottages respond to what Hendrix calls 'a fundamental dissatisfaction with the expressive power of literature', 'Writers' Houses as Media of Expression and Remembrance', 3.

[11] Gail Marshall, 'Women Re-Read Shakespeare Country', in Nicola J. Watson (ed.), *Literary Tourism and Nineteenth-Century Culture* (Basingstoke: Palgrave Macmillan, 2009), 96–7. See Marshall's chapter for a lengthier discussion of Blind's work.

The setting of the Cottage fits perfectly with this narrative. Works like Emma Severn's novel *Anne Hathaway, or, Shakespeare in Love* (1845) featured lengthy descriptions of the Cottage as it figured in the Shakespeares' courtship and, as Julia Thomas notes, Victorian visitors were 'compelled to visit by stories of Shakespeare running through fields of flowers to meet his sweetheart, of the lovers sitting hand in hand in the garden and gazing up at the stars, and of Anne and William snuggling up together on the settle which was still in the house'.[12] The circulation of this myth continues; the most recent brochure for Anne Hathaway's Cottage describes it as 'the most romantic of Shakespeare's family homes where the young William Shakespeare courted his future wife'.[13] In 2014, the 'Love Struck Trail' ran from 14 to 23 February, where 'Couples can follow the Woodland Walk to find a selection of Shakespearian quotes, where one letter in each quote will be highlighted in a red heart for visitors to work out what romantic message the letters make. A special quiz will also be on offer where couples can search for a list of items in the Woodland Walk, which includes a red rose. The trail finishes with the sweetheart tree which will feature red wooden hearts for people to write a message of love on.'[14]

In his work on space, Tim Cresswell points out, 'When humans invest meaning in a portion of space and then become attached to it in some way (naming is one such way) it becomes a place.'[15] By the end of the nineteenth century, the *space* of the Hathaway family farm was fully transformed into Anne Hathaway's Cottage, a *place* that commemorated a pastoral romantic Shakespeare deeply embedded in the 'opening love' of youth and the 'sights and sounds of country life', just in time to fulfil the needs of the next generation. The transformation of Anne Hathaway's Cottage is part of what Nicola J. Watson describes as a 'biographically driven urge to imprint the virtual, readerly experience of Shakespeare onto topographical reality'.[16] During the two world wars, these associations were mobilized

---

[12] Thomas, *Shakespeare's Shrine*, 133.
[13] 'Welcome to Anne Hathaway's Cottage & Gardens', Shakespeare Birthplace Trust Brochure, 2014.
[14] www.shakespeare.org.uk/about-us/press-information/news/perform-romeo-and-juliet.html (last accessed 8 May 2015).
[15] Tim Cresswell, *Place: A Short Introduction* (Malden, MA: Blackwell, 2004), 10.
[16] Watson, 'Shakespeare on the Tourist Trail', 200.

to support patriotic uses of Shakespeare, often conditioned by local economics, politics, and ideologies.

Cultural diplomacy

In the early decades of the twentieth century, Anne Hathaway's Cottage was a destination for international travellers, even in moments of global turmoil. The Visitors' Book, which was begun in 1912 and continued to the end of the Second World War (the last entry is 1954), includes visitors from India, Northern Ireland, Jerusalem, Australia, and New York. Alongside some of the more famous public figures, including early biographers Charlotte and Marie Stopes, Ellen Terry, George Bernard Shaw, Kenneth Clarke, William Poel, Ben Greet, Peggy O'Neill, Lillian Baylis, Stanley Lupino, Charlie Chaplin, and Oliver Hardy, are some intriguing figures of greater political significance. During the First World War, several prominent national dignitaries spent time at the Cottage. Rennie MacInnes, the Anglican Bishop in Jerusalem, signed the guest book on 28 July 1915. He had been appointed Bishop of Jerusalem in 1914 but was prevented from going there owing to the outbreak of the war.[17] Presumably he decided on a tour of the 'country life' of England instead, including Anne Hathaway's Cottage.

In September of 1917, an entourage from Serbia also visited the Cottage, including Prince Alexis Karageorgevitch and his wife, Princess Daria, originally from Cleveland. Prince Alexis served as President of the Serbian Red Cross during the First World War, but fled Serbia during the winter of 1915–16. They spent part of the summer in Stratford – a photo of them survives in Stratford, dated 31 July 1917. Neither

---

[17] MacInnes was appointed the new bishop in Jerusalem in 1914, but war broke out before he got to Jerusalem. According to Lester Pittman, 'Since the Ottoman empire joined the Central Powers against Great Britain and its allies, British missionaries had to leave Palestine, and Bishop MacInnes had to spend the first three years of his episcopate in Egypt.' 'The Formation of the Episcopal Diocese of Jerusalem 1841–1948: Anglican, Indigenous and Ecumenical', in Thomas Hummel, Kevork Hintlian and Ulf Carmesund (eds.), *Patterns of the Past, Prospects for the Future: The Christian Heritage in the Holy Land* (London: Melisende, 1999), 98. Apparently he went on a tour of the midlands before leaving for Egypt. MacInnes coordinated post-war relief efforts in Syria and Palestine, and was instrumental in building ties between Anglican churches in the United States and in Palestine.

MacInnes nor Karageorgevitch left personal records of their reactions to or motivations for visiting the Cottage but, given their respective positions, these trips must have served as respites from the impending pressures of global turmoil, commemorating what Evelyn Waugh called 'the dreaming ancestral beauty of the English country ... something enduring and serene in a world that had lost its reason and would so stand when the chaos and confusion were forgotten'.[18]

During the Second World War, Anne Hathaway's Cottage was adapted to memorialize British perseverance and 'the peaceful sights and sounds of country life' that Dickens described at the end of the nineteenth century. A series of wartime postcards preserves these associations. The interior and exterior of the Cottage are featured on two of the cards, with the interior shot giving a prominent place to the famous courting bench that has long been a symbol of romantic Shakespeare (Figure 15.2). The reverse sides feature Churchill's inspirational words, 'We shall never stop, never weary, never give in', printed in the top left corner.[19] The postcards are undated, but Churchill's speech 'Dieu protège la France' was broadcast on 21 October 1940.

An original photograph of Anne Hathaway's Cottage evokes a similar combination of pastoral country life amid global unrest. The notation on the back of the photograph reads 'American Servicemen at AHC, *c.*1943' (Figure 15.3). Though the identity of the American servicemen is lost, we can surmise that they were probably part of what Simon Barker calls the 'constant stream of military personnel' who were 'established in the countryside around the town' from Canada, the United States, and the other Allied nations.[20]

Attendance at the Cottage fell off dramatically with the start of the war in 1939, but around the time of this photo military personnel were admitted free, and the increased presence of American troops caused

[18] Evelyn Waugh, *Decline and Fall* (London: Penguin, 1928), 148.
[19] Other postcards in the series featured Shakespeare's Birthplace and the Shakespeare Memorial Theatre.
[20] Simon Barker, 'Shakespeare, Stratford, and the Second World War', in Irena R. Makaryk and Marissa McHugh (eds.), *Shakespeare and the Second World War: Memory, Culture, Identity* (University of Toronto Press, 2012), 206. Simon Barker notes that Canadian and US soldiers could have taken courses at the Memorial Theatre in 1944 as well (208). See also Nicholas Fogg, *Stratford: A Town at War, 1914–1945* (Gloucester: Sutton Publishing, 2008), 114–16.

Figure 15.2 Anne Hathaway's Cottage interior, by Brian Gerald. Valentine postcard A. 502.

Figure 15.3 American Servicemen at Anne Hathaway's Cottage, c.1943. By permission of the Shakespeare Birthplace Trust.

340

attendance to rise again.[21] The account of one of the guides at the Cottage during the war years offers a window into how the Cottage fulfilled national and international needs. Emma Salmon remembered giving wounded American servicemen a tour of the Cottage, and she recounts that a doctor regularly brought a coach of American wounded servicemen from a hospital in Birmingham for tours of the Cottage on Sunday afternoons.[22] Roma Innes, who lived at the Shottery Post Office during the war, similarly remembered that 'the coach trade (round the Shakespeare area) really started with a doctor in Birmingham when there were some of the wounded soldiers in Birmingham', who 'thought he'd like to bring them out to see Anne Hathaway's Cottage and he hired a coach'.[23] While no first-hand accounts of this doctor or his patients survive, presumably he was seeking the 'sweet communing with the peaceful sights and sounds of country life' that Charles Dickens evoked.

At least one description does survive about the Cottage's role in commemorating national identity during the war. American serviceman Eugene G. Schulz writes in his memoir about the typical associations American soldiers would have had with Anne Hathaway's Cottage. Schulz, who grew up on a farm in Wisconsin, was drafted

---

[21] Visitors to the Birthplace Trust properties were scarce during the war years; Levi Fox reports that in 1940 only ten American visitors signed the guest book, but 'in 1944, by which time American servicemen had arrived in this country to take part in the Normandy invasion, no fewer than 22,921 G.I.s, as they are called, visited the birthplace'. Levi Fox, *The Shakespeare Birthplace Trust: A Personal Memoir* (Norwich: Jarrold, 1997), 49.

[22] Stratford Society and Shakespeare Birthplace Trust Oral History Project, Interview on 29 November 1990 with Emma Salmon. Salmon began as a guide in 1941, the year her son was shot down. Apparently American soldiers were quite popular in Stratford; according to one resident, American soldiers used to throw candy and gum to the children as their convoy of trucks made their way through the town. 'A Schoolboy in Wartime Stratford,' David Warner, WW2 People's War Oral History project. www.bbc.co.uk/history/ww2peopleswar/about/.

[23] Roma Innes, 'Shottery Post Office in Wartime', WW2 People's War Oral History project, 18 April 2005. Canadian soldiers were apparently not so reverent of Shakespeare. According to one account, 'The Canadian soldiers got drunk one night, and because the locals were too slow in offering billets for them, they took out their resentment on poor old Shakespeare and his bronze characters, whom they knocked off their stone plinths, and gave them a bath in the Avon – Hamlet, Falstaff, and all of them. Did you not wonder why the statues looked so green in the post-war years?' Warner, 'A Schoolboy in Wartime Stratford'.

in 1943 and was a typist in Patton's XX Corps, attached to Patton's Third Army. He writes about the experience of touring the English countryside while stationed in Marlborough in 1944: 'We really enjoyed walking along the lovely English roads and lanes that radiated out from our barracks ... These places were very charming with typical English cottages covered with thatched roofs and tiny front yards showing the early spring roses and other flowers ... I had seen pictures of scenes like this in geography books, and now it was a thrill to actually see these quaint English scenes with my own eyes.'[24] At one point, Schulz expresses the difficulty of remembering their reason for being there as opposed to enjoying the 'peaceful sights' of the countryside: 'We were in England for only one reason, to destroy the tyrant Adolf Hitler, who with his Wehrmacht was destroying the people and lands and cities of Europe ... It was time to get down to the business of war' (76, 74).

Before leaving for the D-Day invasion, Schulz's group of ten American soldiers was given permission to do one last round of authorized sightseeing in early April 1944. After travelling to Stonehenge and Avebury, they stopped in Stratford-upon-Avon. Schulz writes, 'We walked on the streets of this small town, looking at the many sites relating to Shakespeare, including his home and Ann Hathaway's Cottage. There were no tourists, only soldiers, visiting here because all activities concerning this famous dramatist and poet were shut down for the duration of the war' (79). Schulz recalled memorizing Portia's 'Quality of Mercy' speech from his high school days, remarking: 'Wow! This day I had walked on hallowed ground where the author of this play had lived his life. I was on an emotional high during the ride back to camp as I stored these memories into the back of my brain' (80). Schulz's trip to Stratford was indeed a bucolic pause; General Patton arrived in early May to announce their role in his Third Army, in preparation for the D-Day invasion in June. They landed in Normandy and travelled across France, Germany, and Austria, later occupying Germany and liberating the Ohrdruf concentration camp. Schulz was awarded a Bronze Star for service, and made return pilgrimages to many of these sites again later in his life.

---

[24] Eugene G. Schulz, *The Ghost in General Patton's Third Army: The Memoirs of Eugene G. Schulz during his Service in the United States Army in World War II* (Xlibris, 2013), 72. Subsequent page references are given in parentheses in the text.

Anne Hathaway's Cottage was adapted for a further global wartime use, to commemorate England on one of the cover illustrations to the song 'There'll Always Be an England' (1939). 'There'll Always Be an England' was the 'first great hit song of the war', and its legacy extended past the Second World War; it was 'one of the handful of wartime songs still remembered 50 years after the event'.[25] The song posits a stable pastoral place that will always be there, 'Tho' worlds may change and go awry':

> There'll always be an England –
> While there's a country lane;
> Wherever there's a cottage small
> Beside a field of grain.

Written by Ross Parker and Hugh Charles in 1939, the song sold over 200,000 copies within two months and 'became the nation's rallying cry, uniting Britons as one in the fight against the Reich'.[26] Linking Anne Hathaway's Cottage to this song further solidified the Cottage's role in commemorating British perseverance across the Atlantic, since the version of the song with the Cottage on the cover was sold only in the United States, Canada, and Newfoundland.[27]

Local tourism

Outside the United Kingdom, many of the Anne Hathaway Cottages worldwide have adapted the romantic, pastoral, and patriotic associations of the original place, spreading these various commemorative associations worldwide. The replica of Anne Hathaway's Cottage in Wessington Springs, South Dakota, can serve as a model for this global circulation. The cottage was built by faculty and students of Wessington Springs College in 1932 as a retirement home for Professor Clark Shay

---

[25] John Baxendale, '"You and I – All of Us Ordinary People": Renegotiating "Britishness" in Wartime', in Nick Hayes and Jeff Hill (eds.), *'Millions Like Us?': British Culture in the Second World War* (Liverpool University Press, 1999), 295. Baxendale points out that the song's lyrics 'aspire to a timeless and high-minded sense of nationhood' (296).

[26] Steven Seidenberg, Maurice Sellar, and Lou Jones, *You Must Remember This: Songs at the Heart of the War* (London: Boxtree, 1995), 28–9.

[27] This version was published by Gordon V. Thompson in Toronto. The version published in London featured British sailors from the song's premiere in the 1939 film *Discoveries*.

and his wife, Emma, but was initially set up to commemorate Mrs Shay's travel to England. In 1926, at the age of sixty-four, Emma Shay borrowed $1,000 in order to travel to England, entailing a train ride to Milwaukee, Chicago, Toronto, and Montreal; eventually, she crossed the Atlantic by steamer to Liverpool. Mrs Shay travelled alone, and the trip took almost three months. Stratford was one of her first stops in June of 1926. After visiting the birthplace, Holy Trinity Church, and the Memorial Theatre, she made her way to Anne Hathaway's cottage. She noted that 'after many inquiries she found it, and it was just like the picture, with the thatched roof'. She records that 'the guide explained the various rooms', and 'the stone floor, fireplace with oven at the side, places for tinder, were all there, and the courting seat, where all love making was to be made in the presence of the father and mother'.[28] While inside, she was not allowed to take a picture, but did gather some grass and buy some pansies and rosemary. She writes that 'the nurseryman was very kind, he let [her] gather [pansies and rosemary] herself. He told her that they did not know what they would do without the Americans coming to Stratford' (31). According to a memoir about her trip, this was 'her dream of years gone by, to [visit] far away England' (1).

After her return, to commemorate Shakespeare's birthday in 1927, the Shays, students, and faculty began work on the garden. They finished the house in 1932, based on a postcard of the Shottery cottage, and it purports to be the only building in South Dakota with a thatched roof. It is curious that the Shays decided to replicate Anne Hathaway's Cottage to commemorate Emma Shay's Shakespeare journey rather than the birthplace, which she also visited; perhaps the associations she wanted to memorialize were linked to the 'sweet communing' with the countryside and the romantic pastoral Shakespeare associated with the Hathaway homestead.

In 1989 the Shakespeare Garden Society of Wessington Springs was set up to take care of the Shays' cottage, in honour of the South Dakota state centennial. Subsequent use of the cottage suggests evolving commemorative practices related to Shakespeare (mediated through this particular space) in the Great Plains. The cottage now serves as one of several ethnic celebrations in South Dakota, featured in an article

---

[28] Shay's memoir was written by Grace Abrahamson, based on Shay's journal. See *Mrs. Shay Did It!* (Wessington Springs: A. L. Webb, 1976), 30. Subsequent page references are given in parentheses in the text.

entitled 'Celebrating our Ethnic Ways', alongside Czech and other heritages.[29] This South Dakota Hathaway Cottage also functions as a site for marriage and May Day celebrations, further enshrining amorous lore about Shakespeare in upper Midwest America.

Further romantic myths about Shakespeare and his wife, linked to the original Hathaway Cottage, have spread across the Atlantic, most noticeably in the bed and breakfasts that commemorate a domestic version of Shakespeare and celebrate an idealistic fantasy of his marriage that may never have existed. At Anne Hathaway's Cottage Bed and Breakfast Inn in Staunton, Virginia, which advertises 'A little piece of England right here in Staunton!', guests can participate in performative experiences that perpetuate these traditions.[30] The Inn offers special 'Elopement Packages', where guests can stay in one of the 'most romantic rooms', named after Romeo or Juliet, and 'either room is a first choice for wedding nights, anniversaries, and romantic celebrations'. The Inn even offers to arrange an officiant, catering, and flowers for weddings. The testimonies of the guests confirm their enjoyment of the commemorative practices associated with this space. One guest remarks, 'My husband, Chris and I spent a delightful evening at the Anne Hathaway's Cottage in June, immersed in Shakespeare's time. The Anne Hathaway's Cottage B&B is a charming recreation of Shakespeare's original, with a thatched roof, period furnishings and fabrics, and an inviting, authentic English garden, located in the heart of Staunton, VA.' Another guest attests, 'the building itself is so authentic it was hard to believe I wasn't actually vacationing in Stratford-on-Avon'.[31] This replica allows visitors to participate in social practices that keep romantic myths of Shakespeare alive.

The Anne Hathaway Cottage in Green Lake, Wisconsin serves a different and more personal commemorative purpose. This version was built in 1939 by Walter Smith and his wife, Elsie, who was from England,

---

[29] John Andrews, 'Celebrating our Ethnic Ways', *South Dakota Magazine* (May/June 2009): 49–54. This underlines Harald Hendrix's point that houses associated with writers 'not only recall the poets and novelists who dwelt in them, but also the ideologies of those who turned them into memorial sites'. 'Writers' Houses as Media of Expression and Remembrance', 5. See also Watson, 'Tourist Trail', 221–2.

[30] Other Anne Hathaway Cottage bed and breakfasts include Ashland, Oregon, and Perth, Australia. The Anne Hathaway Cottage in Victoria, British Columbia apparently no longer houses guests, but still hosts weddings and other parties.

[31] www.anne-hathaways-cottage.com (accessed 3 February 2014).

and has been described as 'independently wealthy and a woman of descreet [sic] taste'.[32] Although the cottage is currently a rental property open to families in the summer, it has a more complicated past. Elsie Smith spearheaded the construction of the house, hiring an English architect, insisting on a thatched roof, and importing furniture from England. Her English mother, Jane McLennan, enjoyed visiting her daughter in the Hathaway Cottage that commemorated their homeland, but according to one local historian, 'had difficulty being around her son-in-law', Walter Smith, a native of Chicago, who she thought was 'loud, course [sic], and uncouth'. Thus, a second house was built on the property, this time a faux Scottish home called 'Glengary'.[33] In the 1940s, the Hathaway Cottage was sold to Max and Lorraine Rysdon, who 'fell in love with the home' while in Green Lake for a Baptist conference. The Rysdon family rents out the cottage to guests in the summer, using the proceeds to support charitable organizations.[34] This Wisconsin cottage commemorates English heritage, but omits any resonance of a romantic Shakespeare; one publicity blurb describes the property as the 'Anne Hathaway Cottage (inspired by the home of Anne Hathaway, mother of William Shakespeare, in Stratford Upon Avon in England)'.[35]

One of the most intriguing Anne Hathaway Cottages is the one on the grounds of the Grove Park Inn in Asheville, North Carolina. This structure was built to the exact specifications of the cottage in Shottery, but was constructed of local stone. The cottage was completed in 1914, the year after the Grove Park Inn opened for business (on 1 July 1913). Built by architect Fred Loring Seely, the cottage probably owes its origins to the fact that Seely was 'a great Anglophile' and 'spent a great deal of his life in and out of England'.[36] Seely's uncle, Sir John Seely, was a British MP, served as Secretary of State for War during both world wars, and was a good friend of Churchill.[37]

As a component of the Grove Park Inn complex, this Hathaway Cottage was part of 'the Finest Resort Hotel in the World', as its

---

[32] http://www.annehathawaycottage.com/aboutus.shtml (accessed 11 May 2015).

[33] Kathleen Kleinpaste, *Just do it Jessie's Way!: A Story of a Parcel of Land on the Shores of Green Lake, Wisconsin* (K. Kleinpaste, 2003), 124–5, 105.

[34] http://www.annehathawaycottage.com/aboutus.shtml (accessed 11 May 2015).

[35] http://estatesoflawsonia.com/about-the-estates.html (accessed 11 May 2015).

[36] Fred L. Seely Oral History, D. H. Ramsey Library at UNC Asheville Special Collections and University Archives. Interview on 23 June 1983.

[37] Fred L. Seely Oral History.

inaugural brochure proclaimed. Boasting that it was 'built by hand in the old-fashioned way', the brochure claimed that the hotel provided guests with 'rest and comfort and wholesomeness'. Milk was provided by 200 registered Jersey cows from the estate of George Vanderbilt, 400 of the rugs in the inn were made at Aubusson, France, and bed linens were imported Oxford twill. There were 'no radiators to be seen' and 'no electric bulbs to be seen', and the 800 acres of grounds offered 'the finest combination of climate, of comfort and of happiness in surroundings that we believe has ever been made possible'.[38]

One aspect of the 'comfort and happiness' of guests was the absence of children, discouraged in the Inn. As a way to accommodate them, Seely built a series of cottages on the grounds of the Grove Park Inn, suitable for families. When he turned to constructing these cottages, he also turned to the romantic and pastoral associations of Anne Hathaway, naming one of the cottages after Shakespeare's wife, and building it to the exact specifications of the original cottage. Built of stone native to the area, the cottage had three bedrooms and is the only one of the three cottages that remains.

The Anne Hathaway Cottage in Asheville actually did provide a domestic space for the Philippine government during the Second World War, as part of the Grove Park Inn's transformation as a holding space for Axis diplomats and their families, who were kept in 'complete luxury'.[39] The Inn was one of several resorts across the country where foreign diplomats were housed. Beginning in April 1942, the Inn was home to 242 Italian, Hungarian, and Bulgarian diplomats and family members, followed by Japanese and Germans. By October of that year, the Axis diplomats had left, and the US government leased the hotel as a

---

[38] Brochure prepared by the Grove Park Inn, 1913. Biltmore Industries Archive, *The Biltmore Industries Collection (1901–1980)*, D. H. Ramsey Library, Special Collections, University of North Carolina at Asheville 28804. Courtesy of Grovewood Gallery, Inc., 111 Grovewood Road, Asheville NC 28804.

[39] Beginning in April 1942 until June of that year, the Grove Park Inn hosted Italian, Bulgarian, and Hungarian diplomats, including 'their families, servants, pets and private possessions', as well as diplomats from Mexico, Cuba, El Salvador, and Japan. By July 1944 the Inn was leased by the US Army as a place of rest for returning combat veterans until September of 1945. See Richard E. Osborne, *World War II Sites in the United States: A Tour Guide and Directory* (Indianapolis: Riebel-Roque Publishing, 1996), 180–1. The Fred L. Seely Oral History describes the prisoners as living in 'complete luxury'.

rehabilitation site for soldiers wounded in combat.[40] Manuel L. Quezon, President of the Philippines, stayed at the cottage in the spring of 1944, where his government was headquartered for a month.[41] For Quezon, this period did not exactly evoke domestic tranquillity, as he was brought to North Carolina mainly for relief from a serious respiratory illness.[42] Quezon and his staff did not record a response to the fact that the temporary wartime headquarters of their government replicated the family home of Shakespeare's wife across the Atlantic, or that Axis diplomats were housed in a place resonant with associations of Anglo-American culture.

Before and after the war, this Hathaway Cottage continued to host a number of US Presidents and other politicians. In April 1947 General Dwight D. Eisenhower and his wife, Mamie, stayed at this Anne Hathaway Cottage, as did President Herbert Hoover, former President and Chief Justice William Howard Taft, and President Franklin D. Roosevelt and his wife, Eleanor.[43] The Grove Park Inn still commemorates the connection between Anne Hathaway and world politics, in the sign currently standing in front of the cottage, which memorializes both Anne Hathaway and English nostalgia alongside US history and global affairs. Although the cottage was first known as the Hathaway Cottage, most recently it has been named the Presidential Cottage, and current signage simply refers to it as the 'Cottage'.

The physical space of the Hathaway family farm has been adapted to engender narratives that commemorate Shakespeare's wife and his Warwickshire roots far beyond their native country. Had Shakespeare married a woman who lived in the heart of the market town of Stratford, the commemorative practices that propagate the 'peaceful sights and sounds of country life' would not be so easily replicated. Consider the fate of Shakespeare's daughter Judith's house, which is now a retail store on a major street in Stratford rather than a bucolic

---

[40] Bruce E. Johnson, *Built for the Ages: A History of the Grove Park Inn* (Asheville: Archetype Press, 2004), 71.

[41] See Johnson, *Built for the Ages*, 72.

[42] By 1944, Quezon's 'health was visibly failing'. He stayed in Asheville for a couple of weeks but then returned to the Adirondacks on a special train authorized by President Franklin Roosevelt, designed to eliminate bumps and stops. Quezon died in August 1944. Rufino C. Pabico, *The Exiled Government: The Philippine Commonwealth in the United States during the Second World War* (Amherst, NY: Humanity Books, 2006), 102–7, at 104.

[43] Johnson, *Built for the Ages*, 75.

cottage in an idyllic setting. The romantic myths that Anne Hathaway's Cottage has helped maintain and circulate are made possible only by the circumstances of history – the fact that Shakespeare married a woman from the outlying community of Shottery, and the fact that her family home has survived largely intact.[44] In addition, these myths have proved desirable for generations of tourists and others in search of sites of cultural memory where particular constructions of Shakespeare are nurtured and can reside. The many imaginative narratives and compelling uses of Anne Hathaway's Cottage suggest that if the Cottage had not survived, it would need to be recreated (like Shakespeare's Globe Theatre in London, or like New Place in Stratford) to fulfil the desires of readers and tourists alike. As a material space, the Cottage has done the work that the absent archive cannot, by filling in a gap in the documented biography, making possible a narrative of rural, Warwickshire life for Shakespeare, and serving as a stable reminder of pastoral English countryside amid global turmoil.

---

[44] Richard Schoch discusses the development of Shakespeare's birthplace as a heritage site, in light of the absence of New Place, in 'The Birth of Shakespeare's Birthplace', *Theatre Survey* 53 (2012), 181–201. Other discussions of the tourist trade in Stratford include Balz Engler's 'Stratford and the Canonization of Shakespeare', *European Journal of English Studies* 1.3 (1997), 354–66 and Barbara Hodgdon's *The Shakespeare Trade: Performances and Appropriations* (Philadelphia: University of Pennsylvania Press, 1998).

Bibliography

Abrahamson, G., *Mrs Shay Did It!* (Wessington Springs: A. L. Webb, 1976).

Adorno, Theodor W. *In Search of Wagner*, trans. R. Livingstone (London: Verso, 1981).

Andrews, John, 'Celebrating our Ethnic Ways', *South Dakota Magazine* (May/June 2009), 49–54.

Anon. 'A Shakspearean Dinner', *The Press* (Philadelphia), 25 April 1864, 1.

A Tribute to the Genius of William Shakespeare (London: Macmillan, 1916).

'All Sorts of Shorts', *Daily Ohio Statesman*, 31, 19 April 1864, 4.

'Amusements', *The New Regime*, 23 April 1864, 3.

'Another Shakspeare Jubilee', *The Examiner*, 21 April 1816; issue 434. *19th Century British Newspapers*, sourced from British Library: Gale Document Number: BB3200975193. Accessed 19 May 2014.

Anzac Day Commemoration April 25th 1916 Town Hall Sydney. Australian War Memorial Museum, Souvenirs 1 1/1/1.

Anzac Day Matinee, His Majesty's Theatre London, April 25th 1916. Souvenir Programme, Australian War Memorial Museum, Souvenirs 1 1/1/1.

'British Actors Stage Recital for Pope Paul', *The Hartford Courant (1923–1984), ProQuest Historical Newspapers Hartford Courant (1764–1986)* 13 November 1964, 14.

Catholic News Service. Vatican II: 50 Years Ago Today. Accessed 2 June 2014.

'Celebrazione del IV Centenario della Nascita di Shakespeare'. Rai Teche. DVD.

'Celebrazione di Shakespeare alla presenza del Pontefice', *La Stampa*, 13 November 1964, 3.

[= Charles Kelsall], *The First Sitting of the Committee on the Proposed Monument to Shakespeare. Carefully taken in Short-Hand by Zachary Craft, Amanuensis to the Chairman* (Cheltenham: printed for G. A. Williams, 1823).

Charleston Daily Courier, 8 April 1864, 1.

Cleveland Morning Leader, 27 April 1864, 3.

'Count Joannes on Shakspere', *New York Herald*, 24 April 1864, 5.

Daily Picayune [New Orleans], 3 May 1864, 3.

'Essential to Ecumenism is Dialogue, Not Conversion', *Catholic News Service. Vatican II: 50 Years Ago Today.* Accessed 2 June 2014.

Garrick's Vagary: or, England Run Mad, with Particulars of the Stratford Jubilee (London: printed for S. Blade, 1769).

Great Exhibition of 1851, facsimile of *The Art Journal Illustrated Catalogue* (London: The Observer, 1970).

'Interference', *Baptist Times*, October 1963, n.pag.

'IV Centenario della Nascita di William Shakespeare'. Auditorium Palazzo Pio, Roma, 12 Novembre 1964. Programme of the Commemorative Performance.

'Literary Notes', *The Round Table*, 23 April 1864, 297.

'Local Histories: Shakspeare in Norfolk', *The New Regime*, 24 April 1864, 2.

'Local News: The Shakspeare Celebration at Concert Hall', *The Daily Missouri Republican*, 24 April 1864, 3.

'Local News', *Evening Star*, 22 April 1864, 3.

'Local News', *Evening Star*, 23 April 1864, 3.

Lowell Shakespeare Memorial: Exercises on the Tercentenary Celebration of the Birth of William Shakespeare, April 23, 1864, by the Citizens of Lowell, Massachusetts (Lowell, MA: Stone & Huse, 1864).

'Oggi alla TV', *La Stampa*, 12 November 1964, 4. Accessed 2 June 2014.

'Oggi sul video', *Stampa Sera*, 12 November 1964, 1. Accessed 2 June 2014.

'Pius XII and the Jews', *The Tablet*, 11 May 1963, 4. Accessed 2 June 2014.

'Play Report is Denied', *Catholic Herald*, 30 August 1963, 1. Accessed 2 June 2014.

'Polemiche in Inghilterra per un drama su Pio XII', *La Stampa*, 22 September 1963, 5. Accessed 2 June 2014.

'Pope Gets a First Folio of Bard Through Error', *New York Times*, 12 November 1964, n.pag. Accessed 2 June 2014.

'Pope Paul's Affection for England', *The Tablet*, 2 November 1963, 22. Accessed 2 June 2014.

'Pope Play Posters are Defaced', *Daily Telegraph*, 2 October 1963.

Programme for entertainments at the Shakespeare Hut (*c.*1917), Ellen Terry & Edith Craig Archive, National Trust, held at British Library: BL/125/25/2/Ellen Terry Archive/ET/D439.

Punch 45, 24 January 1863.

Punch's Tercentenary Number, 23 April 1864.

Recollections of the Great Exhibition, 1851 (London: Lloyd Bros. & Comp., Sept 1st 1851).

'Shakespeare', *New York Times*, 24 April 1864, 4.

'Shakspeare', *Chicago Tribune*, 25 April 1864, 4.

'Shakspere at the Theatres', *The New York Herald*, 23 April 1864, 8.

Shakespeare's Bouquet: The Flowers and Plants of Shakespeare (1872).

'Shaksperian Celebration', *Evening Star*, 25 April 1864, 3.

Shakespeare Exhibition, 1916: A Catalogue (Victoria and Albert Museum, London, 1916).

'Shaksperian Festivals', *Cincinnati Daily Enquirer*, 25 April 1864, 3.

'Shakespeare Folio Accepted in Error', *The Blade*, 13 November 1964, front page. Accessed 2 June 2014.

Shakespeare. Oration Delivered by the Honorable Joseph Howe at the Request of The Saint George's Society, at the Temperance Hall, Halifax, Nova Scotia, 23rd April 1864, 'Citizen' Printing and Publication Office, 1864.

'Shakspeare. The Tercentenary', *Detroit Advertiser and Tribune*, 25 April 1864, 3.

Shakespeare Tercentenary Observance in the Schools and Other Institutions (London: George W. Jones for the Shakespeare Tercentenary Committee, 1916).

Special Matinee Programme, Tuesday April 25th, 1916, at 2.30. Mander and Mitchenson Collection Bristol Theatre Collection, MM/REF/TH/LO/OLV/11–17 box 45.

'Students', *Caledonian Mercury*, 25 April 1816, citing the *Glasgow Chronicle*: issue 14728. *19th Century British Newspapers*, sourced through British Library: Gale Document Number: BB3205369910. Accessed 19 May 2014.

Tercentenary Celebration of the Birth of William Shakespeare by the New-England Historico-Genealogical Society (Boston: George C. Rand & Avery, 1864).

'The Birthday of Shakspeare', *Cleveland Morning Leader*, 20 April 1864, 3.

'The Malta Report: Report of the Anglican–Roman Catholic Joint Preparatory Commission', 2 January 1968. Accessed 2 June 2014.

'The Shakespeare Tercentenary', *Harper's Weekly*, 7 May 1864, 301.

'The Shakespeare Tercentenary', *New York Times*, 23 April 1864, 8.

'The Shakspeare Jubilee', *The Philadelphia Inquirer*, 25 April 1864, 4.

'The Shaksperian Festival', *The New Regime*, 23 April 1864, 2.

'The Theatres', *The Morning Post*, 24 April 1816: issue 14122. *19th Century British Newspapers*, sourced from the British Library: Gale Document Number: R3209513850. Accessed 19 May 2014.

'The Two Poets', *Harper's Weekly*, 14 May 1864, 309.

'Theatre Gives Catholic View. Anti-Pope Play Controversy', *Catholic Herald*, 20 September 1963, 1. Accessed 2 June 2014.

'Threats to a Theatre "Eichmann"', *Daily Mirror*, 30 October 1964, n.pag.

Tributes to Shakespeare, Collected and arranged by Mary R. Silsby (Harper & Brothers, 1892).

'Un interprete de "Il vicario" chiede protezione alla polizia'. *Stampa Sera*, 2 October 1963, 8.

Welwyn and Woolmer Green Book of Remembrance, (*c*.1918), Imperial War Museums (IWM) War Memorials Database, 20015.

Windsor Castle: A Poem (London: H. Hills, 1708).

Appadurai, Arjun, *Modernity at Large: Cultural Dimensions of Globalization* (Minneapolis: University of Minnesota Press, 1996).

Archer, J. E., *Social Unrest and Popular Protest in England 1780–1840* (Cambridge University Press, 2000).

Archer, William, Robert Lowe and George Halkett, *The Fashionable Tragedian* (Edinburgh: Thomas Gray, 1877).

Auerbach, Jeffrey A., *The Great Exhibition: A Nation on Display* (New Haven: Yale University Press, 1999).

Augusteijn, Joost, *Patrick Pearse: The Making of a Revolutionary* (Basingstoke: Palgrave Macmillan, 2010).

Banerji, Rangana, *The Origins of English Studies in Bengal* (Calcutta: Pages & Chapters, 2012).

Barker, Simon, 'Shakespeare, Stratford, and the Second World War', in Irene R. Makaryk and Marissa McHugh (eds.), *Shakespeare and the Second World War: Memory, Culture, Identity* (University of Toronto Press, 2012), 199–217.

Barnes, P., *Jubilee* (London: Methuen, 2001).

Barracano Schmidt, Dolores and Earl Robert Schmidt, *The Deputy Reader: Studies in Moral Responsibility* (Illinois: Scott, Foresman and Company, 1965).

Bate, Jonathan, 'Shakespeare Nationalised, Shakespeare Privatised', *English* 42 (1993), 1–18.

Shakespearean Constitutions: Politics, Theatre, Criticism, 1730–1830 (Oxford University Press, 1989).

Baxendale, John, '"You and I – All of Us Ordinary People": Renegotiating "Britishness" in Wartime', in Nick Hayes and Jeff Hill (eds.), *'Millions Like Us'?: British Culture in the Second World War* (Liverpool University Press, 1999).

Bea, Augustin Cardinal, *'Text of Cardinal Bea on Draft of Catholic Attitude Toward Jews'*, 19 November 1963. *Catholic News Service. Vatican II: 50 Years Ago Today*. Accessed 2 June 2014.

Bearman, Robert, 'Anne Hathaway's Cottage', in Michael Dobson and Stanley Wells (eds.), *The Oxford Companion to Shakespeare* (Oxford University Press, 2001), 13.

Beisly, Sidney, *Shakspeare's Garden, or the Plants and Flowers named in his Works Described and Defined* (London: Longman, 1864).

Bell, M., 'A brief history of Mason Croft', www.birmingham.ac.uk/schools/edacs/departments/shakespeare/about/mason-croft-history.aspx. Accessed 29 August 2012.

Benjamin, Walter, 'The Task of the Translator', in *Illuminations*, ed. Hannah Arendt, trans. Harry Zohn (London: Fontana, 1977), 69–82.

'Theses on the Philosophy of History', in *Illuminations*, ed. Hannah Arendt, trans. Harry Zohn (London: Pimlico, 1999), 245–55.

Benley, D., http://blogs.coventrytelegraph.net/thegeekfiles/2011/10/roland-emmerichs-anonymous-spa.html.

Benson, E. F., *Mapp and Lucia* (New York, Cambridge, Philadelphia: Perennial Library, 1986).

Bentley, Eric, *The Storm Over The Deputy* (New York: Grove Press, Inc. 1964).

Bergerac, Bernice de, 'In Shakespeare's Garden', *Tercentenary Shakespeare Festival* (Oxford: n.p., 1916).

Bhardwaj, Vishal (dir.), *Haider*. Perf. Shahid Kapoor, Tabu, Shraddha Kapoor and Kay Kay Menon. UTV Motion Pictures and Vishal Bhardwaj Pictures, 2014.

(dir.), *Maqbool*. Perf. Irfan Khan, Tabu and Pankaj Kapoor. Kaleidoscope Entertainment, 2003.

(dir.), *Omkara*. Perf. Ajay Devgan, Kareena Kapoor and Saif Ali Khan. Eros International Entertainment, 2006.

Bishop, Tom, Alexander Huang, Graham Bradshaw and Sukanta Chaudhuri (eds.), *The Shakespearian International Yearbook*, vol. 12 (Farnham: Ashgate, 2012).

Blet, Pierre S. J., *Pius XII and the Second World War* (New Jersey: Paulist Press, 1997).

Blood, S. W., *Making a Shakespeare Garden with his Fragrant Flowers* (New York?: n.p., n.d.).

Bloom, Harold, *The Anxiety of Influence: A Theory of Poetry*. 2nd edn (Oxford University Press, 1997).

Bloom, J. H., *Shakespeare's Garden; Being a Compendium of Quotations and References from the Bard to all Manner of Flower, Tree, Bush, Vine, and Herb, Arranged According to the Month in Which They are Seen to Flourish* (London: Methuen, 1903).

Boaden, J., *Memoirs of the Life of John Philip Kemble, Esq., including a History of the Stage from the time of Garrick to the present period*, 2 vols. (London: Longman, Hurst, Rees, Orme, Brown, and Green, 1825).

Bose, Rajnarain, *Atmacharit* [My Life], in Naresh Jana (ed.), *Atmakatha* [Autobiographies], vol. I (Calcutta: Ananya Prakashan, 1981).

Boswell, J. C., 'Yet Another "New" Shakespeare Image', *Shakespeare Quarterly* 60 (2009), 341–7.

Bowers, Robert Woodger, *A Paper on Shakespeare and Southwark. By ... Robt. W. Bowers ... With a catalogue of the Exhibition held in connexion with the dedication to Shakespeare of a bay in the Reference Department of the Central Library, etc.* (London, 1916).

Brandl, Alois, *Shakespeare and Germany. The British Academy Third Annual Shakespeare Lecture* (London: Humphrey Milford for Oxford University Press, 1913).

Bratton, J. K. S. 'Beating the Bounds: Gender Play and Role Reversal in the Edwardian Music Hall', in Michael R. Booth and Joel H. Kaplan (eds.), *The Edwardian Theatre: Essays on Performance and the Stage* (Cambridge University Press, 1996), 86–111.

New Readings in Theatre History (Cambridge University Press, 2003).

Brereton, Austin, *The Life of Henry Irving*. 2 vols. (London: Longmans, Green, and Co., 1908).

Brewer, Derek and Jonathan Gibson (eds.), *A Companion to the Gawain-Poet* (Cambridge: D. S. Brewer, 1997).

Briggs, Julia, *Reading Virginia Woolf* (Edinburgh University Press, 2006).

Britton, J., 'Essays on the Merits and Characteristics of William Shakspere: also remarks on his birth and burial-place, his monument, portraits, and associations', in *Appendix to Britton's Auto-Biography, Part III* (London: printed for the subscribers to the Britton Testimonial, 1849).

Brown, I. and G. Fearon, *Amazing Monument: A Short History of the Shakespeare Industry* (London, Toronto: Heinemann, 1939).

Browne, Thomas, *Pseudodoxia Epidemica*, 3rd edn (London: R. W. for Nath. Ekins, 1658).

Bruster, Douglas, *Quoting Shakespeare: Form and Culture in Early Modern Drama* (Lincoln, NE, and London: University of Nebraska Press, 2000).

Byron, G. G. Lord, *Byron's Letters and Journals*, ed. L. A. Marchand, vol. V, *1816–1817* (London: John Murray, 1976).

Calvo, C., 'Fighting Over Shakespeare: Commemorating the 1916 Tercentenary in Wartime', *Critical Survey* 24 (2012), 48–72.

'Shakespeare, *lieu de mémoire*', in Christophe Hausermann (ed.), *Shakespeare et la mémoire: Actes de Congrès de la Société Française Shakespeare*, 30 (2013), 209–24. http://shakespeare.revues.org/1961.

'Shakespeare's Church and the Pilgrim Fathers: Commemorating Plymouth Rock in Stratford', *Critical Survey* 24 (2012), 54–70.

Carlson, Marvin, *The Haunted Stage: The Theatre as Memory Machine* (Ann Arbor: University of Michigan Press, 2001).

Carlyle, Thomas, *Heroes and Hero-Worship* (London: Oxford University Press, 1963).

Carter, Angela, *Wise Children* (London: Chatto & Windus, 1991).

Chakravorty, Swapan, *Bangalir Ingreji Sahityacharcha* [The Study of English Literature in Bengal] (Calcutta: Anustup, 2006).

Chattopadhyay, Bankimchandra, *Kapalakundala*, ed. J. K. Chakravarti (Calcutta: Shridhar Prakashani, 1967).

  Rajani, in J. C. Bagal (ed.), *Bankim Rachanavali* [Complete Works] (Calcutta: Sahitya Samsad, 2003), vol. I, 433–80.

  'Shakuntala, Miranda o Desdemona', in J. C. Bagal (ed.), *Bankim Rachanavali* [Complete Works] (Calcutta: Sahitya Samsad, 2004), vol. II, 179–84.

Chattopadhyay, Kshirodbihari, 'Kapalkundala o Miranda', *Bharatvarsha*, Agrahayan 1325/ November–December 1918.

Chaudhuri, Supriya, 'The Absence of Caliban: Shakespeare and Colonial Modernity', in R. S. White, Christa Jansohn and Richard Fotheringham (eds.), *Shakespeare's World / World Shakespeares* (Newark: University of Delaware Press, 2008), 223–36.

  'What Bloody Man is That? *Macbeth, Maqbool*, and Shakespeare in India', in *The Shakespearian International Yearbook*, XII (2012), 97–113.

Chesterton, G. K., 'The Shakespeare Memorial', in G. Marlin, R. P. Rabatin, and J. L. Swan (eds.), *G. K. Chesterton: The Collected Works*, vol. X, *Collected Poetry, Part I* (San Francisco, CA: Ignatius, 1994).

Church, Tony, *A Stage for a Kingdom* (London: Oneiro Press, 2013).

Clarke, E. and C. Nichols, *Herb Garden Design* (London: Francis Lincoln, 1995).

Coates, T. C. and R. S. Well, *Marie Corelli: The Writer and the Woman* (London: Hutchinson, 1903).

Cochrane, Claire, *Shakespeare and the Birmingham Repertory Theatre 1913–1929* (London: Society for Theatre Research, 1993).

Cockin, Katherine, *Edith Craig: Dramatic Lives* (London: Cassell, 1998).

Coffin, David R., *The English Garden: Meditation and Memorial* (Princeton, NJ: Princeton University Press, 1994).

Colbert, Elias, *Scoriae: Eulogy on Shakespeare* (Chicago: Fergus Print Co., 1883).

Collier, John Payne, *Memoirs of the Principal Actors in the Plays of Shakespeare* (London: The Shakespeare Society, 1846).

Colman, G., *Man and Wife: or, the Shakespeare Jubilee* (London: printed for T. Becket and Co. and R. Baldwin, Row, 1770).

Colmer, Francis, *Shakespeare in Time of War: Excerpts from the Plays Arranged with Topical Allusions* (New York: E. P. Dutton & Company, 1916).

Conekin, Becky E., *The Autobiography of a Nation: The 1951 Festival of Britain* (Manchester University Press, 2003).

Conway, M. D., 'The Shakspeare Tercentenary', *Harper's New Monthly Magazine* 29.171 (August 1864), 337–46.

Cook, Dutton, *Nights at the Play* (London: Chatto & Windus, 1883).

Cooper, Thomas, *The Life of Thomas Cooper* (Leicester University Press, 1971).

Corelli, M., *With Shakespeare in his Garden: An Invitation to the Summer Festival at Stratford-upon-Avon, 1916* (Stratford-upon-Avon: n.p., 1916).

Corkery, Daniel, *Synge and Anglo-Irish Literature* (Cork: Mercier, 1966).

Cornwell, John, *Hitler's Pope: The Secret History of Pius XII* (London: Penguin Books, 1999).

Coulter, E. Merton, *The Confederate States of America 1861–1865* (Baton Rouge: Louisiana State University Press, 1950).

Courtney, W. L., 'Foreword', *A Tribute to the Genius of William Shakespeare* (London: Macmillan, 1916).

Cowper, W., *The Poetical Works*, ed. H. S. Milford. 4th edn (London: Oxford University Press, 1934).

Cox, J., *The Tercentenary: A Retrospect* (London: Cassell, Petter, and Galpin, 1865).

Craig, Edward Gordon, *Henry Irving* (London: J. M. Dent & Sons, 1930).

Crane, W., *Flowers from Shakespeare's Garden: A Posy from the Plays* (London: Cassell, 1906).

Cresswell, Tim, *Place: A Short Introduction* (Malden, MA: Blackwell, 2004).

Cunningham, Vanessa, *Shakespeare and Garrick* (Cambridge University Press, 2008).

Curwen, E. Cecil (ed.), *The Journal of Gideon Mantell* (London: Oxford University Press, 1940).

Das, Sisir Kumar, 'Shakespeare in Indian Languages', in P. Trivedi and D. Bartholomeusz (eds.), *India's Shakespeare*, 47–73.

Dávidházi, Péter, '"He drew the Liturgy, and framed the rites": The Changing Role of Religious Disposition in Shakespeare's Reception', *Shakespeare Survey* 54 (2001), 46–56.

  The Romantic Cult of Shakespeare: Literary Reception in Anthropological Perspective (Houndmills, Basingstoke: Macmillan, 1998).

de Bray, L., *Fantastic Garlands: An Anthology of Flowers and Plants from Shakespeare* (Poole: Blandford Press, 1982).

Deelman, Christian, *The Great Shakespeare Jubilee* (London: Michael Joseph, 1964).

Derozio, H. L. V., *Song of the Stormy Petrel: Complete Works of Henry Louis Vivian Derozio*, ed. Abirlal Mukhopadhyay, Amar Dutta, Adhir Kumar and Sakti Sadhi Mukhopadhyay (Calcutta: Progressive Publishers, 2001).

Dickens, C., 'Anne Hathaway's Cottage', *All the Year Round*, 30 April 1892, 420.

Disraeli, Benjamin, *Lothair [1870]* (New York: D. Appleton, 1881).

Dobson, Michael, *The Making of the National Poet: Shakespeare, Adaptation and Authorship, 1660–1769* (Oxford: Clarendon Press, 1992).
     'The Pageant of History: Nostalgia, the Tudors, and the Community Play', in *SEDERI* 20 (2010), 5–25.
     Shakespeare and Amateur Performance: A Cultural History (Cambridge University Press, 2011).

Dogmatic Constitution on the Church Lumen Gentium. 21 November 1964. Accessed 2 June 2014.

Doran, Dr [J.], *Their Majesties' Servants, or, Annals of the English stage: from Thomas Betterton to Edmund Kean*, 2nd edn, revised, corrected and enlarged (London: W. H. Allen, 1865).

Dowden, Edward, *Shakespere: A Critical Study of His Mind and Art* (London: Henry S. King & Co., 1875).

Downes, John, *Roscius Anglicanus, Or An Historical Review of the Stage...* (London: H. Playford, 1708).

Drake, Fabia, *Blind Fortune* (London: William Kimber & Co, 1978).

Dugas, Don-John, *Marketing the Bard: Shakespeare in Performance and Print* (Columbia and London: University of Missouri Press, 2006).

Dutt, Utpal, *Towards a Revolutionary Theatre* (Calcutta: Seagull Books, 2009).

Eccles, Mark, *Shakespeare in Warwickshire* (Madison: University of Wisconsin Press, 1961).

Edmondson, Paul and Stanley Wells, 'The Limitations of the First Folio', in Jansohn, Christa, Lena CowenOrlin and Stanley Wells (eds.), *Shakespeare Without Boundaries: Essays in Honor of Dieter Mehl* (Plymouth: University of Delaware Press and The Rowman and Littlefeld Publishing Group, 2011), 23–34.

Edwards, Ruth Dudley, *James Connolly* (Dublin: Gill & Macmillan, 1981).
     Patrick Pearse: The Triumph of Failure (London: Faber & Faber, 1979).

Ellacombe, H. N., *The Plant-lore and Garden-Craft of Shakespeare* (Exeter: privately printed, 1878).

Emerson, Edward Waldo, *The Early Days of the Saturday Club, 1855–1870* (Boston: Houghton Mifflin, 1918).

England, Martha W., *Garrick's Jubilee* (Columbus, OH: Ohio State University Press, 1964).

Engle, Ron, Felicia Hardison Londré and Daniel J. W. Meier (eds.), *Shakespeare Companies and Festivals: An International Guide* (Westport, CT: Greenwood Press, 1995).

Engler, Balz, 'Shakespeare, Sculpture and the Material Arts', in Mark Thornton Burnett, Adrian Streete, and Ramona Wray (eds.), *The Edinburgh Companion to Shakespeare and the Arts* (Edinburgh University Press, 2011), 435–44.

'Stratford and the Canonization of Shakespeare', *European Journal of English Studies*, 1 (1997), 354–66.

English, Richard, *Irish Freedom: The History of Nationalism in Ireland* (London: Pan, 2007).

Esty, Jed, *A Shrinking Island: Modernism and National Culture* (Princeton University Press, 2003).

Faberman, H. and P. McEvansoneya, 'Isambard Kingdom Brunel's Shakespeare Room', *The Burlington Magazine*, vol. 137, no. 1103 (1995).

Fabian, Johannes, *Time and the Other: How Anthropology Makes its Object* (New York: Columbia University Press, 2002).

Farquhar, George, *Works*, ed. Shirley Strum Kenny. 2 vols. (Oxford: Clarendon Press, 1988).

Faulk, Barry J., *Music Hall and Modernity: The Late-Victorian Discovery of Popular Culture* (Athens, OH: Ohio University Press, 2009).

Fenton, James, '*On Statues*', in his *Leonard's Nephew: Essays on Art and Artists* (Harmondsworth: Penguin Books, 1998).

Figgis, Darrell, *Recollections of the Irish War* (London: Ernest Benn, 1927).

Figueira, Dorothy Matilda, *Translating the Orient: The Reception of Sakuntala in Nineteenth-Century Europe* (Albany: State University of New York Press, 1991).

Fisher, D., 'Pope Pius XII and the Jews', *Catholic Herald*, 17 May 1963, 4. Accessed 2 June 2014.

Fitzgerald, P., *Sir Henry Irving: A Biography* (London: T. Fisher Unwin, 1906).

Florek, Michael, 'Shakespeare Passage Features in Opening Ceremony', *USA Today*, 27 July 2012.

Fogg, Nicholas, *Stratford: A Town at War, 1914–1945* (Gloucester: Sutton Publishing, 2008).

Foster, R. F., *Paddy and Mr Punch: Connections in Irish and English History* (London: Allen Lane, 1993).

Foulkes, Richard, *Performing Shakespeare in the Age of Empire* (Cambridge University Press, 2006).

'Shakespeare and Garibaldi on Primrose Hill', *Camden History Review* 9 (1981), 13–16.

The Shakespeare Tercentenary of 1864 (London: Society of Theatre Research, 1984).

Fox, R. M., *The History of the Irish Citizen Army* (Dublin: James Duffy, 1944).

Foxton, W., *Shakespeare Garden and Wayside Flowers. With Appropriate Quotations for Every Flower. A Complete and Authentic Pocket Guide to Shakespeare Flora* (London: n.p., 1934).

Frayn, Michael, 'Festival', in Michael Sissons and Philip French (eds.), *The Age of Austerity* (London: Hodder and Stoughton, 1963).

Fred L. Seely Oral History, D. H. Ramsey Library at UNC Asheville Special Collections and University Archives. Interview on 23 June 1983.

Freeman, Kirrily, *Bronzes to Bullets: Vichy and the Destruction of French Public Statuary, 1941–1944* (Stanford, CA: Stanford University Press, 2009).

    '"Pedestals Dedicated to Absence": The Symbolic Impact of the Wartime Destruction of French Bronze Statuary', in Patricia M. E. Lorcin and Daniel Brewer (eds.), *France and Its Spaces of War: Experience, Memory, Image* (Houndmills: Palgrave Macmillan, 2009), 163–77.

Furtwangler, Albert, *Assassin on Stage: Brutus, Hamlet, and the Death of Lincoln* (Urbana, IL: University of Illinois Press, 1991).

Fuss, Diane, *The Sense of an Interior: Four Writers and the Rooms that Shaped Them* (New York and London: Routledge, 2004).

García-Periago, Rosa, 'The Re-birth of Shakespeare in India: Celebrating and Indianizing the Bard in 1964', *SEDERI* 22 (2012), 51–68.

Garrick, David, *The Letters of David Garrick*, ed. David M. Little and George M. Kahrl, 3 vols. (London: Oxford University Press, 1963).

    Plays, ed. Harry W. Pedicord and Frederick L. Bergmann, 7 vols. (Carbondale, IL: Southern Illinois University Press, 1980–2).

    The Poetical Works, 2 vols. (London: George Kearsley, 1785).

Gentleman, Francis, *The Stratford Jubilee: A New Comedy of Two Acts* (London: printed for T. Lowndes, 1769).

Gergen, Kenneth J., *The Saturated Self: Dilemmas of Identity in Contemporary Life* (New York: Basic Books, 1991).

Ghairbi, Róisín Ní and Eugene McNulty (eds.), *Patrick Pearse: Collected Plays* (Sallins, Kildare, RoI: Irish Academic Press, 2013).

Gillis, John R., *Commemorations: The Politics of National Identity* (Princeton University Press, 1996).

Giraud, J. E., *The Flowers of Shakespeare* (n.p., 1846).

Golder, J. and R. Madelaine (eds.), *O Brave New World: Two Centuries of Shakespeare on the Australian Stage* (Sydney: Currency, 2001).

Gollancz, Israel, Correspondence, Special Collections, Princeton University Library, Series 1: Correspondence, 1890–1948: Box 1, letter from

Johnston Forbes-Robertson to Gollancz, 21/12/1908; Box 1, letter from Alois Brandl to Gollancz, 29/4/19; Box 3, letter from William Henry Denham Rouse to Gollancz, 29/4/1919.

'Epilogue', in Mrs G. C. West (ed.), *Souvenir of the Shakespeare Ball held at the Albert Hall, June 20, 1911, in support of the Shakespeare Memorial Fund* (London: Shakespeare Ball Committee, 1912).

'Foreword', *Shakespeare Day Festival Matinee at the New Theatre* (London: George W. Jones, 1920).

'"The Shylock of Shakespeare", Lecture delivered by Professor Gollancz before the Jewish Historical Society at University College, Gower Street, W.C. on Monday, 22nd May, 1916', Princeton University Library.

'Statement by Professor I. Gollancz, Hon. Sec. of the Memorial Committee, Mansion House, May 9th, 1906', Princeton University Library.

Grant, S. H., *Collecting Shakespeare: The Story of Henry and Emily Folger* (Baltimore: Johns Hopkins University Press, 2014).

Grant Ferguson, Ailsa, 'Entertaining the Anzacs: Performance for Australian and New Zealand Troops on Leave in London, 1916–1919', in Andrew Maunder (ed.), *British Theatre and the Great War* (London: Palgrave Macmillan, 2015), 234–50.

'Lady Forbes-Robertson's War Work: Gertrude Elliott and the Shakespeare Hut performances, 1916–1919', in Gordon McMullan, Lena Cowen Orlin and Virginia Mason Vaughan (eds.), *Women Making Shakespeare: Text, Performance, Reception* (London: Bloomsbury Arden Shakespeare, 2014), 233–42.

'"When Wasteful War Shall Statues Overturn"': Forgetting the Shakespeare Hut', *Shakespeare* 10 (2014), 276–92.

Greaves, C. Desmond, *The Life and Times of James Connolly* (London: Lawrence and Wishart, 1961).

Gresee, R. E., *Jens Jensen: Maker of Natural Parks and Gardens* (Baltimore: Johns Hopkins University Press, 1992).

Greville, D., Countess of Warwick, *An Old English Garden* (London: Arthur L. Humphreys, 1898).

Grindon, Leopold Hartley, *The Shakespeare Flora* (Manchester: Palmer and Howe, 1883).

Gross, John, *Shylock: Four Hundred Years in the Life of a Legend* (New York: Touchstone, 1992).

Gross, Kenneth, *The Dream of the Moving Statue* (Ithaca, NJ, and London: Cornell University Press, 1992).

Guitton, Jean, *The Pope Speaks: Dialogues of Paul VI with Jean Guitton* (London: Weidenfeld and Nicolson, 1968).

Gullett, H., *The Making of Shakespeare and other Papers* (Sydney: Shakespeare Society of New South Wales, 1905).

H. H., 'The Shakespeare Hut', *The British Journal of Nursing* 57, 16 September 1916, 234.

Hagerman, Anita, 'Monumental Play: Commemoration, Post-War Britain and History Cycles', *Critical Survey* 22 (2010), 105–18.

Hales, M., *Shakespeare in the Garden: A Selection of Gardens and an Illustrated Alphabet of Plants* (New York: Abrams, 2006).

Hall, Melanie and Erik Goldstein, 'Writers, the Clergy, and the "Diplomatization" of Culture: Sub-Structures of Anglo-American Diplomacy, 1820–1914', in John Fisher and Antony Best (eds.), *On the Fringes of Diplomacy: Influences on British Foreign Policy 1800–1945* (Surrey and Burlington: Ashgate, 2010), 127–54.

Halpern, Richard, *Shakespeare Among the Moderns* (Cornell University Press, 1997).

Hancher, Michael, 'College English in India: The First Textbook', *Victorian Literature and Culture* (Cambridge University Press online journal). Accessed at CJO2014. doi:10.1017/S106015031400014X.

Hanchett, William, 'The Diary of John Wilkes Booth, April 1865', *Journal of the Illinois State Historical Society* 72:1 (1979), 39–56.

Hargrove, June, 'Les Statues de Paris', in Pierre Nora (ed.), *Les Lieux de mémoire* (Paris: Éditions Gallimard, 1997), vol. II, 1855–6.

   Les Statues de Paris: La Réprésentation des grands hommes dans les rues et sur les places de Paris (Antwerp: Fons Mercator, and Paris: Albin Michel, 1989).

Hart, Jonathan H., *Columbus, Shakespeare and the Interpretation of the New World* (New York and Houndmills: Palgrave Macmillan, 2003).

Hatcher, Orie Latham, *A Book for Shakespeare Plays and Pageants: A Treasury of Elizabethan and Shakespearean Detail for Producers, Stage Managers, Actors, Artists and Students* (Westport, CT: Greenwood Press, 1916).

Hatton, Joseph, *Henry Irving's Impressions of America*, 2 vols. (Boston, 1884).

Hazlitt, William, *Complete Works of William Hazlitt*, ed. P. P. Howe (London and Toronto: J. M. Dent and Sons, 1930).

Hendrix, Harald, 'Writers' Houses as Media of Expression and Remembrance: From Self-Fashioning to Cultural Memory', in Harald Hendrix (ed.), *Writers' Houses and the Making of Memory* (London: Routledge, 2008), 1–12.

Hershcopf, Judith, 'The Church and the Jews: The Struggle at Vatican Council II', *American Jewish Year Book* 66 (1965), 99–134.

Hewison, Robert, *In Anger: Culture and the Cold War, 1945–60* (London: Weidenfeld and Nicolson, 1981).

   The Culture Industry: Britain in a Climate of Decline (London: Methuen, 1987).

Hiffernan, P., *Dramatic Genius* (London: printed for the author, 1770).

Historic Shakespeare Tercentenary Matinee. New Adelphi Theatre, Wednesday May 3, 1916. Souvenir Programme. Sydney: State Library of New South Wales, 'Shakespeare Society of New South Wales records, 1900–1958, being minute books, correspondence, and newscuttings.' MLMSS 3096.

Hobsbawm, Eric, 'Introduction', in Eric Hobsbawm and Terence Ranger (eds.), *The Invention of Tradition* (Cambridge University Press, 1983).

Hochhuth, Rolf, *The Representative*, trans. Robert David MacDonald (London: Oberon Books, 1988).

Hodgdon, Barbara, *The Shakespeare Trade: Performances and Appropriations* (Philadelphia: University of Pennsylvania Press, 1998).

Hoenselaars, Ton, 'The Pierre Fournier Shakespeare Statue in the City of Paris, 1888–1941: Reflections on Commemoration, Cosmopolitanism, and Urban Development during the Third Republic', *Shakespeare-Jahrbuch* 147 (2011), 105–23.

Hoenselaars, Ton and Clara Calvo, 'Introduction: Shakespeare and the Cultures of Commemoration', *Critical Survey* 22: 2 (2010), 1–10.

  'Shakespeare Eurostar: Calais, the Continent and the Operatic Fortunes of Ambroise Thomas', in W. Maley and M. Tudeau-Clayton (eds.), *This England, That Shakespeare: New Angles on Englishness and the Bard* (Farnham: Ashgate, 2010).

Hogan, Robert and Michael J. O'Neill (eds.), *Joseph Holloway's Abbey Theatre: A Selection from his Unpublished Journal Impressions of a Dublin Playgoer* (Carbondale and Edwardsville: Southern Illinois University Press, 1967).

Holderness, Graham, 'Bardolatry: Or the Cultural-Materialist Guide to Stratford-upon-Avon', in *The Shakespeare Myth*, 1–15.

  Cultural Shakespeare: Essays in the Shakespear Myth (Hatfield: University of Hertfordshire Press, 2001).

  Nine Lives of William Shakespeare (London: Bloomsbury, 2011).

  'Shakespeare Remembered', *Critical Survey* 22 (2010), 39–61.

  Shakespeare's History (Dublin: Macmillan, 1985).

Holderness, Graham (ed.), *The Shakespeare Myth* (Manchester University Press, 1988).

Holland, Peter, 'A History of Histories: From Flecknoe to Nicoll', in W. B. Worthen and Peter Holland (eds.), *Theorizing Practice: Redefining Theatre History* (Basingstoke: Palgrave Macmillan, 2003), 8–29.

Holmes, N. M. McQ. and L. M. Stubbs, *The Scott Monument: A History & Architectural Guide* (Edinburgh: A City of Edinburgh Museums and Art Galleries Publication, 1979).

Holmes, Oliver Wendell, 'Shakespeare', *Atlantic Monthly* 13 (June 1864), 762–3.

Holmesworthe, L., *Shakespeare's Garden; with reference to over a hundred plants* (Leamington: F. Glover, 1906).

Horkheimer, Max and Theodor W. Adorno, *The Dialectic of Enlightenment: Philosophical Fragments* (reprinted London: Verso, 1997).

Hughes, A., *Henry Irving, Shakespearean* (Cambridge University Press, 1981).

Hunt, D., *The Flowers of Shakespeare* (Exeter: Webb & Bower, 1980).

Hunter, R. E., *Shakespeare and Stratford-upon-Avon, A 'Chronicle of the Time': comprising the salient Facts and Traditions, Biographical, Topographical, and Historical, connected with the Poet and his Birth-Place; Together with A Full Record of the Tercentenary Celebration* (London: Whitaker & Co, 1864).

Inglis, K. S., assisted by J. Brazier. *Sacred Places: War Memorials in the Australian Landscape* (Carlton South: Miegunyah, 1999).

Ireland, Samuel, *Picturesque Views on the Upper, or Warwickshire Avon, From its Source at Naseby to its Junction with the Severn at Tewkesbury: With Observations on the Public Buildings, and Other Works of Art in its Vicinity* (London: Faulder and Egerton, 1795).

Ireland, William Henry, *The Confessions of William Henry Ireland* (London, 1895).

Irving, Henry, 'An Actor', 'The Round Table. The Character of Shylock', *The Theatre* (December 1879), 255.

  The Drama: Addresses by Henry Irving (New York: Tait, Sons, & Co., 1896).

Irving, Laurence, *Henry Irving: The Actor and his World* (London: Faber and Faber, 1951).

Jaaware, Aniket and Urmila Bhirdikar, 'Shakespeare in Maharashtra, 1892–1927: A Note on a Trend in Marathi Theatre and Theatre Criticism', *The Shakespearian International Yearbook* XII: 43–52.

Jedin, Hubert, (ed.), *History of the Church. Vol. X. The Church in the Modern Age* (London: Burns & Oates, 1981).

Jensen, Jens, 'A Shakespeare Garden-plan', *Garden Magazine* 3 (April 1916).

Jerrard, Paul, *Flowers from Stratford-on-Avon* (n.p., 1852).

Johnson, Bruce E., *Built for the Ages: A History of the Grove Park Inn* (Asheville: Archetype Press, 2004).

Johnson, G., *A Complete List of Shakespeare's Plants for Use in the Shakespeare Garden at Lightwoods Park, Birmingham* (Birmingham Parks Committee, 1915).

Jones, Henry Arthur, *The Shadow of Henry Irving* (New York: William Morrow & Co., 1931).

Kahan, Jeffrey, *Reforging Shakespeare: The Story of a Theatrical Scandal* (Bethlehem, PA: Lehigh University Press, 1998).

Kahn, Coppélia, 'Remembering Shakespeare Imperially: The 1916 Tercentenary', *Shakespeare Quarterly* 52 (2001), 456–78.

Kaimowitz, Jeremy H. (trans.), *The Odes of Horace*, with an introduction by Ronnie Ancona (Baltimore, MD: The Johns Hopkins University Press, 2008).

Kalidasa, *The Sacontala: or, the Fatal Ring*, trans. William Jones, ed. Jogendra Nath Ghose (Calcutta: Trübner & Co, 1875).

Kear, Jon, 'Une chambre mentale: Proust's Solitude', in Hendrix (ed.), *Writers' Houses and the Making of Memory*, 221–33.

Kerr, J., *Shakespeare's Flowers* (London: Longman, 1969).

Kertzer, David I., *The Popes Against the Jews* (New York: Vintage, 2001).

Kimberley, Michael, *Lord Ronald Gower's Monument to Shakespeare* (Stratford-upon-Avon Society, 1989).

Kirkpatrick, P., *The Sea Coast of Bohemia: Literary Life in Sydney's Roaring Twenties*. (St Lucia: University of Queensland Press, 1992).

Kleinpaste, K., *Just do it Jessie's Way!: A Story of a Parcel of Land on the Shores of Green Lake, Wisconsin* (K. Kleinpaste, 2003).

Klingberg, F. J. and S. B. Hustvedt (eds.), *The Warning Drum: The British Home Front Faces Napoleon: Broadsides of 1803* (Berkeley and Los Angeles: University of California Press, 1944).

Lal, Ananda and Sukanta Chaudhuri (eds.), *Shakespeare on the Calcutta Stage: A Checklist* (Calcutta: Papyrus, 2001).

Langbaine, Gerard, *An Account of the English Dramatick Poets* (Oxford: Printed by L.L. for George West and Henry Clements, 1691).

Larsen, Kenneth J., *Edmund Spenser's 'Amoretti' and 'Epithalamion': A Critical Edition* (Tempe, AZ: Medieval and Renaissance Texts and Studies, 1997).

Law, Ernest, *Shakespeare's Garden, Stratford-upon-Avon, with illustrations* (London: Selwyn & Blount, 1922).

Lee, Sidney, 'The Commemoration of Shakespeare in London', in *Shakespeare and the Modern Stage, and Other Essays* (London: John Murray, 1906), 214–42.

Shakespeare Tercentenary Commemoration, 1616–1916: Shakespeare Birthplace. Catalogue of an Exhibition of Original Documents of the XVth & XVIIth Centuries Preserved in Stratford-upon-Avon, Illustrating Shakespeare's Life in the Town (Stratford-upon-Avon: Edward Fox and Sons, 1916).

Lee, Y. S., 'Sir Walter Scott on the Field of Waterloo', *Nationalism and Irony: Burke, Scott, Carlyle* (Oxford University Press, 2004): published online (Oxford University Press, 2007).

Lefrançois, Michèle, *Paul Landowski: L'Oeuvre sculpté* (Grâne: CREAPHIS Éditions, 2009).

Lessing, Gotthold Ephraim, *Laocoön, Nathan the Wise, Minna von Barn-helm*, ed. W. A. Steel (London: Dent, 1930).

Levenson, Samuel, *James Connolly: A Biography* (London: Martin Brian & O'Keefe, 1973).

Levine, Lawrence, 'William Shakespeare in America', in *Highbrow/Low-brow: The Emergence of Cultural Hierarchy in America* (Cambridge: Harvard University Press, 1988), 11–82.

Lockhart, J. G., *Memoirs of the Life of Sir Walter Scott, Bart.*, 2nd edn, 10 vols. (Edinburgh: R. Cadell; London: J. Murray and Whittaker & Co., 1839).

Lowe, J., *Herbs! Creative Herb Garden Themes and Projects* (Brentwood, TN: Cool Springs Press, 2010).

Lowenthal, David, *The Past is a Foreign Country* (Cambridge University Press, 1985).

Lyons, M., 'Literary Anniversaries: Commemorating Shakespeare and Others, 1900–1940', in M. Lyons and J. Arnold (eds.), *A History of the Book in Australia 1891–1945: A National Culture in a Colonised Market* (St Lucia: University of Queensland Press, 2001), 389–400.

Macaulay, Thomas Babington, *Speeches: with his Minute on Indian Educa-tion*, ed. G. M. Young (Oxford University Press, 1935).

MacBride, Maude Gonne, *A Servant of the Queen: Reminiscences*, ed. A. Norman Jeffares and Anna MacBride White (Gerrards Cross: Colin Smythe, 1994).

Mair, G. H., 'The Music Hall', *The English Review* (1911), 122–9.

Majumdar, Sarottama, 'That Sublime "Old Gentleman": Shakespeare's Plays in Calcutta, 1775–1930', in Trivedi and Bartholomeusz (eds.), *India's Shakespeare*, 260–8.

Majumdar, Shrishchandra, 'Miranda o Kapalakundala', *Bangadarsan*, Shra-van 1287/ July–August 1880.

Malagi, R. A., 'Toward a Terrestrial Divine Comedy: A Study of *The Winter's Tale* and *Shakuntalam*', in Trivedi and Bartholomeusz (eds.), *India's Shakespeare*, 123–40.

Malick, Javed, 'Appropriating Shakespeare Freely: Parsi Theater's First Urdu play *Khurshid*', in Trivedi and Bartholomeusz (eds.), *India's Shakespeare*, 92–105.

Mare, M. L. and W. H. Quarrell, *Lichtenberg's Visit to England* (Oxford: Clarendon Press, 1938).

Marshall, Gail, 'Women Re-Read Shakespeare Country', in Nicola J. Watson (ed.), *Literary Tourism and Nineteenth-Century Culture* (Basingstoke: Palgrave Macmillan, 2009).

Maume, Patrick, *D. P. Moran* (Dublin: Historical Association of Ireland, 1995).

Mayou, B., *Natural History of Shakespeare, being selections of Flowers, Fruits, and Animals* (Manchester: Edwin Slater, 1877).

McDonagh, T., *When the Dawn is Come*, in J. Moran, (ed.), *Four Irish Rebel Plays* (Dublin: Irish Academic Press, 2007).

McElwain, A., 'Rome Letter', *Catholic Herald*, 20 November 1964, 2. http://archive.catholicherald.co.uk/article/20th-november-1964/2/rome-letter. Accessed 2 June 2014.

McIntyre, Ian, *Garrick* (London: Allen Lane, The Penguin Press, 1999).

McLamore, Richard V., 'The Dutchman in the Attic: Claiming an Inheritance in *The Sketch Book of Geoffrey Crayon*', *American Literature* 72 (2000), 31–57.

Michalski, Sergiusz, *Public Monuments: Art in Political Bondage, 1870–1997* (London: Reaktion Books, 1998).

Mitra, Amal, *Kolkatay Bideshi Rangalay* [Foreign Theatres in Calcutta] (Calcutta: Prakash Bhavan, 1967).

Mitra, Dinabandhu, 'Sadhabar Ekadashi' ['The Married Woman's Widow-Rites'] in *Dinabandhu Rachana-sangraha* [Collected Works] (Calcutta: Saksharata Prakashan, 1973), 151–99.

Moncrieff, W. T., *Excursion to Stratford upon Avon* (Leamington: Elliston, 1824).

Montini, Giovanni Battista Cardinal, 'Pius XII and the Jews', *The Tablet*, 29 June 1963, 18. Accessed 2 June 2014.

Moran, James, *Staging the Easter Rising: 1916 as Theatre* (Cork University Press, 2005).

Moran, James (ed.), *Four Irish Rebel Plays* (Dublin: Irish Academic Press, 2007).

Moran, Mabel M., *The Shakespeare Garden Club. Comedy/Fantasy in One Act* (New York: Dramatists Play Service, *c.*1938).

Mukherjee, Sushil Kumar, *The Story of the Calcutta Theatres, 1753–1980* (Calcutta: KP Bagchi, 1982).

Mukhopadhyay, Sakti Sadhan (ed.), *Derozio Remembered: Birth Bicentenary Celebration Commemoration Volume* (Calcutta: Derozio Commemoration Committee and School of Cultural Texts and Records, Jadavpur University, 2008).

Mulryne, J. R. and T. Kozuka (eds.), *Shakespeare, Marlowe, Jonson: New Directions in Biography* (Aldershot: Ashgate, 2006).

Murphy, Andrew, 'Bhíos ag Stratford ar an abhainn: Shakespeare, Douglas Hyde, 1916', in Janet Clare and Stephen O'Neill (eds.), *Shakespeare and the Irish Writer* (University College Dublin Press, 2010), 51–63.

Shakespeare for the People: Working Class Readers, 1800–1900 (Cambridge University Press, 2008).

'Tableaux Vivant: History and Practice'. Art Museum Teaching: a forum for reflecting on practice. 6 December 2012. http://artmuseumteaching. com/2012/12/06/tableaux-vivant-history-and-practice.

Musil, Robert, 'Denkmale', in Robert Musil, *Gesammelte Werke 7: Kleine Prosa. Aphorismen. Autobiographisches* (Hamburg: Rowohlt Verlag, 1978), 506–9.

'Monuments', in *Selected Writings*, trans. and ed. B. Pike (New York: Continuum, 1986), 320–2.

Narasimhaiah, C. D. (ed.), *Shakespeare Came to India* (Bombay: Popular Prakashan, 1964).

Natarajan, U., 'William Hazlitt', in Adrian Poole (ed.), *Great Shakespeareans: Lamb, Hazlitt, Keats*, vol. IV (London and New York: Continuum, 2010), 64–108.

Nevin, Donal, *James Connolly: A Full Life* (Dublin: Gill & Macmillan, 2005).

Nora, Pierre, 'Between Memory and History: *Les Lieux de Mémoire*', *Representations* 26 (1989), 7–24.

O'Brien, Nora Connolly, *James Connolly: Portrait of a Rebel Father* (Dublin: Four Masters, 1975).

Official Programme of the Tercentenary Festival of the Birth of Shakespeare, to be held at Stratford-upon-Avon, commencing on Saturday, April 23, 1864…(London: Cassell, Petter, and Galpin, 1864).

Oram, Alison, *Her Husband was a Woman!: Women's Gender-Crossing in Modern British Popular Culture* (London and New York: Routledge, 2013).

Orgel, Stephen, 'Shylock's Tribe', in Tom Clayton, Susan Brock and Vicente Forés (eds), *Shakespeare and the Mediterranean* (Cranbury, NJ: Associated University Presses, 2004), 38–53.

Osborne, Richard E., *World War II Sites in the United States: A Tour Guide and Directory* (Indianapolis: Riebel-Roque Publishing, 1996).

Oxford Dictionary of National Biography (Oxford University Press, 2004).

Pabico, Rufino C., *The Exiled Government: The Philippine Commonwealth in the United States during the Second World War* (Amherst, NY: Humanity Books, 2006).

Palmeri, F., 'History, Nation, and the Satiric Almanac, 1660–1760', *Criticism* 40 (1998), 377–408.

Paul VI, 'Address of Paul VI for the Fourth Centenary of the Birth of William Shakespeare' www.vatican.va., 12 November 1964. Accessed 2 June 2014.

Paul VI, 'Address of Paul VI to Artists' www.vatican.va. 8 December 1965. Accessed 2 June 2014.

Paul VI and Michael Ramsey, 'Common Declaration of His Holiness Paul VI and His Grace Michael Ramsey, Archbishop of Canterbury' (1966). Accessed 2 June 2014.

Pavis, P., *Dictionary of the Theatre: Terms, Concepts, and Analysis* (University of Toronto Press, 1999).

Pearse, Mary Brigid (ed.), *The Home Life of Pádraig Pearse: As Told by Himself, His Family and Friends* (Dublin & Cork: Mercier, 1979).

Pearse, Patrick, *Patrick Pearse: Collected Plays*, ed. Róisín Ní Ghairbhí and Eugene McNulty (Sallins, Kildare, RoI: Irish Academic Press, 2013).

  The Coming Revolution: The Political Writings and Speeches of Patrick Pearse (Cork: Mercier, 2012).

Pennell, Elizabeth Robins, 'The Pedigree of the Music Hall', *Contemporary Review* 63 (April 1893).

Pettitt, Claire, 'Shakespeare at the Great Exhibition of 1851', in Gail Marshall and Adrian Poole (eds.), *Victorian Shakespeare*, Volume 2: *Literature and Culture* (London: Palgrave, 2003), 61–83.

Pfister, Manfred, '"In States Unborn and Accents Yet Unknown": Shakespeare and the European Canon', in Ladina Bezzola Lambert and Balz Engler (eds.), *Shifting the Scene: Shakespeare in European Culture* (Newark, NJ: University of Delaware Press, 2004), 41–63.

Phayer, Michael, *The Catholic Church and the Holocaust, 1930–1965* (Bloomington: Indiana University Press, 2000).

Pittman, L., 'The Formation of the Episcopal Diocese of Jerusalem 1841–1948: Anglican, Indigenous and Ecumenical', in T. Hummel, K. Hintlian and U. Carmesund (eds.), *Patterns of the Past, Prospects for the Future: The Christian Heritage in the Holy Land* (London: Melisende, 1999).

Plunkett, John, *Queen Victoria: First Media Monarch* (Oxford University Press, 2003).

Poisson, Georges, 'Le Sort des statues de bronze parisiennes sous l'occupation allemande, 1940–1944', *Paris et Île-de-France–Mémoires* 47 (1996), 165–309.

Prendergast, Christopher, 'The World Republic of Letters', in Christopher Prendergast and Benedict Anderson (eds.), *Debating World Literature* (London: Verso, 2004), 1–25.

Rasmussen, Eric, *The Shakespeare Thefts: In Search of the First Folios* (New York: Palgrave Macmillan, 2011).

Rausch, Helke, *Kulturfigur und Nation: Öffentliche Denkmäler in Paris, Berlin und London, 1848–1914* (Munich: R. Oldenbourg Verlag, 2006).

Rawlings, P., *Americans on Shakespeare* (Aldershot: Ashgate, 1999).

Reed, Edwin, *The Truth Concerning Stratford-Upon-Avon and Shaksper* (Boston: Coburn Publishing, 1907).

Richards, Jeffrey (ed.), *Sir Henry Irving: Theatre, Culture and Society* (Keele University Press, 1994).

Richardson, David Lester, *Literary Leaves, or, Prose and Verse chiefly written in India*, 2 vols. (London: W. H. Allen & Co, 1840).

    Selections from the British Poets from the time of Chaucer to the Present Day, with biographical and critical notes by D. L. Richardson (Calcutta: Baptist Mission Press, 1840).

Rigney, A., *The Afterlives of Walter Scott: Memory on the Move* (Oxford University Press, 2012).

Ripley, J., 'From Sheridan to Kemble: The Making of a Production Tradition (1752–1817)', in *Coriolanus on Stage in England and America 1609–1994* (London: Associated University Press, 1998), 94–142.

Risdell, Marcus, 'Picturing Rich', in Berta Joncus and Jeremy Barlow (eds.),'*The Stage's Glory': John Rich, 1692–1761* (Newark: University of Delaware Press, 2011), 266–72.

Ritschel, Nelson Ó Ceallaigh, '*Under Which Flag*, 1916', *New Hibernia Review* 2 (1998), 54–68.

Roach, J., 'Shakespeare and Celebrity Culture,' paper delivered at 'Shakespeare and the Problem of Biography,' conference at the Folger Shakespeare Library, 4 April 2014.

Roberts, W., *Memoirs of the Life and Correspondence of Mrs Hannah More*, 2 vols. (New York: Harper Brothers, 1834).

Roebuck, Thomas, *The Annals of the College of Fort William* (Calcutta: Hindustanee Press, 1819).

Rohde, E. S., *Shakespeare's Wild Flowers, Fairy Lore, Gardens, Herbs, Gatherers of Simples and Bee Lore* (London: The Medici Society, [1935]).

Rose, Paul Lawrence, *Wagner: Race and Revolution* (New Haven, CT: Yale University Press, 1996).

Rowe, Nicholas, 'Some Account of the Life of William Shakespear', in Nicholas Rowe (ed.), *The Works of Mr. William Shakespear*, vol. I (London: Printed for Jacob Tonson, 1709).

Royle, E., *Revolutionary Britannia? Reflections on the Threat of Revolution in Britain, 1789–1848* (Manchester University Press, 2000).

Rumbold, Kate, 'Shakespeare and the Stratford Jubilee', in Fiona Ritchie and Peter Sabor (eds.), *Shakespeare in the Eighteenth Century* (Cambridge University Press, 2012), 254–76.

Ryan, Desmond, *The Man Called Pearse* (Dublin: Maunsel, 1919).

    Remembering Sion: A Chronicle of Storm and Quiet (London: Arthur Barker, 1934).

The Rising: The Complete Story of Easter Week (Dublin: Golden Eagle, 1949).

Savage, F. G., *The Flora and Folk Lore of Shakespeare* (London: E. J. Burrow, 1923).

Savage, Henry L., 'The Shakespeare Society of Philadelphia', *Shakespeare Quarterly* 3 (1952), 341–52.

Sawyer, Robert, 'From Jubilee to Gala: Remembrance and Ritual Commemoration', *Critical Survey* 22 (2010), 25–38.

Scheil, Katherine West, *She Hath Been Reading: Women and Shakespeare Clubs in America* (Ithaca: Cornell University Press, 2012).

Schoch, Richard, 'The Birth of Shakespeare's Birthplace', *Theatre Survey* 53 (2012), 181–201.

Schoenbaum, Samuel, *Shakespeare's Lives* (Oxford: Clarendon, 1970).

Schulz, Eugene G., *The Ghost in General Patton's Third Army: The Memoirs of Eugene G. Schulz during his Service in the United States Army in World War II.* (Xlibris, 2013).

Scott, Clement, *From 'The Bells' to 'King Arthur'* (London: John MacQueen, 1896).

Scott, Walter, *The Antiquary* (1816), ed. David Hewitt (Edinburgh University Press, 1995).

    Paul's Letters to his Kinsfolk (Edinburgh: Constable and Company, and London: Longman, Hurst, Rees, Orme, and Brown, and John Murray, 1816).

Seidenberg, Steven, Maurice Sellar and Lou Jones, *You Must Remember This: Songs at the Heart of the War* (London: Boxtree, 1995).

Select Letters between the late Duchess of Somerset, Lady Luxborough, Mr Whistler, Miss Dolman, Mr R. Dodsley, William Shenstone and others (London: J. Dodsley, 1778).

Sen, Taraknath (ed.), *Shakespeare Commemoration Volume* (Calcutta: Presidency College, 1966).

Shail, Andrew, *Cinema and the Origins of Literary Modernism* (London and New York: Routledge, 2012).

Shakespeare, William, *As You Like It*, ed. Juliet Dusinberre (London: The Arden Shakespeare, 2006).

    The Complete Works, ed. Stanley Wells, Gary Taylor *et al.* (Oxford: Clarendon Press, 1986).

    Hamlet, ed. Ann Thompson and Neil Taylor (London: The Arden Shakespeare, 2006).

    The Merchant of Venice, ed. Stanley Wells (Oxford University Press, 1994).

    The Riverside Shakespeare, 2nd edn, general ed. G. Blakemore Evans (Boston and New York: Houghton Mifflin, 1997).

Shapiro, James, 'Shakespur and the Jewbill', *Shakespeare Survey 48* (1996), 51–60.

Shapiro, James (ed.), *Shakespeare in America* (New York: Library of America, 2014).

Sharpe, William Chapman, *New York Nocturne: The City after Dark in Literature, Painting, and Photography, 1850–1950* (Oxford University Press, 2008).

Shastri, Sivanath, *Ramtanu Lahiri o tatkalin bangasamaj [Ramtanu Lahiri and the Bengali Social World of his Time*: 1904], ed. Baridbaran Ghosh (Calcutta: New Age Publishers, 2007).

Shaw, George Bernard, 'A Dressing Room Secret', in Maurice J. O. Sullivan, Jr. (ed.), *Shakespeare's Other Lives: An Anthology of Fictional Depictions of the Bard* (Jefferson, NC: McFarland and Co., 1997), 104–8.

  Our Theatres in the Nineties. 3 vols. (London: Constable, 1932).

  Pen Portraits and Reviews (London, 1932).

Sheehy-Skeffington, F., '"Under Which Flag?": James Connolly's Patriotic Play', *The Workers' Republic* 1, 46, 8 April 1916.

Shelley, Henry C., *Shakespeare and Stratford* (London: Simpkin, Marshall Hamilton, Kent, 1913).

Sillars, S., *Shakespeare and the Victorians* (Oxford University Press, 2013).

Singleton, E., *The Shakespeare Garden* [1922], (London: Palmer, 1932).

Smialkowska, Monika, '"A Democratic Art at a Democratic Price": The American Celebrations of the Shakespeare Tercentenary, 1916,' *Transatlantica* 1 (2010), accessed online.

Smith, Bruce R., *Roasting the Swan of Avon: Shakespeare's Redoutable Enemies and Dubious Friends* (Washington DC: Folger Shakespeare Library, 1994).

Smith, C. Roach, *Remarks on Shakespeare, his Birthplace etc., suggested by a visit to Stratford-upon-Avon, in the autumn of 1868* (London: privately printed, 1868–9).

Smith, E., 'Introduction', in *King Henry V, Shakespeare in Production* (Cambridge University Press, 2002).

Sorkin, Michael, *Variations on a Theme Park: The New American City and the End of Public Space* (New York: Hill and Wang, 1992).

Sova, Dawn B., *Banned Plays Censorship Histories of 125 Stage Dramas* (New York: Facts on File Inc., 2004).

Stanton, Sarah and Martin Banham, *Cambridge Paperback Guide to Theatre* (Cambridge University Press, 1996).

Stone, G. W., Jr. and G. M. Kahrl, *David Garrick: A Critical Biography* (Carbondale, IL: Southern Illinois University Press, 1979).

Street, L., 'The Enemies of Shakespeare', *The Theatre*, Shakespeare Number, vol. 23, April 1916.

Sturgess, Kim, *Shakespeare and the American Nation* (Cambridge University Press, 2004).

Sullivan, Erin, 'Olympic Performance in the Year of Shakespeare', in Paul Prescott, Paul Edmondson and Erin Sullivan (eds.), *A Year of Shakespeare: Re-living the World Shakespeare Festival* (London: Bloomsbury, 2003), 3–11.

Sullivan, M. J. O., Jr. (ed.), *Shakespeare's Other Lives: An Anthology of Fictional Depictions of the Bard* (Jefferson, NC: McFarland and Co., 1997).

Sutherland, J., *The Life of Walter Scott: A Critical Biography* (Oxford: Blackwell, 1995).

Tagore, Rabindranath, *Jivansmriti* [My Reminiscences], in *Rabindra Rachanavali* [Complete Works] (Calcutta: Vishvabharati, 1954), vol. XVII, 261–432.

'*Shakuntala*', in *Selected Writings on Literature and Language*, ed. and trans. S. Chaudhuri, Oxford Tagore Translations (New Delhi: Oxford University Press, 2001), 237–51.

'*Shakuntala*', in *Rabindra Rachanavali* [Complete Works] (Calcutta: Vishvabharati, 1942), vol. V, 521–37.

Tebeau, Mark, 'Sculpted Landscapes: Art and Place in Cleveland's Cultural Gardens 1916–2000' http://teaching.clevelandhistory.org/files/2009/08/sculpted_gardens_Tebeau_June2009.pdf Last accessed June 2012.

Thomas, Julia, *Shakespeare's Shrine: The Bard's Birthplace and the Invention of Stratford-Upon-Avon* (Philadelphia: University of Pennsylvania Press, 2012).

Thompson, W. I., *The Imagination of an Insurrection* (New York, 1967).

Thorn-Drury, G., *More Seventeenth Century Allusions to Shakespeare and his Works* (London: P. J. and A. E. Dobell, 1924).

Thorndike, S. and R., *Lillian Baylis* (London: Chapman & Hall, 1938).

Tolkien, J. R. R., '*Beowulf*: The Monsters and the Critics', Sir Israel Gollancz Memorial Lecture, British Academy, 1936, *Proceedings of the British Academy*, 22 (1937).

Tolkien, J. R. R., Humphrey Carpenter and Christopher Tolkien (eds.), *The Letters of J. R. R. Tolkien* (London: George Allen & Unwin, 1981).

Tree, H. B., *Diary (of engagements), 1916*. Mander and Mitchenson Collection Bristol Theatre Collection, HBT/000268/1/.

Trivedi, Harish, 'Colonizing Love: *Romeo and Juliet* in Modern Indian Disseminations', in Trivedi and Bartholomeusz (eds.), *India's Shakespeare*, 74–91.

Trivedi, Poonam and Dennis Bartholomeusz (eds.), *India's Shakespeare: Translation, Interpretation and Performance* (Newark: University of Delaware Press, 2005).

Trotter, Mary, *Ireland's Theaters: Political Performance and the Origins of the Irish Dramatic Movement* (Syracuse University Press, 2001).

Tucek, Msgr. James I. 'Discussions on Ecumenism Continue; Liturgy Votes Also Take Place', 20 November 1963, *Catholic News Service*. *Vatican II: 50 Years Ago Today*. Accessed 2 June 2014.

Verma, Rajiv, 'Shakespeare in Hindi Cinema', in Trivedi and Bartholomeusz (eds.), *India's Shakespeare*, 269–90.

'Shakespeare in Indian Cinema: Appropriation, Assimilation, and Engagement', in *The Shakespearian International Yearbook*, vol. XII, 83–96.

Vickers, Brian, *Shakespeare: The Critical Heritage*, 6 vols. (London and Boston: Routledge & Kegan Paul, 1974–81).

Vignaux, Michèle, 'A Southern Shakespeare?' *Transatlantica: Review d'études américaines* 1 (2010). http://transatlantica.revues.org/4879, accessed 10 November 2014.

Viswanathan, Gauri, *Masks of Conquest: Literary Studies and British Rule in India* (Delhi: Oxford University Press, 1998).

Walpole, H., *Private Correspondence*, 3 vols. (London: Henry Colbourn, 1837).

Ward-Jackson, Philip, *Public Sculpture of the City of London* (Liverpool University Press, 2003).

Watson, Nicola J., 'Afterlives', in F. Robertson (ed.), *The Edinburgh Companion to Sir Walter Scott* (Edinburgh University Press, 2012), 143–55.

The Literary Tourist: Readers and Places in Romantic and Victorian Britain (Basingstoke: Palgrave Macmillan, 2006).

'Shakespeare on the Tourist Trail', in Robert Shaughnessy (ed.), *The Cambridge Companion to Shakespeare and Popular Culture* (Cambridge University Press, 2007), 199–226.

'Sir Walter Scott', in Adrian Poole (ed.), *Great Shakespeareans*, vol. V (London: Continuum, 2011), 10–52.

Waugh, Evelyn, *Decline and Fall* (London: Penguin, 1928).

Webster, M., *Johann Zoffany 1733–1810* (New Haven: Yale University Press, 2011).

Weidenthal, Leo, *From Dis's Waggon…a sentimental survey of a poet's corner, the Shakespeare garden of Cleveland* (Cleveland: The Weidenthal Company, 1926).

Weiner, Mark, *Richard Wagner and the Anti-Semitic Imagination* (Lincoln: University of Nebraska Press, 1997).

Weisbord, Robert G. and Wallace P. Sillanpoa, *The Chief Rabbi, the Pope and the Holocaust. An Era in Vatican Jewish Relations* (New Brunswick, NJ: Transactions Publishers, 2008).

Wells, Stanley, *Shakespeare: For All Time* (London: Macmillan, 2002).

Wells, Stanley and Gary Taylor (eds.), *The Oxford Shakespeare*, 2nd edn (Oxford: Clarendon Press, 2005).

West, Anthony James, *The Shakespeare First Folio: The History of the Book. Volume II: A New Worldwide Census of First Folios* (Oxford University Press, 2003).

Whitworth, Geoffrey, *The Making of a National Theatre* (London: Faber, 1951).

Williams, Gordon, *British Theatre in the Great War* (London: Bloomsbury, 2003).

Winstanley, W., *Lives of the Most Famous English Poets* (1687).

Winter, William [Mercutio], 'Drama', *Albion*, 20 February 1864.

Wise, J. R., *Shakspere: His Birthplace and its Neighbourhood* (London: Smith, Elder & Co, 1861).

Wolschke-Bulmahn, J., 'Introduction', in *Places of Commemoration: Search for Identity and Landscape Design* (Washington DC: Dumbarton Oaks, 2001).

Woodward, H., *Songs, Choruses, &c., As they are performed in the new Entertainment of Harlequin's Jubilee* (London: printed for W. Griffin, 1770).

Woolf, Daniel, *Social Circulation of the Past: English Historical Culture 1500–1730* (Oxford University Press, 2003).

Wordsworth, William, *Thanksgiving Ode, January 18, 1816, with other short pieces chiefly referring to recent public events* (London: Longman, Hurst, Rees, Orme, and Brown, 1816).

Worrall, David, *Theatric Revolution: Drama, Censorship, and Romantic Period Subcultures, 1773–1832* (Oxford University Press, 2006).

Wright, Patrick, *On Living in an Old Country: The National Past in Contemporary Britain* (London: Verso, 1985).

Yeats, W. B., *The Collected Poems of W. B. Yeats*, ed. R. J. Finneran (Basingstoke: Palgrave, 1983).

The Collected Works of W. B. Yeats, gen. eds. R. Finneran and G. M. Harper (New York: Scribner, 2007).

Yeaxlee, Basil. Letter to Professor I. Gollancz, 3 March, 1916. National Theatre Archive, SMNT/2/2/55.

Young, Alan R., *'Punch' and Shakespeare in the Victorian Era* (Berlin: Peter Lang, 2007).

Index

Note: 'fig' indicates an illustration; documents and foreign words and phrases are given in italics.